Humanities 1102

Write It Review
A Process Approach
to College Essays with Readings

Fourth Edition

Linda Strahan
Kathleen Moore

University of California, Riverside

Michael Heumann

Imperial Valley College

Kendall Hunt
publishing company

Cover image © Shutterstock, Inc.

Kendall Hunt
publishing company

www.kendallhunt.com
Send all inquiries to:
4050 Westmark Drive
Dubuque, IA 52004-1840

Copyright © 2006, 2007, 2009, 2015 by Kendall Hunt Publishing Company

ISBN 978-1-4652-6762-7

Printed in the United States of America

Contents

Part 2 WRITING ASSIGNMENTS 67

Assignment #3: "Competition and Happiness" by Theodore Isaac Rubin   169

Assignment #4: "I Wish They'd Do It Right" by Jane Doe   221

Part 3   CASE STUDIES   443

Preface

The goal of *Write It Review* is to reinforce the academic reading and writing skills you learned in *Write It*. Each section of *Write It Review*, just as in *Write It*, helps you develop a range of writing strategies. As you are guided through the writing process, you learn how to use each stage to maximize its benefits. Using the strategies this book teaches will help you strengthen the confidence and understanding you need to write effective academic essays. As you work through the assignments and exercises in *Write It Review*, be sure to complete all the activities, and give special attention to activities devoted to building reading comprehension and idea development skills. If you have already worked through *Write It*, you likely have adjusted some of the stages in the writing process to suit your own methods and approaches to writing assignments; however, it is important that you reassess the process you are using. In this way, you will focus on areas that need improvement and thereby maximize the potential of *Write It Review*.

As you work through the writing process for each assignment, remember the series of skills we introduced in *Write It* that are necessary for producing a successful essay: focused reading, critical thinking, careful analysis, marshaling of evidence, drafting and editing. *Write It Review*'s exercises will guide you through each stage in the production of an essay, and will encourage you to practice each skill, one stage at a time. As you go through the writing process step by step, remember that writing is always a recursive activity and THAT when you begin a paper you may not always begin at step one with your topic and proceed in a linear way, one step at a time, to proofreading. As you move through the guiding exercises *Write It Review* provides, new ideas will come to you. Don't set these discoveries aside, but carry them forward into the remaining exercises. As you relate old and new information, you will explore each assignment's topic from several angles so that your ideas will build on one another. In this way the steps, though done in isolation, will come together in a unified perspective. The organization of this book is intended to help reinforce your understanding of essay-building as a process AND not a formula, the stages as necessary steps to internalize until each becomes an intuitive part of writing itself.

Write It Review's activities, exercises, and assignments will be familiar to those of you who have used *Write It*. The book is organized to guide you through each stage in the writing process, each unit beginning with a central reading and then moving through a sequence for essay development, from "Questions to Guide Your Reading," to "Questions to Guide Your Writing." A peer draft review form and a personal assessment form will help you revise and edit your essay. You will also find class discussion and homework activities that reinforce grammar, comprehension, and critical thinking skills. Following the assignment units is a section that contains student essays, and you will be able to read and evaluate the essays other students have written in response to similar essay topics. Like *Write It, Write It Review* is designed to encourage you not just to become a writer of college essays, but also to become a reader and writer in college. We hope that, as you become a proficient college writer, and exchange ideas with others in the academic community, you will both shape and be shaped by that community. Your experiences are unique to you, and your writing will reflect the knowledge you've accumulated from those experiences as you engage with others in defining the world in which we all live.

Here Is How to Use This Skill-Building Book

Write It Review is presented in three parts.

Part 1: BASIC INFORMATION AND DOCUMENTATION that presents information and guidance for completing reading and writing assignments in your English classes. Included in Part 1 are:

- A Step-by-Step Strategy for Reading Thoughtfully
- A Reminder of the Definitions of Plagiarism and Copyright Infringement
- A Review of the Resources in a Handbook
- A Review of the Argument Essay Structure and Two Alternatives
- A Review of Strategies for Writing a Timed Essay
- A Review of the Elements of the Conventional Argument Essay.
- A Review of an Introduction in an Argument Essay
- A Review of the Guidelines for Writing a Directed Summary
- Strategies for Developing Your Ideas
- Writing Supporting Paragraphs for Your Thesis Statement
- A Review of Logical Fallacies
- Transitions
- Conclusions
- Strategies for Participating in a Rough Draft Workshop
- A Sample Scoring Rubric
- Strategies for Proofreading Your Essay for Mistakes in Grammar, Punctuation, and Mechanics
- Grammar Diagnostic Tests and Self-Assessment Forms

Part 2: SEVEN ASSIGNMENT UNITS that contain a central essay to read and analyze and a writing assignment to respond to with your own essay. For each of these, the book will lead you through the writing process as you:

- read for comprehension and learn to recognize and evaluate a writer's argument.
- develop your own position and supporting evidence.
- organize your ideas into an effective essay structure.
- revise and edit for coherence and clarity.
- incorporate supplemental readings to expand and broaden the scope and complexity of your essay response.
- participate in class discussion activities at the end of each supplemental reading selection.

Part 3: CASE STUDIES that provide student writing examples to highlight strategies other students have used to construct essays. This section gives you an opportunity to practice applying criteria from the scoring rubric to evaluate others' essays. By evaluating the writing of others, you will become better at evaluating your own writing.

The step-by-step lessons in this skill-building workbook will provide you with a strong foundation for good writing. The book's techniques have been widely tested and proven successful. In a recent survey on our campus, students awarded first place in their success on an important writing exam to the lessons in this book. We are confident that this book will work for you, too.

Acknowledgments

This text is in many ways a collaborative effort, so we wish first of all to thank the faculty of the University Writing Program at the University of California, Riverside, for their inspiring ideas and contributions. For this edition we wish to acknowledge in particular Benedict Jones, for his commitment, tenacity, and perspicacity in producing the final version of the manuscript, and Jerry Winter and Terry Spaise, for their creative ideas about the best ways to teach this material. We also want to recognize the Kendall Hunt managerial and editorial team; without their support, the book could not have come into existence. We are especially grateful for the reliability and professionalism of Christine Bochniak and Linda Chapman, whose tireless efforts and good advice guided us through the process and made this book possible.

Foreword

Engineers tell us that they spend half of their time on the job writing reports, proposals, and job-related messages to their colleagues. Much of that work is "writing on demand," which must be completed rapidly, accurately, and in a way that helpfully addresses the requirements of the task. In many walks of life, the ability to respond quickly in writing, doing that work in a way that truly addresses the issue at hand, is what eventually distinguishes the rising professional, entrepreneur, craftsman, teacher, and civic leader, as well as the effective employee. Writing on demand also prepares us to speak in job-related settings. It readies us to formulate and express our thoughts in spoken words that others find useful, informative, and persuasive.

Your work in this course will improve your chances of thriving at the University, which holds in high esteem the ability to compose thoughts with dispatch, accuracy, relevance, and verve. Your preparation will help you become a better reader, for good writers see more when they read. Conversely, the more you learn to read attentively, the better the writer you will become. What you learn in this class will also help you articulate your ideas and express yourself in aspects of your life that have little to do with the world of work or academics. A trained proficiency in writing and reading will give you greater access to the ideas and experiences of others.

Your lecture class, your workshop sessions, and your online studies will prepare you to succeed in this class and prepare you for Freshman English. You will need to be patient as well as dedicated; many students need more than one quarter to become proficient writers. Remember that the goal of this book is to help all students reach proficiency as quickly as possible. We look forward to seeing you in Freshman English.

Professor John Briggs
Director of the University Writing Program
University of California, Riverside

Basic Information

Part 1 of *Write It Review* is designed to be used as a writing reference section. We advise you to work through it carefully. It contains many of the basic strategies and conventions for academic writing. As such, you can rely on many of its basic elements to complete academic writing assignments in any discipline. For your purposes in this course, however, the strategies and information in this section should be practiced as fundamental writing strategies that you will be asked to apply in completing Part 2's essay assignments. We urge you to turn back frequently to Part 1 as you work on the essays in Part 2; these pages will support your prewriting, drafting, and revising as you move through the writing process, and they will supplement and reinforce the writing support pages in each of the units in Part 2.

The information in Part 1 is organized around the stages of the writing process and includes guidance on building each of the conventional essay parts that come together to form the essay's overall structure.

Part 1 contains the following information:

A Review of Some Basic Guidelines

> A Step-by-Step Strategy for Reading Thoughtfully
> A Reminder of the Definitions of Plagiarism and Copyright Infringement
> A Review of the Resources in a Handbook
> A Review of the Argument Essay Structure and Two Alternatives
> A Review of Strategies for Writing a Timed Essay

A Review of the Elements of the Conventional Argument Essay

> A Review of an Introduction in an Argument Essay
> A Review of the Guidelines for Writing a Directed Summary
> Strategies for Developing Your Ideas
> Writing Supporting Paragraphs for Your Thesis Statement
> A Review of Logical Fallacies
> Transitions
> Conclusions
> Strategies for Participating in a Rough Draft Workshop
> A Sample Scoring Rubric

A Review of Sentence-Level Control

> Proofreading Your Essay for Mistakes in Grammar, Punctuation, and Mechanics
> Assessing Your Grammar Awareness

A Review of Basic Information
A Step-by-Step Strategy for Reading Thoughtfully

Students tell us that one of the most challenging aspects of working through this book and writing successful essays is the reading selections. Most of these readings are not particularly difficult to read, nor are they overly long. The difficulty lies in fully comprehending the arguments they contain. Because each of the writing topics in Part 2 asks you to respond to a particular reading selection, it will be important for you to spend some time with the reading. Work through it several times until you fully understand the writer's central argument and are able to identify the argument's supporting evidence. Until that understanding is reached, you will not be able to respond appropriately in your own essay.

We all read—on a daily basis and without much effort—common things such as signs, text messages, e-mails, and menus without thinking about them very much. In an academic setting, however, reading becomes an activity that requires effort and thought. Use the steps below to ensure that your reading is focused and productive.

1. **Consider the title given to the material you are to read.**
   It should suggest a particular topic or issue. Think about what you already know about the topic. Think about what else you need to know about the topic in order to have an informed opinion about it. Look at the title again and ask yourself what its wording suggests about the writer's opinion and perhaps his or her reason for writing about the topic.

2. **Learn about the author.**
   If biographical information about the writer is presented with the reading, look for biographical information that may have influenced the content and perspective of the reading. Sometimes you can better evaluate a writer's argument by taking into account his or her level of expertise or personal connection to the subject of the essay.

3. **Read through the material once quickly.**
   This first rapid reading gives you an overview of the subject, the writer's attitude toward the subject, and the nature of the supporting evidence that the reading contains.

4. **Read again to identify the thesis.**
   For your second reading, you need a pen or highlighter and not just your eyes. Your first task on the second reading is to find and mark the thesis. The thesis states the writer's position on the topic. Often, it is contained in a single sentence, but, in some cases, it takes several sentences to make clear the point of the work. There are times when the writer does not state his or her thesis explicitly, but you should be able to state it after reading through the essay once. You might want to note the thesis in the margin.

5. **Read slowly and methodically through the rest of the material.**
   Each paragraph has a topic sentence that expresses the main point of the paragraph. The topic sentence is usually found at the beginning of the paragraph, but it can be anywhere within the paragraph. You should note the point (or topic sentence) of each paragraph as you work through your second reading. The remainder of the paragraph contains evidence to support the topic sentence. While you read, your job is to evaluate this evidence for its logic and validity. For future reference, you may find it useful to make comments in the margins regarding the strength and weakness of the paragraph's evidence.

6. **Read again for review.**

Now that you have thought through the ideas and evidence supporting the ideas in your reading, read the whole thing again. Watch for any anomalies—statements or points that don't fit with your overall understanding of the material. If you find any, take time to determine whether the material is the writer's error or a misreading on your part. You may find that you need to go back to Step 4 and begin working through the reading again. Once you are certain that your reading is accurate, you are prepared to discuss, summarize, and respond to the reading with your own essay.

Look over the following essay and notice the way that one writer used *Write It Review*'s guidelines to underline main ideas and make notations in the margins. These notes help identify the essay's argument and supporting details.

An Example

Do Women in Politics Face a Glass Ceiling?

LIZ CHADDERDON POWELL

Liz Chadderdon Powell is vice president of political strategies with BatesNiemand, Inc., a Democratic consulting firm in Washington, DC. This reading selection originally appeared in Winning Campaigns Magazine.

Is there a glass ceiling for women in the political consulting industry? **(This is a rhetorical question that the thesis statement will answer.)**

(This is introductory material.) Whenever an article is written about the professional glass ceiling for women, men get jumpy. They defensively point to articles written about women sportscasters interviewing male football players in the locker room, female soldiers fighting alongside their male counterparts, and wives outearning their husbands. They usually say this with a look on their face clearly saying, "C'mon, what more do you want?" **(The thesis statement has to be inferred: For women, there is a glass ceiling in politics. So the answer to the opening rhetorical question is "yes," in Powell's opinion.)**

(Here is the Controlling Idea Sentence.) There are plenty of examples of women succeeding in traditionally male-dominated professions. **(The next two sentences are Careful Description Statements defining "success" in terms of how the writer is using the term.)** But let's define success as actually running the company, the corporation, or even the country. You know—the good jobs with the power and sweet paychecks. **(The next five sentences are Corroborating Details.)** There are nineteen female CEOs running Fortune 500 companies. This sounds good until you remember there are 500 companies in the Fortune 500 (thus the name) and women only run nineteen of them. That is only 3.8%. And then there are the celebrated seventy-four women in Congress. Seventy-four seems applause-worthy unless you count all 535 seats in both the House and Senate. That means women hold only 13.8% of Congress while being 52% of the voting population of America. (**This final sentence is the Connection Sentence that ties back to and supports the thesis.**) We may have come a long way, baby, but we still have a very long way to go before we have an equal share of the real power in this country. (**This paragraph is compelling—probably because it uses all four of the 4Cs.**)

(**Here is the Controlling Idea, but "that" is a bit unclear. A noun would have been clearer, especially as the sentence is the first in a new paragraph and the referent is unclear.**) (**The rest of this paragraph, except for the last sentence, gives Corroborating Details in the form of examples.**) That is very true in the political consulting industry. Women are making inroads, but the victories are small. Mary Beth Cahill managed John Kerry's presidential campaign, but all-male consultants surrounded her. More disturbing, she was the only female in a visible, top-level role among the '04 Democratic presidential nominees. While Karen Hughes played an advisory role for President Bush, she was always second to Karl Rove, who definitely got all the credit for Bush's victory. Furthermore, there is not one female in a high level position on Bush's internal White House staff. (**The final sentence ties back to the thesis, but the too-informal tone of it detracts somewhat from the point it is trying to make.**) And while Secretary Rice's influence is impressive, let me know when she gets Rummy's job. (**Note: This paragraph would have been stronger if it had spent more time on Careful Explanation of Why the Details Are Significant. The writer gives the details and assumes that readers will interpret them in the way she has.**)

At the political committees, women are scattered through the organization, usually in fundraising positions. But there are no female Executive Directors or Political Directors at any of the four committees (DSCC, DCCC, RNCC, RSCC), and neither national party has a woman Executive Director or Party Chairperson. So women work there, but none have achieved the most visible, and most profitable, positions. Women are working for the cause. They are just not leading it. (**The 4Cs are here, but the ideas could be more fully developed.**)

(**Here is another observation about the Controlling Idea in the previous paragraph. The writer has many Corroborating Details and Careful Explanation of Why the Details Are Significant, so she extends the topic to a second paragraph.**) I see three primary causes of the political consulting industry's glass ceiling: (**These are Corroborating Details and Careful Explanation of Why the Details Are Significant presented together in a list of causes and a list of solutions.**) 1) women have children, which means they are not available to their clients 24/7/365 and lose that edge to their male competitors; 2) being a committee executive director or a partner in a firm requires a killer instinct, and some women shy away from being that aggressive; and 3) people in powerful positions (usually men) are loath to move out and give others a leg up. It is a societal issue, not just a political consulting issue, that children hurt mommies in the workplace more than daddies. The idea of men being able to work late nights with no adverse effects to their family because the wife will always handle it is archaic. Women in every professional industry will remain trapped beneath the glass until their male counterparts share equally in parenting. Men are no longer the sole breadwinners, so why should women be the sole caregivers? (**This is a good question, really—a good point to make.**) As to women not being aggressive enough, I know there are plenty of aggressive women in the political business. But there are plenty more who fear the label of "bitch" or "hard-ass," which prevents them from making the tough decisions and rising to the top positions. By now, we should be wise to this age-old male defense mechanism. Women need to move past this and see it for what it is—an intimidation tactic, not to mention a load of horse crap. (**Too informal!**) So the solutions to breaking the glass ceiling require effort on everyone's part.

Women need to get over the stigma of being aggressive and close the deal. Men need to stay home and change a few diapers. And consultants who worked for George McGovern or Richard Nixon need to retire. This will immediately usher in many new women to top positions.

(In this paragraph, the writer continues with the same topic and gives more solutions for the problem.) Furthermore, women consultants need to work together to train and support the next generation of female campaign operatives. We all know how tough it is to get that first campaign job and to live "on the road" for a few years while building your résumé. Women tend to get off the road and take safe jobs far more often than men. I envision training seminars exclusively for female operatives given exclusively by female consultants. After the training, these operatives would receive mentoring support from a female consultant, giving them advice and encouraging them to stick it out, even when they want to take a "real" job. Then perhaps young women would stay on the road longer and get the experience they need to get the higher-level jobs. I would also encourage female candidates and female-oriented political action committees to work only with female consultants. If we don't help our own, we will never be successful at tearing down walls. Men have been hiring men exclusively for years, and I think it's high time we follow their lead. In 2001, a male staff member at the DSCC told me I could not run one of the top Senate races because I was female and none of his candidates would take orders from a woman. If that is true, then female candidates should stop "taking orders" from male managers and male consultants and start working with more women.

(Conclusion type: a Request for Action. This is an effective way to end—it assumes that change can happen.) I am not interested in sparking a "gender war" within this industry. I am interested in seeing the Campaigns and Elections "Rising Star" list have as many women as men. I am interested in seeing the C & E Political Pages list at least ten Democrat media firms with named female partners. I am interested in seeing 278 women in the Senate and House, to reflect the fifty-two percent of the voting population that women represent. I am interested in never being asked again whether there is a glass ceiling for women in the political consulting industry.

Application

1. After reading the selection on women in politics, write your own annotations in its margin. Then, compare your margin notes to the ones given in the parentheses within the reading. How similar are they? How do you account for any differences you notice?

2. Discuss with a classmate your responses to these questions: Have you used annotating in the past? If so, do you see a way to modify this strategy to improve its effectiveness? If you haven't been using this strategy, do you think that you might try it in the future to better aid your comprehension? Explain your responses.

3. Build an outline for "Do Women in Politics Face a Glass Ceiling?" Then, discuss with a classmate how effective the outline is in helping you to understand Powell's argument. Which strategy was most effective for you, annotating or outlining? Would you choose to use both strategies? Explain.

A Reminder of the Definitions of Plagiarism and Copyright Infringement

You may be aware of the requirement that all work you turn in for credit must be your own, but sometimes students inadvertently commit plagiarism because they are unclear about what constitutes plagiarism or infringement of copyright laws. Review the following definitions and rules, and check to see that your own paper meets all the requirements of intellectual and academic honesty.

Copyright refers to the legal ownership of published material. Any writing—a play, an essay, a pamphlet, a website—is the intellectual property of the person who wrote it. If, in your paper, you borrow that property by quoting, summarizing, or paraphrasing, you must give credit to the original author. The *fair use* laws allow you to borrow *brief passages* without infringing on copyright, but you must credit the source and document it properly. Your handbook will show you the correct form to use for each and every source.

Plagiarism can occur in different ways. For example, some students make poor choices and turn in another student's work as their own. Institutions of higher learning have strict policies regarding this type of plagiarism, and the consequences for this action can be significant. Plagiarism may also be committed by oversight; a student may have forgotten where he or she found the particular material or even that the material was not his or her own. It is important during your research that you include all the source information in your notes so that you will not accidentally commit plagiarism and be held accountable for it.

Remember to acknowledge the following:

> *Ideas*—any idea or concept that you learned elsewhere that is not common knowledge
> *Words and Phrases*—exact reproduction of another author's writing
> *Charts/Tables/Statistic/Other Visuals*—other forms of work done by an author
> *Your Own Work*—with permission from your instructor, work of your own done for a different assignment or purpose

Intellectual property is the result of work people do with their heads rather than their hands; nevertheless, the result of that work still belongs to the person who did it. If a carpenter made a chair, that chair is owned by its maker. You would consider taking that chair an act of theft. Try to think of printed material as a similar object, and show that property the same respect you would any other. By doing so, you will avoid plagiarism and copyright infringement.

A Review of the Resources in a Handbook

How to Use a Handbook

Many students have never bothered to buy a handbook, or they own one but never use it. This may be because they do not realize what a powerful tool a handbook is for writers. A good handbook contains a great deal of information. It presents the conventions for formatting an academic essay, it suggests some good prewriting activities to help YOU develop ideas, it includes a grammar and punctuation guide, and it shows you how to use and cite quotations and paraphrases in your essays. It is important to become familiar with the extensive resources available in a handbook, and to take the time and care to follow all the guidelines that govern academic writing. Many of these you already know; your handbook will be able to refresh your memory when you aren't sure of yourself, and it will give you information that you may meet for the first time.

A handbook helps at every stage of the writing process. It has sections that show you how to get started by defining your purpose and your audience. Your handbook has chapters that can aid you as you make a plan for your writing and chapters that can lead you through the drafting process. When your rough draft is completed, your handbook will give you ideas and techniques for improving and revising the work you have done. Most importantly, a handbook contains all the information and explanations of the conventions of written English. You will want to consult your handbook extensively as you correct and edit your final draft.

You need to familiarize yourself with two important features of your handbook: the **table of contents** and the **index.** Learning how to use them and training yourself to consult them will save you time and improve your writing.

The Table of Contents

The table of contents appears at the beginning of your handbook. It gives the title (topic) of each chapter and lists the subtopics covered in each of the chapters. A page number follows each listing for easy access to the information.

Example:
Your instructor has given a general assignment for your paper. You are to write a research paper on the novel *The Sun Also Rises* by Ernest Hemingway, but you are expected to come up with your own topic. You have no idea where to begin, so you look at your handbook's table of contents. You find a section devoted to Writing Topics. There are subheadings, such as:

> "Finding a Topic"
> "Selecting a Topic"
> "Narrowing the Topic"

Because you do not have any particular topic in mind, you follow the activities the handbook suggests to help you think about subjects for your paper. It suggests you first try some of the following activities to generate a topic that interests you:

> *freewriting*
> *brainstorming*
> *mapping*

listing
browsing
questioning

You try them all, but the final technique, using the question words, produces the following:

Who? Jake Barnes
When? 1920s
Where? Paris
What? Expatriate
Why? Physical/mental wounds
How? World War I

The penultimate question, "Why?" produces a relevant and researchable, though still quite broad, topic. "Jake's wound." You can begin by thinking and researching more on that topic. Once you have gathered information from secondary sources and the primary text, you can then return to the section in the handbook for ideas on ways to narrow your subject and begin to refine and limit your topic.

Once you have decided on your topic, your handbook can also help you produce a thesis that is appropriate and manageable in terms of your assignment.

Index

The index appears at the very end of your handbook. It contains an alphabetical listing of every topic, concept, and problem addressed within the handbook's pages. A page number or a sequence of page numbers follows each listing. These numbers indicate pages where information on a particular listing can be found.

Example:
You are writing about your chemistry study group and want to discuss the commitment of all the members. You have written the following sentence:

My study group, named "Good Chemistry," brings their textbooks to each meeting.

You are unsure about your pronoun choice. Should it be "their" or "its"? You know that "group" is a collective noun. You use your handbook to find the answer. In the index, you find alphabetical listings for the following:

"Pronoun-antecedent agreement
      collective nouns and"
"Collective nouns
      pronoun agreement with"

Both listings direct you to the same page. On that page, you discover that collective nouns such as "group" can take both the singular and plural pronoun, depending on the content and meaning of the sentence. If the unit (collective noun) functions as a whole, or one, the singular pronoun is correct. If the members of the group act individually, the plural pronoun is needed. In your sentence, the group has members that must show commitment by each completing certain actions on their own Remembering to bring the book is an action completed separately by the individuals in the group. Which pronoun would be correct?

A Review of the Argument Essay Structure and Two Alternatives

The Conventional Argument Essay Structure

The most commonly used structure for a thesis-centered essay is established by convention. That is, the thesis essay format has an introduction that contains the thesis statement, followed by body paragraphs that support it, and ending with a conclusion that gives closure to the essay. The majority of college writing assignments anticipate this structure.

An Introduction That Contains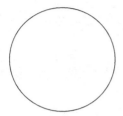

an **INTRODUCTORY SENTENCE** that introduces the reading selection's title, author, and subject.

a **DIRECTED SUMMARY** of the reading selection that includes an answer to the first part of the writing topic.

your thesis statement in response to the writing topic.

Body Paragraphs, Each of Which Includes

a **TOPIC SENTENCE** that gives the paragraph's ONE central point that supports your thesis statement.

CONCRETE EVIDENCE, EXPLAINED so that it supports the central point and ties that point to the thesis statement.

A Conclusion That Gives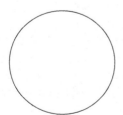

a **RESTATEMENT** of the reading selection's argument and your argument.

a sense of **CLOSURE** for the essay

The conventional academic structure delivers its central, overarching point in the opening of the essay. Its direct and efficient presentation of the essay's main point is followed by the step-by-step logic and evidence that have led the writer to the conclusion he or she has reached, the insight or revelation that has determined the thesis statement of the essay. Writers might use this structure when they are writing for purposeful readers who are reading for intellectual insight, rather than for entertainment or for general, thoughtful commentary on current issues of social interest.

Example

You will meet the following reading selection in a different context in Part 2 of this book. For now, examine it as an essay written in the academic essay format.

The Ethics of Work-Life Balance

BRUCE WEINSTEIN

> *Bruce Weinstein received a BA from Swarthmore College and a PhD from Georgetown University. From 2006 to 2012, he contributed to* Bloomberg Businessweek's *online edition, which also posted his twelve-episode series* Ask the Ethics Guy. *He is now a blogger at the* Huffington Post *and is a professional public speaker, lecturing on ethics and leadership. His latest book,* Ethical Intelligence, *was published in 2011. The essay below appeared on* Bloomberg Businessweek *in 2009.*

We are a nation in pain. According to a March 12 Gallup poll, the number of people in this country classified as "suffering" has increased by three million over the past year. Managers and business owners experienced the greatest loss of well-being; 60.8% of businesses were thriving in the first quarter of 2008, but this number decreased by almost 14% by the fourth quarter. Given the difficult economic climate and the number of jobs being lost daily, most of us are feeling the pressure to work harder than ever. But in spite of the increasing intensity of our economic crisis, it is not only unfortunate to give in to such pressure. It's unethical.

It's not too late to make a change for the better, though.

It may seem misplaced to discuss work-life balance in a column about ethics. But recall that one of five fundamental ethical principles is fairness, and that we demonstrate fairness in everyday life by how we allocate scarce resources. The most precious commodity you have is time, both in your professional and your personal life. It's also your most critical nonrenewable resource. As a manager, you must constantly ask yourself how you should allocate your time. You know it's wrong to spend so much time on one project at the expense of equally critical ones, or to spend so much time managing one employee that you're unable to manage others.

But a good manager should be, first and foremost, a good human being. Just as managing your career well means allocating your time wisely among the different projects and people you oversee, managing your life wisely means giving due time not just to work but to family, friends, community, self, and spirit. You wouldn't think of spending most of your work day talking with one client on the phone. Why, then, is it okay to devote so much time to your job when you don't give non-work-related things the attention they deserve?

Ethics isn't just about how you treat others. It's also about how you treat yourself—at work and beyond. You're not being fair to others and yourself if you haven't had a vacation in a long time, or if you force yourself to work when you've got the flu. You're also not being fair to others and yourself if you spend so much time being a good manager that you're not able to be a good parent, spouse, or friend. And let's face it: You can't do your job to the best of your ability if you're thoroughly exhausted, and that's not fair to your coworkers or your employer. But working to the exclusion of all else isn't just unfair (and thus unethical). It's also tragic, because the time you spend away from the other meaningful relationships in your life is time you can never get back. ⌐ Thesis

Let's now look at some of the common excuses people give for working so much and how to get beyond them.

"I want to make sure I keep my job."

More than 2.5 million jobs were lost in 2008, and the losses continue to mount. What could be wrong with working all the time in such a climate if it will mean hanging onto your job? Speaking of ethics, isn't there an ethical obligation to keep your job? After all, what would be ethical about not paying bills, or your mortgage, or not being able to take care of your family?

Of course it's important to remain an employee in good standing. But you shouldn't assume that there is a direct correlation with the number of hours you work and the likelihood that you'll hold onto your job. Downsizing is largely a function of economics rather than of job performance; companies are letting people go to cut their losses and hit budget targets. (And yes, letting go of good employees raises other ethical issues, but that deserves its own column.) Working twelve-hour days six or seven days a week isn't going to guard against getting downsized.

In fact, it could even backfire. You might look like someone who can't manage his or her time or isn't up to the responsibilities of the job. And if you work without any letup, you will reach the point of diminishing returns. This isn't a time to be less than a stellar employee, but working overtime won't get you there.

"I need to work more to make what I did last year."

Many of the recently downsized are taking lower-paying jobs because that's all that is available. Some are even taking second jobs and still not making what they did a year ago. But how important is it now to live in the manner to which you have become accustomed? It's one thing to have to work seventy hours a week just to put food on the table and pay the rent or mortgage. It's another to work so much to be able to afford lavish trips, expensive clothes, or a certain lifestyle. Instead of working longer, couldn't you shift your priorities so that you're able to spend more time with family and friends, exercise more often, or even just read some of those books you've been thinking about?

"I have a demanding job."

Gone are the days when leaving your office meant leaving work behind. Many of us choose to use our BlackBerrys, iPhones, laptops, and social networking sites to remain constantly available to our bosses, clients, and colleagues, but this can get out of control. It's flattering to believe that you're indispensable to your company, and that only you can do the work you spend so much time doing. This is rarely true, however painful that may be to accept. Be honest with yourself: Are you spending so much time on the job because you must, or because of habit, ego, or some other reason? We owe it to ourselves and the people we care about (and who care about us) to work smarter, not harder.

"I just love to work."

It's a blessing to be able to say this, but all passions should have limits. A fully human life is a life in balance, and that means giving due time to all of the things that enrich us, fulfill us, and make our lives worth living. When Freud said that work and love were essential components of a happy life, he didn't mean that these were one and the same thing.

There is a time to work and a time to leave work behind. The good manager leaves time to do both.

Discussion Questions

1. Identify the thesis statement in Weinstein's article. Restate his claim in your own words. Discuss your initial response to it. What are some identifying labels (such as "provocative," "unexpected," "commonplace," etc.) you would attach to his thesis? Explain your answer.

2. Summarize in a few sentences the argument of "The Ethics of Work-Life Balance."

3. Why do you think Weinstein wrote this essay? How does the placement of the thesis in his essay help make his readers more open to the position he takes?

4. Weinstein uses the second person in his essay. Who do you think he images that he is addressing when he says "you"? Discuss what types of readers might be interested in reading this essay. Although the second person is not conventionally used in academic writing, why do you think this writer chooses to use it in this essay?

Two Alternative Structures

Although it is most common in an argumentative essay to place the thesis early—usually towards the end of the first paragraph—there are alternative structures can be used in an argument essay. Each of the two alternative essay structures in this section contains a clear thesis statement, but neither thesis can be found at the beginning of the essay. The first essay uses what we call the "hourglass structure," and the second uses what we call the "funnel structure." You might notice that several of the reading selections in this book use one of these alternative structures, in part because the articles were not written for an academic readership. In your own essays, however, we recommend that you use the conventional academic essay structure.

A First Alternative: The Hourglass Structure

One alternative structure for an essay places the thesis statement somewhere in the middle of the essay. Here is a diagram of this type of essay.

An Introduction That Contains

> an **ANECDOTE** that is related to the subject of the essay
>
> a **HINT** about the writer's position on the issue

Body Paragraphs That Include

> **TOPIC SENTENCES**
>
> concrete **EVIDENCE** that supports the writer's position
>
> additional **EXAMPLES** that support the writer's position
>
> **A THESIS STATEMENT**

More Body Paragraphs That Include

> **TOPIC SENTENCES**
>
> concrete **EVIDENCE** that supports the writers's position
>
> added **EXAMPLES** that support the writer's position

A Conclusion That Gives

> a **REMINDER** of the writer's position
>
> a sense of **CLOSURE** for the essay

With the hourglass structure, writers ask readers to read a fair portion of the essay before they come to the essay's central point. Writers begin talking about a subject, offering assertions, anecdotes, and observations whose significance isn't yet clear. These assertions and observations are meant to create a path to the central point—stated in a thesis statement—followed by more corroborating assertions and observations.

Writers might use this structure when their thesis is controversial and they do not want to risk losing dissenting readers up front. To persuade readers who disagree, a writer tries to draw them in by offering material more widely agreed upon and accessible. You will want to notice when a writer uses an alternative essay structure because it will help you to identify the argument and the linking ideas that support it.

Example

 ### Time to Cerebrate

BENEDICT JONES

> *Benedict Jones received a double bachelor's degree from the University of California, San Diego, and earned an English MA at the University of California, Riverside, where he is now a lecturer in the University Writing Program. His scholarly work focuses on Victorian-era prehistoric fiction and evolutionary theories, but he has written articles, reviews, and conference papers on a variety of topics.*

The race was on: My ten-page literature paper was due at noon the next day. I had been stewing about the essay for days, reading and rereading the poems to be analyzed, and scribbling down random ideas. I often just stared off into space and simply thought about the project, afraid to commit and dreading to start. But I still hadn't typed a word, and I had under twenty-four hours left.

This type of delayed start was my *modus operandi*, and I therefore considered myself something of a failure as a college student. Sure, I was smart. No question of that. And I loved academics and especially literature, my area of focus; I spent hours and hours thinking about what I had read and what I planned to write. But when a due date loomed, I habitually procrastinated and agonized, waiting until the deadline was hard upon me before I could force myself to sit down and actually tap out a product.

I did not delay on purpose, nor was I indifferent about my grade. I truly wanted to do well. I longed to begin writing earlier and avoid the seemingly inevitable all-nighter, the day-long last-minute mad dash to both start and finish. If only I could be sensible, I thought. If I could bring myself to start writing a week earlier, I would produce a couple of pages a day and still have time left to revise and edit—and I would never again have to face the terrifying possibility of *not* finishing. Breaking up the project well before the due date would mean low stress, plenty of sleep, and my best work possible: the perfect combination. However, no amount of logic penetrated my dense skull, so I continued as I was, hating myself with a passion but always sliding under the wire at the eleventh hour. The system did work, even if it made me uncomfortable and ashamed. After all, I usually earned As and never got below a B.

After dropping out of school and taking several years off, I reentered the university as a working student—and still found that many of my essays were last-minute affairs completed in the wee, small hours of the morning they were due. Although my second attempt at academic life was certainly challenged by both the ten-week quarter system and a full-time job, it seemed that not much else had changed. Even in graduate school, I would spend weeks doing research, taking notes, and thinking, thinking, thinking about a project, but I would allow only a few days to actually write the essay.

Now I teach my own students, and many of them seem to be on the same path I was on. They make plans to see me in office hours for advice but often e-mail me to say that they cannot make it because they are still writing the first draft. They skitter into class ten minutes late with a paper they have just barely finished. Or they submit an assignment on time but note that their last-minute scheduling did not allow time for editing and proofreading, so "it might have a few mistakes." Perhaps nothing much *has* changed.

But I'm beginning to think it actually has. I am gradually coming to the conclusion that I was not as dramatic a procrastinator as I have always thought. After all, I spent hours, days, even weeks thinking about my projects, although the writing took only a short time. In contrast, the final product that my students now expect me to grade is often superficial, with indifferent organization, jumbled paragraphs, and discrete points that don't always add up to a cohesive whole. Most of these essays do not seem to have required much time to write and do not appear to have invited much thought. And that, I think, might be a key difference between me and my students: the time we take to think.

To prepare for my various writing assignments, I always allowed long periods of rumination, and I truly doubt that very many of my students do the same. Before writers ever get to the drafting stage, they should reserve a generous portion of the project's allotted time for focused reflection. Some students will require less time and some more; some will think more in the middle of the project than in the beginning. Some will think IN the shower, and some on the bus. But careful, uninterrupted thought is still the absolute best guarantee of high-quality content.

I don't often see such results, so I wonder whether thinking has lately become an eccentric pursuit, the butt of jokes. Oddly enough, I see evidence of this trend on television—on *The Big Bang Theory*, a program devoted to the brainiac experience. For example, a sequence in an episode called "The Pirate Solution" shows Sheldon, a string-theory physicist, and Raj, an astrophysicist, comically practicing the manly art of mental exercise.

In his cluttered university office, Sheldon declares, "We're doing serious research which requires complete and utter focus."

"All right," agrees Raj, "let's buckle down and work."

And with that, audiences are treated to a rousing musical excerpt from "The Eye of the Tiger," accompanied by various shots of the two scientists standing, sitting, leaning, all while staring intently at equations on a dry erase board. The laugh track tells viewers that this sequence is very funny indeed.

In another episode, "The Pulled Groin Extrapolation," supergeek and social disaster Amy Farrah Fowler, a neurobiologist, sits on the couch in Sheldon and Leonard's apartment while Leonard works at his computer, his back to her. Amy sits erect, with her hands on her thighs, staring blankly at nothing in particular. Finally, the increasingly uncomfortable Leonard cannot help himself. "Amy?" he says tentatively.

"Yo," replies Amy, her concentration momentarily broken.

"You okay?"

"Oh, sure," she says with confidence, and goes back to staring.

Leonard persists: "I thought you were reading."

"I was," she replies, and adds with obvious satisfaction, "Now I'm *thinking* about what I read." Again the laugh track tells us to respond with hilarity. Is the number one comedy in America, supposedly a paean to geekdom, telling its audience that thinking is funny?

I laughed, and still do, because I can relate. What Raj and Sheldon and Amy do, I also do, minus the equations but probably with the same dorky, far-off look in my eyes. Busy as I am, I still take time to sit and think, to *percolate*. I contemplate what I have read, how I need to spend my day, what I want to cover in class, what I want my students to get out of an assignment. I ponder my writing projects, too, often for long periods of apparent inactivity. When a problem is particularly knotty, I get up and pace around while I exercise my little gray cells. While walking back and forth, I often talk out the problem: I am thinking out loud.

That's why I think the TV scenes are funny; they are a slice right out of my own nerdy life. But now I wonder exactly what everyone else is laughing about. Is mental reflection really so funny? Is it an alien occupation, something to poke fun at? Do people laugh because they see Raj and Sheldon's idea of labor as not worthy of the label "work" because "work" must refer to significant physical activity rather than intellectual exertion? I expect that for most viewers, the answer to all of these questions is a resounding "yes." I also suspect that fewer and fewer people simply sit and think; our young people, and even middle-aged geezers like me, are busy filling in their mental interstices with external stimulation from their technological gadgets. It seems that every spare minute is filled with texting, googling, facebooking, youtubing, browsing. While I have nothing against these pursuits in their proper place, they seem to have taken over, leaving no space for contemplation. In addition, writing on a computer seems to encourage sloppy products, since students are not obliged to think carefully about their essays before committing them to paper, as they would need to do when working on a typewriter. In short, I worry that lengthy rumination is becoming a thing of the past, especially among college students.

I'll admit that this might not be much of a tragedy for most people, but it is a travesty for our universities. I may come across as an elitist for believing as I do, but universities are geared primarily toward people who like to think, people whose ability to ruminate helps them to flourish in their disciplines. What will happen if that population is rapidly diminishing? I am concerned that by filling in every mental pause with rapid-fire gadget-centered interactions, my own students are robbing themselves of the ability to think deeply or for sustained periods of time. I believe I can say that in recent years, the overall quality of thinking-on-paper has diminished noticeably in my classes—and I worry about what that trend means for higher education, for good old American ingenuity or, indeed, for the world. It is still too early to be sure what long-term effects our technology will have on our thinking, but the preliminary conclusions of various recent studies do not inspire confidence.

Looking back on my past life as a student, I feel that the hours that I used to devote to simply thinking about my own undergraduate essays were well spent. I was engaged by interesting issues and problems. I learned how to make connections between ideas and how to organize my thoughts. I learned to reason effectively and, occasionally, write my way out of a corner. As a result, I became a strong critical thinker. I should also note that my essays generally did not read like the work of a single day—because they weren't. They tended to earn high grades because they were the product of hours, days, or weeks of careful introspection even if the execution was a little rushed. I procrastinated on the writing but not on the mental preparation that led up to the writing.

⌈ Consequently, I do wish that my writing students would manage their time a bit differently and fill their quiet moments with less browsing and more brooding. Not everyone has the same process, but thinking deeply about their writing projects should be an essential component of all students' creative process and will improve their mental acuity, the quality of their work, probably their grades, and perhaps even their future professions and personal lives. ⌉

Now that nerds are achieving a semi-mythic status in American culture, we ought to recognize the value of some of their strongest characteristics—among them the ability to simply ponder. Student writers in particular must take an occasional sustained break from gadget heaven and devote time to think more deeply about their writing projects before ever penning—or, more likely, typing—a draft. I'm not saying to ditch the devices; they are here to stay, and they are valuable tools and entertaining toys in twenty-first-century life. But if Raj and Sheldon and their friends can be heavily invested in their electronic devices and still allow time for sustained deep thinking, I am sure that my own students can do the same. Focused thinking should be included in every writer's toolbox. In the lingo of *The Big Bang Theory*, America's next episode should be "The Cerebration Celebration."

Works Cited

"The Pirate Solution." *The Big Bang Theory*. CBS. KFMB, San Diego, 12 Oct. 2009. Television.

"The Pulled Groin Extrapolation." *The Big Bang Theory*. CBS. KFMB, San Diego, 29 Sept. 2011. Television.

Discussion Questions

1. Identify the thesis statement in Jones's article. Restate his claim in your own words. Discuss your initial response to it. Do you think the position he takes is controversial? Explain.

2. Summarize in a few sentences the argument of "Time to Cerebrate."

3. Where, specifically, did Jones choose to place the thesis? How does the placement of the thesis in this particular position help make his readers more open to the position he takes in the article? Who are the readers Jones imagines he is writing to, in your opinion? Explain your answer.

A Second Alternative: The Funnel Structure

Another alternative structure for an argument essay is one that places its thesis somewhere within the conclusion of the essay. Here is a diagram of this type of essay structure.

An Introduction That Contains

One of the following
  an **ANECDOTE**
  an **EXAMPLE**
  a **SUMMARY** of the topic
  INFORMATION related to the topic

Body Paragraphs That Include

TOPIC SENTENCES

other **ANECDOTES** that point toward a position on the subject

facts, statistics, or other **INFORMATION** that points toward a particular position on the subject

additional **EXAMPLES** that point toward a particular position on the subject

concrete **EVIDENCE** that points toward a particular position on the subject

A Conclusion That Gives

a clear statement of the author's **THESIS**

a sense of **CLOSURE** for the essay

With the funnel structure, writers pile up the evidence piece by piece but do not draw the significance of this evidence until the end. Writers might use this structure to present the reasonableness of their argument to a hostile audience, to lead an uninformed audience to form the writer's desired conclusion on an issue, or simply to prepare readers to accept a surprising conclusion.

Example

Grammar Gets Real

JEROME WINTER

Jerome Winter is a PhD candidate at the University of California, Riverside. For the last few years, he has been involved in teaching entry-level writing at the college level in various capacities: in the University Writing Program and Writing Across the Curriculum Program at UCR, in instruction at writing laboratories, and in basic writing courses. His studies center on the intersection of globalization and contemporary speculative fiction (SF). In this regard, he is the editor of Speculative Fiction *for the* Los Angeles Review of Books *and contributed a chapter on SF art and illustration to the* Oxford Handbook of Science Fiction *(2014). He has published articles, reviews, and interviews in* Science Fiction Studies, Extrapolation, *and* Journal of Fantastic in the Arts.

The story goes that Winston Churchill replied to an editor's insistence that one of his sentences should not end with a preposition with this genius one-liner: "This is the kind of tedious nonsense up with which I will not put." The comeback sticks in my mind probably because it reminds me that the best offense against Grammar Nazis is a good defense. For the sentence misattributed to Churchill is, on a purely technical level, grammatically correct. It fails, however, at achieving clarity and concision, our prime directive as far as the purpose of good writing goes. The tortured sentence clearly calls into question the rule of rearranging word order so as never to end sentences with a preposition.

Such questioning finds support in Dilin Liu's "Making Grammar Instruction More Empowering", published in the May 2011 issue of the journal *Research in the Teaching of English*. Liu is a so-called "descriptivist" who believes usage reflects a naturally evolving set of bottom-up norms that help writers communicate their meanings with the least amount of possible confusion. Liu therefore joins the academic fight against the overly nitpicky teaching of grammar still common in schools, which dates back at least to the nineteenth-century version of the Grammar Nazi archetype, the learned G. P. Quackenbos. This practice garnered support well into the late twentieth century with the writings of the eminent Henry Watson Fowler. The overly picky approach, so the complaint lodged against these so-called "prescriptivists" goes, has become widely enforced through a series of "Dos" and "Don'ts" scrawled on a whiteboard. These rules are then blandly memorized and regurgitated in the bubbled pencil lead of multiple-choice Scantrons. Liu therefore conducted research on the use of searchable databases of grammatical usage in the college classroom. Students who used these vast databases of acceptable usage to answer their grammatical queries reported their shock when real-world grammar frequently debunked the idea that certain usages are off-limits, for example, split infinitives, beginning sentences with "but" or "because," or placing commas after "therefore."

But the tendency to rigidly cling to such rules still exists; therefore, the grammar of sentences such as this one remains uncertain to a shrinking minority of readers. Other sources of pointless controversy on the subject of English and American lexicogrammatical rules are legendary. Should commas be placed after any prepositional phrases or only those prepositional phrases with five words or more? Does "begging the question" mean provoking follow-up questions, or does the phrase mean, in its more philosophically rigorous sense, conflating a proven conclusion with an assumed premise? To indicate a possessive, does one put an apostrophe after an "s" for a name that ends in "s," or does one add an apostrophe and another "s"? That is, is it Hopkins' or Hopkins's? Should "due to" be used only as an adjectival phrase in the mode of "attributable to," or can it also be used like the preposition "because of"? Can "hopefully" be used only as an adjective or adverb ("she asked hopefully"), or can it be used also as an initial position to modify an entire sentence—as in the phrase: "Hopefully, the grammar is not atrocious"? If you haven't answered this harangue with your own impatiently begged question—namely, "who cares?"—then you might want to do so now. A nagging doubt arises, then: "Is all attention to grammatical issues hairsplitting and nitpicky?" You don't have to be a Grammar Nazi to answer that question with a decisive negative.

Stephen King claims that the main rule he followed when he taught grammar in high school was a straightforward one, "Keep it Simple, Stupid." The writer surely means no disrespect to his or his students high intelligence by these words that beginning college writers should live by. As readers, writers often absorb standard usage through immersion in reading. However, when certain grammatical issues fail to sink in, then major breakdowns in clarity can occur. The most severe problems are not the trivial peccadilloes discussed above at all. Major errors include the usual suspects every writer invested in being understood clearly should be vigilant in avoiding, including sentence fragments, run-on sentences, subject-verb disagreement, mixed construction, pronoun confusion, tense errors, and comma splices. When writers revise drafts with a handy checklist of major errors such as these, the final drafts will be not only significantly more polished but also more comprehensible.

It is small wonder, then, that contemporary researchers suggest that beginning writers should avoid learning grammar out of context. Make no mistake; no one is suggesting that an academic or professional writer should resort to casual textspeak of liberally applied "LOL"s sprinkled with emoticons. The correction of severe grammatical problems is not a petty concern, and when college instructors demand the elimination of such grammatical mistakes, they are not being arbitrary. Severe grammatical errors fatally impair the author's ability to communicate clearly and appropriately to readers. However, a fussy obsession with memorizing grammar rules can undermine the writer's goal of developing meaningful and complex insights. The writer runs the risk of recreating the Churchill anecdote. Clarity comes from the lengthy and involved process of drafting and revising language, while also exploring ideas, rather than from a strict and unwavering faithfulness to a set of grammar rules that have been studied and memorized by rote.

Discussion Questions

1. Identify the thesis statement in Winter's article. Restate his claim in your own words. Discuss your initial response to it; do you think the position he takes is controversial? Explain.

2. Summarize in a few sentences the argument of "Grammar Gets Real."

3. Where, specifically, did Winter choose to place the thesis? How does the placement of the thesis in this particular position help make his readers more open to the position he takes in the article?

Applications

1. Using a couple of the reading selections from this book, identify which of the three structures each one uses, and speculate on the possible reasons for each writer's choice.

2. As a class, list some possible reasons why the conventional argument essay structure is most often expected in college writing assignments.

A Review of Strategies for Writing a Timed Essay

When writing an essay under time constraints, you need a clear and thoughtful strategy. Look over the following suggestions, and then write a plan of your own that takes into consideration your particular strengths and weaknesses.

1. **Read the questions in the writing topic**. Circle the interrogatives (question words: who, what, where, when, why, and how) in the first part of the writing topic.

2. **Read the essay** and underline the information that specifically answers the question(s). Make margin notes.

3. **Write your summary** in a manner that responds directly to the question(s) asked.

4. **Reread the writing topic**. Determine which point of the author's argument you are being asked to take a position on. Think about what you believe and why you believe the way you do. Write your thesis to express that position clearly.

5. **Write a series of paragraphs** that offer developed reasons and concrete examples that support your thesis. In each paragraph, be sure to show the connection between your reasons, your examples, and your thesis.

6. **Write a conclusion**. It should provide a sense of closure for your essay. It can be a restatement of your thesis or a recalling of certain important information in your summary. It must, however, leave no doubt as to your own position on the topic.

7. **Proofread your complete essay.** Then, double-check grammar and spelling by reading from the end of your essay to the beginning. Read your essay again to check that your ideas are fully developed and logically connected.

One Way You Might Budget Your Time

Here is one person's time plan for a timed final essay exam lasting two hours and forty-five minutes. You should arrange your own time plan in a way that works best for your particular skills and the time you have.

> **Step 1:** Reading the question—5 minutes
> **Step 2:** Reading/marking the reading selection—20 minutes
> **Step 3:** Writing the summary—15 minutes
> **Step 4:** Writing the thesis—10 minutes
> **Step 5:** Supporting the thesis—60 minutes
> **Step 6:** Writing the conclusion—10 minutes
> **Step 7:** Proofreading the essay—45 minutes

When creating your own time schedule, carefully consider your strengths and weaknesses. If you need more time for, say, understanding the reading selection, but are generally strong when it comes to writing clear, correct sentences, you might plan to spend thirty or more minutes examining and marking the reading selection, and thirty or less on proofreading your essay.

Once you create your time schedule, try to stick with it so that you take advantage of all of the stages of the writing process yet still finish on time. If you use your schedule, you won't run out of time, but neither will you waste some of the time you are given because you rushed through and neglected some important elements related to relevance, development, support, or sentence clarity and correctness. You may discover that you left something out, or that you made a mistake in the way you presented an idea or used a vocabulary word. We tend to hurry when doing timed writing, and often our hand struggles to keep up with our thoughts. It is too easy to make mistakes that will have an impact on how the essay is received by readers.

A Review of the Elements of the Conventional Argument Essay

A Review of an Introduction in an Argument Essay

Even if you are already familiar with the elements of a good introduction, review the guidelines below. Also, be sure to look back at these guidelines once your draft is completed. At that point in the writing process, you are more likely to understand your argument better than when you began to draft. For this reason, many writers draft their introduction after they have written their body paragraphs.

The introduction is often the most difficult part of an essay to draft. A paper's opening creates a first impression for readers, and deciding how to begin can be difficult. The introduction should do three things: capture readers' attention, set the stage for the paper's argument, and present the thesis statement. Length is also an important consideration: An introductory paragraph should be only as long as necessary to provide a context for the argument that the paper will develop. Too much detail or background information will bog down your introduction and leave readers feeling confused. Save the details for the paper's body.

Customarily, the last sentence of the introduction is the *thesis statement*. A strong thesis statement is essential to developing, organizing, and writing a successful persuasive paper. An essay isn't successful simply because its grammar is correct or because it has an introduction, a set of body paragraphs, and a conclusion. These components must have a thesis statement to tie them together and give them significance. The thesis statement is an important part of the introduction because it unifies the essay and gives it a purpose. Including it at the end of the introduction ensures that readers clearly understand the paper's purpose at the outset.

The essays you are assigned to write in *Write It Review* will follow the same format, and the introduction for each essay assignment will be effective if you follow these steps:

1st: Introduce the reading selection by giving the author's first and last name and the selection's title.
2nd: Give a directed summary of the reading selection (see the next page).
3rd: Present your thesis statement (be sure it answers the question or questions in the writing topic).

Hints

- **Don't offer a flat explanation of what you will cover in the paper:**
  "This essay will discuss. . . ."
- **Avoid clichés:**
  "It is certainly true that love is blind."
- **Avoid meaningless platitudes:**
  "People often find it difficult to get along with others in this world."
- **Do not resort to overly broad statements:**
  "Since the beginning of time, humans have tried to live peacefully."

A Review of the Guidelines for Writing a Directed Summary

The summary guidelines we give here are based on a specific type of writing assignment, one that asks you to read a persuasive piece of writing and respond to its argument in an essay of your own. We have said that the techniques that you learn in this book can be used for any persuasive academic writing assignment, and that is true. However, you should always take into consideration the specific context of any assignment because you will have to adjust your response to satisfy the particular requirements of that assignment.

The writing topics in *Write It Review* have a common set of requirements, as you will see. One of these requirements is that, for each unit's assignment, you will asked to write a *focused* summary of a reading, meaning a summary of a particular aspect of a reading designated in the writing topic that follows it. In other words, while a general summary asks you to take an entire reading into account, each of the assignments in Part 2 asks for a *directed* summary of a specific aspect of a reading.

To write a directed summary that is complete and correct, follow the steps below:

Preparation

Step 1: Carefully read through the reading selection and the writing topic questions that follow it.
Step 2: Underline the key terms in the first question.
Step 3: Locate in the essay the specific sentences that provide information relevant to answering the first question.
Step 4: Decide on the answer to that question. Be sure you have read through the essay more than once and are ready to provide a thorough and correct response.

Writing

Step 1: In or near the opening sentence, include the title of the essay (in quotation marks) and the full name of the author (after the first mention, the author should be referred to by last name only).
Step 2: In your own words, fully answer the first question in the writing topic.
Step 3: Explain this answer using careful reasoning.
Step 4: Use direct quotation sparingly and only when appropriate, to emphasize the answer the author provides to the question.

Hints

- Do not include minor details or points.
- Do not insert your own opinions or ideas and attribute them to the author.
- Do not ordinarily include examples.

Applications

Examine the following student-written introductions, taken from the case studies in Part 3 of this book. Using the two sets of guidelines given above, "A Review of an Introduction in an Argument Essay" and "A Review of the Guidelines for Writing a Directed Summary," discuss some of the strengths and weaknesses of these four introductions. If you wish, you can turn to Part 3 and familiarize yourself with the reading selections and the writing topics each of the students is responding to.

1. In "How Male and Female Students Participate in Class," Deborah Tannen places men and women into two separate, conflicting categories when it comes to learning preferences. She believes that women are more likely to participate in open discussions with a minimum amount of challenges and debates. Men, conversely, appreciate being attacked publicly, and find it more rewarding to debate since it adds to defense skills. I agree with Tannen's representation of behavior in the classroom; men are bolder and willing to stand out while women are more reluctant to participate in class if they believe they will be "attacked."

2. According to Deborah Tannen, in the article, How Male and Female Students Participate in Class, she elaborates on the differences the way men and women think and feel speaking in class. Tannen explains that in general men are very aggressive and women are quiet and soft. Girls have a tendency to easily become friends by telling each other secrets as boys have a tendency to pick on each other. Deborah Tannen's explanation of these differences help me understand student behavior in the classroom not only because of the article but because she states facts that I have even observed in some of my classes. So, is it true what Tannen is elaborating on? Well, I've come to a conclusion that she has a very good perspective on how men and women behave in a classroom.

3. In "What Management Doesn't Know", Devun Hackleton writes about the communication breakdowns that occur because management doesn't understand their employee's jobs and associated stresses. The author believes that managers should have hands-on experience in a variety of jobs that are part of the business before holding supervisor positions. Managers need hands-on experience so they make correct judgements and decisions, because college degrees can't be substituted for years of experience.

4. In the essay "What Management Doesn't Know," the author describes the lack of communication between employers and employees and the lack of hands-on experience of many employers. He writes that if employers don't have any experience in the fields they're managing, there is a lack of communication with the employees. Managers do not know the kind of stress and dangers their employees go through every day. This problem occurs because managers and supervisors are hired straight out of college and do not know the workings of a company. Many are also hired straight out of college to create cost-cutting plans. They have no idea how the field works and do not create the most cost effective plans. Employees who have been in the field for a long time are the best for management because of the experience and the knowledge of the tasks involved in the field. Manager should understand and experience the work of their employees before taking the role of a supervisor. I agree with the author's argument because I have been employed in a case where the manager had no hands-on experience and in a case where he did.

Strategies for Developing Your Ideas

Students often say that they know *how* to write an essay—that is, they know it should have an introduction, thesis statement, supporting body paragraphs, and a conclusion—but they don't have anything to write *about*. They don't know what to say, and they can't think of any experiences they have had that they can use. Consider using the techniques below for exploring your thoughts and finding strategies that work whenever you are faced with a challenging writing assignment.

Time is the crucial element here. It takes time to think carefully and systematically about a subject. You will have to focus your thoughts and have patience in order for your mind to work, to develop insights that go beyond surface impressions and quick, easy judgments. You should do much of your thinking in writing—this aspect is very important. Writing your thoughts down will give them definition and clarity.

If you find yourself without good ideas about a subject, try these strategies. You might not use all of them for any given assignment. Instead, look them over and choose those that seem most promising for the particular piece of writing you are developing:

1. *Focus*: Write down the issue of the reading selection that you want to explore; a simple phrase might be enough.
2. *Response*: Look over the selection again (and the reading and summary questions you have answered) and list its ideas. Write down
   a. any questions and/or doubts you have about these ideas, and list your reasons.
   b. any points the writer makes that you find persuasive, and the reasons you find them convincing.
   c. your thoughtful impression of the reading selection.
   d. a final conclusion about the selection's argument, its weaknesses, and its strengths.

Hint

Your responses here do not have to be polished. Allow yourself to write freely, putting down all ideas that come to you. You will sort them out later.

3. *Reflection*: Now you need some data, some basic observations from your own experience that you can examine and use to draw conclusions or insights. First, write down, in a rough list, any personal memories you have that seem to relate to the subject you are writing on. Do a few minutes of freewriting to explore these memories. Try some *focused freewriting*, whereby you keep the essay's general subject in mind but write down everything that you can, even things you roughly associate with the subject. Stay with it until you feel you have something substantial, something your readers will find thoughtful and compelling.
   If you need more structure, try using these general guidelines for each incident:
   a. Begin by simply recounting what you remember: Make it as brief as possible, but don't omit anything that seems important.

   b. Now expand your thinking: Try to speculate about the importance of the memory and its relevance to the subject you are exploring.

   c. Look over what you have written: Underline the ideas that you think are important. Think about the way they relate to the reading selection's ideas. How are your ideas like the selection's? How are they different?

   d. Take note: Consider any judgment words in your freewriting, such as *sometimes, always, seems to, might mean, only when, but if.* These will help you formulate the position you want to take in your thesis statement.

4. *Expansion*: Keeping the subject in mind, write down any relevant experiences you can think of from the world at large. Do you know of any examples from books, the news, movies, and your cultural awareness in general? Freewrite for each example that comes to mind.

5. *A Reconsideration of Your Freewriting*

   a. First, begin by simply recounting the event or text, summarizing its main elements as briefly as you can without omitting important elements.

   b. Now move beyond the basic facts and try to explore the implications of each for the subject. What thoughts come to mind as you reflect on the event or text? What do those thoughts suggest about the subject? Take your freewriting as far as you can for each event or text you have listed.

   c. Then, look over all that you have written. Underline the ideas that you think are important. Try to explain in writing how they relate to the reading selection's ideas. How are they like the reading selection's? How are they different?

   d. Finally, look for the judgment words. These will help you formulate the position you want to take in your thesis statement. What seems to be your strongest feeling about the subject, the one most dominant in your freewriting?

6. *Shape*: Consider what you have underlined and the judgment words you found. What significance do they have once you consider them all together? What do they "add up to"?

   a. Group parts of your freewriting together. Find some main ideas that you came back to two or three times using different experiences, examples, or texts. Try to identify all of the main ideas you find, and write out the connection between them and the underlined portions of your freewriting.

   b. Explore the parts you underlined and the implications you noted by asking yourself the following questions:

      • Which parts seem important, and why?
      • How do the lists you made fit together, or what do they add up to?
      • Do any parts of your freewriting contradict other parts, or do parts have similar ideas?
      • What do either the contradictions or the similarities suggest?

   c. Identify the ideas that you feel strongly about. Write about the reasons they are important and the way they relate to the subject you are exploring.

Hint

Sometimes it is too restrictive to think in terms of "for or against" the reading selection's issue. There are often more than two positions on a topic, and disagreeing with the position taken in the reading selection may mean that, while the selection's ideas may be sound, the conclusions drawn are not as convincing, in your mind, as the conclusions you want to draw.

Hint

Your goal is to uncover what you know and develop it so that you can show your readers how you arrived at your main ideas and how your ideas led to your thesis statement.

Once you've done some freewriting and located important topics and supporting details, you have the foundation pieces to create an outline.

When you are assigned an essay from a unit in Part 2, the writing support pages that are in the unit will guide you to develop your ideas on the relevant issue presented in the lead essay. But do not forget the strategies given here in Part 1. They may be useful to you as you work to complete any of the assignments in Part 2.

Writing Supporting Paragraphs for Your Thesis Statement

The body paragraphs make up the largest part of an essay, and each paragraph should develop one important point in support of the thesis statement. Paragraphs should be unified around a central point and should contain concrete evidence that clarifies and supports that central point. Readers need concrete evidence as examples that help them to understand your ideas. Therefore, body paragraphs usually open with a topic sentence, and include evidence, a discussion of the evidence, and an explanation of how the paragraph's subject matter connects to your thesis claim. Writing a well-developed paragraph can be easy once you understand the paragraph's conventional structure. Here is a useful memory device that will help you construct well-developed body paragraphs:

Remember the 4Cs:

Controlling idea sentence
Corroborating details
Careful explanation of why the details are significant
Connection to the thesis statement

Once you determine your thesis statement, you can develop your supporting paragraphs using the following guidelines:

Controlling idea sentence

First, write a topic sentence that announces the point you want to make in the paragraph.

Corroborating details

Then, think of one or more specific examples that will help you explain and prove the point.

Careful explanation of why the details are significant

Now, carefully explain how each example proves the point you are making in the paragraph.

Connection to the thesis statement

Be sure to connect your examples and explanation to the position you have taken in your thesis statement. Tell your reader what the paragraph's point and examples have to do with your argument.

Here's an example:

Thesis: The violence on television desensitizes viewers to violence and can ultimately lead to a thoughtless and uncaring society.

Controlling idea sentence for a paragraph supporting the thesis statement
Write a sentence stating the point you want to make in the paragraph:

After seeing casual violence repeatedly on television, viewers come to see real-life violence in terms of entertainment rather than real human tragedy.

Corroborating details

Think of some examples that will show that people see violence in terms of entertainment rather than real tragedy. Here are some sample sentences:

- A couple of weeks ago, there was a pause in the traffic flow because there was an accident on the freeway and people like to slow down and look.

- The last time I watched the evening news, reporters spent most of the time reporting on acts of violence in our society rather than on more positive events, I think because more people want to hear about violence.

Careful explanation of why the details are significant

Explain how these examples show that people see violence in terms of entertainment rather than real-life tragedy.

Connection to the thesis statement

Explain how we can understand this view of violence as an indication of society's growing lack of thought and care (paragraph's controlling idea), and how this is a direct result of television violence (tie to thesis statement).

Here is a sample body paragraph from a student paper on the issue of genetic cloning and its use. See if you can follow the 4Cs paragraph development.

Essay

> The paper's thesis statement: I agree with McMillan that, in spite of the excitement about cloning, it shouldn't be used right now because our limited knowledge makes it too dangerous.

(Controlling Idea Sentence) Although many experts are excited about pushing forward with the uses of cloning, the promise of cloning is still far on the horizon, and much more work must be done before it is widely used with confidence. (***Corroborating Details***) At a recent biotechnology conference, one expert said, "I am convinced that human cloning is going to play a critical role in the future of our species. We cannot afford to ignore the potential benefits of this science. It may well mean the ultimate survival of our species" (McDermott 29). Many people agree with him. In fact, scientists all over the world are experimenting with animals, and even humans, to gain some of the benefits that our early stages of knowledge allow, but cloning is still primarily a matter of trial and error, and successful attempts have been few. Methods of cloning are still very crude, and only a mere 3% of the successfully reconstructed embryos reach the birth stage (Doyle 69). The first attempt made to clone an animal, a sheep now named "Dolly," took 276 cloning attempts. (***Careful Explanation of Why the Details are Significant***) The chances of serious mistakes, with such a low success rate, suggest caution is necessary. The responsibility attached to such a powerful tool is enormous, and scientists must be careful as they move forward, and wait to introduce such a significant ability to widespread social use. (***Connection to the Thesis Statement***) Hence, in spite of the excitement about genetic cloning, we must, for now, keep genetic cloning limited to laboratory experiment because our limited knowledge makes it too dangerous to use.

Remember that you should use the 4Cs with great flexibility, rather than rigidly as a set formula. Each paragraph in an argument essay requires its own stylized structure and application of these basic elements. The goal, after all, is to maximize the support of your thesis statement. You may find, for example, that you have more than one corroborating detail to add to support the topic of a paragraph and you may decide to include most or all of it to support your topic sentence. Sometimes, too, one sentence will be all you will need to show the paragraph's relevance to your thesis statement; other times, you may need several sentences. Think of the 4Cs as layers in a paragraph, elements that must be present, but that may intertwine and develop in creative and even necessary ways that are different each time you use them to build a supporting paragraph.

Application

1. Look over several of the supporting paragraphs in the essays in this book. Evaluate the strengths or weaknesses: Are the paragraphs fully developed? Are the topic sentences clear? Are the corroborating details convincing? Are there enough of them to support the writer's assertions? Is the writer able to tie the paragraphs to the overarching argument of the paper?

2. Rewrite one of the paragraphs you feel is weak, or restructure a set of short, incomplete paragraphs to make one strong one. Explain your revision.

A Review of Logical Fallacies

A writer's job is to provide as much evidence and support as possible for his or her thesis. However, the argument that a writer offers to defend that thesis must be sound. If some of the arguments the writer presents are illogical or unfair, the writer will undermine his or her own position and lose credibility with readers.

Arguments that lack reason or justice are called *fallacies*. Fallacies are simply false arguments. Often, writers are so enthusiastic about their own position that they make false claims, unethical arguments, or assertions that cannot be proven by the evidence at hand. The best way to guard against spurious arguments is to become familiar with some of the most common types of fallacies and learn to recognize them in your own writing and the writing of others.

Fallacies fall into two categories. The first category contains unethical arguments. These arguments attempt to manipulate the reader emotionally or attack the opposing position in some way that is unjust. Here are some examples of fallacies that are manipulative or unfair:

1. *Ad hominem*—attacking the person rather than the argument itself
   example: A well-known plant pathologist, Harold Weber, has written a book discussing the relationship between plant health and human disease, but his ideas should not be taken seriously because he gambles too much in Las Vegas.
   example: The members of the Glee Club are a bunch of prima donnas, so, of course, they would oppose spending money to charter a bus instead of using cars to go to Disneyland for Senior Ditch Day.

Hint

Check to see if your argument remains focused on ideas and reason rather than the character of an individual.

2. *Birds of a feather*—using guilt by association to blame the person for actions of friends or family
   example: Lupe Santiago belonged to a Girl Scout troop whose leader embezzled money from the cookie fund, so Lupe should not be the treasurer of our club.
   example: John Smith's sister has a drug problem, so even though he is a qualified nurse, he shouldn't be trusted in a job that requires him to administer prescribed narcotics to dying patients.

Hint

Check to see that your rejection of a point of view is based on its merit rather than its supporters.

3. *Sob story*—using a sad situation or dramatic case to manipulate the readers' emotions

> example: A wildfire set by an arsonist cost Kenji Yamamoto his house and his family, so you should agree to go with him to the prom.
>
> example: Santiago Cortez was the only member of his family to survive a horrific plane crash, so he is the best candidate for mayor of our town.

Hint

Check to see if you are appealing to the audience's reason rather than their pity.

The majority of fallacies are illogical because the thinking behind their arguments is flawed; the conclusions offered by these fallacies follow neither inductive nor deductive reasoning. Here are some examples of false reasoning:

1. *Circular reasoning*—restating the same argument in other words instead of giving evidence or proof

> example: *The Big Bang Theory* is my favorite television show, so it is the best show on television because I like it a lot.
>
> example: The president has thought a lot about health care, so his plan is the most well-thought-out plan available.

Hint

Check to see that you support your argument with evidence, not repetition.

2. *Post hoc, ergo propter hoc* (Latin for "after this, therefore because of this")—assuming because one event follows another, the first causes the second

> example: The night before the midterm, Karl Johnson played a game of baseball with his friends. The next day, he performed badly on his test. Karl failed the exam because he played baseball.
>
> example: On Saturday night, Eun Hee went to the movies with her girlfriends, and on Sunday her boyfriend Jun Ho broke up with her. Jun Ho ended his relationship with Eun Hee because she went out with her friends.

Hint

Check to see that the relationship between two occurrences is causal, not temporal.

3. *False dichotomy*—assuming an either/or choice so that the writer's position seems the only correct one

> example: Olmsted Hall is not earthquake safe. Either we tear it down, or students will die.

example: Either we eradicate the Pit Bull breed altogether, or children playing outside will not be safe from dog attacks.

Hint

Check to see that there are no other alternatives to the two options you are asking the audience to choose between.

4. *Hasty generalization*—basing a conclusion on limited evidence
   example: The girls in my college dorm wrote their lab notes in green ink; therefore, green is the color of ink used by college girls in biology lab.
   example: My dog leaves the carrots in his bowl when I give him my leftover beef stew. Therefore, dogs do not eat vegetables.

Hint

Check to see that the sample you are using to draw your conclusion IS not overly small.

5. *False authority*—citing a source that has no validity in terms of the subject
   example: Edmund Craft, the Pulitzer Prize-winning journalist, wears Brock loafers, so they must be comfortable.
   example: Li'l' Hound, a popular rapper, took his mother to Mexico for expensive cancer drug treatments unapproved by the FDA, so the medicine must really work.

Hint

Check to see that the source you use is recognized as having authority on the subject under discussion.

Transitions

Connect or Correct

Essays need transitions to link the ideas in individual sentences to each other and to tie paragraphs together. Transitions are the words or phrases that help relate thoughts and ideas to each other. Without transitions, sentences are merely lists, and paragraphs can seem disconnected from each other.

Transitions link concepts in one of two ways: They can signal that individual sentences or paragraphs extend a train of thought (***connect***), or they can predict for the reader that whatever follows will change the direction of thought (***correct***). Careful use of transitions improves the overall coherence of your essay.

There are a number of categories of transitional words that ***connect*** sentences and paragraphs. Here are some of the kinds of transitions and some examples of words and phrases that ***connect***:

Relationship	Transition Word
time	afterward, later, meanwhile, next, now, suddenly, then
continuation	also, finally, furthermore, in addition, secondly
reasons	for this reason, in order to, to that end
examples	for example, for instance, to illustrate, to show that
assertion	in fact, indeed, to tell the truth
repetition	as already noted, in other words
similarity	in the same way, likewise, similarly
space	here, near, opposite

Here are some kinds of transitions and some examples of words and phrases that ***correct***:

alternative	besides, not, or
contrast	however, in contrast, on the other hand, to the contrary

Smooth transitions between sentences and paragraphs can be achieved in other ways besides the use of particular transitional words and phrases. Here are some other ways to link ideas and thoughts.

repetition	repeating a word or phrase from the previous sentence or the previous paragraph in the new construction
parallelism	using a similar structure in consecutive sentences or paragraphs
	In other words, begin paragraphs with very similar sentences or with sentences noticeably similar in structure. Within a paragraph, repetition of sentence structure can be used for emphasis and to highlight the connection between ideas.

Hint

To check that you have provided transition words when necessary, identify the relationship you see between each sentence and the one that follows it, and between each paragraph and the one that follows it. Then, make sure you have provided a transition word when needed to help the reader see that relationship.

Application

Turn back to Weinstein's "The Ethics of Work-Life Balance" and find three good places to insert transition words. Rewrite the sentences in the space below, including the transition words; then, compare the new version to the original version. Discuss with a classmate the changes each of you made. Consider, based on your discussion, how transitions may be used to smooth out the flow of your sentences, and how they can also be overused so that your sentences become wordy or too long. You will want to develop a good sense of when to use transition words, and when to let your sentences stand more independently from one another.

Conclusions

The conclusion's primary purpose is to provide closure for your essay, but there are several effective ways to accomplish that goal. Consider the strategies below so that you can call on the most appropriate one for every essay you write.

Any essay that includes discussion of more than one point, idea, or example requires a conclusion. Without a conclusion, the reader has no sense of closure, no certainty that you have come to the end of your argument. It is important that you let the reader know that your essay is complete, not because you have run out of things to say or time to say them, but because you have fully explored and supported your thesis. The conclusion of the essay is also the place for you to impress upon the reader the importance of considering your ideas.

A good conclusion accomplishes two tasks:

1. It makes the reader aware of the finality of your argument.

2. It leaves the reader with an understanding of the significance of your argument.

Hint

Check to see that the conclusion of your essay fulfills the promise suggested by your introduction.

Writing the conclusion of your essay will offer you many choices and many challenges. You may choose a simple, formal ending, or you may choose to be somewhat creative and less conventional. Familiarize yourself with the possibilities below, and then decide which works best for your particular essay:

Types of Conclusions

Brief Summary	"In conclusion. . . ." "To summarize briefly. . . ."
Significance of Subject	"All these matters need to be understood because. . . ."
Most Important Point	"Lastly, remember that. . . ."
Request for Action or Opinion	X must be changed. . . ."
Useful Quotation	"In the words of Y. . . ."
Emotional Statement	an outcry, appeal, or plea such as "Let's all move to. . . ." or "Please. . . ."

Interesting Anecdote	a short relevant story, or a reference to a story mentioned in the introduction
Directive	"In the future. . . ." or "From now on. . . ."

Application

1. Look at the conclusions of the student essays in one of the case studies of Part 3 of this book, and identify which type of conclusion each one uses (a call to action, a summary, and so on).

2. Choose the one conclusion you feel is most effective and share your choice, and the reasons for that choice, with your classmates.

Strategies for Participating in a Rough Draft Workshop

After you have completed the first draft of your essay, your instructor may ask you to bring that rough draft to class for a workshop. Giving and receiving feedback is an important part of the writing process. While it is helpful to have friends and relatives who are not in your class read and comment on what you have written, other members of the class can better evaluate your writing in ways that are focused on the material and assignments for your particular course.

The process of reading and evaluating your classmates' papers provides you with a valuable learning experience and requires you to think again about the assignment as you read responses to it by your peers. You will be able to bring the insight you gained from this activity to your own work.

While you are reading papers written by members of your class, they will be reading and commenting on your paper. It is important that you seriously consider the critique you receive, and use it to improve your essay. If you disagree with a suggested change, you must make sure that you can give a good reason for not taking your reader's suggestion. You have to remember that the reader is judging your response to the assignment solely by the words on the printed page. Something that may seem clear to you in your own head but is confusing to the reader requires more thought on your part. Remember that the reader's remarks are intended to help you improve your work and are not meant as criticism of your writing ability.

How to Get the Most out of Your Rough Draft Workshop

As a Reader:

- Come prepared with your textbook, the assignment sheet, and writing apparatus.
- Listen to and carefully follow the directions given by your instructor.
- Do a quick first read through the essay you are reviewing without writing on either the draft itself or a review sheet.
- Then, carefully consider the questions or issues you have been instructed to evaluate one by one. As you consider each question, issue, section, or paragraph, make notes on your observations about the things that are working and the things that need more attention.
- The more specific the comment, the more helpful it will be to the writer. Ask what the writer intended in a particular sentence or passage, if it isn't clear; try to identify *why* a sentence or passage isn't clear or doesn't logically work; praise something that works and say why it does; avoid overused and unhelpful words such as "good," "nice," or "okay."
- Finally, think about the work as a whole and provide a written summary that clarifies the successes and problems you see in the draft as it is.

As a Writer:

- Bring a complete and readable draft of your own essay.
- When you get your paper back from your reader, if there are comments that are not clear to you, ask for a verbal explanation from your reviewer.
- Consider the suggestions carefully, and try to understand what in your essay led your reader to react in that particular way to the words on your paper.

- When you begin to revise, go back to the written peer review you have been given. Start with the final overview of the paper. Then, ask yourself whether you need to begin by rethinking the whole concept of your essay or by simply working to improve individual sections.
- Finally, use your handbook to review any grammatical or technical errors in your essay that were obvious to the reader. Once you feel that you understand the rules, make any necessary corrections.

A Sample Scoring Rubric

High Pass (A, A-, B+)

This score indicates superior writing skills. An essay receiving a high pass has a sophisticated style marked by variety in sentence structure, effective word usage, and mastery of the conventions of written English. The content of the essay responds directly to the writing topic with a persuasive argument and reasoned examples that address and explore the issue in a focused, organized, and thoroughly developed manner.

Pass (B, B-)

This score indicates strong writing skills. A passing essay characteristically shows some variety of usage in syntax and vocabulary and demonstrates competence in grammar and mechanics. It presents a response to the writing topic that is thoughtful and appropriate. Its argument is well developed with relevant examples and clear reasoning.

Low Pass (C+, C)

This score indicates satisfactory writing skills, which may be marginal in some areas. It often has some sentence-level errors, but these errors do not interfere with comprehension, and, for the most part, there is control of grammar and mechanics. The content provides an appropriate but sometimes partial or somewhat abbreviated answer to the writing topic. There is an attempt to focus and organize, but ideas and examples may not be logically sequenced or may be so brief as to lack clarity.

High Fail (C-)*

This score indicates a problem in one or more of the following areas. Sentences may lack variety, may use vocabulary in an imprecise manner, or may contain an unacceptable number of grammar and mechanical errors. The content of the essay might not adequately respond to the writing topic due to some misreading of the topic, or it may fail to develop its ideas with logic and/or examples. The essay may lack focus because it offers no thesis or central idea, it digresses, or it provides no discernible pattern of organization.

Fail (D+, D)

This score indicates clearly inadequate writing skills. Sentences tend to be simplistic and structurally repetitive. Errors in grammar, mechanics, and word choice are numerous. The essay's content reveals a misunderstanding of the writing topic itself. There may not be sufficient examples or any other details or ideas relevant to the topic. Paragraphs are often disconnected, and the point, or thesis, of the essay is not clear.

Low Fail (D-, F)

This score indicates a complete lack of familiarity with the conventions of written English. There is no control of grammar, mechanics, or vocabulary, and the sentences may be unintelligible. The content of the essay fails to respond to the writing topic in any logical manner, and it ordinarily fixates on a single idea or detail. There often is no organizational pattern, and what development there is comes from repetition of a digression stemming from the single idea or detail.

*Some schools accept a C- as a passing grade.

A CLOSER LOOK AT YOUR CONTROL AT THE SENTENCE LEVEL

Proofreading Your Essay for Mistakes in Grammar, Punctuation, and Mechanics

Students often feel that their work is completed once they have revised their rough draft by honing the content and arguments it contains, but they should still carefully examine their sentences to eliminate any errors. Frequently, errors in the rough draft are overlooked during the revision process because writers are focused on idea development and structure. Any writer should review her or his work several times to omit grammatical, mechanical, and spelling errors. While word processing programs can be helpful in finding some mistakes, computers are limited in this area. It is, therefore, the writer's responsibility to proofread and edit before printing out a final draft.

Here are a few strategies to focus your editing:

- Read your essay aloud, word for word, being careful to say exactly what you wrote, and not what you meant to write.
- Let the draft sit for a while after it is drafted; getting away from it will allow you to return to it with more objectivity.
- Be sure to edit using a paper copy; mistakes will be easier to find.
- For the errors you know you often make, read your draft several times, each time focusing on one error at a time.

Examine the following ten errors commonly made by writers.

Becoming familiar with these errors will help you to avoid them.

1. Verb Errors
   Underline the verbs and then
   - check to see that they agree with their subjects. (For help, consult a handbook.)
   - make sure you have used the correct verb tense. (For help, consult a handbook.)
   - when possible, change "to be" verbs (is, are, was, etc.) to action words.
     - *Flat*:   Gloria Watkins is a good writer.
     - *Active*:   Gloria Watkins writes brilliantly.
2. Use of Inappropriate or Informal Language
   Mark sentences that contain informal language or slang. Rewrite them using more formal language.
   - *No*:   Kids' fairy tales are, like, really great to hear when you're a kid.
   - *Yes*:   We all enjoyed listening to fairy tales when we were young.
3. Pronoun Agreement or Reference Errors
   Circle all the pronouns in your draft and then
   - check to be sure that the nouns they refer to are clear; if they aren't, change the unclear pronouns to nouns.
   - be sure that each pronoun agrees with its referent.
     - *No*:   Even though a person may witness an accident, <u>they</u> will not be able to remember exactly what happened.
     - *Yes*:   Even though a person may witness an accident, he or she will not be able to remember exactly what happened.

4. Unwanted Repetition

   Identify sentences close to one another in the paper that use the same word two or more times (ignoring common words such as "the" or "to"). Eliminate the repetition by
   - looking for synonyms to replace repeated words.
   - seeing if you can combine two sentences into one and eliminate repetition that way.

5. Overuse of Sentences Similar in Construction

   To vary the pace of your sentences, try changing the construction of three or four of your sentences. For example, you can reorder the wording or turn sentences into phrases or dependent clauses.

   > Every culture has its own celebrations and rituals to mark special days.
   > Celebrations and rituals mark special days in every culture.
   > A writer might revise a paper several times before he or she submits it for a class.
   > Before submitting a paper for a class, a writer might revise it several times.

6. Comma Splice Errors

   Be sure there are no commas joining two complete sentences. For each comma splice, use one of the following methods to correct the error:

   > *comma splice error:*   Barbara decided to run for public office, however, she knew that the odds were against her winning.

   - Change the comma to a semicolon.
     > Barbara decided to run for public office; however, she knew that the odds were against her winning.
   - Change the comma to a period and a capital letter.
     > Barbara decided to run for public office. However, she knew that the odds were against her winning.
   - Link the sentences with a coordinating conjunction (for, and, nor, but, or, yet, so)
     > Barbara decided to run for public office, but she knew that the odds were against her winning.
   - Turn the second sentence into a dependent clause or phrase.
     > Although she knew that the odds were against her winning, Barbara decided to run for public office.

7. Unwanted Use of "You"

   Rewrite any sentence where "you" is used; eliminate "you" by replacing it with "I," "we," or another noun or pronoun.

   > *No:*   You can always identify a person who is wearing a uniform.
   > *Yes:*   We can always identify a person that is wearing a uniform.
   > *Yes:*   Everyone can identify a person that is wearing a uniform.

8. Word Choice Errors

   Use a dictionary to look up words you are unsure of and to make sure you've used them correctly.

9. Spelling Errors

   Use spell check to eliminate misspelled words.

10. Punctuation Errors

    Be sure all sentences begin with a capital letter and have the appropriate punctuation mark at the end.

Assessing Your Grammar Awareness

Below are two diagnostic tests that check grammar mastery. Take Test #1. Next, check your answers with an answer key (your instructor will supply one) and mark those you got wrong. Then, fill in the assessment sheet to identify your grammar weaknesses. The assessment sheet will give you a focus for further study. You might, for example, use the index in your handbook to find out why you made the errors you made and how to correct them.

Identify each item as correct or incorrect. If it is correct, then simply write "OK" on the lines below. If a sentence is incorrect, then rewrite the whole sentence and make it correct.

Verb Tense and Form

1. Homer was a blind poet of ancient Greece whose works are passing down in the oral tradition.

    Homer was a blind Poet of Ancient Greece whose works were Passed down in the oral tradition

2. It may be that his epics are the compilations of stories by many authors.

    OK

3. Many works of art inspired by Homer's subject matter are hanged in museums all over the world.

    Many works of art inspired by Homer's subject matter are hung in museums all over the world

4. The Trojan War had an economic basis even though the excuse the Greeks used was that Paris had stealed Helen.

    The trojan War had economic basis even though the excuse Greeks used was that Paris had stolen Helen

5. In Homer's version, the Greeks say that Paris has kidnapped Helen, but the truth is that Helen loves the handsome, charming Paris.

In Homers version, the Greeks say that Paris has kidnapped Helen, but the truth is that Helen loved the handsome charming Paris

Subject-Verb Agreement

6. *The Iliad* begins when the flotilla of Greek ships ~~are~~ ⁱˢ ready to leave for Troy, but the ships are becalmed.

7. Agamemnon consults the priest, who tells him that he must sacrifice his sixteen-year-old daughter, Iphigenia, to bring the winds.

8. When Iphigenia dies, the winds come; the Greeks reach Troy and ~~camps~~ ᶜᵃᵐᵖ on the beach.

9. The battles in *The Iliad* often involves one-on-one combat between Greek and Trojan heroes.

The battles in the Iliad often involve one on one combat between Greek and Trojan heroes

10. The residents of Troy are able to watch the bloody battles from the walls of the city.

OK

Pronoun Agreement

his or her

11. Everyone in Troy is able to watch ~~their~~ loved ones die on the battlefield.

OK

12. The Trojans reinforce when they see the Greeks getting ready to leave.

OK

13. Some soldiers build a great wooden horse and conceal soldiers in them.

Some soldiers built a great wooden house and conceal soldiers in it.

14. The Greek army pretends to leave after they roll the horse up to the city gates.

The Greek Army pretends to leave after they roll the horse up to the city gates

15. Someone in the crowd of soldiers says they think it might be a trick, but no one listens.

Someone in the crowd of soldiers says he or she ~~thinks it~~ might be a trick but no one listens

Pronoun Reference

16. The Trojans bring the horse, a gift from the Greeks, into their city.

OK

17. The Trojans party when they see the Greek ships leave and know they are safe.

Knowing they are safe, the Trojans party when they see the Greek ships leave

18. In the middle of the night, the Greek soldiers come out of the great horse and attack the Trojans, and they are killed.

In the middle of the night, the Greek soldiers come out of the

19. As the Greek soldiers find reinforcements, many Trojan soldiers are killed or enslaved, and their anger further ignites the war.

OK

20. Since Homer wrote this story, something is called a "Trojan horse" because it is a ruse.

OK

Dangling and Misplaced Modifiers

21. Having defeated the Trojans, the Greek ships depart after the war.

OK

22. Odysseus has angered the Gods, throwing them off course.

Odysseus had angered the Gods, throwing them off course

23. Enduring many hardships and adventures, Odysseus wanders for ten years.

Enduring many hardships and adventures Odysseus wundered for ten years

24. The English word "odyssey" is derived from Odysseus's name meaning a long wandering.

The English word "odyssey" is derived from Odysseus's name, which means a long wandering

25. Often seeming crafty or sly, Homer describes Odysseus using the adjective "wily" in the epic poem.

OK

Parallelism

26. Odysseus and his men face great dangers on their journey and dependent on the wind.

Odysseus and his men face great dangers on their journey and depend on the wind

27. Imprisoned in Polyphemus's cave, they watch their comrades being eaten, realize they will soon share the same fate because they have no weapons of defense.

Imprisoned in polyphemus's cave, they watch their comrades being eaten and realize they will soon share the same fate because they have no weapons of defense

28. Odysseus blinds the Cyclops, devises his escape by tucking himself under the sheep in the cave, and finds freedom when the sheep go out to graze.

O|C

29. Next, Odysseus and his ship reach the Aeolian Isles, whose inhabitants are hospitable and entertain them.

O|C

30. To help Odysseus on his way and speeding his return to Ithaca, Aeolus, Keeper of the Wind, gives Odysseus a west wind.

O|C

Fused (Run-On) Sentences

31. Storms blow Odysseus's ships past Ithaca, and in ten days they reach the land where the lotus-eaters live, the men go ashore and eat the magic lotus that induces memory loss.

    OK

32. Odysseus orders other sailors to shore they have to drag the original search party back to the ship.

    Odysseus orders other sailors to shore. They have to drag the original search Party back to shore

33. When they come to an island inhabited by aggressive, fierce, one-eyed giants known as Cyclopes, one of the giants, Polyphemus, imprisons Odysseus and his twelve men in a cave.

    OK

34. While Polyphemus is sleeping, Odysseus steals a piece of the giant's staff and sharpens it he makes the point red hot in the fire.

    While Polyphemus is Sleeping odysseus steals a piece of the giants staff and Sharpens it. He makes the point red hot in the fire

35. Using the hot point, Odysseus burns out the giant's eye, and now Polyphemus is blind.

    OK

Comma Splices

36. Back at the palace in Ithaca, Odysseus's wife Penelope has her own problems, her many suitors are pressing her to pick one of them as a husband.

Back at the Palace in Ithaca, Penelope has her own Problems. Her many suitors are pressing her to Pick one of them as a husband

37. Many of the suitors stay at the palace, and they squander Odysseus's wealth on riotous living and sumptuous banquets.

OK

38. Penelope, as wily as Odysseus, staves off the suitors by declaring that first she must weave a shroud for Odysseus's father, every night she unravels what she has woven that day.

Penelope, as wily as odysseus, starves off the suitors by declaring that first she must weave a shroud. Every night she unravels what she has woven

39. Some servants betray Penelope to the suitors, who angrily force Penelope to make a decision.

OK

40. Penelope is smart and has a secret strategy, she says she will marry the man who can pull Odysseus's bow and send the arrow flying through the holes of twelve aligned ox blades.

Penelope is smart and has a secret strategy. She says she will marry the man who can pull odysseus's bow and send the arrow flying through the hole of twelve aligned ox blades

Problem	Needs Review	Needs Study	Completed
Verb Tense and Form			
Subject-Verb Agreement			
Pronoun Agreement			
Pronoun Reference			
Dangling and Misplaced Modifiers			
Parallelism			
Fused (Run-On) Sentences			
Comma Splices			

Identify each sentence as correct or incorrect. If a sentence is correct, write **"OK"** on the line below. If the sentence is incorrect, then rewrite the whole sentence and make it correct.

Verb Tense

1. Charles Dickens, the famous novelist, was born in Kent on February 7, 1812, but he moves to London when he is nine.

   _____

   _____

   _____

2. Dickens's father spent more than he made, so the whole family had been sent to debtors' prison in 1824.

   _____

   _____

   _____

3. For a short time while his family was living in prison, young Dickens is working in a blacking warehouse.

   _____

   _____

   _____

4. Many young children in Dickens's novels share a similar fate; for example, Oliver Twist is raised in a workhouse, and he later joins a gang of pickpockets.

   _____

   _____

   _____

Subject-Verb Agreement

5. *Great Expectations*, one of Dickens's autobiographical novels, tell the story of Pip, a poor, rural orphan boy with a job he hates.

6. Visiting his parents' grave, Pip meets Magwitch, an escaped convict.

7. Neither trust the other, but Pip steals food and a file as Magwitch orders.

8. When Magwitch is caught, he protects Pip and take the blame for the theft.

Pronoun Agreement

9. Since Pip is an orphan, he lives with his older sister and their husband Joe, a blacksmith who apprentices Pip.

10. Joe is a good man, but nobody can seriously claim that his wife, known as Mrs. Joe, is a nice woman, for she is mean and abusive.

_____

_____

_____

11. Someone viciously attacks Mrs. Joe; perhaps they meant to kill her, but she survives and becomes a mute invalid.

_____

_____

_____

12. Orlick, a journeyman who works for Joe, is responsible for attacking Mrs. Joe, threatening Pip, and planning to kill Pip; besides these, he does many other evil deeds.

_____

_____

_____

Pronoun Reference

13. Pip is invited to play at Satis House, a place much different from his country home, which makes him feel special.

_____

_____

_____

14. Miss Havisham lives there with her ward, Estella, and she always wears a wedding dress and keeps the clocks stopped at a certain hour.

_____

_____

_____

15. Miss Havisham is unusual, and Estella is beautiful; Pip dreams of their wedding.

_____

_____

_____

16. Miss Havisham does not believe that Estella and Pip will ever marry, and, indeed, she says that she does not love Pip.

_____

_____

_____

Dangling and Misplaced Modifiers

17. Expecting to be a blacksmith for the rest of his life, a lawyer tells Pip that a secret benefactor has paid for the boy to be educated in London as a gentleman.

_____

_____

_____

18. After moving from Joe's home to London, Herbert Pocket becomes Pip's best friend.

_____

_____

_____

19. To live the life of a gentleman, former friends and relations are ignored by Pip.

_____

_____

_____

20. Using his newly acquired fortune, Pip helps Herbert buy a business.

_____

_____

_____

Parallelism

21. Herbert and Pip lead a life of drinking, gambling, and run up debts.

_____

_____

_____

22. Mrs. Joe dies, and Pip returns home for the funeral, overcome by grief, remorse, and by shame.

_____

_____

_____

23. One night, Magwitch breaks into Pip's room, announces that he, not Miss Havisham, is the benefactor, and again wants Pip's help.

_____

_____

_____

24. Magwitch needs a safe place to hide, for he is pursued by his former partner Compeyson, the police, and will be put to death for returning to England.

_____

_____

_____

Comma Splices

25. Estella marries an upper-class fellow, Bentley Drummle, he treats her badly.

   _____

   _____

   _____

26. Miss Havisham bends over her fireplace, her clothing catches on fire, causing her, too, to go up in flames.

   _____

   _____

   _____

27. She survives, and she spends her remaining days feeling sorry for her past misdeeds.

   _____

   _____

   _____

28. Caught by the police, Magwitch is again sentenced to death, Pip loses his fortune.

   _____

   _____

   _____

Fused (Run–On) Sentences

29. Pip chooses to go abroad with Herbert they will work in the mercantile trade.

   _____

   _____

   _____

30. Many years later, Pip returns, and he encounters Estella in the garden of Satis House.

    _____

    _____

    _____

31. Drummle is dead Estella is now free.

    _____

    _____

    _____

32. Dickens originally wrote a different outcome this is the revised ending.

    _____

    _____

    _____

Sentence Skills Assessment for Diagnostic Test #2

Problem	Needs Review	Needs Study	Completed
Verb Tense			
Subject-Verb Agreement			
Pronoun Agreement			
Pronoun Reference			
Dangling and Misplaced Modifiers			
Parallelism			
Comma Splices			
Fused (Run-On) Sentences			

Writing Assignments

Those of you who are familiar with *Write It* will recognize the writing process pages in each of the units in Part 2. We hope that you continue to use them in ways that work for you. Those of you new to these writing strategies will want to work carefully with the writing process pages in each of the assignment units because the writing process is crucial if you want to write successful essays. As you may already know, composition studies have identified four basic stages of the writing process—prewriting, drafting, revising, and editing. Successful writers use these stages either explicitly or implicitly whenever they write.

The writing support pages in this section of *Write It Review* will guide you to perfect your use of the writing process, or to develop a writing process of your own. The activities in each of the units will guide you to develop your ideas, formulate them into a conventional argument form, and present them to readers with clarity and effectiveness. You will find that, the more deliberate you become at making use of the writing process, the stronger your writing will become in both form and content. We encourage you to continue to practice your writing skills and to deepen your engagement with the critical reading and thinking that are so integral a part of successful academic writing.

A note on the organization of Part 2: If you have worked in the past with *Write It*'s format, you will already be familiar with the way each unit in *Write It Review* introduces you to a new topic using a lead reading selection followed by a writing assignment in the form of a writing topic based on that reading. For those of you who have not worked with *Write It* before, each writing topic is followed by worksheets that guide you through the writing process and help you to 1) clarify and deepen your understanding of the lead essay, 2) develop your own ideas about the issue contained in the lead essay, 3) focus your ideas and formulate a clear and well-developed thesis statement that responds to the writing assignment, 4) find specific and compelling support for your thesis statement, and 5) build concrete plans for drafting and revising your essay. For each unit's writing assignment, additional reading material is provided in the "Extending the Discussion" section. These supplemental readings are meant to provide a context for the argument in the main reading selection and help you explore the subject of that selection in greater depth.

A note on the importance of careful reading:

In general, college students today read less than ever before. Yet reading is the primary way that knowledge is communicated in an academic setting. Hence, we are hearing that college students report, on graduating, that they have learned very little in their four or five years spent in college. We urge you to be a tenacious and careful reader. For many of you, this will take some self-discipline and practice, but, as with anything difficult, your increasing proficiency as a reader will bring you not only intrinsic rewards but also a sense of success, increased learning, and ultimately higher grades. As with any challenging skill, reading sometimes-difficult college-level material will get easier with determined practice. Remember that it is unlikely that any reading selection, short or long, can be fully understood when read only once. Decide now to read everything you are assigned in this book two or three times initially, and then to go back to it frequently to refresh your memory and confirm your understanding of its ideas.

Assignment #1

"WHY WE CRAVE HORROR MOVIES"

For this assignment, you will write an essay responding to Stephen King's argument in a reading selection titled "Why We Crave Horror Movies." To complete the assignment successfully, be sure to read the essay and the writing topic carefully. Then carefully complete the assignments that follow. They will help you to understand the essay's ideas, think about the topic, and respond thoughtfully in your own essay.

The "Extending the Discussion" section for this assignment contains reading selections that explore King's subject from various points of view. Read these essays and compare their ideas to the ideas expressed in "Why We Crave Horror Movies." These supplementary readings will get you thinking about issues that relate to King's argument and that may be useful as you begin to develop your own essay in response to the writing topic.

WHY WE CRAVE HORROR MOVIES

STEPHEN KING

Stephen King is a best-selling writer, screenwriter, columnist, producer, and director. He is best known as a writer of horror fiction, using the genre to confront some of the basic concerns of modern society. He has sold over 350 million copies of his books. Many of his stories have been adapted for movies, television series, and comic books. King has also written under the pen names of Richard Bachman and John Swithen. In 2003, he received The National Book Foundation's Medal for Distinguished Contribution to American Letters. He lives in Maine, the state of his birth. The following well-known essay has appeared in a number of publications, including several widely used composition textbooks.

I think that we're all mentally ill; those of us outside the asylums only hide it a little better, after all. We've all known people who talk to themselves, people who sometimes squinch their faces into horrible grimaces when they believe no one is watching, people who have some hysterical fear—of snakes, the dark, the tight place, the long drop . . . and, of course, those final worms and grubs that are waiting so patiently underground.

When we pay our four or five bucks and seat ourselves at tenth-row center in a theater showing a horror movie, we are daring the nightmare. Why? Some of the reasons are simple and obvious. To show that we can, that we are not afraid, that we can ride this roller coaster. Which is not to say that a really good horror movie may not surprise a scream out of us at some point, the way we may scream when the roller coaster twists through a complete 360 or plows through a lake at the bottom of the drop. And horror movies, like roller coasters, have always been the special province of the young; by the time one turns forty or fifty, one's appetite for double twists or 360-degree loops may be considerably depleted.

We also go to reestablish our feelings of essential normality; the horror movie is innately conservative, even reactionary. Freda Jackson as the horrible melting woman in *Die, Monster, Die!* confirms for us that no matter how far we may be removed from the beauty of a Robert Redford or a Diana Ross, we are still light-years from true ugliness.

And we go to have fun.

Ah, but this is where the ground starts to slope away, isn't it? Because this is a very peculiar sort of fun, indeed. The fun comes from seeing others menaced—sometimes killed. One critic has suggested that if pro football has become the voyeur's version of combat, then the horror film has become the modern version of the public lynching.

It is true that the mythic, "fairy tale" horror film intends to take away the shades of gray. . . . It urges us to put away our more civilized and adult penchant for analysis and to become children again, seeing things in pure blacks and whites. It may be that horror movies provide psychic relief on this level because this invitation to lapse into simplicity, irrationality, and even outright madness is extended so rarely. We are told we may allow our emotions a free rein . . . or no rein at all.

If we are all insane, then sanity becomes a matter of degree. If your insanity leads you to carve up women like Jack the Ripper or the Cleveland Torso Murderer, we clap you away in the funny farm (but neither of those two amateur-night surgeons was ever caught, heh-heh-heh); if, on the other hand, your insanity leads you only to talk to yourself when you're under stress or to pick your nose on your morning bus, then you are left alone to go about your business . . . though it is doubtful that you will ever be invited to the best parties.

The potential lyncher is in almost all of us (excluding saints, past and present; but then, most saints have been crazy in their own ways), and every now and then, he has to be let loose to scream and roll around in the grass. Our emotions and our fears form their own body, and we recognize that it demands its own exercise to maintain proper muscle tone. Certain of these emotional muscles are accepted—even exalted—in civilized society; they are, of course, the emotions that tend to maintain the status quo of civilization itself. Love, friendship, loyalty, kindness—these are all the emotions that we applaud, emotions that have been immortalized in the couplets of Hallmark cards and in the verses (I don't dare call it poetry) of Leonard Nimoy.

When we exhibit these emotions, society showers us with positive reinforcement; we learn this even before we get out of diapers. When, as children, we hug our rotten little puke of a sister and give her a kiss, all the aunts and uncles smile and twit and cry, "Isn't he the sweetest little thing?" Such coveted treats as chocolate-covered graham crackers often follow. But if we deliberately slam the rotten little puke of a sister's fingers in the door, sanctions follow—angry remonstrance from parents, aunts, and uncles; instead of a chocolate-covered graham cracker, a spanking.

But anticivilization emotions don't go away, and they demand periodic exercise. We have such "sick" jokes as "What's the difference between a truckload of bowling balls and a truckload of dead babies?" (You can't unload a truckload of bowling balls with a pitchfork . . . a joke, by the way, that I heard originally from a ten-year-old.) Such a joke may surprise a laugh or a grin out of us even as we recoil, a possibility that confirms the thesis: If we share a brotherhood of man, then we also share an insanity of man. None of which is intended as a defense of either the sick joke or insanity but merely as an explanation of why the best horror films, like the best fairy tales, manage to be reactionary, anarchistic, and revolutionary all at the same time.

The mythic horror movie, like the sick joke, has a dirty job to do. It deliberately appeals to all that is worst in us. It is morbidity unchained, our most base instincts let free, our nastiest fantasies realized . . . and it all happens, fittingly enough, in the dark. For those reasons, good liberals often shy away from horror films. For myself, I like to see the most aggressive of them— *Dawn of the Dead*, for instance—as lifting a trap door in the civilized forebrain and throwing a basket of raw meat to the hungry alligators swimming around in that subterranean river beneath.

Why bother? Because it keeps them from getting out, man. It keeps them down there and me up here. It was Lennon and McCartney who said that all you need is love, and I would agree with that.

As long as you keep the gators fed.

Writing Topic

Explain the "dirty job" horror movies perform for us, according to King. Do you think horror movies potentially benefit all of us in the way he claims? Be sure to support your position with specific details taken from your own experiences, including the media, your observations of others, and your reading.

Vocabulary Check

Use a dictionary to find the meanings of the following words from King's essay. Choose the meaning or meanings that you think are useful in gaining a full understanding of King's ideas. Then, explain the way each of the definitions you wrote down is key to understanding his argument.

1. *province*

   definition: _____

   _____

   explanation: _____

   _____

   _____

   _____

2. *innately*

   definition: _____

   _____

   explanation: _____

   _____

   _____

   _____

3. *reactionary*

   definition: _____

   _____

   explanation: _____

   _____

   _____

   _____

4. *penchant*

   definition: _____

   _____

   explanation: _____

   _____

   _____

5. *exalted*

definition: _____

_____

explanation:

_____

_____

_____

6. *couplets*

definition: _____

_____

explanation:

_____

_____

_____

7. *covet*

definition: _____

_____

explanation:

_____

_____

_____

8. *remonstrance*

definition: _____

_____

explanation:

_____

_____

_____

9. *anarchistic*

    definition: _____

    _____

    explanation:

    _____

    _____

    _____

10. *voyeur*

    definition: _____

    _____

    explanation:

    _____

    _____

    _____

11. *subterranean*

    definition: _____

    _____

    explanation:

    _____

    _____

    _____

Questions to Guide Your Reading

Answer the following questions so you can gain a thorough understanding of "Why We Crave Horror Movies."

Paragraph 1

What are some of the behaviors that signal the hidden mental illness we all share, according to King? Have you noticed any other everyday behaviors that might fall into this category?

Paragraph 2

What does King claim is the obvious reason young people go to see a horror movie? Explain age as a factor defining the audience for this genre.

Paragraphs 3–4

According to King, what are some other reasons people watch horror movies? Can you think of any other reasons that he may have omitted?

Paragraph 5

Explain why King says it is "peculiar" to have "fun" watching a horror movie.

Paragraph 6

How do horror movies invite us to react in a childlike manner to their content, according to King?

Paragraphs 7–9

Explain the relationship King believes exists between degrees of sanity and emotions. How are humans in a civilized society taught to control their negative impulses?

Paragraph 10

What is another acceptable outlet for negative emotions, according to King? In what way can this outlet, along with horror movies, be seen as "reactionary, anarchistic, and revolutionary"?

Paragraph 11

Explain King's analogy of the hungry alligators.

Prewriting for a Directed Summary

It is always important to look carefully at a writing topic and spend some time ensuring that you understand what it is asking. Your essay must provide a thorough response that responds to all parts of the writing topic. The writing topic that follows "Why We Crave Horror Movies" contains three parts. The first part asks you about a central idea from the reading. To answer this part of the writing topic, you will have to summarize part of King's argument. In other words, you will write a *directed* summary, meaning one that responds specifically to the first question in the writing topic.

> first part of the writing topic:
>
> *Explain the "dirty job" horror movies perform for us, according to King.*

Do not stray too far from this question when writing your summary. Notice that it doesn't ask you to summarize the entire essay. Rather, it asks you to explain what particular job horror movies do for us. Use the questions below to help plan your response. They will guide you in identifying King's ideas.

Hint

It will be helpful to review Part 1's "A Review of the Guidelines for Writing a Directed Summary."

Focus Questions

1. According to King, is anyone completely mentally healthy?

2. How do civilized societies teach us to behave sanely and control, though not entirely eliminate, our negative emotions?

3. What is the relationship between THE maintenance of sanity and the socially acceptable release of base instincts?

4. How do horror movies help with that process?

Developing an Opinion and Working Thesis Statement

The second question in the topic asks you to consider the author's position, think about the reasons he gives for taking this position, and decide if you are convinced that he is right.

> second part of the writing topic:
>
> *Do you think horror movies potentially benefit all of us in the way he claims?*

Make sure you answer this part of the question directly; your response to it will be your thesis statement. It is very important that you write a clear thesis statement, one that focuses on "anticivilization emotions" (as King calls them), their presence in our lives, and our strategies for dealing with them. In order to do this, you should take into account King's ideas about such emotions and the need to deal with our own "insanity."

1. Use the following thesis frame to formulate the basic elements of your thesis statement:
   a. What is the issue of "Why We Crave Horror Movies" that the writing topic asks you to consider?

   _____

   b. What is King's opinion about that issue?

   _____

   _____

   c. What is your opinion about the issue, and will you agree or disagree with King's opinion?

   _____

   _____

   _____

2. Now use the elements you isolated in 1a, b, and c to write a thesis statement. You likely will have to revise it several times until it captures your idea clearly.

   _____

   _____

Prewriting to Find Support for Your Thesis Statement

The last part of the essay topic asks you to develop and support the position you took in your thesis statement by drawing on your own experience and readings.

last part of the writing topic:

Be sure to support your position with specific details taken from your own experiences, including the media, your observations of others, and your reading.

Use the guiding questions below to develop your ideas and find concrete support for them. The proof or evidence you present is an important element in supporting your argument and a significant aspect of making your ideas persuasive for your readers.

1. As you begin to develop your own examples, think about your attraction to—or revulsion for—watching horror and violence in movies and in other forms of media. In the space below, make a list of personal experiences you or others have had with experiences such as the ones King discusses.

    How much fun have you had watching horror movies, reading horror novels, or telling/listening to what King calls "sick jokes"? List some of the horror movies you have seen. Which one would you say is your favorite? Why? Try to identify what you enjoy about these films.

    If you do not enjoy horror films, list some reasons you avoid them. Take into account some of the advertisements and trailers you have seen for these movies. What images, sounds, or language were used to entice people to see them? Then make a list of reasons others might enjoy them—based on your own observations of family or friends who like them.

    Any experience you have had that says something about this central idea can provide you with an example to support your thesis. List as many ideas as you can, and freewrite about the significance of each.

    Once you've written your ideas, look them over carefully. Try to group the ideas you've listed or developed in your freewriting into categories. Then, give each category a label. That is, cluster ideas that seem to have something in common and, for each cluster, identify that shared quality by giving it a name.

2. Now make another list, but this time focus on examples from your studies, the media, your reading (especially the supplemental readings in this section), and your knowledge of contemporary society. Do any of these examples affirm King's ideas? For example, do the plots of novels, films, or TV shows you are familiar with seem to be doing the "dirty job" that King claims they do? Do any of your examples challenge King's ideas and offer other ways of understanding fear and horror novels, and sick jokes.

What views do the supplemental essays in this section take? Review their arguments and supporting evidence, and compare them to King's. Are any of them especially convincing for you? If so, list them here. (If you refer to any of their ideas in your essay, remember to cite them.) List and/or freewrite about all the relevant ideas you can think of, even those about which you are hesitant.

Once you've written your ideas, look them over carefully. Try to group the ideas you've listed, or developed in your freewriting, into categories. Then give each category a label. That is, cluster ideas that seem to have something in common and, for each cluster, identify that shared quality by giving it a name.

3. Now that you've developed categories, look through them and select two or three to develop in your essay. Make sure they are relevant to your thesis and are important enough to persuade your readers. Then, in the space below, briefly summarize each item in your categories and explain how it supports your thesis statement.

The information and ideas you develop in this exercise will become useful when you turn to planning and drafting your essay.

Revising Your Thesis Statement

Now that you have spent some time working out your ideas more systematically and developing some supporting evidence for the position you want to take, look again at the working thesis statement you crafted earlier to see if it is still accurate. As your first step, look again at the writing topic, and then write your original working thesis on the lines that follow it.

writing topic:

Explain the "dirty job" horror movies perform for us, according to King. Do you think horror movies potentially benefit all of us in the way he claims? Be sure to support your position with specific details taken from your own experiences, including the media, your observations of others, and your reading.

working thesis statement:

_____

_____

Remember that your thesis statement must answer the second question in the writing topic while taking into consideration the writing topic as a whole. The first question in the topic identifies the issue that is up for debate, and the last question reminds you that, whatever position you take on the issue, you must be able to support it with specific examples.

Often, after extensive prewriting and focused thought, you will find that the working thesis statement is no longer an accurate reflection of what you plan to say in your essay. Sometimes, only a word or phrase must be added or deleted; other times, the thesis statement must be significantly rewritten. The subject or the claim portion may be unclear, vague, or even inaccurate. When we draft, we work out our thoughts as we write them down; consequently, draft writing is almost always wordy, unclear, or vague. Look at your working thesis statement through the eyes of your readers and see if it actually says what you want it to say.

After examining it and completing any necessary revisions, check it one more time by asking yourself the following questions:

a. Does the thesis statement directly identify King's argument?

b. Does it state your position on the issue?

c. Is your thesis well punctuated, grammatically correct, and precisely worded?

Write your polished thesis on the lines below and look at it again. Is it strong and interesting?

_____

_____

Planning and Drafting Your Essay

Now that you have examined King's argument and thought at length about your own views, draft an essay that responds to all parts of the writing topic. Use the material you developed in this section to compose your draft. Don't forget to turn back to Part 1, especially "The Conventional Argument Essay Structure," for further guidance.

Do take the time to develop an outline because it will give you a basic structure for incorporating all the ideas you have developed in the preceding pages. An outline will also give you a bird's-eye view of your essay and help you spot problems in development or logic. The form below is modeled on "The Conventional Argument Essay Structure" in Part 1, and it can guide you as you plan your essay.

Hint

This outline doesn't have to contain polished writing. You may want to fill in only the basic ideas in phrases or terms.

Creating an Outline for Your Draft

I. **Introductory Paragraph**

   A. An opening sentence that gives the reading selection's title and author and begins to answer the writing topic:

   _____

   B. Main points to include in the directed summary:
      1.

      2.

      3.

      4.

   C. Write out your thesis statement. (Look back to "Revising Your Thesis Statement," where you reexamined and improved your working thesis statement.) It should clearly agree or disagree with the argument in King's essay and state a clear position using your own words.

   _____

II. **Body Paragraphs**

   A. The paragraph's one main point that supports the thesis statement:

   _____

   1. <u>C</u>ontrolling idea sentence:

   _____

   _____

   2. <u>C</u>orroborating details:

   _____

   _____

   _____

   _____

   3. <u>C</u>areful explanation of why the details are significant:

   _____

   _____

   _____

   _____

   4. <u>C</u>onnection to the thesis statement:

   _____

   _____

   _____

   _____

B. The paragraph's one main point that supports the thesis statement:

_____

   1. <u>C</u>ontrolling idea sentence:

   _____

   _____

   2. <u>C</u>orroborating details:

   _____

   _____

   _____

   _____

3. Careful explanation of why the details are significant:

_____

_____

_____

_____

4. Connection to the thesis statement:

_____

_____

_____

_____

C. The paragraph's one main point that supports the thesis statement:

_____

1. Controlling idea sentence:

_____

_____

2. Corroborating details:

_____

_____

_____

_____

3. Careful explanation of why the details are significant:

_____

_____

_____

_____

4. Connection to the thesis statement:

_____

_____

_____

_____

D. The paragraph's one main point that supports the thesis statement:

_____

1. Controlling idea sentence:

_____

_____

2. Corroborating details:

_____

_____

_____

_____

3. Careful explanation of why the details are significant:

_____

_____

_____

_____

4. Connection to the thesis statement:

_____

_____

_____

_____

Repeat this form for any remaining body paragraphs.

III. Conclusion (Look back to "Conclusions" in Part 1. It will help you make some decisions here about what type of conclusion you will use.)

    A. Type of conclusion to be used:

       _____

    B. Suggestions, or key words or phrases to include:

       _____

Use the following guidelines to give a classmate feedback on his or her draft. Read the draft through first, and then answer each of the items below as specifically as you can.

Name of draft's author: _____

Name of draft's reader: _____

The Introduction

1. Within the opening sentences:
   a. King's first and last name are given.   yes   no
   b. the reading selection's title is given and
      placed within quotation marks.   yes   no
2. The opening contains a summary that:
   a. explains King's idea of human nature.   yes   no
   b. explains why he thinks we benefit from
      watching horror films.   yes   no
3. The opening provides a thesis that makes clear the draft writer's
   opinion regarding King's argument.   yes   no

If the answer to #3 above is yes, state the thesis below as it is written. If the answer is no, explain to the writer what information is needed to make the thesis complete.

_____

_____

_____

The Body

1. How many paragraphs are in the body of this essay? _____
2. To support the thesis, this number is   sufficient   not enough
3. Do paragraphs contain the 4Cs?

Paragraph 1	Controlling idea sentence	yes	no
	Corroborating details	yes	no
	Careful explanation of why the details are significant	yes	no
	Connection to the thesis statement	yes	no
Paragraph 2	Controlling idea sentence	yes	no
	Corroborating details	yes	no
	Careful explanation of why the details are significant	yes	no
	Connection to the thesis statement	yes	no

Paragraph 3	Controlling idea sentence	yes	no
	Corroborating details	yes	no
	Careful explanation of why the details are significant	yes	no
	Connection to the thesis statement	yes	no
Paragraph 4	Controlling idea sentence	yes	no
	Corroborating details	yes	no
	Careful explanation of why the details are significant	yes	no
	Connection to the thesis statement	yes	no
Paragraph 5	Controlling idea sentence	yes	no
	Corroborating details	yes	no
	Careful explanation of why the details are significant	yes	no
	Connection to the thesis statement	yes	no

(Continue as needed.)

4. Identify any of the above paragraphs that are underdeveloped (too short). _____

5. Identify any of the above paragraphs that fail to support the thesis. _____

6. Identify any of the above paragraphs that are redundant or repetitive. _____

7. Suggest any ideas for additional paragraphs that might improve this essay.

_____

_____

_____

The Conclusion

1. Does the final paragraph avoid introducing new ideas and examples that really belong in the body of the essay?   yes   no

2. Does the conclusion provide closure (let readers know that the end of the essay has been reached)?   yes   no

3. Does the conclusion leave readers with an understanding of the significance of the argument?   yes   no

4. State in your own words what the draft writer considers to be important about his or her argument.

_____

_____

_____

5. Identify the type of conclusion used (see the guidelines for conclusions in Part 1).

_____

Editing

1. During the editing process, the writer should pay attention to the following problems in sentence structure, punctuation, and mechanics:
     fragments
     fused (run-on) sentences
     comma splices
     misplaced, missing, and unnecessary commas
     misplaced, missing, and unnecessary apostrophes
     incorrect quotation mark use
     capitalization errors
     spelling errors
2. While editing, the writer should pay attention to the following areas of grammar:
     verb tense
     subject-verb agreement
     irregular verbs
     pronoun type
     pronoun reference
     pronoun agreement
     noun plurals
     misplaced and dangling modifiers
     prepositions

Final Draft Checklist

Content

	My essay has an appropriate title.
_____	I provide an accurate summary of King's position on the issue presented in "Why We Crave Horror Movies."
_____	My thesis states a clear position that can be supported by evidence.
_____	I have enough paragraphs and argument points to support my thesis.
_____	Each body paragraph is relevant to my thesis.
_____	Each body paragraph contains the 4Cs.
_____	I use transitions whenever necessary to connect ideas to each other.
_____	The final paragraph of my essay (the conclusion) provides readers with a sense of closure.

Grammar, Punctuation, and Mechanics

_____	I use the present tense to discuss King's argument and examples.
_____	I use verb tenses correctly to show the chronology of events.
_____	I have verb tense consistency throughout my sentences.
_____	I have checked for subject-verb agreement in all of my sentences.
_____	I have revised all fragments and mixed or garbled sentences.
_____	I have repaired all fused (run-on) sentences and comma splices.
_____	I have placed a comma after introductory elements (transitions and phrases) and all dependent clauses that open a sentence.
_____	If I present items in a series (nouns, verbs, prepositional phrases), they are parallel in form.
_____	If I include material spoken or written by someone other than myself, I have correctly punctuated it with quotation marks, using the MLA style guide's rules for citation.

Reviewing Your Graded Essay

After your instructor has returned your essay, you may have the opportunity to revise your paper and raise your grade. Many students, especially those whose essays receive nonpassing grades, feel that their instructors should be less "picky" about grammar and should pass the work on content alone. However, most students at this level have not yet acquired the ability to recognize quality writing, and they do not realize that content and writing actually cannot be separated in this way. Experienced instructors know that errors in sentence structure, grammar, punctuation, and word choice either interfere with content or distract readers so much that they lose track of content. In short, good ideas badly presented are no longer good ideas; to pass, an essay must have passable writing. So even if you are not submitting a revised version of this essay to your instructor, it is important that you review your work carefully in order to understand its strengths and weaknesses. This sheet will guide you through the evaluation process.

You will want to continue to use the techniques that worked well for you and to find strategies to overcome the problems that you identify in this sample of your writing. To recognize areas that might have been problematic for you, look back at the scoring rubric in this book. Match the numerical/verbal/letter grade received on your essay to the appropriate category. Study the explanation given on the rubric for your grade.

Write a few sentences below in which you identify your problems in each of the following areas. Then, suggest specific changes you could make that would improve your paper. Don't forget to use your handbook as a resource.

1. **Grammar/punctuation/mechanics**
   My problem:

   My strategy for change:

2. **Thesis/response to assignment**
   My problem:

   My strategy for change:

3. Organization
My problem:

My strategy for change:

4. Paragraph development/examples/reasoning
My problem:

My strategy for change:

5. Assessment
In the space below, assign a grade to your paper using a rubric other than the one used by your instructor. In other words, if your instructor assigned your essay a grade of *High Fail*, you might give it the letter grade you now feel the paper warrants. If your instructor used the traditional letter grade to evaluate the essay, choose a category from the rubric in this book, or any other grading scale that you are familiar with, to show your evaluation of your work. Then, write a short narrative explaining your evaluation of the essay and the reasons it received the grade you gave it.

Grade: _____

Narrative: _____

_____

_____

_____

_____

Extending the Discussion: Considering Other Viewpoints

Reading Selections

"Fear" by Phil Barker
"Sugar and Spice and a Parent's Worst Fears" by John Balzar
"A Peaceful Woman Explains Why She Carries a Gun" by Linda M. Hasselstrom
"Anxiety: Challenge by Another Name" by James Lincoln Collier
"The Solstice Blues" by Akiko Busch
"Inhibitions, Symptoms, and Anxiety" by Sigmund Freud
"The Tell-Tale Heart" by Edgar Allan Poe

FEAR

PHIL BARKER

In 2003, when this informative research article was published, Phil Barker was a graduate student in political science at the University of Colorado, Boulder, and was part of the research staff at the Conflict Research Consortium.

What Is Fear?

Fear is "an unpleasant and often strong emotion caused by anticipation or awareness of danger."[1] Fear is completely natural and helps people to recognize and respond to dangerous situations and threats. However, healthy fear—or fear which has a protective function—can evolve into unhealthy or pathological fear, which can lead to exaggerated and violent behavior.

Dr. Ivan Kos lays out several different stages of fear. The first is real fear, or fear based on a real situation. If someone or something hurts you, you have a reason to fear it in the future. Second is realistic, or possible fear. This is fear based in reality that causes a person to avoid a threat in the first place (i.e., waiting to cross a busy road for safety reasons). Next, exaggerated or emotional fear deals with an individual "recalling past fears or occurrences and injecting them into a current situation."[2] This type of fear is particularly relevant to conflict. Emotional fear affects the way people handle conflictual situations.

Causes of Fear

Conflict is often driven by unfulfilled needs and the fears related to these needs. The most common fear in intractable conflict is the fear of losing one's identity and/or security. Individuals and groups identify themselves in certain ways (based on culture, language, race, religion, and so on), and threats to those identities arouse very real fears—fears of extinction, fears of the future, fears of oppression, and so forth.

For many people, the world is changing rapidly, and their lives are being altered as a result. For some religious people, this change leads to the fear that young people will abandon the Church or Mosque, that the media will become more important and influential in the lives of their children, and that they are losing control of their own future. These threats to identity result in fear.[3]

Similarly, in many ethnic conflicts, a history of "humiliation, oppression, victimhood, feelings of inferiority, persecution of one's group, and other kinds of discrimination" lead to a fear of similar wrongdoing in the future.[4] These historical memories shape how groups and people see each other. As a result, historical violence between Israelis and Palestinians, Hutus and Tutsis, and Protestants and Catholics in Northern Ireland affects how these groups look at one another and often leads to fear of one another. Group fears often translate into individual fears, as group extinction is often associated with individual extinction.

Barker, Phil. "Fear." *Beyond Intractability*. Eds. Guy Burgess and Heidi Burgess. Conflict Information Consortium, University of Colorado, Boulder. Posted: July 2003 <http://www.beyondintractability.org/essay/fear>

These examples illustrate the important role that history plays in the development of fear. Memories of past injustices lead individuals to anticipate future oppression or violence with a sense of anxiety and dread.

Why Fear Matters

Fear is a very important factor in intractable conflict. Emotions like fear can often cause extreme and seemingly irrational behavior in people, which can result in escalating conflict. According to James F. Mattil, the managing editor of *Flashpoints: Guide to World Conflicts,* "The common thread that weaves violent political movements together is fear. It is not the only motivating factor behind political violence, nor necessarily the most obvious, but it is virtually always there. Whenever we ask why people hate, or why they are willing to kill or die for a cause, the answer is invariably fear."[5]

People are social in nature, with shared values, religion, tradition, language, and so on. Whenever the basic characteristics that tie a group together are threatened, the group will fear for its survival. As a result, the group will also attempt to get rid of the threat, sometimes through distorted or violent means.

History plays an important role in this process. Historical experiences shape how groups view threats. If a group has been hurt or wounded in the past, it affects their outlook today. For example, historical tensions and wrongdoing affect the way Israelis and Palestinians see each other today. Oftentimes, history is exaggerated—meaning one group is portrayed as extremely heroic and another group is portrayed as barbarian or inhuman. This in turn leads to more mistreatment, as it is easier to abuse or hurt a group that has been dehumanized. A cycle develops—someone is hurt, resulting in fear and the demonization of the person or group that hurt them. This, in turn, makes it easier for future wrongdoing to occur.

It is also important to note the impact that elites, or leaders, have on fear and conflict. Oftentimes, leaders use fear to their political advantage. Leaders need support from those they lead, and one way to gain this support is by playing on the fears of the people. Leaders in Northern Ireland can use the fear of either the Protestants or the Catholics to their own political advantage. Many have asserted that George Bush used the fear of another 9/11 to support the second US war in Iraq. Leaders can even intentionally deepen these fears for their own purposes. Doing so can aggravate the already existing fears and lead to future difficulties.[6]

Dealing with Fear

Individuals: There are many ways of approaching fear in the context of conflict. However, since fear is such a personal issue, most approaches focus on the individual. There are various ways to deal with your own fear, including

- becoming aware of it,
- identifying the ways you express fear,
- recognizing the situations which trigger fear, and
- using behavioral techniques to reduce fear and stress.[7]

In order to overcome fears, individuals and groups must first come to terms with their own fears and understand just how destructive they can be. However, it is equally important to be aware of others' fears. Being aware of other people's fear allows you to deal with it appropriately. One of the most effective ways of handling the fear of others is through empathy, or seeing things from the other person's perspective. Once one does that, one can recognize actions of one's own that might be unnecessarily causing fear on the other side. By toning down one's language, or clarifying one's interests and needs, it is possible to dispel unwarranted fears, thereby helping the other side feel more secure. Empathy is also important in any attempt at reconciliation or mediation because it helps to foster a positive interaction between people.[8] It is also important to share your own fears so that others can empathize with you in return, and alter their behavior in ways that will lessen that fear as well.

Officials: Public support is essential for political leaders. One way leaders can gain this support is by addressing, playing off of, or even causing the fears of their people. As a result, leaders can play an important role in the creation and/or calming of fears, particularly in ethnic or intergroup conflicts. It is important that leaders be aware of the consequences of using fear as a motivational tool. Because fear is such a powerful emotion, leaders must be extremely cautious about playing on the fears of people. The former Yugoslavia is a perfect example of how the fears of the people can be used by leaders for power. Serb leaders often played on Serb fears in order to strengthen their power and to push people to do things they might otherwise have refused to do.[9] Contrast this with the very famous quotation of Franklin Roosevelt: "We have nothing to fear but fear itself." This is an overstatement; fear can be real and justified, but it is far too dangerous to exploit for other aims.

Third Parties: Mediators and third parties can play an important part in helping people to overcome their fears. By understanding the ways in which fear can create and escalate conflict, third parties can address these issues in a constructive manner. One way this can be accomplished is by assuring that people on both sides of a conflict feel that their individual needs and fears are being addressed. Oftentimes, this is done through no-fault discussions, wherein people are not allowed to discuss who is wrong in a situation, but only ways in which they may move toward a peaceful resolution. Neither side should have to sacrifice in areas that it considers to be an important need or fear. Solutions must always "satisfy fundamental needs and allay deepest fears."[10]

It is also important to remember that an issue such as identity and the fears associated with it are not zero-sum. In other words, the calming of one group's fear does not necessarily mean that another group has more reason to fear. Usually, quite the opposite is true. The more secure one group feels, the less it feels a need to attack other groups. Thus, security can actually be a win-win or positive-sum game: The more one side has, the more the other side has, too. This is true from the bully on the playground—who is usually an insecure child—to the bully in the international system.

Through empathy and understanding, groups in conflict can learn about the fears and needs of others and, in the process, overcome their own fears as well.

Endnotes

[1] *Merriam-Webster Online* book on-line (accessed 7 March 2003); available from http://www.webster.com; Internet.

[2] Paul Wahrhaftig, *Belgrade Combating Fear Project* article on-line (accessed 11 March 2003); available from http://www.conflictres.org/vol181/belgrade.html; Internet.

[3] James F. Mattil, *What in the Name of God?: Fundamentalism, Fear & Terrorism* article on-line (accessed 7 March 2003); available from http://www.flashpoints. info/issue_briefings/Analysis%20&%20Commentary/Analysis-Religion_main.htm; Internet.

[4] Steve Utterwulghe, *Rwanda's Protracted Social Conflict: Considering the Subjective Perspective in Conflict Resolution Strategies* article on-line (accessed 7 March 2003); available from http://www.trinstitute.org/ojpcr/2_3utter.htm; Internet.

[5] James F. Mattil, *What in the Name of God?: Fundamentalism, Fear & Terrorism* article on-line (accessed 7 March 2003); available from http://www.flashpoints.info/issue_briefings/Analysis%20&%20Commentary/Analysis-Religion_main.htm ; Internet.

[6] Herbert Kelman, "Social-Psychological Dimensions of International Conflict," in *Peacemaking in International Conflict: Methods and Techniques,* eds. I. William Zartman and J. Lewis Rasmussen (Washington, D.C.: United States Institute of Peace Press, 1997), 197.

[7] **Endnote missing

[8] Herbert Kelman, "Social-Psychological Dimensions of International Conflict," in *Peacemaking in International Conflict: Methods and Techniques,* eds. I. William Zartman and J. Lewis Rasmussen (Washington, D.C.: United States Institute of Peace Press, 1997), 199.

[9] Anthony Oberschall, *The manipulation of ethnicity: from ethnic cooperation to violence and war in Yugoslavia* article on-line (accessed 13 March 2003); available from http://www.unc.edu/courses/2002fall/soci/326/039/manipulation_of_ethnicity.pdf; Internet.

[10] Herbert Kelman, "Social-Psychological Dimensions of International Conflict," in *Peacemaking in International Conflict: Methods and Techniques,* eds. I. William Zartman and J. Lewis Rasmussen (Washington, D.C.: United States Institute of Peace Press, 1997), 197.

Discussion Questions

1. What are the three categories of fear identified by Dr. Ivan Kos? Which category of fear does Barker feel accounts for many of the conflicts that result in war? Do you think his explanation is a reasonable way of understanding historical violence? Support your answer with a past and a current example.

2. How does Barker suggest we should deal with personal fears? Can you give an example of someone you know that may have benefited from following Barker's advice? If you don't think these strategies for dealing with fear would be helpful, explain your position.

3. Examine Barker's documentation style—the numbering system he uses to document his sources in the text of his essay, and the way he arranges his sources at the end. If you were giving him advice on documenting sources in MLA style, what would his citations and his works cited list look like? How might he have benefitted by using a formal style guide such as MLA or APA to cite his sources?

4. Which of King's reasons for watching horror movies relates to fear? Now consider the following list of synonyms for the word "fear": dread, anxiety, horror, distress, fright, panic, alarm, trepidation, apprehension. Choose words from this list that could be used to apply to fear as King uses it. Which of the words on the list apply to fear as discussed by Barker? Explain the difference between your two lists.

SUGAR AND SPICE AND A PARENT'S WORST FEARS

John Balzar

John Balzar is a correspondent for the Los Angeles Times. *He was awarded the Scripps-Howard Foundation Prize for human interest writing. He has worked as a river boatman in Alaska and sailed across the Pacific. The essay below appeared in the* Los Angeles Times *on May 4, 2002.*

I'm struggling to raise a daughter in this chilling summer of 2002. I can protect her, or so I tell myself. The odds are with me. But I'm not so sure I can protect her childhood.

We throw fences around our little girls, and our boys, too. We don't let them venture beyond our gaze, and maybe not even that far. We plan their movements. We supervise their activities. We give them a code word so they won't be fooled and walk off with a Big Bad Wolf who says Papa is hurt and needs help. We tell them not to worry about lost puppies. We tell them about little girls stolen out of their yards and grabbed out of their kitchens, and about big girls kidnapped from lovers' lane. We scare them for their own good. And if we don't, someone else will.

Einstein was asked what he thought was the most important question concerning the future of humanity. His reply was, "Is the universe friendly?" In my search for an answer, I turn to the steadiest voice I know, sociologist Barry Glassner: In reality, he says, "Kids are more likely to die falling off a bicycle without a helmet on the way to the park than they are to be abducted when they get there. They're more likely to be hit by lightning." He should know; he wrote the book on it, *The Culture of Fear.* The trouble is that Glassner's odds of "less than one in a million" make sense in our heads, but we aren't gamblers with something so close to our hearts.

Last year, it was shark attacks. This year, the world stops for cable TV to feed off the kidnapping, assault, murder, and rescue of girls. And our children are watching. It is "the flowers, the crying, that's what they mention," says my friend Susan about the first- and second-graders she teaches. "They see it on TV; they hear people talk about it. But they won't say a thing unless you bring it up. They hold it inside." How heavy does this burden inside weigh? How do we protect our children from fear? We mobilize to safeguard our children from stray maniacs, but how do we also protect the good-nights and sleep-tights of their childhoods from the emotional bombardment of the tabloid echo chamber? Television and newspapers tell me that it is not enough to teach my daughter how to swim and ride a bicycle. I'm told I now must instruct her on how to kick a man in the groin.

"Missing," "raped," "molested," "murdered"; I fear the loss of childhood. Children know more the meaning of a circling helicopter than they do a robin's song.

Discussion Questions

1. What are the things that Balzar fears? How do his fears influence his behaviors? Explain why you think the actions he takes are either sane and reasonable, or bordering on paranoia.

2. What, according to Balzar, does Einstein think is the most important question about humanity's future? What does Balzar think is meant by a "friendly" universe? Describe your vision of a "friendly" universe.

3. In what ways does Balzar believe the media are changing childhood? Why do you think that television and the media, including the horror movies King discusses, are having either a positive or negative effect on children's mental well-being?

4. Compare King's idea of the strategies we use for dealing with fear to Balzar's idea of the strategies we give to our children for dealing with fear. Which writer's ideas are more compelling to you? Why?

A PEACEFUL WOMAN EXPLAINS WHY SHE CARRIES A GUN

Linda M. Hasselstrom

Linda M. Hasselstrom is a rancher, an active environmentalist, and a writer of nonfiction and poetry. She writes about the Western landscape and environment and has said that she hopes her writing brings people to respect the life of the prairies and plains and live moderately so as to protect our resources. The following essay is taken from her book Land Circle: Writing Collected from the Land *(1991).*

I am a peace-loving woman. But several events in the past ten years have convinced me I'm safer when I carry a pistol. This was a personal decision, but because handgun possession is a controversial subject, perhaps my reasoning will interest others.

I live in western South Dakota on a ranch twenty-five miles from the nearest town; for several years, I spent winters alone here. As a free-lance writer, I travel alone a lot—more than 100,000 miles by car in the last four years. With women freer than ever before to travel alone, the odds of our encountering trouble seem to have risen. Distances are great, roads are deserted, and the terrain is often too exposed to offer hiding places.

A woman who travels alone is advised, usually by men, to protect herself by avoiding bars and other "dangerous situations," by approaching her car like an Indian scout, by locking doors and windows. But these precautions aren't always enough. I spent years following them and still found myself in dangerous situations. I began to resent the idea that just because I am female, I have to be extra careful.

A few years ago, with another woman, I camped for several weeks in the West. We discussed self-defense, but neither of us had taken a course in it. She was against firearms, and local police told us Mace was illegal. So we armed ourselves with spray cans of deodorant tucked into our sleeping bags. We never used our improvised Mace because we were lucky enough to camp beside people who came to our aid when men harassed us. But on one occasion we visited a national park where our assigned space was less than fifteen feet from other campers. When we returned from a walk, we found our closest neighbors were two young men. As we gathered our cooking gear, they drank beer and loudly discussed what they would do to us after dark. Nearby campers, even families, ignored them; rangers strolled past, unconcerned. When we asked the rangers pointblank if they would protect us, one of them patted my shoulder and said, "Don't worry, girls. They're just kidding." At dusk, we drove out of the park and hid our camp in the woods a few miles away. The illegal spot was lovely, but our enjoyment of that park was ruined. I returned from the trip determined to reconsider the options available for protecting myself.

At that time, I lived alone on the ranch and taught night classes in town. Along a city street I often traveled, a woman had a flat tire, called for help on her CB radio, and got a rapist who left her beaten. She was afraid to call for help again and stayed in her car until morning.

For that reason, as well as because CBs work best along line-of-sight, which wouldn't help much in the rolling hills where I live, I ruled out a CB.

As I drove home one night, a car followed me. It passed me on a narrow bridge while a passenger flashed a blinding spotlight in my face. I braked sharply. The car stopped, angled across the bridge, and four men jumped out. I realized the locked doors were useless if they broke the windows of my pickup. I started forward, hoping to knock their car aside so I could pass. Just then another car appeared, and the men hastily got back in their car. They continued to follow me, passing and repassing. I dared not go home because no one else was there. I passed no lighted houses. Finally, they pulled over to the roadside, and I decided to use their tactic: fear. Speeding, the pickup horn blaring, I swerved as close to them as I dared as I roared past. It worked; they turned off the highway. But I was frightened and angry. Even in my vehicle, I was too vulnerable.

Other incidents occurred over the years. One day, I glanced out at a field below my house and saw a man with a shotgun walking toward a pond full of ducks. I drove down and explained that the land was posted. I politely asked him to leave. He stared at me, and the muzzle of the shotgun began to rise. In a moment of utter clarity I realized that I was alone on the ranch, and that he could shoot me and simply drive away. The moment passed; the man left.

One night, I returned home from teaching a class to find deep tire ruts in the wet ground of my yard, garbage in the driveway, and a large gas tank empty. A light shone in the house; I couldn't remember leaving it on. I was too embarrassed to drive to a neighboring ranch and wake someone up. An hour of cautious exploration convinced me the house was safe, but once inside, with the doors locked, I was still afraid. I kept thinking of how vulnerable I felt, prowling around my own house in the dark.

My first positive step was to take a kung fu class, which teaches evasive or protective action when someone enters your space without permission. I learned to move confidently, scanning for possible attackers. I learned how to assess danger and techniques for avoiding it without combat.

I also learned that one must practice several hours every day to be good at kung fu. By that time I had married George; when I practiced with him, I learned how *close* you must be to your attacker to use martial arts, and decided a 120-pound woman dare not let a six-foot, 220-pound attacker get that close unless she is very, very good at self-defense. I have since read articles by several women who were extremely well trained in the martial arts, but were raped and beaten anyway.

I thought back over the times in my life when I had been attacked or threatened and tried to be realistic about my own behavior, searching for anything that had allowed me to become a victim. Overall, I was convinced that I had not been at fault. I don't believe myself to be either paranoid or a risk taker, but I wanted more protection.

With some reluctance, I decided to try carrying a pistol. George had always carried one, despite his size and his training in martial arts. I practiced shooting until I was sure I could hit an attacker who moved close enough to endanger me. Then I bought a license from the county sheriff, making it legal for me to carry the gun concealed.

But I was not yet ready to defend myself. George taught me that the most important preparation was mental: convincing myself I could actually *shoot a person*. Few of us wish to hurt or kill another human being. But there is no point in having a gun—in fact, gun possession might increase your danger—unless you know you can use it. I got in the habit of rehearsing, as I drove or walked, the precise conditions that would be required before I would shoot someone.

People who have not grown up with the idea that they are capable of protecting themselves—in other words, most women—might have to work hard to convince themselves of their ability, and of the necessity. Handgun ownership need not turn us into gunslingers, but it can be part of believing in, and relying on, *ourselves* for protection.

To be useful, a pistol has to be available. In my car, it's within instant reach. When I enter a deserted rest stop at night, it's in my purse, with my hand on the grip. When I walk from a dark parking lot into a motel, it's in my hand, under a coat. At home, it's on the headboard. In short, I take it with me almost everywhere I go alone.

Just carrying a pistol is not protection; avoidance is still the best approach to trouble. Subconsciously watching for signs of danger, I believe I've become more alert. Handgun use, not unlike driving, becomes instinctive. Each time I've drawn my gun—I have never fired it at another human being—I've simply found it in my hand.

I was driving the half-mile to the highway mailbox one day when I saw a vehicle parked about midway down the road. Several men were standing in the ditch, relieving themselves. I have no objection to emergency urination, but I noticed they'd dumped several dozen beer cans in the road. Besides being ugly, cans can slash a cow's feet or stomach.

The men noticed me before they finished and made quite a performance out of zipping their trousers while walking toward me. All four of them gathered around my small foreign car, and one of them demanded what the hell I wanted.

"This is private land. I'd appreciate it if you'd pick up the beer cans."

"I don't see no beer cans. Why don't you get out of there and show them to me, honey?" said the belligerent one, reaching for the handle inside my door.

"Right over there," I said, still being polite, "—there, and over there." I pointed with the pistol, which I'd slipped under my thigh. Within one minute, the cans and the men were back in the car and headed down the road.

I believe this incident illustrates several important principles. The men were trespassing and knew it; their judgment may have been impaired by alcohol. Their response to the polite request of a woman alone was to use their size, numbers, and sex to inspire fear. The pistol was a response in the same language. Politeness didn't work; I couldn't match them in size or number. Out of the car, I'd have been more vulnerable. The pistol just changed the balance of power. It worked again recently when I was driving in a desolate part of Wyoming. A man played cat-and-mouse with me for thirty miles, ultimately trying to run me off the road. When his car passed mine with only two inches to spare, I showed him my pistol, and he disappeared.

When I got my pistol, I told my husband, revising the old Colt slogan, "God made men *and women*, but Sam Colt made them equal." Recently, I have seen a gunmaker's ad with a similar sentiment. Perhaps this is an idea whose time has come, though the pacifist inside me will be saddened if the only way women can achieve equality is by carrying weapons.

We must treat a firearm's power with caution. "Power tends to corrupt, and absolute power corrupts absolutely," as a man (Lord Acton) once said. A pistol is not the only way to avoid being raped or murdered in today's world, but intelligently wielded, it can shift the balance of power and provide a measure of safety.

Discussion Questions

1. What fears cause Hasselstrom to carry a gun? What do you think of her means for managing her fear?

2. What are some of the alternatives Hasselstrom uses to try to protect herself from the things she fears? Which of Barker's suggestions for managing fear is she adapting to her individual situation?

3. Taking into consideration the benefits King believes result from watching horror movies, what impact do you think that activity would have on Hasselstrom's decision to arm herself?

4. Hasselstrom's piece is autobiographical and recounts events that really happened. Do such real-life accounts have the same effects on readers as King says horror movies have? viewers?

ANXIETY: CHALLENGE BY ANOTHER NAME

JAMES LINCOLN COLLIER

James Lincoln Collier graduated from Hamilton College and is a journalist, author, and professional jazz musician.

Between my sophomore and junior years at college, a chance came up for me to spend the summer vacation working on a ranch in Argentina. My roommate's father was in the cattle business, and he wanted Ted to see something of it. Ted said he would go if he could take a friend, and he chose me.

The idea of spending two months on the fabled Argentine Pampas was exciting. Then I began having second thoughts. I had never been very far from New England, and I had been homesick my first few weeks at college. What would it be like in a strange country? What about the language? And besides, I had promised to teach my younger brother to sail that summer. The more I thought about it, the more the prospect daunted me. I began waking up nights in a sweat.

In the end, I turned down the proposition. As soon as Ted asked somebody else to go, I began kicking myself. A couple of weeks later I went home to my old summer job, unpacking cartons at the local supermarket, feeling very low. I had turned down something I wanted to do because I was scared, and had ended up feeling depressed. I stayed that way for a long time. And it didn't help when I went back to college in the fall to discover that Ted and his friend had had a terrific time.

In the long run, that unhappy summer taught me a valuable lesson out of which I developed a rule for myself: Do what makes you anxious; don't do what makes you depressed. I am not, of course, talking about severe states of anxiety or depression, which require medical attention. What I mean is that kind of anxiety we call stage fright, butterflies in the stomach, a case of nerves—the feelings we have at a job interview, when we're giving a big party, when we have to make an important presentation at the office. And the kind of depression I am referring to is that downhearted feeling of the blues, when we don't seem to be interested in anything, when we can't get going and seem to have no energy.

I was confronted by this sort of situation toward the end of my senior year. As graduation approached, I began to think about taking a crack at making my living as a writer. But one of my professors was urging me to apply to graduate school and aim at a teaching career. I wavered. The idea of trying to live by writing was scary—a lot more scary than spending a summer on the Pampas, I thought. Back and forth I went, making my decision, unmaking it. Suddenly, I realized that every time I gave up the idea of writing, that sinking feeling went through me; it gave me the blues. The thought of graduate school wasn't what depressed me. It was giving up on what deep in my gut I really wanted to do. Right then, I learned another lesson. To avoid that kind of depression meant, inevitably, having to endure a certain amount of worry and concern.

The great Danish philosopher Søren Kierkegaard believed that anxiety always arises when we confront the possibility of our own development. It seems to be a rule of life that you can't advance without getting that old, familiar, jittery feeling. Even as children, we discover this when we try to expand ourselves by, say, learning to ride a bike or going out for the school play. Later in life, we get butterflies when we think about having that first child, or uprooting the family from the old hometown to find a better opportunity halfway across the country. Any time, it seems, that we set out aggressively to get something we want, we meet up with anxiety. And it's going to be our traveling companion, at least part of the way, into any new venture.

When I first began writing magazine articles, I was frequently required to interview big names—people like Richard Burton, Joan Rivers, sex authority William Masters, baseball great Dizzy Dean. Before each interview, I would get butterflies, and my hands would shake. At the time, I was doing some writing about music. And one person I particularly admired was the great composer Duke Ellington. On stage and on television, he seemed the very model of the confident, sophisticated man of the world. Then I learned that Ellington still got stage fright. If the highly honored Duke Ellington, who had appeared on the bandstand some ten thousand times over thirty years, had anxiety attacks, who was I to think I could avoid them?

I went on doing those frightening interviews, and one day, as I was getting onto a plane for Washington to interview columnist Joseph Alsop, I suddenly realized to my astonishment that I was looking forward to the meeting. What had happened to those butterflies? Well, in truth, they were still there, but there were fewer of them. I had benefited, I discovered, from a process psychologists call "extinction." If you put an individual in an anxiety-provoking situation often enough, he will eventually learn that there isn't anything to be worried about. Which brings us to a corollary to my basic rule: You'll never eliminate anxiety by avoiding the things that caused it. I remember how my son Jeff was when I first began to teach him to swim at the lake cottage where we spent our summer vacations. He resisted, and when I got him into the water he sank and sputtered and wanted to quit. But I was insistent. And by summer's end he was splashing around like a puppy. He had "extinguished" his anxiety the only way he could—by confronting it.

The problem, of course, is that it is one thing to urge somebody else to take on those anxiety-producing challenges; it is quite another to get ourselves to do it. Some years ago, I was offered a writing assignment that would require three months of travel through Europe. I had been abroad a couple of times on the usual "If it's Tuesday, this must be Belgium" trips, but I hardly could claim to know my way around the continent. Moreover, my knowledge of foreign languages was limited to a little college French. I hesitated. How would I, unable to speak the language, totally unfamiliar with local geography or transportation systems, set up interviews and do research? It seemed impossible, and with considerable regret, I sat down to write a letter begging off. Halfway through, a thought—which I subsequently made into another corollary to my basic rule—ran through my mind: You can't learn if you don't try. So I accepted the assignment. There were some bad moments. But by the time I had finished the trip, I was an experienced traveler. And ever since, I have never hesitated to head for even the most exotic of places, without guides or even advanced bookings, confident that somehow I will manage.

The point is that the new, the different, is almost by definition scary. But each time you try something, you learn, and as the learning piles up, the world opens to you. I've made parachute jumps, learned to ski at forty, flown up the Rhine in a balloon. And I know I'm going to go on doing such things. It's not because I'm braver or more daring than others. I'm not. But I don't let the butterflies stop me from doing what I want. Accept anxiety as another name for challenge, and you can accomplish wonders.

Discussion Questions

1. Explain the time that James Lincoln Collier gave in to his fears. What was the result? What rule did he form because of this experience? Tell about a time when you made a decision based on your fear and anxiety. What was the result of your decision? With hindsight, did you make the right choice?

2. How did Collier use his rule to make a career choice? Describe the possible safe career, and possible anxiety-producing career, you are considering. After reading Collier, which career do you think you will choose? Explain the reason for your choice.

3. Explain the psychological term "extinction." How do you think King might use it to explain the value of horror movies?

THE SOLSTICE BLUES

Akiko Busch

Akiko Busch taught at the University of Hartford and Bennington College and is now a faculty member of the MFA program at the School of Visual Arts. She is a widely published writer in the field of design, culture, and nature. Among other things, she wrote a book of essays about science and stewardship, titled The Incidental Steward: Reflections on Citizen Science *(2013) that was published by Yale University Press. She is also the author of* Geography of Home: Writings on Where We Live *(1999),* Nine Ways to Cross a River *(2007), and* Patience: Taking Time in an Age of Acceleration *(2010).*

In mid-June, the twilight seems to go on forever, the sky awash with translucent shades of rose, pearl, gray. These are evenings of enchantment—but also of apprehension. The moment the sun reaches its farthest point north of the Equator today is the moment the light starts to fade, waning more each day for the following six months. If the summer solstice doesn't signal the arrival of winter, surely it heralds the gradual lessening of light, and with that, often, an incremental decline in disposition.

It is easy to associate sundown with melancholy, to believe that temper can be so closely tied to degrees of illumination. The more floodlit our nights, the more we seem to believe that a well-lit world is part of our well-being. But equating the setting of the sun with that of the spirit may be misguided, at variance with some essential need humans have for darkness and shadow.

In his book *The End of Night*, Paul Bogard notes that two-thirds of Americans "no longer experience real night" (9). "Most of us go into the dark armed not only with 'a light,'" he writes, "but with so much light that we never know that the dark, too, blooms and sings" (271).

Certainly, that is true where I live in a rural area of the Hudson Valley in New York. It may be the country, but the gas station and convenience store down the road emit a halo of orange light; across the street at Stop & Shop, high-intensity-discharge lighting casts a radiant glow across the parking lot and beyond. The garish gleam of illuminated signs and street lighting further drenches the crossroad. Illumination, albeit artificial, bathes my world.

It occurs to me now that such an extravagance of light can work to diminish our comfort with nightfall, encouraging us to link darkness to fear, brightness to security. But it is a flawed connection.

In his 1933 anthem to obscurity, *In Praise of Shadows*, the Japanese writer Junichiro Tanizaki cataloged the oppressiveness of the illuminated world. An advocate for opacity, he lamented the bright, shining sterility of hotels, hospitals, Western living rooms and bathrooms, the glitter of diamonds, the glare of silver, steel and nickel tableware. "Were it not for shadows," he wrote, "there would be no beauty" (Tanizaki 46).

Tanizaki's appreciation for the subtleties of the shadow world resonate all the more today, when we tend to equate light with clarity and transparency, and assume that brightness and exposure in the environment have some corollary lucidity in thought and behavior. But of course, that is not so. We have a need for the shadow world, those things that cannot be easily explained, those things we suspect or imagine but do not know. And all those other areas in our lives that are defined by their gradations of uncertainty. Such ambiguity has a place in human thought and perception.

Here, when the sun finally falls, is the time one hears more acutely the cry of the coyotes, the courtship call of the barred owls. And if I am far enough away from the crossroads, from the floodlights of the town park and the headlight beams of traffic, I can make out the distant pinpoints of Orion, the dim shadows the white pines make in the moonlight, the random flicker of fireflies. The water in the marsh catches just a bit of the star shine.

One can have a similar experience in a city. Linnaea Tillett, a lighting designer in New York, spoke to me of a nighttime walk in Central Park, of listening more keenly to bird calls, the screech owls, foxes. But most of all, she spoke of understanding more fully night as a place of life. All species have their own cycles, and nocturnal rhythms are part of that, she said. "Standing at the edge of the pond, I heard an animal plunge into the water, maybe a raccoon or badger, I don't know. It is still a mystery."

Such experiences, she said, are important at a time when many of us are looking for ways to reconnect with the complex ecologies around us. Light, and its absence, are essential parts of this, and of the weeks that lie ahead now, Ms. Tillett said. "It's not about going from light to dark, but of being more sensitive to this progression of light, looking more acutely at the degrees of twilight, being more attentive to the nuances of half light."

The summer solstice may be a good time to recalibrate the impulse we often have to equate dusk with depression. Perhaps it makes sense to use the coming months of declining light as an opportunity to recognize the value of nightfall, the blooming and singing of the dark, in an increasingly illuminated world.

Works Cited

Bogard, Paul. *The End of Night: Searching for Natural Darkness in an Age of Artificial Light.* New York: Little Brown, 2013. Print.
Tanizaki, Junichiro. *In Praise of Shadows.* 1933. New York: Vintage-Random, 2001. Print.

Discussion Questions

1. For the most part, what mental states and ways of thinking are associated with darkness? How does Akiko Busch feel about that connection?

2. Before reading "The Solstice Blues," how did you feel about being alone in the deep dark? How has your reading this article changed the way you perceive darkness? How would you explain any changes you may have in regard to your thinking/behavior and darkness after reading this article? If it is unlikely that there will be any changes, explain the reason for the lack of change.

3. Notice the several ways that "darkness" has been used in this unit's readings to represent a part of the human psyche and hence of human life. The writers focus on different approaches and strategies for dealing with this dark side of life: King, choosing a light tone to present a serious subject, suggests going to horror films; Hasselstrom carries a firearm; Collier recommends facing it head-on and finds it educational; Balzar makes it a priority in raising his child. How would you summarize Busch's depiction of darkness and her strategy for dealing with it? Discuss the different perspectives in these readings, and contrast their various approaches.

INHIBITIONS, SYMPTOMS, AND ANXIETY

SIGMUND FREUD

Sigmund Freud (1856–1939) was an Austrian-born physician and founder of the psychoanalytic school of psychology. Psychoanalysis is a clinical practice that uses patient-psychoanalyst dialogue to cure various forms of psychological disturbance. He is particularly remembered for his influential theories of the unconscious mind and its use of repression as a defense mechanism. He also argued that sexual desire, displaced through a wide spectrum of objects, is a key motivator in human beings. The excerpt below is from Freud's essay originally published in 1926.

The biological factor is the long period of time during which the young of the human species is in a condition of helplessness and dependence. Its intra-uterine existence seems to be short in comparison with that of most animals, and it is sent into the world in a less finished state. As a result, the influence of the real external world upon it is intensified, and an early differentiation between the ego and the id is promoted. Moreover, the dangers of the external world have a greater importance for it, so that the value of the object which can alone protect it against them and take the place of its former intra-uterine life is enormously enhanced. The biological factor, then, establishes the earliest situations of danger and creates the need to be loved, which will accompany the child through the rest of its life.

The existence of the second, phylogenetic, factor is based only upon inference. We have been led to assume its existence by a remarkable feature in the development of the libido. We have found that the sexual life of man, unlike that of most of the animals nearly related to him, does not make a steady advance from birth to maturity, but that, after an early efflorescence up till the fifth year, it undergoes a very decided interruption; and that it then starts on its course once more at puberty, taking up again the beginnings broken off in early childhood. This has led us to suppose that something momentous must have occurred in the vicissitudes of the human species which has left behind this interruption in the sexual development of the individual as a historical precipitate. This factor owes its pathogenic significance to the fact that the majority of the instinctual demands of this infantile sexuality are treated by the ego as dangers and fended off as such, so that the later sexual impulses of puberty, which in the natural course of things would be ego-syntonic, run the risk of succumbing to the attraction of their infantile prototypes and following them into repression. It is here that we come upon the most direct etiology of the neuroses. It is a curious thing that early contact with the demands of sexuality should have a similar effect on the ego to that produced by premature contact with the external world.

The third, psychological, factor resides in a defect of our mental apparatus which has to do precisely with its differentiation into an id and an ego, and which is therefore also attributable ultimately to the influence of the external world. In view of the dangers of [external] reality, the ego is obliged to guard against certain instinctual impulses in the id and to treat them as dangers. But it cannot protect itself from internal instinctual dangers as effectively as it can from some piece of reality that is not part of itself. Intimately bound up with the id as it is, it can only fend off an instinctual danger by restricting its own organization and by acquiescing in the formation of symptoms in exchange for having impaired the instinct. If the rejected instinct renews its attack, the ego is overtaken by all those difficulties that are known to us as neurotic ailments.

Further than this, I believe, our knowledge of the nature and causes of neurosis has not as yet been able to go.

Discussion Questions

1. What is the biological factor that Freud uses to explain the human need for love? Give your own explanation for the desire to love and be loved.

2. Use Freud's account of the id and the ego guarding against the dangers of the external world to explain the somewhat ordinary behaviors King terms manifestations of insanity. In what ways do Freud and King seem to share an understanding of human nature?

3. What is the definition of repression? How do you think King would see horror movies as aiding in the process of repression?

THE TELL-TALE HEART

EDGAR ALLAN POE

Edgar Allan Poe (1809–1849) was an American poet, author, literary critic, and editor. Now revered as a master of the short story, he was among the first writers in America to use that form and believed that the finest stories should be readable in one sitting. He is now best known for his mysteries and tales of the macabre and is considered the inventor of the genre of detective fiction; his fictional detective C. Auguste Dupin predates even Sherlock Holmes. Poe was determined to make his living solely by writing and is the first well-known American writer to attempt it. As a result, his life was difficult, both financially and professionally.

TRUE! nervous, very, very dreadfully nervous I had been and am; but why WILL you say that I am mad? The disease had sharpened my senses, not destroyed, not dulled them. Above all was the sense of hearing acute. I heard all things in the heaven and in the earth. I heard many things in hell. How then am I mad? Hearken! and observe how healthily, how calmly, I can tell you the whole story.

It is impossible to say how first the idea entered my brain, but, once conceived, it haunted me day and night. Object there was none. Passion there was none. I loved the old man. He had never wronged me. He had never given me insult. For his gold I had no desire. I think it was his eye! Yes, it was this! One of his eyes resembled that of a vulture—a pale blue eye with a film over it. Whenever it fell upon me my blood ran cold, and so by degrees, very gradually, I made up my mind to take the life of the old man, and thus rid myself of the eye for ever.

Now this is the point. You fancy me mad. Madmen know nothing. But you should have seen me. You should have seen how wisely I proceeded—with what caution—with what foresight, with what dissimulation, I went to work! I was never kinder to the old man than during the whole week before I killed him. And every night about midnight I turned the latch of his door and opened it oh, so gently! And then, when I had made an opening sufficient for my head, I put in a dark lantern all closed, closed so that no light shone out, and then I thrust in my head. Oh, you would have laughed to see how cunningly I thrust it in! I moved it slowly, very, very slowly, so that I might not disturb the old man's sleep. It took me an hour to place my whole head within the opening so far that I could see him as he lay upon his bed. Ha! Would a madman have been so wise as this? And then when my head was well in the room I undid the lantern cautiously—oh, so cautiously—cautiously (for the hinges creaked), I undid it just so much that a single thin ray fell upon the vulture eye. And this I did for seven long nights, every night just at midnight, but I found the eye always closed, and so it was impossible to do the work, for it was not the old man who vexed me but his Evil Eye. And every morning, when the day broke, I went boldly into the chamber and spoke courageously to him, calling him by name in a hearty tone, and inquiring how he had passed the night. So you see he would have been a very profound old man, indeed, to suspect that every night, just at twelve, I looked in upon him while he slept.

Upon the eighth night I was more than usually cautious in opening the door. A watch's minute hand moves more quickly than did mine. Never before that night had I felt the extent

The Tell-Tale Heart by Edgar Allan Poe, (1843).

of my own powers, of my sagacity. I could scarcely contain my feelings of triumph. To think that there I was opening the door little by little, and he not even to dream of my secret deeds or thoughts. I fairly chuckled at the idea, and perhaps he heard me, for he moved on the bed suddenly as if startled. Now you may think that I drew back—but no. His room was as black as pitch with the thick darkness (for the shutters were close fastened through fear of robbers), and so I knew that he could not see the opening of the door, and I kept pushing it on steadily, steadily.

I had my head in, and was about to open the lantern, when my thumb slipped upon the tin fastening, and the old man sprang up in the bed, crying out, "Who's there?"

I kept quite still and said nothing. For a whole hour I did not move a muscle, and in the meantime I did not hear him lie down. He was still sitting up in the bed, listening; just as I have done night after night hearkening to the death watches in the wall.

Presently, I heard a slight groan, and I knew it was the groan of mortal terror. It was not a groan of pain or of grief—oh, no! It was the low stifled sound that arises from the bottom of the soul when overcharged with awe. I knew the sound well. Many a night, just at midnight, when all world slept, it has welled up from my own bosom, deepening, with its dreadful echo, the terrors that distracted me. I say I knew it well. I knew what the old man felt, and pitied him although I chuckled at heart. I knew that he had been lying awake ever since the first slight noise when he had turned in the bed. His fears had been ever since growing upon him. He had been trying to fancy them causeless, but could not. He had been saying to himself, "It is nothing but the wind in the chimney, it is only a mouse crossing the floor," or, "It is merely a cricket which has made a single chirp." Yes, he has been trying to comfort himself with these suppositions; but he had found all in vain. ALL IN VAIN, because Death in approaching him had stalked with his black shadow before him and enveloped the victim. And it was the mournful influence of the unperceived shadow that caused him to feel, although he neither saw nor heard, to feel the presence of my head within the room.

When I had waited a long time very patiently without hearing him lie down, I resolved to open a little—a very, very little crevice in the lantern. So I opened it—you cannot imagine how stealthily, stealthily—until at length a single dim ray like the thread of the spider shot out from the crevice and fell upon the vulture eye.

It was open, wide, wide open, and I grew furious as I gazed upon it. I saw it with perfect distinctness—all a dull blue with a hideous veil over it that chilled the very marrow in my bones, but I could see nothing else of the old man's face or person, for I had directed the ray as if by instinct precisely upon the damned spot.

And now have I not told you that what you mistake for madness is but over-acuteness of the senses? Now, I say, there came to my ears a low, dull, quick sound, such as a watch makes when enveloped in cotton. I knew that sound well, too. It was the beating of the old man's heart. It increased my fury as the beating of a drum stimulates the soldier into courage.

But even yet I refrained and kept still. I scarcely breathed. I held the lantern motionless. I tried how steadily I could maintain the ray upon the eye. Meantime the hellish tattoo of the heart increased. It grew quicker and quicker, and louder and louder, every instant. The old man's terror must have been extreme! It grew louder, I say, louder every moment!—do you mark me well? I have told you that I am nervous: So I am. And now at the dead hour of the night, amid the dreadful silence of that old house, so strange a noise as this excited me to uncontrollable terror. Yet, for some minutes longer I refrained and stood still. But the beating grew louder, louder! I thought the heart must burst. And now a new anxiety seized me—the sound would be heard by a neighbor! The old man's hour had come! With a loud yell, I threw open the lantern and leaped into the room. He shrieked once—once only. In an instant I dragged him to the floor, and pulled the heavy bed over him. I then smiled gaily, to find the deed so far done. But for many minutes the heart beat on with a muffled sound. This, however, did not vex me; it would not be heard through the wall. At length it ceased. The old man was dead. I removed the bed and examined the corpse. Yes, he was stone, stone dead. I placed my hand upon the heart and held it there many minutes. There was no pulsation. He was stone dead. His eye would trouble me no more.

If still you think me mad, you will think so no longer when I describe the wise precautions I took for the concealment of the body. The night waned, and I worked hastily, but in silence.

I took up three planks from the flooring of the chamber, and deposited all between the scantlings. I then replaced the boards so cleverly, so cunningly, that no human eye—not even his—could have detected anything wrong. There was nothing to wash out—no stain of any kind—no blood-spot whatever. I had been too wary for that.

When I had made an end of these labors, it was four o'clock—still dark as midnight. As the bell sounded the hour, there came a knocking at the street door. I went down to open it with a light heart, —for what had I now to fear? There entered three men, who introduced themselves, with perfect suavity, as officers of the police. A shriek had been heard by a neighbor during the night; suspicion of foul play had been aroused; information had been lodged at the police office, and they (the officers) had been deputed to search the premises.

I smiled, —for what had I to fear? I bade the gentlemen welcome. The shriek, I said, was my own in a dream. The old man, I mentioned, was absent in the country. I took my visitors all over the house. I bade them search—search well. I led them, at length, to his chamber. I showed them his treasures, secure, undisturbed. In the enthusiasm of my confidence, I brought chairs into the room, and desired them here to rest from their fatigues, while I myself, in the wild audacity of my perfect triumph, placed my own seat upon the very spot beneath which reposed the corpse of the victim.

The officers were satisfied. My MANNER had convinced them. I was singularly at ease. They sat and while I answered cheerily, they chatted of familiar things. But, ere long, I felt myself getting pale and wished them gone. My head ached, and I fancied a ringing in my ears; but still they sat, and still chatted. The ringing became more distinct: I talked more freely to get rid of the feeling: but it continued and gained definitiveness—until, at length, I found that the noise was NOT within my ears.

No doubt I now grew VERY pale; but I talked more fluently, and with a heightened voice. Yet the sound increased—and what could I do? It was A LOW, DULL, QUICK SOUND—MUCH SUCH A SOUND AS A WATCH MAKES WHEN ENVELOPED IN COTTON. I gasped for breath, and yet the officers heard it not. I talked more quickly, more vehemently but the noise steadily increased. I arose and argued about trifles, in a high key and with violent gesticulations; but the noise steadily increased. Why WOULD they not be gone? I paced the floor to and fro with heavy strides, as if excited to fury by the observations of the men, but the noise steadily increased. O God! what COULD I do? I foamed—I raved—I swore! I swung the chair upon which I had been sitting, and grated it upon the boards, but the noise arose over all and continually increased. It grew louder—louder—louder! And still the men chatted pleasantly, and smiled. Was it possible they heard not? Almighty God! —no, no? They heard! —they suspected! —they KNEW! —they were making a mockery of my horror! —this I thought, and this I think. But anything was better than this agony! Anything was more tolerable than this derision! I could bear those hypocritical smiles no longer! I felt that I must scream or die! —and now—again—hark! louder! louder! louder! LOUDER! —

"Villains!" I shrieked, "dissemble no more! I admit the deed! —tear up the planks! —here, here! —it is the beating of his hideous heart!"

Discussion Questions

1. Discuss the ways the narrator of the story attempts to convince the readers of his sanity. What impressions do readers form as a result of his attempts?

2. Discuss the fear—and the fearlessness—exhibited by the narrator through the course of the story. Consider the way the narrator's different experiences relating to fear illustrate Phil Barker's discussion of fear in the opening paragraph of his essay "Fear."

3. Explain the benefits you think King would attribute to reading "The Tell-Tale Heart." Suggest a reason of your own that might explain the time-honored popularity of Poe's horror stories.

Assignment #2

"THE PROTESTANT WORK ETHIC: JUST ANOTHER 'URBAN LEGEND'?"

This assignment focuses on the subject of work and its place in our lives. As you explore the reading selections in this unit, note the definitions of work each one presents, and the importance each places on work. Think about the work you do in your life, perhaps in a paid job, in your dedication to your studies, at home, or in playing a sport or a musical instrument. You will have to decide how you will define work, and how you will evaluate it in your life.

Begin by carefully reading the lead reading selection, "The Protestant Work Ethic: Just Another 'Urban Legend'?"—we recommend that you read it more than once—and pay attention to Klemens's definition of work and the position he takes on it. Also note the kinds of evidence he uses to support his position, and decide just how compelling you find his argument overall. Then, look carefully at the writing topic that follows it, and spend some time thinking about how you might respond. If you don't yet know what position you want to take, your ideas will develop as you move through the writing process using the activities pages that follow Klemens's essay. The group of reading selections that you will find at the end of the unit will be helpful, too, as you work out your own views and try to formulate a thesis statement and supporting evidence for your position.

THE PROTESTANT WORK ETHIC: JUST ANOTHER "URBAN LEGEND"?

Jonathan Klemens

Jonathan Klemens is a practicing pharmacist currently serving as clinical pharmacist at CVS/Caremark. In the past, he has been a pharmacy instructor and a director of pharmacy. Also a writer, he has published many essays, articles, and works of fiction. The essay below was first published on eZine in 2008.

"Hi Ho! Hi Ho! It's off to work we go!" Like the words in the Disney cartoon melody, every day some people merrily trek to a job they apparently enjoy. Are these people misguided social dwarfs out of synch with the rest of the workforce? Even though we often give lip service to the work ethic, it really does exist, and it is stronger than one might expect. Frank Lloyd Wright, the famous twentieth-century architect, stated, "I know the price of success: dedication, hard work, and an unremitting devotion to the things you want to see happen."[1]

The work ethic is personified by those who have found work that provides both a service to society and personal satisfaction. It is their passion—their life calling. Our calling can follow any career path—writer, accountant, missionary, teacher, auto mechanic, carpenter, cook, social worker, attorney, or brain surgeon. It takes commitment and hard work, but we enjoy it and it feels like the right fit. We may actually become so intensively involved and committed that our calling becomes one with the company or organization's mission. Encompassing centuries, this commitment and dedication to hard work has been exemplified in such societies as the Amish, Mennonites, Hutterites, and Shakers. The Shaker phrase attributed to Mother Ann Lee, the founder of the Shaker sect—"Put your hands to work, and your hearts to God"—encourages a simple life of hard work and spirituality. We might also identify with Ben Franklin, who espoused his philosophy of avarice and a strong work ethic.

How could this concept of a work ethic develop and endure in a society where the concept of entitlement now seems to be so prevalent? The roots begin with Max Weber, one of the leading founders of modern sociology, and his renowned work on modern social science, *The Protestant Ethic and the Spirit of Capitalism*. In the 1930s, after the book was translated into English, the US workforce began its ongoing love affair with the work ethic—a social trait that would become the backbone of American enterprise and world leadership. The arduous work of capitalism, according to Weber, is closely associated with intrinsic Protestant religious beliefs and behavior. He states, "However, all the peculiarities of Western capitalism have derived their significance in the last analysis only from their association with the capitalistic organization of labor."[2] Only in the West has rationalization in science, law, and culture developed to the extent where political, technical, and economic conditions depend on highly trained government officials.

Historically, certain Protestant denominations had a strong influence on the members' development of business acumen and the ethic of hard work. These Protestants developed a sense of economic rationalism that emphasized diligent and dedicated work. Each and every

Sunday, Methodist and Presbyterian ministers extolled the virtues of the work ethic to their congregations through lengthy and tedious sermons. According to Weber, the following traits characterize a strong work ethic:

- Focus on Work
  We know how precious our time is and that it is limited. We must have a passion and must strive for excellence in our work. Work time should be used efficiently and wisely with a desire to make money as a fruit of our labor and not spend it irresponsibly.

- Unpretentious and Modest
  We should act and dress appropriately—dress should not be flashy to attract attention or cause distraction to others.

- Honest and Ethical
  One should possess and exhibit strong ethical beliefs and a moral code of behavior, i.e., the Ten Commandments. We must do the "right thing" when no one is watching.[3]

The power of a free labor force has made capitalism a very powerful force in our society. Riding high on the wave of post-WWII patriotism and intense business competition, we became rightfully proud of our fast-growing economy and the image of hard-working Americans. We take pride in who we were and what we produce as a nation, the greatest and most successful nation on earth. Although the original religious aspects eventually faded, the work ethic is firmly entrenched as a powerful and valued American social trait.

Unquestionably, we do not desire a workforce dominated by mindless "robots" even with a good work ethic. We need innovative thinkers and committed leaders that can guide us through the twenty-first-century and beyond. It is essential that we continue to build a strong labor force committed to an indomitable work ethic—workers that are honest, ethical, and rational. We also need leaders that will not be afraid to work and who will take the responsibility to guide new projects and develop employee potential to exceed projected goals. We need people passionate about a mission. A good work ethic is essential to a strong economy and a strong vibrant society.

Notes:

[1] ThinkExist.com Quotations Online 1 Jan. 2011. 2 Feb. 2011 http://thinkexist.com/quotes/ frank_lloyd_wright/
[2] Weber, Max. *The Protestant Ethic and the Spirit of Capitalism*. BN Publishing, 2008, p. 22.
[3] Weber 35.

Writing Topic

Explain Klemens's definition of the American work ethic. Do you agree with his claim that this work ethic is "firmly entrenched as a powerful and valued American social trait"? Be sure to support your position with specific details taken from your own experiences, the media, your observations of others, and your reading, including the reading selections from this course.

Vocabulary Check

Good writers choose their words carefully so that their ideas will be clear. In order for you to understand Klemens's ideas, it is important to think about the key vocabulary terms and the way he uses them to communicate his argument. Words can have a variety of meanings, or they can have specialized meanings in certain contexts. Look up the definitions of the following words or phrases from "The Protestant Work Ethic: Just Another 'Urban Legend'?" Choose the meaning that you think Klemens intended when he selected that particular word or phrase for use in this reading selection. Then, explain the way the meaning or concept behind the definition is key to understanding Klemens's argument.

1. *unremitting*

   definition: _____

   _____

   explanation: _____

   _____

   _____

   _____

2. *personify*

   definition: _____

   _____

   explanation: _____

   _____

   _____

   _____

3. *espouse*

   definition: _____

   _____

   explanation: _____

   _____

   _____

   _____

4. *prevalent*

   definition: _____

   _____

explanation:

_____

_____

_____

5. *arduous*

definition: _____

_____

explanation:

_____

_____

_____

6. *intrinsic*

definition: _____

_____

explanation:

_____

_____

_____

7. *derive*

definition: _____

_____

explanation:

_____

_____

_____

8. *acumen*

definition: _____

_____

explanation:

_____

_____

_____

9. *extoll*

definition: _____

_____

explanation:

_____

_____

_____

10. *entrench*

definition: _____

_____

explanation:

_____

_____

_____

11. *indomitable*

definition: _____

_____

explanation:

_____

_____

_____

Questions to Guide Your Reading

Answer the following questions to gain a thorough understanding of "The Protestant Work Ethic: Just Another 'Urban Legend'?"

Paragraph 1

How do the lyrics from a song from Disney's *Snow White and the Seven Dwarfs* relate to Klemens's view of work?

The lyrics relate to klemen's view of work since klemens, in his argument, is saying that in the American work ethic, we take pride in the work we do and we have this image that we are hard working

Paragraph 2

According to Klemens, what qualities are shared by groups and individuals who exhibit a strong work ethic? What do they give to their work, and what does their work give back to them?

The qualities shared by groups and individuals exhibiting a strong work ethic are focusing on work and being unpretentious, modest, honest and ethical. In their work they give their full effort and devote the needed time and the work gives the individual satisfaction

Paragraph 3

What are the historical roots of the work ethic, as Klemens presents them? Explain the place the work ethic has in the American economic system.

The historical roots of the work ethic are Max weber's book: The Protestant work Ethic and the spirit of Capitalism. The place work ethic has in American economic system is that it is the backbone of the American economic system

Paragraph 4

Based on Klemens's essay, identify and explain Max Weber's understanding of what constitutes a strong work ethic.

Max weber's beleves that the constituents of a strong work ethic are focus on work, the behavior should be unProtentious and honest

Paragraph 5

and work that is honest and ethical

According to Klemens, what kind of a workforce is important both to society and its economy?

According to Klemens, the kind of workforce that has innovative thinkers, a strong labor force that embodies what it means to have a strong work ethic as well as leaders who are willing to take responsibility to lead projects and develope employee Potential to exceed goals and people who are passionate about a goal

Prewriting for a Directed Summary

Now that you have used the questions above to understand "The Protestant Work Ethic: Just Another 'Urban Legend'?" as a whole, use the following questions as a guide to focus your attention on a particular perspective in the essay. This perspective will be important when you are working on your own essay in response to the writing topic for this assignment. Be sure to use the answers you give below when it is time to write a clear and coherent directed summary in response to the writing topic's first question:

> first part of the writing topic:

> *Explain Klemens's definition of the American work ethic.*

This first part asks you to explain Klemens's explanation of a particular concept. It doesn't ask you to summarize his entire essay. Be sure to keep two aspects in mind as you construct your answer: you will have to *explain*, not just identify, the meaning of the American work ethic *as Klemens's defines it*.

Hint

Don't forget to look back to Part 1's "A Review of the Guidelines for Writing a Directed Summary."

Focus Questions

1. What particular behaviors and beliefs developed into the work ethic, according to Klemens?

   - Focus on work
   - unpretentious, honest behavior
   - Honest, ethical work

2. What characteristics does Klemens associate with a strong work ethic?

3. In Klemens's view, how do these traits produce a strong economy and society?

Developing an Opinion and Working Thesis Statement

The second question in the writing topic for "The Protestant Work Ethic: Just Another 'Urban Legend'?" asks you to take a position of your own. Your response will form the thesis statement of your essay, so it is important to spend some time ensuring that what you write is an accurate reflection of the position you want to take on the place of work in people's lives. Use the framework below to develop your working thesis, but keep an open mind as you complete the prewriting pages that follow this one and read the positions other writers take in the essays in the "Extending the Discussion" section of this unit. You may find that, after giving more thought to the idea of work, you want to modify your position.

> second part of the writing topic:
>
> *Do you agree with his claim that this work ethic is "firmly entrenched as a powerful and valued American social trait"?*

Do you agree with Klemens that the work ethic is a pervasive value in the lives of most Americans? As you think about the position you want to take in your working thesis statement, keep in mind that the topic asks you to take a position on whether Klemens's idea of a work ethic is still a dominant American trait. In other words, do Americans *today*—not historically or in the recent past—demonstrate that the work ethic is still valued and continues to shape the way they live? Do notice the writing topic's use of the terms "firmly entrenched," "powerful," and "valued" as you develop your thoughts and decide on the position you will take in your essay.

1. Use the following thesis frame to identify the basic elements of your working thesis statement:
   a. What is the issue of "The Protestant Work Ethic: Just Another 'Urban Legend'?" that the writing topic question asks you to consider?

   _____

   b. What is Klemens's opinion about that issue?

   _____

   c. What is your position on the issue, and will you agree or disagree with Klemens's opinion?

   _____

   _____

   _____

2. Now use the elements you isolated in 1a, b, and c to write a thesis statement. You may have to revise it several times until it captures your idea clearly.

   _____

   _____

Prewriting to Find Support for Your Thesis Statement

The last part of the writing topic asks you to support the position you put forward in your thesis statement. Well-developed ideas are crucial when you are making an argument because you will have to be clear, logical, and thorough if you are to be convincing. As you work through the exercises below, you will generate much of the 4Cs material you will need when you draft your essay's body paragraphs.

You might want to take some time now to go back to Part 1 and review the 4Cs.

last part of the writing topic:

Be sure to support your position with specific details taken from your own experiences, the media, your observations of others, and your reading, including the reading selections from this course.

Complete each section of this prewriting activity; your responses will become the material you will use in the next stage—planning and writing the essay.

1. As you begin to develop your own examples, consider, first, your own work ethic.

   - How much value do you place on work, and what kinds of work do you think are important? Note that the concept of work doesn't just refer to a particular job. It can also refer to anything that requires a commitment of your time and energy in the completion of a task.
   - Where and how did you learn the values you have about work? Do you find a value in the many kinds of work you have done?
   - Do you believe that you already work hard enough, or are you always trying to push yourself to do more? How much of your day, on average, is spent working? Write out your thoughts.
   - How do you make decisions about scheduling relaxation or fun time into your week? Do you think you have enough relaxation time? Does it intrude on your ability to get your work done? How do you feel about this? Write out your thoughts and try to get a sense of your own commitment to a work ethic.
   - List or freewrite about personal experiences that involved your friends and your family in regard to work. Can you recall ways that you think demonstrate how strongly they have internalized a work ethic?

Once you've written your ideas, look them over carefully. Try to group your ideas into categories. Then, give each category a label. In other words, cluster ideas that seem to have something in common and, for each cluster, identify that shared quality by giving it a title.

2. The writing topic asks you to consider how influential the work ethic is in American society as a whole, so you will want to broaden your focus to extend beyond you and your family and friends. Individuals in your life may be exceptions to a rule that is more pervasive. List or freewrite about examples from your studies, your readings, and your knowledge of current events.

- Do you see a value placed on work in the training of the young people around you? What observations can you make about that training? Try to include specific examples that demonstrate your ideas.
- Have you observed any people new to this country? How do you think they respond to the culture of work in America? Note one or two specific examples you can use to support your conclusions.
- What message about hard work do we get when we watch or read the news? What do we learn to be especially proud of as Americans? How do young people come to understand what makes a good, successful life? How is that reflected in the media?
- Think about TV shows, movies, ads, music, and books you are familiar with. Do any of them suggest, directly or indirectly, that hard work has value? Spend some time analyzing one or two examples that you think are especially relevant. What messages about work do these examples give us?

Now think about examples of a work ethic in a larger context. What different perceptions of work do you see in others? How does a person's work ethic appear to influence his or her life? Do you think the people you know and observe work hard simply for the benefits of hard work, or do they work hard only because they need money? What specific observations have led you to your impressions? Is the difference in motivation significant? Why? Based on your observations, try to come to a conclusion about how pervasive the work ethic is in the people around you.

Once you've written your ideas, look them over carefully. Try to group your ideas into categories. Then, give each category a label. In other words, cluster ideas that seem to have something in common and, for each cluster, identify that shared quality by giving it a title.

3. Now that you've created topics by clustering your ideas into categories, go through them and pick two or three specific ones to develop in your essay. Make sure that they are relevant to your thesis and that they have enough substance to be compelling to your reader. Then, in the space below, briefly summarize each item.

Hint

Once you've decided which categories and items you will use in your essay, take some time to explain below how each category and its items connect to your thesis statement. You will use these details for the next stage.

Revising Your Thesis Statement

Now that you have spent some time working out your ideas more systematically and developing some supporting evidence for the position you want to take, look again at the working thesis statement you crafted earlier to see if it is still accurate. As your first step, look again at the writing topic and then write your original working thesis on the lines that follow it:

writing topic:

Explain Klemens's definition of the American work ethic. Do you agree with his claim that this work ethic is "firmly entrenched as a powerful and valued American social trait"? Be sure to support your position with specific details taken from your own experiences, the media, your observations of others, and your reading, including the reading selections from this course.

your working thesis statement:

_____

_____

Remember that your thesis statement must answer the second question in the writing topic while taking into consideration the writing topic as a whole. The first question in the topic identifies the issue that is up for debate, and the last question reminds you that, whatever position you take on the issue, you must be able to support it with specific examples.

Now that you've completed the prewriting exercises and given the writing topic some extensive and focused thought, you might find that the working thesis statement is no longer an accurate reflection of your ideas and of the position you want to take in your essay. You might need to change only a few words or phrases to correct the problem, but it's possible that the thesis statement must be significantly rewritten. Don't try to force your thoughts to fit a working thesis statement that no longer reflects your beliefs; instead, take some time and make your thesis the best representation of your thoughts. The subject or the claim portion may be unclear, vague, or even inaccurate. Look at your working thesis statement through the eyes of your readers and see if it actually says what you want it to say.

After examining it and completing any necessary revisions, check it one more time by asking yourself the following questions:

a. Does the thesis directly identify Klemens's argument?

b. Do you make clear your opinion about the issue?

c. Is your thesis well punctuated, grammatically correct, and precisely worded?

Write your polished thesis on the lines below and look at it again. Is it strong and interesting?

_____

_____

Planning and Drafting Your Essay

The rough draft of an essay is often the most difficult part of the writing process because this is where you move from exploring and planning to getting your ideas down in a unified, coherent shape. Be sure to begin with an outline because it will give you a basic structure to follow as you try to incorporate all the ideas you have developed in the preceding pages. An outline will also give you a bird's-eye view of your essay and help you spot problems in development or logic.

This outline doesn't have to contain polished writing. You may want to fill in only the basic ideas in phrases or terms. Try using the form below.

Creating an Outline for Your Draft

I. **Introductory Paragraph:**
    A. An opening sentence that gives the reading selection's title and author and begins to answer the writing topic question:

    _____

    B. Main points to include in the directed summary:
        1.

        2.

        3.

        4.

        (Continue as necessary.)

    C. Write out your thesis statement. (Look back to "Revising Your Thesis Statement," where you reexamined and refined your working thesis statement.) It should clearly agree or disagree with "The Protestant Work Ethic: Just Another 'Urban Legend'?" and state a clear position using your own words.

II. **Body Paragraphs**

    A. The paragraph's one main point that supports the thesis statement:

    _____

        1. Controlling idea sentence:

        _____

        _____

2. Corroborating details:

_____

_____

_____

_____

3. Careful explanation of why the details are significant:

_____

_____

_____

_____

4. Connection to the thesis statement:

_____

_____

_____

_____

B. The paragraph's one main point that supports the thesis statement:

_____

1. Controlling idea sentence:

_____

_____

2. Corroborating details:

_____

_____

_____

_____

3. Careful explanation of why the details are significant:

_____

_____

_____

_____

4. Connection to the thesis statement:

_____

_____

_____

_____

C. The paragraph's one main point that supports the thesis statement:

_____

1. Controlling idea sentence:

_____

_____

2. Corroborating details:

_____

_____

_____

_____

3. Careful explanation of why the details are significant:

_____

_____

_____

_____

4. Connection to the thesis statement:

_____

_____

_____

_____

D. The paragraph's one main point that supports the thesis statement:

_____

1. Controlling idea sentence:

_____

_____

  2. Corroborating details:

_____

_____

_____

_____

  3. Careful explanation of why the details are significant:

_____

_____

_____

_____

  4. Connection to the thesis statement:

_____

_____

_____

_____

Repeat this form for any remaining body paragraphs.

III. Conclusion

   A. Type of conclusion to be used:

_____

   B. Key words or phrases to include:

_____

Use the following guidelines to give a classmate feedback on his or her draft. Read the draft through first, and then answer each of the items below as specifically as you can.

Name of draft's author: _____

Name of draft's reader: _____

The Introduction

1. Within the opening sentences,
   a. Klemens is correctly identified by first and last name.   yes   no
   b. the writing selection's title is included and placed within
      quotation marks.   yes   no
2. The opening contains a summary that
   a. explains Klemens's definition of a "work ethic"   yes   no
   b. explains the importance Klemens places on this ethic   yes   no
3. The opening provides a thesis that
   a. offers a concise summary of Klemens's thesis.   yes   no
   b. gives the draft writer's position on the issue.   yes   no

If the answers to #3 above are yes, state the thesis below as it is written. If the answer to one or both of these questions is no, explain to the draft writer what information is needed to make the thesis complete.

_____

_____

_____

The Body

1. How many paragraphs are in the body of this essay? _____
2. To support the thesis, this number is   sufficient   not enough
3. Do paragraphs contain the 4Cs?

Paragraph 1	Controlling idea sentence	yes	no
	Corroborating details	yes	no
	Careful description of why the details are significant	yes	no
	Connection to the thesis statement	yes	no
Paragraph 2	Controlling idea sentence	yes	no
	Corroborating details	yes	no
	Careful description of why the details are significant	yes	no
	Connection to the thesis statement	yes	no

Paragraph 3	Controlling idea sentence	yes	no
	Corroborating details	yes	no
	Careful description of why the details are significant	yes	no
	Connection to the thesis statement	yes	no
Paragraph 4	Controlling idea sentence	yes	no
	Corroborating details	yes	no
	Careful description of why the details are significant	yes	no
	Connection to the thesis statement	yes	no
Paragraph 5	Controlling idea sentence	yes	no
	Corroborating details	yes	no
	Careful description of why the details are significant	yes	no
	Connection to the thesis statement	yes	no

(Continue as needed.)

4. Identify any of the above paragraphs that are underdeveloped (too short). _____

5. Identify any of the above paragraphs that fail to support the thesis. _____

6. Identify any of the above paragraphs that are redundant or repetitive. _____

7. Suggest any ideas for additional paragraphs that might improve this essay.

_____

_____

_____

The Conclusion

1. Does the final paragraph avoid introducing new ideas and examples that really belong in the body of the essay?   yes   no
2. Does the conclusion provide closure (let readers know that the end of the essay has been reached)?   yes   no
3. Does the conclusion leave readers with an understanding of the significance of the argument?   yes   no

4. State in your own words what the draft writer considers to be important about his or her argument.

_____

_____

_____

5. Identify the type of conclusion used (see the guidelines for conclusions in Part 1).

_____

Editing

1. During the editing process, the writer should pay attention to the following problems in sentence structure, punctuation, and mechanics:

    fragments
    fused (run-on) sentences
    comma splices
    misplaced, missing, and unnecessary commas
    misplaced, missing, and unnecessary apostrophes
    incorrect quotation mark use
    capitalization errors
    spelling errors

2. While editing, the writer should pay attention to the following areas of grammar:

    verb tense
    subject-verb agreement
    irregular verbs
    pronoun type
    pronoun reference
    pronoun agreement
    noun plurals
    misplaced and dangling modifiers
    prepositions

Final Draft Checklist

Content

_____ My essay has an appropriate title.

_____ I provide an accurate summary of Klemens's position on the topic presented in "The Protestant Work Ethic: Just Another 'Urban Legend'?"

_____ My thesis states a clear position that can be supported by evidence.

_____ I have enough paragraphs and concrete examples to support my thesis.

_____ Each body paragraph is relevant to my thesis.

_____ Each body paragraph contains the 4Cs.

_____ I use transitions whenever necessary to connect ideas to each other.

_____ The final paragraph of my essay (the conclusion) provides readers with a sense of closure.

Grammar, Punctuation, and Mechanics

_____ I use the present tense to discuss Klemens's argument and examples.

_____ I use verb tenses correctly to show the chronology of events.

_____ I have verb tense consistency throughout my sentences.

_____ I have checked for subject-verb agreement in all of my sentences.

_____ I have revised all fragments and mixed or garbled sentences.

_____ I have repaired all fused (run-on) sentences and comma splices.

_____ I have placed a comma after introductory elements (transitions and phrases) and all dependent clauses that open a sentence.

_____ If I present items in a series (nouns, verbs, prepositional phrases), they are parallel in form.

_____ If I include material spoken or written by someone other than myself, I have correctly punctuated it with quotation marks, using the MLA style guide's rules for citation.

Reviewing Your Graded Essay

After your instructor has returned your essay, you may have the opportunity to revise your paper and raise your grade. Many students, especially those whose essays receive nonpassing grades, feel that their instructors should be less "picky" about grammar and should pass the work on content alone. However, most students at this level have not yet acquired the ability to recognize quality writing, and they do not realize that content and writing actually cannot be separated in this way. Experienced instructors know that errors in sentence structure, grammar, punctuation, and word choice either interfere with content or distract readers so much that they lose track of content. In short, good ideas badly presented are no longer good ideas; to pass, an essay must have passable writing. So, even if you are not submitting a revised version of this essay to your instructor, it is important that you review your work carefully in order to understand its strengths and weaknesses. This sheet will guide you through the evaluation process.

You will want to continue to use the techniques that worked well for you and to find strategies to overcome the problems that you identify in this sample of your writing. In order to help yourself recognize areas that might have been problematic for you, look back at the scoring rubric in this book. Match the numerical/verbal/letter grade received on your essay to the appropriate category. Study the explanation given on the rubric for your grade.

Write a few sentences below in which you identify your problems in each of the following areas. Then, suggest specific changes you could make that would improve your paper. Don't forget to use your handbook as a resource.

1. **Grammar/punctuation/mechanics**
   My problem:

   My strategy for change:

2. **Thesis/response to assignment**
   My problem:

   My strategy for change:

3. **Organization**
   My problem:

My strategy for change:

4. **Paragraph development/examples/reasoning**

My problem:

My strategy for change:

5. **Assessment**

In the space below, assign a grade to your paper using a rubric other than the one used by your instructor. In other words, if your instructor assigned your essay a grade of *High Fail*, you might give it the letter grade you now feel the paper warrants. If your instructor used the traditional letter grade to evaluate the essay, choose a category from the rubric in this book, or any other grading scale that you are familiar with, to show your evaluation of your work. Then, write a short narrative explaining your evaluation of the essay and the reasons it received the grade you gave it.

Grade: _____

Narrative: _____

_____

_____

_____

_____

Extending the Discussion: Considering Other Viewpoints

Readings

"The American Work Ethic" by Peter Kirsanow
"Work in an Industrial Society" by Eric Fromm
"The Ethics of Work-Life Balance" by Bruce Weinstein
"Time Off for the Overworked American" by Courtney E. Martin
"The Importance of Work" by Betty Friedan
"Woe Is the American Worker" by Paul Waldman
"Men at Work" by Anna Quindlen

THE AMERICAN WORK ETHIC

Peter Kirsanow

Peter N. Kirsanow received his BA from Cornell University and his JD from Cleveland State University's Cleveland-Marshall College of Law, where he also acted as articles editor of the Cleveland State Law Review, *a scholarly journal focusing on legal scholarship and research. He is a practicing attorney, a partner in a law firm, and a member of the US Commission on Civil Rights. In addition, he served on the National Labor Relations Board from 2006 to 2008. This 2013 article was published in the* National Review Online *in the magazine's blog, called* The Corner.

For more than a century, much of the world has marveled at the American work ethic and American productivity. How long will that continue?

Probably like most *Corner* readers, as a kid, when I wasn't in school, I worked. Starting at age five, I began doing yard work and odd jobs for neighbors and local businesses. When I got a bit older, I got summer and after-school jobs (the latter when not involved in sports). Obviously, I had no skills, so most of the jobs involved manual labor, much of it fairly arduous.

On the occasions when I couldn't find a job, I became self-employed—painting houses, digging trenches, mowing lawns, putting up fences. Almost all of my friends had jobs or were self-employed also. Not working was a source of deep embarrassment. Once, the summer after eighth grade, I had no work for maybe one to two weeks, and not for lack of effort (we typically began lining up summer jobs the preceding October and November). One of my best friends chided me for "being on welfare." The statement stung so much—so profound was the stigma of not working—that we almost came to blows.

Is that changing? An observation: When I bought my house years back, two neighborhood boys appeared almost instantly to rake leaves, cut grass, paint the tool shed, and so on. They worked hard and well—both after school and during breaks. When they moved away, another boy performed some of the same work for about a year.

For the last twenty years, however, no one's asked to do any work, even though it's clear to anyone in the neighborhood there's work to be had. I've sought kids out who, it's plain to see, have no jobs, but I have been largely unsuccessful. For example, I recently asked two teenage boys who'd spent most of the summer playing basketball at a nearby playground if they wanted to earn some cash doing some yard work. They promise to come over Saturday morning. Saturday arrives, no call, no show. I try again the next week. More promises, but again, no call, no show.

I've heard similar stories in recent years from lots of friends and employers. Yes, several anecdotes don't amount to statistical evidence, and I encounter hardworking kids all the time. But the *expectation*, the *presumption* of hard work doesn't appear to be anywhere near as pervasive as in the past.

Is it more likely or less likely that this phenomenon will persist (or perhaps get worse) when much of the major media and an entire political party drive a narrative that productive Americans aren't "paying their fair share"; when a president lauds a twenty-six-year-old's ability to stay on his parents' insurance plan; when nearly fifty million Americans access food stamps benefits with a slick-looking card; when unemployment benefits continue interminably;

when government encourages citizens to access "free" benefits; when stigma or shame attaches almost as readily to the productive as the nonproductive?

Discussion Questions

1. According to Peter Kirsanow, how does the rest of the world view America in terms of work habits and the results they produce? Discuss the work ethic in the community where you grew up, whether here in the United States or elsewhere.

2. From his experiences and those of his friends, how does he think American children have changed in their attitude towards work? What specific personal examples have led him to his conclusion? Explain why you think that the anecdotes on which he bases his conclusion are sufficient or insufficient to warrant such a conclusion. Relate an anecdote of your own that supports or contradicts his conclusion.

3. Who does the author feel is at least partially responsible for the changing attitude toward work? What specifics does he point out as evidence? What concerns do you think Klemens would have about the effect of these things on America's future?

WORK IN AN INDUSTRIAL SOCIETY

Erich Fromm

Erich Fromm was born in Germany and trained as a psychoanalyst in Berlin. He taught at Yale and Columbia and became a well-known psychoanalyst and writer. The following essay is adapted from his book The Sane Society (1955).

Craftsmanship, especially as it developed in the thirteenth and fourteenth centuries, constitutes one of the peaks in the evolution of creative work in Western history. During the Middle Ages, the Renaissance, and the eighteenth century, work was not only a useful activity, but one which carried with it a profound satisfaction. The main features of craftsmanship as it existed before the Industrial Revolution have been very lucidly expressed by C. W. Mills:

> There is no ulterior motive in work other than the product being made and the processes of its creation. The details of daily work are meaningful because they are not detached in the worker's mind from the product of the work. The worker is free to control his own working action. The craftsman is thus able to learn from his work; and to use and develop his capacities and skills in its prosecution. There is no split of work and play, or work and culture. The craftsman's way of livelihood determines and infuses his entire mode of living.

By contrast, what happens to the industrial worker today, in 1955? He spends his best energy for seven or eight hours a day in producing "something." He needs his work in order to make a living, but his role is essentially a passive one. He fulfills a small, isolated function in a complicated and highly organized process of production, and is never confronted with "his" product as a whole—at least not as a producer, but only as a consumer, provided he has the money to buy "his" product in a store. He is concerned neither with the whole product in its physical aspects nor with its wider economic and social aspects. He is put in a certain place, has to carry out a certain task, but does not participate in the organization or management of the work. He is not interested in, nor does he know, why he produces this commodity instead of another one—what relation it has to the needs of society as a whole. The shoes, the cars, the electric bulbs, are produced by "the enterprise," using the machines. He is part of the machine, rather than its master as an active agent.

For today's industrial worker, work is a means of getting money, not in itself a meaningful human activity. P. Drucker, observing workers in the automobile industry, expresses this idea very succinctly:

> For the great majority of automobile workers, the only meaning of the job is in the pay check, not in anything connected with the work or the product. Work appears as something unnatural, a disagreeable, meaningless, and stultifying condition of getting the pay check, devoid of dignity as well as of importance. No wonder that this puts a premium on slovenly work, on slowdowns, and on other tricks to get the same pay check with less work. No wonder that this results in an unhappy and discontented worker—because a pay check is not enough to base one's self-respect on.

The alienated and profoundly unsatisfactory character of modern industrial work results in two reactions: one, the ideal of complete laziness; the other, a deep-seated, though often unconscious, hostility toward work and everything and everybody connected with it.

It is not difficult to recognize the widespread longing for the state of complete laziness and passivity. Our advertising appeals to it even more than to sex. There are, of course, many useful and labor-saving gadgets. But this usefulness often serves only as a rationalization for their appeal to complete passivity and receptivity. A package of breakfast cereal is advertised as "new—easier to eat." An electronic toaster is advertised with these words: "the most distinctly different toaster in the world! Everything is done for you with this new toaster. You need not even bother to lower the bread. Power-action, through a unique electric motor, gently takes the bread right out of your fingers!" Everybody knows the picture of the elderly couple in an advertisement of a life-insurance company, who have retired at the age of sixty, and spend their life in the complete bliss of having nothing to do except just travel.

But there is a far more serious and deep-seated reaction to the meaninglessness and boredom of work. It is hostility toward work that is much less conscious than our craving for laziness and inactivity. Many a businessman feels himself the prisoner of his business and the commodities he sells; he has a feeling of fraudulence about his product and a secret contempt for it. He hates his customers, who force him to put up a show in order to sell. He hates his competitors because they are a threat; he hates his employees as well as his superiors because he is in a constant competitive fight with them. Most important of all, he hates himself because he sees his life passing by without making any sense beyond the momentary intoxication of success. Of course, this hate and this contempt—for others and for oneself, and for the very things one produces—are mainly unconscious. Only occasionally do these feelings come up to awareness in a fleeting thought that is sufficiently disturbing to be set aside as quickly as possible.

Discussion Questions

1. According to Fromm, in what ways did the relationship between worker, work, and product differ during preindustrial times from what it was in Fromm's day (1955)? Do you think he may be idealizing the past? Explain your answer. Give your assessment of the relationship that exists today between the worker and his work.

2. What two reactions does Fromm suggest are the result of performing work in an industrialized society? Relate examples in which you demonstrated one of these reactions yourself or were the recipient of behavior resulting from one of these reactions.

3. Explain the differences in the relationships between workers and work in the discussions of Fromm and Klemens. How would what Klemens calls a "strong work ethic" alter the way the automobile factory workers, observed by Drucker, see themselves and their work?

THE ETHICS OF WORK-LIFE BALANCE

BRUCE WEINSTEIN

Bruce Weinstein received a BA from Swarthmore College and a PhD from Georgetown University. From 2006 to 2012, he contributed to Bloomberg Businessweek's *online edition, which also posted his twelve-episode series* Ask the Ethics Guy. *He is now a blogger at the* Huffington Post *and is a professional public speaker, lecturing on ethics and leadership. His latest book,* Ethical Intelligence, *was published in 2011. The essay below appeared on* Bloomberg Businessweek *in 2009.*

We are a nation in pain. According to a March 12 Gallup poll, the number of people in this country classified as "suffering" has increased by three million over the past year. Managers and business owners experienced the greatest loss of well-being; 60.8% of businesses were thriving in the first quarter of 2008, but this number decreased by almost 14% by the fourth quarter. Given the difficult economic climate and the number of jobs being lost daily, most of us are feeling the pressure to work harder than ever. But in spite of the increasing intensity of our economic crisis, it is not only unfortunate to give in to such pressure. It's unethical.

It's not too late to make a change for the better, though.

It may seem misplaced to discuss work-life balance in a column about ethics. But recall that one of five fundamental ethical principles is fairness, and that we demonstrate fairness in everyday life by how we allocate scarce resources. The most precious commodity you have is time, both in your professional and your personal life. It's also your most critical nonrenewable resource. As a manager, you must constantly ask yourself how you should allocate your time. You know it's wrong to spend so much time on one project at the expense of equally critical ones, or to spend so much time managing one employee that you're unable to manage others.

But a good manager should be, first and foremost, a good human being. Just as managing your career well means allocating your time wisely among the different projects and people you oversee, managing your life wisely means giving due time not just to work but to family, friends, community, self, and spirit. You wouldn't think of spending most of your work day talking with one client on the phone. Why, then, is it okay to devote so much time to your job when you don't give non-work-related things the attention they deserve?

Ethics isn't just about how you treat others. It's also about how you treat yourself—at work and beyond. You're not being fair to others and yourself if you haven't had a vacation in a long time, or if you force yourself to work when you've got the flu. You're also not being fair to others and yourself if you spend so much time being a good manager that you're not able to be a good parent, spouse, or friend. And let's face it: You can't do your job to the best of your ability if you're thoroughly exhausted, and that's not fair to your coworkers or your employer. But working to the exclusion of all else isn't just unfair (and thus unethical). It's also tragic, because the time you spend away from the other meaningful relationships in your life is time you can never get back.

Let's now look at some of the common excuses people give for working so much and how to get beyond them.

"I want to make sure I keep my job."

More than 2.5 million jobs were lost in 2008, and the losses continue to mount. What could be wrong with working all the time in such a climate if it will mean hanging onto your job? Speaking of ethics, isn't there an ethical obligation to keep your job? After all, what would be ethical about not paying bills, or your mortgage, or not being able to take care of your family?

Of course it's important to remain an employee in good standing. But you shouldn't assume that there is a direct correlation with the number of hours you work and the likelihood that you'll hold onto your job. Downsizing is largely a function of economics rather than of job performance; companies are letting people go to cut their losses and hit budget targets. (And yes, letting go of good employees raises other ethical issues, but that deserves its own column.) Working twelve-hour days six or seven days a week isn't going to guard against getting downsized.

In fact, it could even backfire. You might look like someone who can't manage his or her time or isn't up to the responsibilities of the job. And if you work without any letup, you will reach the point of diminishing returns. This isn't a time to be less than a stellar employee, but working overtime won't get you there.

"I need to work more to make what I did last year."

Many of the recently downsized are taking lower-paying jobs because that's all that is available. Some are even taking second jobs and still not making what they did a year ago. But how important is it now to live in the manner to which you have become accustomed? It's one thing to have to work seventy hours a week just to put food on the table and pay the rent or mortgage. It's another to work so much to be able to afford lavish trips, expensive clothes, or a certain lifestyle. Instead of working longer, couldn't you shift your priorities so that you're able to spend more time with family and friends, exercise more often, or even just read some of those books you've been thinking about?

"I have a demanding job."

Gone are the days when leaving your office meant leaving work behind. Many of us choose to use our BlackBerrys, iPhones, laptops, and social networking sites to remain constantly available to our bosses, clients, and colleagues, but this can get out of control. It's flattering to believe that you're indispensable to your company, and that only you can do the work you spend so much time doing. This is rarely true, however painful that may be to accept. Be honest with yourself: Are you spending so much time on the job because you must, or because of habit, ego, or some other reason? We owe it to ourselves and the people we care about (and who care about us) to work smarter, not harder.

"I just love to work."

It's a blessing to be able to say this, but all passions should have limits. A fully human life is a life in balance, and that means giving due time to all of the things that enrich us, fulfill us, and make our lives worth living. When Freud said that work and love were essential components of a happy life, he didn't mean that these were one and the same thing.

There is a time to work and a time to leave work behind. The good manager leaves time to do both.

Discussion Questions

1. On what basis does Bruce Weinstein claim that we are "a nation in pain"? From what he and other authors you have read in this unit have to say, offer what evidence you can find to support his statement.

2. From your own experiences and observations, in real life and the media, provide a detailed example of one individual's overcommitment to work and the effects on the people around him or her.

3. What principle of ethics does Weinstein apply to overwork? How does he believe Americans are being unethical in this regard? Discuss his assessment of the excuses and their validity that people give for violating this principle. Explain how one or more of the characteristics of a strong work ethic, which are detailed in Klemens's essay, are being violated by the unethical work behavior that concerns Weinstein.

4. How might Klemens respond to Weinstein.

TIME OFF FOR THE OVERWORKED AMERICAN

Courtney E. Martin

Courtney E. Martin received a BA in political science and sociology from Barnard College and earned an MA in writing and social change from New York University's Gallatin School of Individualized Study. Her latest book, Do It Anyway: The New Generation of Activists *(2010), focuses on Martin's main passion, social change. She has written many articles for various publications, including the* New York Times, *the* Washington Post, *and the* American Prospect, *whose online division published the article below in 2007. In addition, she is an accomplished public speaker who often addresses issues of body image and youth, also the focus of her first book.*

Remember riding hip to hip with your brothers and sisters in the back of the family van, eating the snacks too soon, fighting over the music selection, losing tiny, indispensable pieces of travel games? Or maybe your family was not of the road trip ilk. Perhaps you remember exciting trips on airplanes, a special pin from the stewardess, watching the clouds take shape out of your own oval window, your grandparents waiting feverishly for your arrival in the sprawling Portland or Poughkeepsie or even Paris airport. As much as you may have resented it then, the family vacation is as quintessentially American as homemade apple pie. It is also just about as rare in this age of store-bought desserts and workaholism.

Last year, twenty-five percent of American workers got no paid vacation at all, while forty-three percent didn't even take a solid week off. A third fewer American families take vacations together today than they did in 1970. American workers receive the least vacation time among wealthy industrial nations. And it is no thanks to the US government—127 other countries in the world have a vacation law. We—the crackberry denizens and Protestant ethic superstars—do not.

A growing movement of nonprofits, citizen advocacy groups, and trade associations is trying to change all that. Take Back Your Time, a national organization with over ten thousand members, has declared getting a federal vacation law that guarantees Americans at least three week paid vacation a top priority issue in 2007. They are joined by Joe Robinson, author of the 2003 book *Work to Live* and a work/life balance coach, and the Adventure Travel Trade Association, among others.

This is not just a plea for more beach time. It is a movement that recognizes that Americans' lives are diminished by our work-above-all-else orientation. Dissatisfaction with work/life balance cuts across class boundaries, leaving too many Americans feeling estranged from the things they believe are most important—family, friends, well-being, spiritual practice. In what journalist Keith H. Hammonds calls our "postbalance world," most Americans live their lives in unsatisfying feast or famine. Unfortunately, there is more famine when it comes to relaxation, exploration, and rejuvenation these days—no thanks to federal policy. John Schmitt, senior economist and co-author of "No-Vacation Nation," a recent study by the Center for Economic Policy Research, says, "It's a national embarrassment that 28 million Americans don't get any paid vacation or paid holidays."

We don't get much time at home; and at work, we feel significantly unsupported. In the latest Pew Research Center survey on work, a near majority of workers (forty-five percent) now says benefits are worse than they had been twenty or thirty years ago. This includes a gamut of policies—health care, paternity leave, flextime—all of which America is pathetically behind other industrialized countries in legislating. There has certainly been a growing conversation about these issues, thanks to the mothers' movement led by groups like MomsRising, but legislated vacation time is often last on the list of demands. (Not so surprising when you consider how difficult it is for most mothers to believe they deserve a rest.)

Not only does less vacation time mean we have less time to develop our most critical and lasting relationships with family members and friends, but our physical health is in jeopardy when we refuse to unchain ourselves from the cubicle. Vacations cut down on stress, which any medical expert will tell you is at the center of so many of America's most pernicious health crises. Two researchers at the State University of New York at Oswego showed that an annual vacation can cut the risk of death from heart disease in women by fifty percent and in men by thirty-two percent. Taking time out, exploring new horizons, getting away from your desk and moving around, reconnecting with close friends and family are all safeguards against burnout and depression. But this kind of rejuvenation takes time—two weeks, most studies indicate. The average vacation in the United States is now only a long weekend, which just isn't long enough.

Cali Williams Yost, author of the 2005 book *Work+Life: Finding the Fit That's Right for You* and a coach on work/life balance, asserts that it is not just taking vacation that is important, but how we operate while on it that makes the big difference. She advises corporate clients on how to "avoid having technology become the Grinch that Stole Your Christmas (or Hanukkah, or Kwanzaa)" by setting personal goals around technology usage: "We all need to be much more conscious when we go on vacation."

But it's not all about self control; it's also about government control. Why does the government need to get involved? Because in this cutthroat economic environment, vacation—like parental leave—goes the way of the wimp. Even if workers are employed by companies that guarantee vacation time, many of them are afraid to take advantage because they might be seen as slackers. A culture of self-sacrifice has cropped up in so many careers, leaving those who take their full two weeks looking uncommitted and ineffective.

In truth, they are probably *better* employees for taking the time off. Three-week vacations have proven to be a boost to productivity and profits at enlightened American firms where the culture truly supports the practice. Especially in the knowledge economy, clear thinking and a fresh perspective are critical to best practice. How can anyone expect to get the newest ideas and most innovative approaches from workers who get only the occasional weekend getaway, cell phones still permanently attached to their ears?

Some companies are already reporting hard-and-fast evidence of the phenomenon, according to Robinson. Jancoa, a Cincinnati-based cleaning services company, extended its vacation benefits for its 468 employees to three weeks at a total cost of seven cents. Productivity and morale increased so much that the company was able to eliminate overtime and cut its retention and recruiting costs. The H Group, a management firm founded in 1990 and based in Salem, Oregon, has seen profits double since owner Ron Kelemen pushed his three-week vacation program.

The movement rallying around this issue hopes to get vacation law into the 2008 presidential conversation as well. They are framing it not only as a quality of life issue, but as an indispensable ingredient of global competition. The fastest growing economy in the world, China, offers three weeks off, which they call "Golden Weeks."

Robinson quips, "President Bush knows the value of vacation time. He enjoys his trips to his ranch. He ought to be the first to step up and say, 'Send me this bill and I'll sign it.'"

Discussion Questions

1. Compare the vacation time of American workers with that of workers in other wealthy nations. In terms of time off, was the percentage of American workers taking time to go on a family vacation what you expected it to be? Why or why not? Tell about the last time your family went on a vacation together.

2. How does the author feel the lack of sufficient "beach time" is harmful to Americans? Do you think the benefits of less time off outweigh the negatives she raises? Explain your answer.

3. Do you think workers at all jobs should get the same amount of vacation, or do you think the number of vacation days should be determined by seniority or the kind of work the person does? Justify your answer.

4. Do you think the Protestant work ethic Klemens discusses is responsible for creating a society of overworked Americans? Do you think, as Martin does, that Americans are unwilling to take time away from their jobs? Why? Consider the way many Japanese companies arrange group vacations for their workers. Do you think American companies should institute practices to encourage their employees to take a vacation?

THE IMPORTANCE OF WORK

Betty Friedan

Betty Friedan (1921–2006) was one of the founders of the National Organization for Women. She attended Smith College, graduating with a degree in psychology, and did graduate study at the University of California, Berkeley. Friedan is a well-known feminist, public speaker, and writer whose essays have appeared in numerous periodicals. Her books include It Changed My Life *(1976),* The Second Stage *(1981), and* The Feminine Mystique *(1963), which many attribute to starting the "second wave" of the feminist movement and which is excerpted below.*

The question of how a person can most fully realize his own capacities and thus achieve identity has become an important concern of the philosophers and the social and psychological thinkers of our time—and for good reason. Thinkers of other times put forth the idea that people were, to a great extent, defined by the work they did. The work that a man had to do to eat, to stay alive, to meet the physical necessities of his environment, dictated his identity. And in this sense, while work was seen merely as a means of survival, human identity was dictated by biology.

But today the problem of human identity has changed. For the work that defined man's place in society and his sense of himself has also changed man's world. Work, and the advance of knowledge, has lessened man's dependence on his environment; his biology and the work he must do for biological survival are no longer sufficient to define his identity. This can be most clearly seen in our own abundant society; men no longer need to work all day to eat. They have an unprecedented freedom to choose the kind of work they will do; they also have an unprecedented amount of time apart from the hours and days that must actually be spent in making a living. And suddenly one realizes the significance of today's identity crisis—for women, and increasingly, for men. One sees the human significance of work—not merely as the means of biological survival, but as the giver of self and the transcender of self, as the creator of human identity and human evolution.

For "self-realization" or "self-fulfillment" or "identity" does not come from looking into a mirror in rapt contemplation of one's own image. Those who have most fully realized themselves, in a sense that can be recognized by the human mind even though it cannot be clearly defined, have done so in the service of a human purpose larger than themselves. Men from varying disciplines have used different words for this mysterious process from which comes the sense of self. The religious mystics, the philosophers, Marx, Freud—all had different names for it: Man finds himself by losing himself; man is defined by his relation to the means of production; the ego, the self, grows through understanding and mastering reality through work and love.

The identity crisis, which has been noted by Erik Erikson and others in recent years in the American man, seems to occur for lack of, and be cured by finding, the work, or cause, or purpose that evokes his own creativity. Some never find it, for it does not come from busy-work or punching a time clock. It does not come from just making a living, working by formula, finding a secure spot as an organization man. The very argument, by Riesman and others, that man no longer finds identity in the work defined as a paycheck job, assumes that identity for man comes through creative work of his own that contributes to the human community: The core of the self becomes aware, becomes real, and grows through work that carries forward human society.

Work, the shopworn staple of the economists, has become the new frontier of psychology. Psychiatrists have long used "occupational therapy" with patients in mental hospitals; they have recently discovered that to be of real psychological value, it must be not just "therapy," but real work, serving a real purpose in the community. And work can now be seen as the key to the problem that has no name. The identity crisis of American women began a century ago, as more and more of the work important to the world, more and more of the work that used their human abilities and through which they were able to find self-realization, was taken from them.

Until, and even into, the last century, strong, capable women were needed to pioneer our new land; with their husbands, they ran the farms and plantations and Western homesteads. These women were respected and self-respecting members of a society whose pioneering purpose centered in the home. Strength and independence, responsibility and self-confidence, self-discipline and courage, freedom and equality were part of the American character for both men and women, in all the first generations. The women who came by steerage from Ireland, Italy, Russia, and Poland worked beside their husbands in the sweatshops and the laundries, learned the new language, and saved to send their sons and daughters to college. Women were never quite as "feminine," or held in as much contempt, in America as they were in Europe. American women seemed to European travelers, long before our time, less passive, childlike, and feminine than their own wives in France or Germany or England. By an accident of history, American women shared in the work of society longer, and grew with the men. Grade- and high-school education for boys and girls alike was almost always the rule; and in the West, where women shared the pioneering work the longest, even the universities were coeducational from the beginning.

The identity crisis for women did not begin in America until the fire and strength and ability of the pioneer women were no longer needed, no longer used, in the middle-class homes of the Eastern and Midwestern cities, when the pioneering was done and men began to build the new society in industries and professions outside the home. But the daughters of the pioneer women had grown too used to freedom and work to be content with leisure and passive femininity.

It was not an American, but a South African woman, Mrs. Olive Schreiner, who warned at the turn of the century that the quality and quantity of women's functions in the social universe were decreasing as fast as civilization was advancing; that if women did not win back their right to a full share of honored and useful work, woman's mind and muscle would weaken in a parasitic state; her offspring, male and female, would weaken progressively, and civilization itself would deteriorate.

The feminists saw clearly that education and the right to participate in the more advanced work of society were women's greatest needs. They fought for and won the rights to new, fully human identity for women. But how very few of their daughters and granddaughters have chosen to use their education and their abilities for any large creative purpose, for responsible work in society? How many of them have been deceived, or have deceived themselves, into clinging to the outgrown, childlike femininity of "Occupation: housewife"?

It was not a minor matter, their mistaken choice. We now know that the same range of potential ability exists for women as for men. Women, as well as men, can find their identity only in work that uses their full capacities. A woman cannot find her identity through others—her husband, her children. She cannot find it in the dull routine of housework. As thinkers of every age have said, it is only when a human being faces squarely the fact that he can forfeit his own life, that he becomes truly aware of himself, and begins to take his existence seriously. Sometimes this awareness comes only at the moment of death. Sometimes it comes from a more subtle facing of death: the death of self in passive conformity, in meaningless work. The feminine mystique prescribes just such a living death for women. Faced with the slow death of self, the American woman must begin to take her life seriously.

"We measure ourselves by many standards," said the great American psychologist William James, nearly a century ago. "Our strength and our intelligence, our wealth and even our good luck, are things which warm our heart and make us feel ourselves a match for life. But deeper than all such things, and able to suffice unto itself without them, is the sense of the amount of effort which we can put forth." If women do not put forth, finally, that effort to become all that they have it in them to become, they will forfeit their own humanity. A woman today who has no goal, no purpose, no ambition patterning her days into the future, making her stretch and grow beyond that small score of years in which her body can fill its biological function, is committing a kind of suicide. For that future half a century after the child-bearing years are over is a fact that an American woman cannot deny. Nor can she deny that as a housewife, the world is indeed rushing past her door while she just sits and watches. The terror she feels is real, if she has no place in that world.

The feminine mystique has succeeded in burying millions of American women alive. There is no way for these women to break out of their comfortable concentration camps except by finally putting forth an effort—that human effort that reaches beyond biology, beyond the narrow walls of home, to help shape the future. Only by such a personal commitment to the future can American women break out of the housewife trap and truly find fulfillment as wives and mothers—by fulfilling their own unique possibilities as separate human beings.

Discussion Questions

1. How does Friedan explain the change in the significance of work from the past to the present?

2. Does Friedan find all kinds of work to be equally satisfying? Where, according to Klemens, is job satisfaction found? Identify and discuss the points of disagreement in their positions.

3. Who, according to Friedan, were the early feminists, and in what ways did they succeed in reconstructing our ideas about women and work? How has the relationship between women and work changed in the history of America? How does Friedan feel about this change? Explain why you do or do not think her perspective has validity.

4. How does the relationship between work and identity that Friedan discusses correspond with Klemens's idea of the work ethic? Explain why you believe his idea to be either gender biased or gender neutral.

WOE IS THE AMERICAN WORKER

Paul Waldman

Paul Waldman was a senior fellow at Media Matters for America and an associate director of the Annenberg Public Policy Center at the University of Pennsylvania. His work has appeared in several different newspapers, and his most recent book is Being Right Is Not Enough: What Progressives Must Learn from Conservative Success *(2008). He is now a contributing editor and daily blogger for the* American Prospect, *where the essay below appeared online in 2007.*

These are not good times for American workers. Real wages are lower today than they were before the recession of 2001, and barely higher than they were thirty-five years ago. Health insurance is more expensive and harder to obtain than ever before. Manufacturing jobs continue to move overseas. The unions whose efforts might arrest these trends continue to struggle under a sustained assault that began when Ronald Reagan fired striking air-traffic controllers in 1981, in effect declaring war on the labor movement.

This is a story with which you are probably familiar. But these are in no small part symptoms of a larger transformation of the relationship between employers and employees, in which Americans increasingly sign away their humanity when they sign an employment contract.

Let's take just one component of today's work environment that most people have simply come to accept: drug testing. An article published last year on *Time* magazine's website titled "Whatever Happened to Drug Testing?" reports that in the last decade, the proportion of employers testing their employees for drug use has declined to sixty-two percent, after having exploded to over eighty percent in the 1990s.

That's right—"only" sixty-two percent of employers make their employees pee into a cup (or fork over a lock of hair, the current state of the art). The recent decline notwithstanding, the fact remains that most Americans work at places where drug testing is standard practice.

But the classic justifications for drug testing—that it will reduce accidents, absenteeism, and overall productivity—turn out to have very little support. When this study was released ten years ago, it got a certain amount of attention for what the authors referred to as a "surprising" finding. In their survey of high-tech firms, they found that those that performed drug testing on their employees had *lower* productivity than those that didn't test. Forget all the rhetoric about pot-addled employees missing work and stumbling their way around the office.

But I'd bet that most people who work weren't too surprised. Think about the jobs you've had. Where were you the most productive? Was it when you worked for a boss and an organization that treated you with respect, that valued your contributions, where you actually felt that you were part of something useful? Or were you more productive when you worked for a boss and an organization that governed by fear, that treated you with suspicion and contempt? Most adults have worked for the latter kind, while only some have had the good fortune to work for the former. And many if not most of them do just enough work to stay out of trouble and avoid the wrath of their superiors. That's the spirit fostered in a workplace where employees are treated like criminals.

There is an ideology inherent in the way employers treat their workers, one reflected in the relative amounts of attention paid by the news media to labor issues and the ups and downs of the stock market. Wall Street, of course, makes heroes out of executives who cut benefits and sack workers, like the monstrous "Neutron Jack" Welch, formerly of General Electric. A corporate barbarian of the first order, Welch pocketed hundreds of millions of dollars while firing more than 100,000 employees, then went on to write a series of best-selling books gobbled up by junior executives looking for the secret battle plan to slash their way to the top. He's just one among many; another such executive, who laid off nine thousand people when he was CEO of Halliburton, later became vice president of the United States.

If you are one of those left behind, you get called an "associate" instead of a clerk. In the place of paid vacation, you get company-sponsored activities whose absurdity can only make you more depressed. In the place of a union to represent you, you get assurances that the company considers you part of the "family." Your samples will be analyzed, your movements surveilled, your e-mail read, all in the name of enhancing productivity and rooting out the bad apples. And should they decide your time is done, they will send a security guard to march you out the door in a ritual of public humiliation, lest you decide to pilfer a stapler as a memento of your service.

There is no labor section of the newspaper to tell the stories of the families devastated by layoffs and the workers ground down by the daily parade of indignities. But in the morally inverted world of Wall Street, what's bad for workers is good for stocks, and the cable news "money honeys" will bare their gleaming teeth as they report the inevitable upward swing in share prices that accompanies a mass firing or benefit cut.

It would be positively revelatory to hear a presidential candidate truly speak to the conditions Americans find themselves in at work, to say firmly that companies that treat their employees like dirt are undermining our national spirit. They are the ones who have the ability to change our national conversation on topics like these. What if, instead of simply talking about "creating jobs," expanding health care, or increasing the minimum wage—important goals all—they actually attempted to speak to how people feel about their jobs? When candidates say the American dream is getting harder to attain, one often wonders if they understand all the reasons why that is so.

The Republicans certainly know the kind of workplace they admire. It's one in which power—not values, principles, or fairness, but raw power—determines how people are treated. They find deeply troubling anything that constrains employers from exploiting their workers to whatever degree they see fit. They despise unions precisely because they alter that balance of power in the worker's favor, providing some check on the ability of organizations to intimidate and humiliate, underpay and overwork. But so far, Democrats haven't articulated their vision of what a progressive workplace in the twenty-first century is supposed to look like—and what they're willing to do to create it. I'd be eager to hear.

Discussion Questions

1. In what way, according to Paul Waldman, has the relationship between the American workers and employers changed? Give an example of a place where you or someone you know has worked that supports Waldman's view of the employer-employee relationship. Give an example that contradicts his view. For which of the two categories did you find that more examples came to mind?

2. What was one result of drug testing that was "surprising"? Explain your reasons for thinking that drug testing by employers should, or should not, continue.

3. Explain, in your own words, the relationship between Wall Street and the treatment of workers. How does this example of the practice of capitalism deviate from the practice by both leaders and workers of the work ethic Klemens finds essential for the future of America?

MEN AT WORK

ANNA QUINDLEN

Anna Quindlen graduated from Barnard College at Columbia University and has worked as a reporter and columnist for the New York Post, *the* New York Times, *and* Newsweek. *Her* New York Times *column, "Public and Private," received a Pulitzer Prize for Commentary in 1992. She is now a full-time best-selling novelist. The following essay is from a collection of her work titled* Thinking Out Loud: The Personal, the Political, the Public, and the Private *(1993).*

The five o'clock dads can be seen on cable television these days, just after that time in the evening the stay-at-home moms call the arsenic hours. They are sixties sitcom reruns, Ward and Steve and Alex, and fifties guys. They eat dinner with their television families and provide counsel afterward in the den. Someday soon, if things keep going the way they are, their likenesses will be enshrined in a diorama in the Museum of Natural History, frozen in their recliner chairs. The sign will say, "Here sit lifelike representations of family men who worked only eight hours a day."

The five o'clock dad has become an endangered species. A corporate culture that believes presence is productivity, in which people of ambition are afraid to be seen leaving the office, has lengthened his workday and shortened his home-life. So has an economy that makes it difficult for families to break even at the end of the month. For the man who is paid by the hour, that means never saying no to overtime. For the man whose loyalty to the organization is measured in time at his desk, it means goodbye to nine to five.

To lots of small children it means a visiting father. The standard joke in one large corporate office is that dads always say their children look like angels when they're sleeping because that's the only way they ever see them. A Gallup survey taken several years ago showed that roughly twelve percent of the men surveyed with children under the age of six worked more than sixty hours a week, and an additional twenty-five percent worked between fifty and sixty hours. (Less than eight percent of the working women surveyed who had children of that age worked those hours.)

No matter how you divide it up, those are twelve-hour days. When the talk-show host Jane Wallace adopted a baby recently, she said one reason she was not troubled by becoming a mother without becoming a wife was that many of her married female friends were "functionally single," given the hours their husbands worked. The evening commuter rush is getting longer. The 7:45 to West Backofbeyond is more crowded than ever before. The eight o'clock dad. The nine o'clock dad.

There's a horribly sad irony to this, and it is that the quality of fathering is better than it was when the dads left work at five o'clock and came home to café curtains and tuna casserole. The five o'clock dad was remote, a "Wait until your father gets home" kind of dad with a newspaper for a face. The roles he and his wife had were clear; she did nurture and home, he did discipline and money.

The role fathers have carved out for themselves today is a vast improvement, a muddling of those old boundaries. Those of us obliged to convert behavior into trends have probably been a little heavy-handed on the shared childbirth and egalitarian diaper-changing. But fathers today do seem to be more emotional with their children, more nurturing, more open. Many say, "My father never told me he loved me," and so they tell their own children all the time that they love them—when they're home.

There are people who think that this is changing even as we speak, that there is a kind of *perestroika* of home and work that we will look back on as beginning at the beginning of the 1990s. A nonprofit organization called the Families and Work Institute advises corporations on how to balance personal and professional obligations and concerns, and Ellen Galinsky, its cofounder, says she has noticed a change in the last year. "When we first started doing this the groups of men and women sounded very different," she says. "If the men complained at all about long hours, they complained about their wives' complaints. Now if the timbre of the voice was disguised I couldn't tell which is which. The men are saying: 'I don't want to live this way anymore. I want to be with my kids.' I think the corporate culture will have to begin to respond to that."

This change can only be to the good, not only for women but especially for men, and for kids, too. The stereotypical five o'clock dad belongs in a diorama, with his "Ask your mother" and his "Don't be a crybaby." The father who believes hugs and kisses are sex-blind and a dirty diaper requires a change, not a woman, is infinitely preferable. What a joy it would be if he were around more.

"This is the man's half of having it all," says Don Conway-Long, who teaches a course at Washington University in St. Louis about men's relationships that drew 135 students this year for thirty-five places. "We're trying to do what women want of us, what children want of us, but we're not willing to transform the workplace." In other words, the hearts and minds of today's fathers are definitely in the right place. If only their bodies could be there, too.

Discussion Questions

1. Why does Quindlen say that the "five o'clock dad" has become an endangered species?

2. What irony does Quindlen see in the relationship these new "visiting" fathers have with their children?

3. What change does Quindlen identify, and how does she explain this shift in men's attitude toward work versus time expectations? What do you think Klemens would say about the work ethic of these men? Why do you feel the change they desire either can, or cannot, be made without harming the economic future of America?

Assignment #3

"COMPETITION AND HAPPINESS"

This assignment asks you to write an essay in response to a reading selection that takes up the topic of competition and its place in our lives. Once again, there are several essays in the "Extending the Discussion" section that your instructor may assign or that you may read on your own. These readings will help you explore the subject of Rubin's argument in greater depth and develop your own ideas on the controversy that he addresses.

Whether you are assigned to read the supplemental readings or not, we encourage you to continue using all of the prewriting activities provided. They will ensure that you develop your thoughts and organize them within an effective essay format.

COMPETITION AND HAPPINESS

Theodore Isaac Rubin

Theodore Rubin is a writer of both fiction and nonfiction. He is a psychoanalyst and a former president of the American Institute of Psychoanalysis. The essay below is adapted from his book Reconciliation: Inner Peace in an Age of Anxiety *(1980).*

Our culture has come to believe that competition "brings out the best" in people. I believe that it brings out the worst. It is intimately linked to envy, jealousy, and paranoia, and blocks the evolution and development of self. It ultimately has a depleting and deadening effect on self as its unrelenting demands are met and self-realizing needs are ignored.

In competition, the focus of one's life is essentially outside one's self. The use of our time and energy is determined by our competitors rather than by ourselves and our own real needs. This weakens our own sense of identity, and to compensate for this ever-increasing feeling of emptiness and vulnerability, we compete still more, perpetuating a self-depleting cycle. When enough depletion takes place to preclude further "successful" competition, we feel hopeless and futile, and our lives seem purposeless. Despite talk about good sportsmanship, competition is totally incompatible with the kind of easy aliveness that is the aim of this book.

Competition is a residual of a primitive past, and it is *not* a genetic residual. It is passed on to us through training in our society from generation to generation. This training starts early and can usually be seen in very early sibling rivalry. I do not believe that rivalry among children of the same family is instinctual. I believe that it is engendered by parents who themselves are caught in the same trap: They spend enormous time and energy getting ahead of the Joneses. Small wonder so many children are pressured into Little League or equivalent competitive structures—all with the rationalization that these activities will promote their self-development, well-being, and health. Actually, these activities and organizations nearly always serve as vicarious vehicles designed to satisfy *parental* craving for competitive success.

People brought up in this way feel lost if they are suddenly thrust into a situation of low competitive tension. Because they exist to compete and they've lost their *raison d'être* in the new situation, they invent hierarchies and games to provide the stimulation they need to "keep the motor running," even if these inventions are ultimately destructive to inner peace and personal health.

I am reminded of my own medical school experience as part of a group of about eighty Americans studying at the university in Lausanne, Switzerland. The system was noncompetitive. People who received passing grades in the required premedical or foundation courses were accepted into the school. Two series of examinations—one in the basic sciences one and one half years after admission, and the other after studies were completed—determined qualification for graduation. Students were allowed to postpone these examinations as long as they felt was necessary. To pass, students were required to demonstrate adequate knowledge of the material. The atmosphere was totally benevolent, with no coercion or intimidation whatsoever. There was no "curve," and students were not graded relative to each other.

The Swiss students exhibited great camaraderie among themselves, helped each other, and for the most part demonstrated great proficiency in grasping and integrating the material. There were no "tricks" whatsoever, no surprise quizzes or exams. Indeed, there were no examinations at all, other than the two sets of standardized government exams. Requirements for passing the examinations were well defined for everyone. Instruction was superb.

We Americans arrived as graduates of a highly competitive system. Few of us could believe that medical school could be a straightforward, noncompetitive activity, and that we would be required to learn only the material we were told to learn. Stimulation addicts like ourselves found little motivation in the Swiss system—so we formed competitive cliques. Some people convinced themselves and others that the Swiss professors were tricky and that the two sets of exams could never be passed. People kept secret from each other the ready availability of course notebooks. Bets were made as to who would and who would not get through. People tried to convince other people that they would never get through and should return home. There was much gossip about absences from classes and who was and who wasn't dedicated to medical school and his chosen field. Former friends who came to Switzerland together stopped talking to each other because they now saw each other as competition. The Swiss went on as they always did. The Americans did also. They had re-created American competition in Switzerland.

Competition damages people other than students. It provides a stressful, isolating, and paranoid atmosphere that is the very antithesis of peace of mind. Competitive strivings are not always felt directly or blatantly. They do not occur solely when we are locked in antagonistic embrace with adversaries—we have, after all, come a considerable distance from the dinosaurs. But the subtle influence of competitive standards to be met and our consciousness of how the next guy is doing—in terms of earnings, position, accomplishments, notoriety, possessions, or whatever—work their subtle and not-so-subtle corrosive effects. They provide constant pressure and undermine our efforts to build a self-realizing value system. This means that we are more involved with how the next fellow is doing than with knowing what *we* really want to do. We are more concerned with how *they* feel about us than how we feel about ourselves.

Competition also makes it very difficult to accept and to feel the nourishing effects of give-and-take, and often makes much-needed help from others impossible to accept. Our culture in large measure has made this paranoid closure to nourishment from others a virtue, often rationalized by ideas about independence and self-reliance. Independence and self-reliance are indeed valuable assets, but often they are actually cover-ups for fear of other people and are functions of sick pride invested in rejection of other people's much-needed help.

Writing Topic

How does competition limit people's ability to lead happy and satisfying lives, according to Rubin? Do you agree with his views? Be sure to support your position with evidence taken from your own experience, your observations of others, and your reading, especially the reading from this course.

Vocabulary Check

Use a dictionary to find the meanings of the following words from Rubin's essay. Choose the meaning or meanings that you think are useful in gaining a full understanding of Rubin's ideas. Then, explain the way each of the definitions you wrote down is key to understanding his argument.

1. *depleting*

    definition: _____

    _____

    explanation:

    _____

    _____

    _____

2. *unrelenting*

    definition: _____

    _____

    explanation:

    _____

    _____

    _____

3. *compensate*

    definition: _____

    _____

    explanation:

    _____

    _____

    _____

4. *futile*

definition: _____

_____

explanation:

_____

_____

_____

5. *instinctual*

definition: _____

_____

explanation:

_____

_____

_____

6. *engender*

definition: _____

_____

explanation:

_____

_____

_____

7. *raison d'être*

definition: _____

_____

explanation:

_____

_____

_____

8. *hierarchy*

   definition: _____

   _____

   explanation:

   _____

   _____

   _____

9. *benevolent*

   definition: _____

   _____

   explanation:

   _____

   _____

   _____

10. *coercion*

   definition: _____

   _____

   explanation:

   _____

   _____

   _____

11. *intimidation*

   definition: _____

   _____

   explanation:

   _____

   _____

   _____

12. *camaraderie*

    definition: _____

    _____

    explanation:

    _____

    _____

    _____

13. *corrosive*

    definition: _____

    _____

    explanation:

    _____

    _____

    _____

Questions to Guide Your Reading

Answer the following questions so you can gain a thorough understanding of "Competition and Happiness."

Paragraph 1

What effect do most people believe that competition has on individuals? What does Rubin believe?

Paragraph 2

Why does Rubin think that competition is a destructive force in our lives?

Paragraph 3

What does Rubin see as the origin of competition in society, and what has enabled it to continue from generation to generation?

Paragraph 4

According to Rubin, what happens when people who are used to competing are placed in situations where there is no competition?

Paragraphs 5-7

Discuss the author's and the other Americans' medical school experience in Switzerland. Consider the ways that medical school there differs from medical school in the United States.

Paragraph 8

In what ways does the author feel competition damages people? Can you think of any other ill effects of competition?

Paragraph 9

What problems does the author think are created by privileging independence and self-reliance in our competitive society?

Prewriting for a Directed Summary

It is always important to look carefully at a writing topic and spend some time ensuring that you understand what it is asking. Your essay must provide a thorough response to all parts of the writing topic. The writing topic that follows "Competition and Happiness" contains three parts. The first part asks you about a central idea from the reading. To answer this part of the writing topic, you will have to summarize part of Rubin's argument. In other words, you will write a *directed* summary, meaning one that responds specifically to the first question in the writing topic.

> first question in the writing topic:
>
> *How does competition limit people's ability to lead happy and satisfying lives, according to Rubin?*

Notice that the question doesn't ask you to summarize the entire essay or simply explain Rubin's definition of competition. Rather, it asks you to explain Rubin's reason(s) for claiming that competition undermines happiness. The questions below will help you plan your response. They will guide you in identifying what you should include in your directed summary.

Focus Questions

1. What emotions does the author believe that competition evokes in people?

2. What are the effects of competition on people's personal lives, according to Rubin?

3. What group of Americans does the author especially point to as suffering from the competitive nature of our society?

4. In what way, according to Rubin, does a competitive society make interpersonal relationships difficult?

Developing an Opinion and Working Thesis Statement

The second question in the writing topic asks you to respond to Rubin's central claim by taking a position of your own:

> second part of the writing topic:
>
> *Do you agree with his views?*

You will have to explore your ideas about competition and decide what position you want to take in your essay. Do you agree with Rubin that competition undermines our happiness and diminishes our lives? Be sure to answer this part of the question directly because it will become the thesis statement for your essay. You will want to be as clear as possible.

It is likely that you aren't yet sure what position you want to take in your essay. If this is the case, it will be helpful to do your best to draft a working thesis statement now. There will be a chance later to revise or even change it completely once you've used the writing process to develop your thoughts a little more.

1. Use the following thesis frame to formulate the basic elements of your thesis statement:
   a. What is the issue of "Competition and Happiness" that the writing topic asks you to consider?

   _____

   b. What is Rubin's opinion about that issue?

   _____

   c. What is your opinion about the issue, and will you agree or disagree with Rubin's opinion?

   _____

   _____

   _____

2. Now use the elements you isolated in 1a, b, and c to write a thesis statement. You likely will have to revise it several times until it captures your idea clearly.

   _____

   _____

Prewriting to Find Support for Your Thesis Statement

The last part of the writing topic asks you to develop and support the position you took in your thesis statement by drawing on your own experience and readings.

last part of the writing topic:

Be sure to support your position with evidence taken from your own experience, your observations of others, and your reading, especially the reading from this course.

Use the guiding questions below to develop your ideas and find concrete support for them. The proof or evidence you present is an important element in supporting your argument and making your ideas persuasive for your readers.

1. As you begin to develop your own examples, think about how competition connects to your own life and the lives of those you know. In the space below, make a list of personal experiences you or others have had with competition. How significant are Rubin's concerns in your life and in the lives of those you know? What strategies have you or others used to deal with competition? List as many ideas as you can, and freewrite about the significance of each.

    Once you've written your ideas, look them over carefully and see if you can group them into categories. Then, give each category a label. In other words, cluster ideas that seem to have something in common and, for each cluster, identify that shared quality by giving the cluster a name.

2. Now make another list, but this time focus on examples from your studies, the media, your reading (especially the supplemental readings in this section), and your knowledge of contemporary society. Do any of these examples affirm Rubin's ideas? For example, do you recall any novels or films whose theme is the harmful effects of competition? Do you know of any examples that challenge Rubin's view and portray competition as positive? Explore a couple of TV shows that pit contestants against one another. What do they show about competition? What views do the supplemental essays in this section take? Review their arguments and supporting evidence, and compare them to Rubin's. Are any of them especially convincing for you? If so, list them here. (Remember to cite any of their ideas you include in your essay.) List and/or freewrite about all the relevant ideas you can think of, even those about which you are hesitant.

    As you did in #1, examine your ideas and try to arrange them in groups. Then, title each group according to the ideas they have in common.

3. Look back at the categories you created in #1 and #2, and decide which of them to develop in your essay; look for ones that will enable you to develop your argument and convincingly and concretely support your thesis statement. In the space below, briefly summarize how each chosen category supports your thesis statement.

The information and ideas you develop in this exercise will be the core of your body paragraphs when you turn to planning and drafting your essay.

Revising Your Thesis Statement

Now that you have spent some time working out your ideas more systematically and developing some supporting evidence for the position you want to take, look again at the working thesis statement you crafted earlier to see if it is still accurate. As your first step, look again at the writing topic, and then write your original working thesis on the lines that follow it.

> writing topic:
>
> *How does competition limit people's ability to lead happy and satisfying lives, according to Rubin? Do you agree with his views? Be sure to support your position with evidence taken from your own experience, your observations of others, and your reading, especially the reading from this course.*

working thesis statement:

_____

_____

Remember that your thesis statement must answer the second question in the writing topic but take into consideration the writing topic as a whole. The first question in the topic identifies the issue that is up for debate, and the last question reminds you that, whatever position you take on the issue, you must be able to support it with specific examples.

Now that you have spent some time thinking about competition, your draft thesis statement may not represent the position you want to take in your essay. Sometimes, only a word or phrase must be added or deleted; other times, the thesis statement must be significantly rewritten. The subject or the claim portion may be unclear, vague, or even inaccurate. Draft writing is almost always wordy, unclear, or vague. Look at your working thesis statement through the eyes of your readers, and see if it actually says what you want it to say.

After examining it and completing any necessary revisions, check it one more time:

a. Does the thesis statement directly identify Rubin's argument?

b. Does your thesis state your position on the issue?

c. Is your thesis well punctuated, grammatically correct, and precisely worded?

Write your polished thesis on the lines below and look at it again. Is it strong and interesting?

_____

_____

Planning and Drafting Your Essay

Now that you have examined Rubin's argument and thought at length about your own views, draft an essay that responds to all parts of the writing topic. Use the material you developed in this section to compose your draft. Don't forget to turn back to Part 1, especially "The Conventional Argument Essay Structure," for further guidance on the essay's conventional structure.

Do not skip this step in the process because drafting an outline will give you a basic structure for incorporating all the ideas you have developed in the preceding pages. An outline will also give you an overview of your essay and help you spot problems in development or logic. The form below is modeled on "The Conventional Argument Essay Structure" in Part 1, but you may want to use your own outline form. Be sure to plan the body paragraphs, including the examples that will provide the concrete evidence to support your assertions. Once you complete your outline, you will be set to construct your rough draft.

Hint

This outline doesn't have to contain polished writing. You may want to fill in only the basic ideas in phrases or terms.

Creating an Outline for Your Draft

I. **Introductory Paragraph**

   A. An opening sentence that gives the reading selection's title and author and begins to answer the writing topic:

   _____

   B. Main points to include in the directed summary:

   1.

   2.

   3.

   4.

   C. Write out your thesis statement. (Look back to "Revising Your Thesis Statement," where you reexamined and refined your working thesis statement.) It should clearly agree or disagree with Rubin's position, and it should state your position using your own words. Remember that your essay will have to develop and argue for a single point of view. You should not simply discuss competition offering both pro and con views in relation to Rubin. Avoid writing an essay that is inconclusive, one that merely examines both sides of the issue.

   _____

II. Body Paragraphs

A. The paragraph's one main point that supports the thesis statement:

_____

_____

   1. Controlling idea sentence:

_____

_____

   2. Corroborating details:

_____

_____

_____

_____

   3. Careful explanation of why the details are significant:

_____

_____

_____

_____

   4. Connection to the thesis statement:

_____

_____

_____

_____

B. The paragraph's one main point that supports the thesis statement:

_____

   1. Controlling idea sentence:

_____

_____

   2. Corroborating details:

_____

_____

_____

3. Careful explanation of why the details are significant:

_____

_____

_____

_____

4. Connection to the thesis statement:

_____

_____

_____

_____

C. The paragraph's one main point that supports the thesis statement:

_____

1. Controlling idea sentence:

_____

_____

2. Corroborating details:

_____

_____

_____

_____

3. Careful explanation of why the details are significant:

_____

_____

_____

_____

4. Connection to the thesis statement:

_____

_____

_____

_____

D. The paragraph's one main point that supports the thesis statement:

_____

1. **C**ontrolling idea sentence:

_____

_____

2. **C**orroborating details:

_____

_____

_____

_____

3. **C**areful explanation of why the details are significant:

_____

_____

_____

_____

4. **C**onnection to the thesis statement:

_____

_____

_____

_____

Repeat this form for any remaining body paragraphs.

III. Conclusion

A. Type of conclusion to be used:

_____

B. Suggestions, or key words or phrases to include:

_____

Getting Feedback on Your Draft

Use the following guidelines to give a classmate feedback on his or her draft. Read the draft through first, and then answer each of the items below as specifically as you can.

Name of draft's author: _____

Name of draft's reader: _____

The Introduction

1. Within the opening sentences:
   a. Rubin's entire name is given.   yes   no
   b. the reading selection's title is given and
      placed within quotation marks.   yes   no
2. The opening contains a summary that:
   a. explains Rubin's view of competition and of its negative
      impact on our lives   yes   no
   b. explains why Rubin supports this position   yes   no
3. The opening provides a thesis that makes clear the draft writer's
   opinion regarding Rubin's argument.   yes   no

If the answer to #3 above is yes, state the thesis below as it is written. If the answer is no, explain to the writer what information is needed to make the thesis complete.

_____

_____

_____

The Body

1. How many body paragraphs are in the body of this essay? _____
2. To support the thesis, this number is   sufficient   not enough
3. Do paragraphs contain the 4Cs?

Paragraph 1	Controlling idea sentence	yes	no
	Corroborating details	yes	no
	Careful explanation of why the details are significant	yes	no
	Connection to the thesis statement	yes	no
Paragraph 2	Controlling idea sentence	yes	no
	Corroborating details	yes	no
	Careful explanation of why the details are significant	yes	no
	Connection to the thesis statement	yes	no

Paragraph 3	Controlling idea sentence	yes	no
	Corroborating details	yes	no
	Careful explanation of why the details are significant	yes	no
	Connection to the thesis statement	yes	no
Paragraph 4	Controlling idea sentence	yes	no
	Corroborating details	yes	no
	Careful explanation of why the details are significant	yes	no
	Connection to the thesis statement	yes	no
Paragraph 5	Controlling idea sentence	yes	no
	Corroborating details	yes	no
	Careful explanation of why the details are significant	yes	no
	Connection to the thesis statement	yes	no

(Continue as needed.)

4. Identify any of the above paragraphs that are underdeveloped (too short). _____

5. Identify any of the above paragraphs that fail to support the thesis. _____

6. Identify any of the above paragraphs that are redundant or repetitive. _____

7. Suggest any ideas for additional paragraphs that might improve this essay.

_____

_____

_____

The Conclusion

1. Does the final paragraph avoid introducing new ideas and examples that really belong in the body of the essay?   yes   no

2. Does the conclusion provide closure (let readers know that the end of the essay has been reached)?   yes   no

3. Does the conclusion leave readers with an understanding of the significance of the argument?   yes   no

4. State in your own words what the draft writer considers to be important about his or her argument.

_____

_____

_____

5. Identify the type of conclusion used (see the guidelines for conclusions in Part 1).

_____

Editing

1. During the editing process, the writer should pay attention to the following problems in sentence structure, punctuation, and mechanics:
   fragments
   fused (run-on) sentences
   comma splices
   misplaced, missing, and unnecessary commas
   misplaced, missing, and unnecessary apostrophes
   incorrect quotation mark use
   capitalization errors
   spelling errors

2. While editing, the writer should pay attention to the following areas of grammar:
   verb tense
   subject-verb agreement
   irregular verbs
   pronoun type
   pronoun reference
   pronoun agreement
   noun plurals
   misplaced and dangling modifiers
   prepositions

Final Draft Checklist

Content

_____ My essay has an appropriate title.

_____ I provide an accurate summary of Rubin's position on the issue presented in "Competition and Happiness."

_____ My thesis states a clear position that can be supported by evidence.

_____ I have enough paragraphs and argument points to support my thesis.

_____ Each body paragraph is relevant to my thesis.

_____ Each body paragraph contains the 4Cs.

_____ I use transitions whenever necessary to connect ideas to each other.

_____ The final paragraph of my essay (the conclusion) provides readers with a sense of closure.

Grammar, Punctuation, and Mechanics

_____ I use the present tense to discuss Rubin's argument and examples.

_____ I use verb tenses correctly to show the chronology of events.

_____ I have verb tense consistency throughout my sentences.

_____ I have checked for subject-verb agreement in all of my sentences.

_____ I have revised all fragments and mixed or garbled sentences.

_____ I have repaired all fused (run-on) sentences and comma splices.

_____ I have placed a comma after introductory elements (transitions and phrases) and all dependent clauses that open a sentence.

_____ If I present items in a series (nouns, verbs, prepositional phrases), they are parallel in form.

_____ If I include material spoken or written by someone other than myself, I have correctly punctuated it with quotation marks, using the MLA style guide's rules for citation.

Reviewing Your Graded Essay

After your instructor has returned your essay, you may have the opportunity to revise your paper and raise your grade. Many students, especially those whose essays receive nonpassing grades, feel that their instructors should be less "picky" about grammar and should pass the work on content alone. However, most students at this level have not yet acquired the ability to recognize quality writing, and they do not realize that content and writing actually cannot be separated in this way. Experienced instructors know that errors in sentence structure, grammar, punctuation, and word choice either interfere with content or distract readers so much that they lose track of content. In short, good ideas badly presented are no longer good ideas; to pass, an essay must have passable writing. So even if you are not submitting a revised version of this essay to your instructor, it is important that you review your work carefully in order to understand its strengths and weaknesses. This sheet will guide you through the evaluation process.

You will want to continue to use the techniques that worked well for you and to find strategies to overcome the problems that you identify in this sample of your writing. To recognize areas that might have been problematic for you, look back at the scoring rubric in this book. Match the numerical/verbal/letter grade received on your essay to the appropriate category. Study the explanation given on the rubric for your grade.

Write a few sentences below in which you identify your problems in each of the following areas. Then, suggest specific changes you could make that would improve your paper. Don't forget to use your handbook as a resource.

1. **Grammar/punctuation/mechanics**
   My problem:

   My strategy for change:

2. **Thesis/response to assignment**
   My problem:

   My strategy for change:

3. Organization
My problem:

My strategy for change:

4. Paragraph development/examples/reasoning
My problem:

My strategy for change:

5. Assessment

In the space below, assign a grade to your paper using a rubric other than the one used by your instructor. In other words, if your instructor assigned your essay a grade of *High Fail*, you might give it the letter grade you now feel the paper warrants. If your instructor used the traditional letter grade to evaluate the essay, choose a category from the rubric in this book, or any other grading scale that you are familiar with, to show your evaluation of your work. Then, write a short narrative explaining your evaluation of the essay and the reasons it received the grade you gave it.

Grade: _____

Narrative: _____

_____

_____

_____

_____

Extending the Discussion: Considering Other Viewpoints

Reading Selections

"Dating as Competition" by Beth Bailey
"The Cost of High Stakes on Little League Games" by C. W. Nevius
"The Power of Two" by Joshua Wolf Shenk
"The Joy of Graduating" by Kate Stone Lombardi
"Securing the Benefits of Global Competition" by R. Hewitt Pate
"An Objective Look at the Benefits of Competition in the Workplace" by Carmine Coyote

DATING AS COMPETITION

Beth Bailey

Beth Bailey was for several years a professor of American studies at the University of New Mexico. She is now a professor of history at Temple University. The following passage is from her book From Front Porch to Back Seat: Courtship in Twentieth-Century America *(1988).*

In the early twentieth century, the gloomiest critics of the new system of male/female socialization called "dating" feared only that it would make it harder for youth to negotiate the true business of courtship: marriage. They worried that poor but ambitious and worthy young men could not attract suitable partners without spending vast sums on entertainment and that every theater ticket and late supper meant less money set aside toward the minimum figure needed to marry and start a family.

The critics were right, but in some ways, their criticisms were irrelevant. During the 1920s and 1930s, for mainstream, middle-class young people, dating was not about marriage and families. It wasn't even about love—which is not to say that American youth didn't continue to fall in love, marry, and raise families. But before World War II, long-term commitments lay in the future for youth and were clearly demarcated from the dating system. In the public realm, in the shared culture that defined the conventions of dating and gave meaning and coherence to individual experience, dating was not about marriage. Dating was about competition.

Shortly after World War II ended, anthropologist Margaret Mead gave a series of lectures on American courtship rituals. Although the system she described was already disappearing, she captured the essence of what dating meant in the interwar years. Dating, Mead stressed, was not about sex or adulthood or marriage. Instead, it was a "competitive game," a way for girls and boys to "demonstrate their popularity." This was not a startling revelation to the American public. Americans knew that dating was centered on competition and popularity. These were the terms in which dating was discussed, the vocabulary in which one described a date.

In 1937, in the classic study of American dating, sociologist Willard Waller gave this competitive system a name: "the campus rating complex." His study of Penn State detailed a "dating and rating" system based on very clear standards of popularity. To be popular, men needed outward, material signs: an automobile, the right clothing, fraternity membership, money. Women's popularity depended on building and maintaining a reputation for popularity. They had to *be seen* with popular men in the "right" places, indignantly turn down requests for dates made at the "last minute" (which could be weeks in advance), and cultivate the impression that they were greatly in demand.

Although Waller did not see it, the technique of image building was not always limited to women. For men, too, nothing succeeded like success. *Guide Book for the Young Man about Town* advised: "It's money in the bank to have lots of girls on the knowing list and the date calendar. . . . It means more popularity for you." As proof, the author looked back on his own college days, recalling how a classmate won the title of "Most Popular Man" at a small coed college by systematically going through the college register and dating every girl in the school who wasn't engaged.

Bailey, Beth L. *From Front Porch to Back Seat: Courtship in Twentieth-Century America*, pp. 25–26, 28–30. © 1988 The John Hopkins University Press. Reprinted with permission of John Hopkins University Press.

The concept of dating value had nothing to do with the interpersonal experience of a date—whether or not the boy (or girl, for that matter) was fun or charming or brilliant was irrelevant. Instead, the rating looked to others, to public perceptions of success in the popularity competition. Popularity was clearly the key—and popularity defined in a very specific way. It was not earned directly through talent, looks, personality, or importance in organizations, but by the way these attributes translated into dates. These dates had to be highly visible, and with many different people, or they didn't count.

The rating-dating system, and the definition of popularity on which it was based, did not remain exclusively on college campuses. High school students of the late 1930s and 1940s were raised on rating and dating. Not only did they imitate the conventions of older youth, they were advised by some young columnists, who spoke with distinctly nonparental voices, that these conventions were natural and right. *Senior Scholastic*, a magazine used in high schools all over the United States, began running an advice column in 1936. "Boy Dates Girl" quickly became the magazine's most popular feature.

The advice in "Boy Dates Girl" always took the competitive system as a given. Its writer assumed that girls would accept any *straightforward* offer of a date if not already "dated" for the evening, and that boys, in trying for the most popular girl imaginably possible, would occasionally overreach themselves. The author once warned girls never to brush off any boy, no matter how unappealing, in a rude way, since "he may come in handy for an off-night."

Discussion Questions

1. What problem did some of the critics of the early twentieth century's new system of dating predict? Whom did they think would be most adversely affected? Did future events show their concerns to be valid? Explain your answer.

2. What had dating been about before World War II? What was the purpose of dating during the interwar years? Do you think dating in the twenty-first century has more in common with the years before or after World War II? Explain your choice.

3. Explain "the campus rating complex." When people use such a scale, what characteristics earn a high rating? What attributes are valueless on this scale? If you were to devise your own dating-rating scale, what would it look like?

THE COST OF HIGH STAKES ON LITTLE LEAGUE GAMES

C. W. NEVIUS

C. W. Nevius is a writer and journalist. His column appears regularly in the San Francisco Chronicle. *The following essay was published in 2000.*

When he was ten years old, Joseph Matteucci had a coach for his Castro Valley Little League team who was a "screamer." Joseph's mother, Alexandra, had concerns, but as a single parent, she wanted to encourage her son to meet and play with other kids, so she didn't complain. Another parent did not hold back, however. In the parking lot after a game, he confronted the coach about the yelling at his son. The coach got out of the car and began throwing punches. The father went down in the barrage, and when his wife rushed out to aid him, the coach slugged her, too.

Joseph Matteucci, sitting in the car, saw it all and burst into tears. He quit Little League the next day. Alexandra Matteucci was relieved. Thank God she'd gotten her son out of that violent environment. Six years later, Joseph was dead. An innocent bystander, he stopped by a spring Little League game for sixteen-year-old players to pick up a friend. A brawl broke out after the game, the result of excessive taunting from spectators. A player swung a bat at one of his tormentors, he ducked, and Matteucci was hit in the back of the head. He died in less than twenty-four hours.

Some might call that 1993 incident a fluke, but the reality is the tragedy on that Castro Valley playground had all the elements of what has become an ugly trend in youth sports. Violence has become commonplace on the fields of play in America, and the formula is simple, direct, and brutal. Taunting from the sidelines escalates, coaches and spectators fail to quell the rising tensions, umpires or referees cannot control the situation, and, finally, rage boils over. "Before it was coaches helping the kids who were having trouble controlling their emotions," says Jim Thompson, director of Stanford's Positive Coaching Alliance. "Now it is, 'Let's provide leadership to help the coaches control the parents.'"

The incidents of enraged parents are so out of proportion that they sound absurd. Orlando Lago, an assistant coach with the Hollywood, Florida, All-Stars, broke the jaw of umpire Tom Dziedzinski after a disputed call at third base in a Connie Mack game between high school teams. Last January, police were called to a gym in Kirkland, Washington, when a heated confrontation at a wrestling match became so violent that a coach head-butted a parent and broke his nose. The wrestlers were six years old. And the most shocking display took place in Reading, Massachusetts, last July when Thomas Junta, a parent, beat to death Michael Costin, a hockey coach, at an ice rink. Junta, who was furious because he felt that Costin was allowing rough play, beat the coach to unconsciousness as his children begged him to stop. Junta, forty-two, has pleaded not guilty to charges of manslaughter.

But those are just the headlines. Anyone who has been to a youth sports game lately knows the truth. Parents are out of control. They scream at their kids, yell at the officials, and, in more cases than anyone would like to admit, something troubling happens. Worse, every indicator shows it is becoming more common. Bob Still, spokesman for the National Association of Sports Officials, says his organization gets "between one and three" reports of physical assaults on an official each week. "These are what we would call assaults as defined by law," says Still, whose organization has been tracking the numbers for twenty-five years. "The verbal attacks have always been there. But people acting out, coming on the field, there is a definite trend to more violence."

Kill the ump? It isn't so funny. Still says it has reached the point that in 1998 his association began offering "assault insurance" to its nineteen thousand members. The policy pays medical bills, provides counseling, and offers legal advice about how to prosecute attackers. It doesn't take much imagination to project the short-term result. Would you want to be a referee in this climate? "Finding referees is the single most important thing we have to deal with right now," says Bob Maas, president of Pleasanton's highly competitive Ballistic United Soccer League. "You get out there, some parent yells at you, and you think, 'You know, I am missing the 49ers game right now.'"

But the referee shortage is the symptom, not the problem. Fueled by unrealistic expectations and an unhealthy obsession with winning, parents have gone from cheerleaders to taskmasters. Having invested large sums in clinics and private instruction for their kids, anything but success is unacceptable. Alexandra Matteucci, who now runs the Joseph Matteucci Foundation, was speaking to a group in Los Angeles when she heard a recent example. A mother, watching her son in a baseball game for twelve- to fifteen-year-olds, was furious when her son was taken out. "She went out and sat on second base and refused to move until they put her son back in," Matteucci said. "They didn't know what to do, so they put him back in the game."

That kind of acting out may have worked in that case, but how many kids want their parent to become a laughingstock? The yelling, the gestures, and the intense pressure can drive even avid athletes out of organized sports. "I can't tell you how many times I have heard kids say, 'Shut up, Dad!'" says Danville's John Wondolowski, whose under-eleven soccer team won the State Cup last spring. When dad won't pipe down, the next step is off the field. Many kids drop sports—an estimated seventy percent quit before they reach the age of twelve—but some also find another outlet. Skateboarders, mountain bikers, and surfers are just part of an emerging X Games generation. There are fewer rules, less structure, and—best of all—dad doesn't know the first thing about it. "That's the protection," says Positive Coaching Alliance's Thompson. "No adults. It is not hypercompetitive. Fifteen or twenty years ago, adults didn't know anything about soccer. Now you've got guys who think they know all about it. My son is into surfing, skating, and snowboarding. His point was: Do I want to stand in line, wait to bat, and have the coach yell at me? Or do I want to sit out in the ocean?"

A kinder, gentler approach was the idea behind "Silent Sunday" last October in a Cleveland suburb. Coaches and parents in the 217-team league were told not to yell at the players, not even to cheer good plays. Was it hard to break old habits? Well, some parents, afraid they couldn't resist the temptation, put duct tape over their mouths. Another soccer coach turned the tables on his parents. He put them on the field for a practice and let the kids scream instructions at them as they scrambled to kick the ball. Reportedly, the parents were ready for the exercise to stop long before the kids.

Are those the only choices? Do kids either have to drop out of sports or duct tape their parents' mouths shut? Well no, there are options, proposed by groups like Thompson's PSA and the Matteucci Foundation. It begins with what groups like Ballistic Soccer call "zero tolerance" for attacks on officials, but more than anything, it involves changing perceptions for parents. "After all," says Thompson, "when you go to a spelling bee, nobody screams at the officials. It isn't done." "We turn our heads," says Still of the Association of Sports Officials. "We say, 'I'm going to let it go. It is no big deal. Bill is a good guy, he just lost it that one time.'" That, says facilitators like Matteucci, has to stop.

A clear ethics code must be established before the season begins, and the parents must go over it. Expecting them to read a handout isn't enough. Matteucci advocates reading the code aloud before every game. Second, parents who get out of control need to be told so, and in a way that makes it clear that they are out of step with the entire group. And if the coach, or some of the other parents, cannot calm the transgressor down, enforce the rules and call a forfeit. "Call the game," says Matteucci. "If we do, life goes on."

But most important, parents need to monitor their level of involvement with an eye toward scaling it down. Chances are, their son or daughter is not going to get a college scholarship, or appear on a Wheaties box. In ten years, the best you can hope is that the kids still enjoy staying physically active and look back fondly on their sports career.

What's fun about sports if you don't win? Thompson recommends changing the goal. He worked with a soccer team that was so outclassed that it lost every game. Instead of winning, or even scoring, the team decided to make its objective to get the ball over midfield five times in one game. When they finally did it, cheers rang up and down their sideline, puzzling the opposing parents. "They were asking, 'What are they so happy about?'" Thompson said. "Aren't we beating them by eight goals?" Yes, but they were playing a different game.

Discussion Questions

1. Describe the kinds of behavior of the Little League parents or the soccer parents that concern Nevius. How do the details of their behavior relate to the case Rubin is trying to make about competition?

2. Because of the emphasis on winning in organized children's sports, what choice do seventy percent of the players make, according to Nevius? What other activities does Nevius think these kids prefer? Why? When you were twelve, what were your favorite activities? Why?

3. What change does Thompson recommend for children's sports? Do you think Rubin would like to see this change? Why or why not?

THE POWER OF TWO

Joshua Wolf Shenk

Joshua Wolf Shenk is the author of Powers of Two: Finding the Essence of Innovation in Creative Pairs, *recently published by Eamon Dolan Books/Houghton Mifflin Harcourt.*

In the fall of 1966, during a stretch of nine weeks away from the Beatles, John Lennon wrote a song. He was in rural Spain at the time, on the set of a movie called *How I Won the War,* but the lyrics cast back to an icon of his boyhood in Liverpool: the Strawberry Field children's home, whose sprawling grounds he'd often explored with his gang and visited with his Aunt Mimi. In late November, the Beatles began work on the song at EMI Studios, on Abbey Road in London. After four weeks and scores of session hours, the band had a final cut of "Strawberry Fields Forever." That was December 22.

On December 29, Paul McCartney brought in a song that took listeners back to another icon of Liverpool: Penny Lane, a traffic roundabout and popular meeting spot near his home. This sort of call-and-response was no anomaly. He and John, Paul said later, had a habit of "answering" each other's songs. "He'd write 'Strawberry Fields,'" Paul explained. "I'd go away and write 'Penny Lane' . . . to compete with each other. But it was very friendly competition."

It's a famous anecdote. Paul, of course, was stressing the collaborative nature of his partnership with John (he went on to note that their competition made them "better and better all the time"). But in this vignette, as in so many from the Beatles years, it's easy to get distracted by the idea of John and Paul composing independently. The notion that the two need to be understood as individual creators, in fact, has become the contemporary "smart" take on them. "Although most of the songs on any given Beatles album are usually credited to the Lennon-McCartney songwriting team," Wikipedia declares, "that description is often misleading." Entries on the site about individual Beatles songs take care to assert their "true" author. Even the superb rock critic Greg Kot once succumbed to this folly. John and Paul "shared songwriting credits but little else," he says, writing in 1990, "and their 'partnership' was more of a competition than a collaboration."

Kot makes that observation in a review of *Beatlesongs,* by William J. Dowlding— a high-water mark of absurdity in the analysis of Lennon-McCartney. Dowlding actually tries to quantify their distinct contributions, giving 84.55 credits to John—"the winner," he declares—and 73.65 to Paul. (His tally also includes 22.15 credits for George Harrison, 2.7 for Ringo Starr, and 0.45 for Yoko Ono. For a few lines in the song "Julia," Dowlding gives 0.05 credits to the Lebanese poet Kahlil Gibran.)

For centuries, the myth of the lone genius has towered over us, its shadow obscuring the way creative work really gets done. The attempts to pick apart the Lennon-McCartney partnership reveal just how misleading that myth can be, because John and Paul were so obviously more creative as a pair than as individuals, even if at times they appeared to work in opposition to each other. The lone-genius myth prevents us from grappling with a series of paradoxes about creative pairs: that distance doesn't impede intimacy, and is often a crucial ingredient of it; that competition and collaboration are often entwined. Only when we explore this terrain can we grasp how such pairs as Steve Jobs and Steve Wozniak, William and Dorothy Wordsworth, and Martin Luther King, Jr., and Ralph Abernathy all managed to do such creative work. The essence of their achievements, it turns out, was relational. If that seems far-fetched, it's because our cultural obsession with the individual has obscured the power of the creative pair.

John and Paul epitomize this power. Geoff Emerick—who served as the principal engineer for EMI on *Revolver*, *Sgt. Pepper's Lonely Hearts Club Band*, some of *The White Album*, and *Abbey Road*—recognized from the outset that the two formed a single creative being. "Even from the earliest days," he wrote in his memoir, *Here, There and Everywhere*, "I always felt that the artist was John Lennon and Paul McCartney, not the Beatles."

One reason it's so tempting to try to cleave John and Paul apart is that the distinctions between them were so stark. Observing the pair through the control-room glass at Abbey Road's Studio Two, Emerick was fascinated by their odd-couple quality:

> *Paul was meticulous and organized: He always carried a notebook around with him, in which he methodically wrote down lyrics and chord changes in his neat handwriting. In contrast, John seemed to live in chaos: He was constantly searching for scraps of paper that he'd hurriedly scribbled ideas on. Paul was a natural communicator; John couldn't articulate his ideas well. Paul was the diplomat; John was the agitator. Paul was soft-spoken and almost unfailingly polite; John could be a right loudmouth and quite rude. Paul was willing to put in long hours to get a part right; John was impatient, always ready to move on to the next thing. Paul usually knew exactly what he wanted and would often take offense at criticism; John was much more thick-skinned and was open to hearing what others had to say. In fact, unless he felt especially strongly about something, he was usually amenable to change.*

The diplomat and the agitator. The neatnik and the whirling dervish. Spending time with Paul and John, one couldn't help but be struck by these sorts of differences. "John needed Paul's attention to detail and persistence," Cynthia Lennon, John's first wife, said. "Paul needed John's anarchic, lateral thinking."

Paul and John seemed to be almost archetypal embodiments of order and disorder. The ancient Greeks gave form to these two sides of human nature in Apollo, who stood for the rational and the self-disciplined, and Dionysus, who represented the spontaneous and the emotional. Friedrich Nietzsche proposed that the interaction of the Apollonian and the Dionysian was the foundation of creative work, and modern creativity research has confirmed this insight, revealing the key relationship between breaking and making, challenging and refining, disrupting and organizing.

John was the iconoclast. In early live shows, he would fall into the background, let Paul charm the audience, and then twist up his face, adopt a hunchback pose, and play dissonant chords. Sometimes, he deliberately kept his guitar slightly out of tune, which contributed to what the composer Richard Danielpour calls "that raw, raunchy sound." He was difficult with the press, at times even impossible. In the studio, he clamored constantly to do things differently. He wanted to be hung from the ceiling and swung around the mic. He wanted to be recorded from *behind*.

While John broke form, Paul looked to make it. He was the band's *de facto* musical director in the studio and, outside, its relentless champion. "Anything you promote, there's a game that you either play or you don't play," he said. "I decided very early on that I was very ambitious and I wanted to play." Among the Beatles, he said, he was the one who would "sit the press down and say, 'Hello, how are you? Do you want a drink?,' and make them comfortable." Distinctions are a good way to introduce ourselves to a creative pair. But what matters is how the parts come together. So it's not right to focus on how John insulted reporters while Paul charmed them.

John was able to insult reporters *because* Paul charmed them. Their music emerged in a similar way, with single strands twisting into a mutually strengthening double helix.

The work John initiated tended to be sour and weary, whereas Paul's tended to the bright and naive. The magic came from interaction. Consider the home demo for "Help!"—an emotionally raw, aggressively confessional song John wrote while in the throes of the sort of depression that he said made him want "to jump out the window, you know." The original had a slow, plain piano tune, and feels like the moan of the blues. When Paul heard it, he suggested a countermelody, a lighthearted harmony to be sung behind the principal lyric—and this fundamentally changed its nature. It's not incidental that in the lyrics John pleaded for "somebody . . . not just anybody." He knew he was at risk of floating away, and Paul helped put his feet back on the ground.

And John knocked Paul off his, snorting at his bromides (as with Paul's original "She was just seventeen / Never been a beauty queen") and batting against his sweet, optimistic lyrics, as in the song "Getting Better." "I was sitting there doing 'Getting better all the time,'" Paul remembered, "and John just said, in his laconic way, 'It couldn't get no worse.' And I thought, *Oh, brilliant! This is exactly why I love writing with John.*"

John lived most of his youth in his Aunt Mimi's house, a prim, stuffy place, protected—or so Mimi thought—from the wreckage of his charming but dissolute parents. Even as a boy, John was a mischief-maker, a gang leader. When he discovered music, he wanted to get his gang onstage. He insisted that his best friend, Pete Shotton, join his band, the Quarry Men, even though Pete protested that he could hardly play. John didn't mind. He could hardly play himself.

Paul, by contrast, came from a warm, close-knit family. Music occupied a central place in the McCartney home, in the form of the upright piano that dominated the tiny living room. Music for Paul was family sing-alongs and brass-band concerts with his dad. When he began to write songs, Paul wasn't thinking about rock and roll. He wanted to write for Sinatra.

John's rebellious impulse took him in dangerous directions. By the time he met Paul, his boyhood pranks had progressed to shoplifting. He said later that had he not wound up in a truly outstanding band—which is to say, had he not met Paul—he probably would have ended up like his father, a likable ne'er-do-well jostling between odd jobs and petty crime.

Paul, for his part, might have ended up teaching, or doing some other job for which he could rely on his smarts and still live inside his own mind. He was studied and careful. Even his moments of abandon (his imitations of Little Richard, say) were conducted more or less by the book. John was twenty months older—a world apart for a teenager. He was the badass older brother Paul never had. For John, Paul was a studious and charming sidekick who could do something rare: keep up with him.

Alongside their many differences, John and Paul shared uncannily similar musical tastes and drives to perform. The chemistry between them was immediate. A member of John's band who watched them on the day they met later recalled that they "circled each other like cats."

But distance doesn't necessarily hinder creativity; often, it drives a pair forward. We flourish with an ongoing stream of new influences, new ideas. It's also true that we're affected by not just what people explicitly say to us, or their overt contributions to our work, but also the way they get in our heads. One sure way this happens is through competition—or what's known in business as "co-opetition," whereby two entities at once oppose and support each other. George Martin, the Beatles's longtime producer, noticed this element in John and Paul's relationship. "Imagine two people pulling on a rope, smiling at each other and pulling all the time with all their might," he said. "The tension between the two of them made for the bond."

That tension took on varying forms during the course of the Lennon-McCartney partnership. The two spun, time and again, through the same cycle. As the alpha, John would establish his dominance, and then Paul, like a canny prime minister under a tempestuous king, would gradually assert himself and take charge—until John, often suddenly, struck back.

This dynamic helped give birth to the two albums that represent the best of John and Paul's work together: *Sgt. Pepper's Lonely Hearts Club Band* and *The White Album*. In popular lore, *Sgt. Pepper* represents the zenith of the partnership ("It was a peak," John said), while *The White Album* represents its nadir ("the tension album," Paul called it). But the truth is that the two albums were born of the same cycle, just at different points in it.

Despite the tension—*because of* the tension—the work was magnificent. Though the *White Album* recording sessions were often tense and unpleasant (Emerick disliked them so much that he flat-out quit), they yielded an album that is among the best in music history. The album is notable for a number of role-raiding songs, with John doing the sort of ballads associated with Paul ("Julia" and "Goodnight"), and Paul drenching himself in the noise and aggression usually associated with John ("Helter Skelter," "Why Don't We Do It in the Road"). No matter how thick the tension got, it kept serving a creative purpose.

Discussion Questions

1. According to Joshua Wolf Shenk, what role did competition play in the song writing partnership of John Lennon and Paul McCartney? Explain the way this type of partnership could be responsible for the writing of such songs as "Strawberry Fields" and "Penny Lane." Considering that these particular songs were written in the late 1960s, how effectively do these examples support Shenk's argument?

2. Discuss the different personalities of John and Paul. How can their differences be considered archetypal? What is the relationship between these differences and a competition that results in increased production? Do you agree with Shenk's conclusion that the differences in character of John and Paul explain, in part, their creative genius? Explain your answer.

3. By applying Theodore Rubin's argument that competition must have placed limits on John's and Paul's satisfaction and happiness, what conclusion would you be forced to assume about their contentment with their careers as Beatles? Explain why you think that Rubin's point is, or is not, applicable to creative endeavors.

THE JOY OF GRADUATING

Kate Stone Lombardi

Kate Stone Lombardi is a freelance writer in New York. She has a master's degree from the Columbia University Graduate School of Journalism. This essay was published in the New York Times *in 2008.*

Danielle Gorman is musing about what it takes to secure the number one spot at her highly ranked, competitive high school. "Valedictorians are the type of people who take on too much and are unwilling to fail," she says. She should know. Danielle is this year's valedictorian at Moorestown High School, in Moorestown, New Jersey. She often studied until two in the morning.

Danielle, eighteen, took one Advanced Placement class in her sophomore year, five her junior year, and four senior year. Why not five? Because her math class, Multivariable Calculus and Differential Equations, covered material beyond what the AP tests measure.

On top of her studies, there was mock trial, model Congress, and the debate team, along with four years on the track team. Oh yes, and there were those relaxing summers, like the one after her sophomore year, when she took a course on international law at Harvard Summer School, while at the same time completing a fifty-hour internship with a law firm.

Danielle, who will attend MIT this fall, says she chose challenging courses and pushed herself because she wasn't sure what she ultimately wanted to do. She wasn't shocked to find out she had been named valedictorian—she knew she was one of the three top students—but tried to keep herself from wanting the honor too intensely. "I really conditioned myself to not want it or expect it," Danielle says. "I take things pretty stoically. It didn't set in for a while, and then I was really happy."

Another valedictorian season has come to a close, with students throughout the region having proudly stepped up to the podium to deliver their graduation speeches and receive the accolades that come from being the highest academic performer in their school. But as the path to that honor has intensified over recent years, some administrators are beginning to question the valedictorian tradition. Several factors—including the increase in the number of high school students, grade inflation, intense competition for college acceptances, and a savvier student body—have changed the game.

Some students strategize to win, taking on a heavy load of AP courses, which are weighted when grade point averages are calculated. Some avoid more creative courses, like art or photography, where grading can be subjective and a B could ruin their shot at the top spot. There have been conflicts about how to measure the transcripts of transfer students who come from schools with different grading systems. In a handful of cases, the zeal for valedictorian honors has led to lawsuits.

Take Danielle's high school in Moorestown, which landed in the national spotlight five years ago, when a high school senior sued the district in an effort to be named valedictorian. Blair L. Hornstine was awarded sixty thousand dollars by the Moorestown School District to settle a federal lawsuit that she filed after the district tried to name a student with a lower grade point average as co-valedictorian.

Ms. Hornstine had been home-schooled, and her lawyer said she suffered from chronic fatigue syndrome. Critics claimed she manipulated the system, and her lawsuit caused an uproar in the community. Ms. Hornstine was so vilified—there was even a website that chronicled her case called *The Blair Hornstine Project*, a play on the film *The Blair Witch Project*—that she skipped her graduation.

Later that summer, Ms. Hornstine's acceptance to Harvard was withdrawn after accusations that articles she had written for the local newspaper were plagiarized. She ended up going to St. Andrews University in Scotland, where she graduated in 2006 with a degree in classics.

Danielle remembers the controversy and has some sympathy for her predecessor. "I felt really bad for her," Danielle says. "She ended up being valedictorian but losing a lot of other things. I remember everyone said she shouldn't care so much because it ended up hurting her."

This year at Horace Greeley High School in Chappaqua, New York, Susannah Rudel and Brett Rosenberg are co-valedictorians, and they share the honor with apparent grace. Though no one would speak for the record, the stories circulated about contested grade point averages and smothered resentment, yet Susannah and Brett presented a united front, describing how delighted they were that as best "study buddies" they would both be honored.

In an interview including her co-valedictorian, Susannah, seventeen, says, "I would have felt terrible if it was just me. I genuinely don't believe I would have succeeded as much without Brett. I spend hours on the phone going over math problems with her." Brett, seventeen, says that if she alone had been named, "It definitely would have been empty in a way, and it wouldn't have been fair because it was such a collaborative relationship." Those words are balm to high school administrators, who had to calculate the top grade point averages to the third decimal point to determine the girls were tied. Nineteen students at Horace Greeley High had perfect 4.0 grade point averages or higher; Susannah and Brett each had a 4.1.

Each girl took seven APs in high school. Susannah was captain of the varsity swim team, placed in the state championships, earned her Gold Award from the Girl Scouts, and played the flute. Brett was captain of the cross country team, captain of the nationally ranked academic challenge team, and a bass clarinet player. Susannah will attend Amherst College this fall; Brett will go to Harvard. "The two of them had an exact numerical tie," says Andrew Selesnick, the high school principal. "It's pretty remarkable. You just want to be sure, you don't want to make a mistake."

The high school has reason to be cautious. Five years ago, the valedictorian and the salutatorian were named at a cum laude ceremony in the fall. But a week later, the students were called to the principal's office and told a mistake had been made in calculating the grade point averages. A teacher, who traditionally changed final class grades based on students' performance on the AP test, had delayed reporting an upgrade. The new grade—a fraction of a point—changed the equation for several students in the tight competition at the top of the class. The students were told, based on recalculations, that there would be two valedictorians and two salutatorians. All four students gave speeches. "I remember thinking it was a little odd," says Dan Adler, the originally named valedictorian. "But I clearly appreciated it when I was given the honor, so for someone else who deserved it not be granted it was a little absurd."

When the differences between the top student and the tenth come down to hundredths of a point, some administrators are questioning how meaningful the valedictorian distinction is. "We have had valedictorians and salutatorians when it's less than a hundredth of a point apart," says Carol Burris, principal of South Side High School in Rockville Centre.

South Side, like many schools in New York, New Jersey, and Connecticut, has eliminated class ranking on transcripts because administrators believe a rank reduces students to a number and prefer that colleges take a close look at student transcripts and consider the broader student. Still, they maintain the grade point averages to determine the number one and number two spots. "Our community has been happy with eliminating ranking, but naming the valedictorian is a strong tradition," Dr. Burris says. "If you're going to have student speakers, it really is an honor and you have to have some objective way of choosing them."

Given all the drama over the honor, how do valedictorians fare in the long term? Karen D. Arnold, an associate professor of higher education at Boston College, spent more than fifteen years studying valedictorians who graduated in 1981 from high schools across Illinois. Dr. Arnold found that high school valedictorians consistently did well in college and were generally well-rounded, successful people. They were not a group, however, who were particularly creative or who would achieve great distinction in life. "They're kind of like wonderful organizational achievers," Dr. Arnold says. "They're hard workers. They're not going to remold your organization, but they might lead it."

Dr. Arnold says she is familiar with the arguments in favor of eliminating valedictorians but believes the tradition should be maintained. "There aren't many academic honors, and it is one of those labels that follows you through life, like the Heisman Trophy or Rhodes Scholar," she says. "To get rid of the one meaningful designation for what school is really all about seems like something we should do only with great caution."

Mr. Adler, Horace Greeley's 2003 co-valedictorian, works in management consulting. He graduated last year from Yale, where he found himself in the company of hundreds of other valedictorians. ("I think I dated at least two of them," he says.) "I'm still extremely proud of the honor, but if I were to give someone advice about how to think about it in the right way, it's that you have to think about this as a validation of what you're capable of and keep it in the back of your mind as a motivation," he says. "But you can't be haughty about it, because there are so many people who you are going to meet who are just as smart as you."

Discussion Questions

1. How does Danielle Gorman, a valedictorian quoted by the author, describe the traits common to valedictorians? Do you think her assessment is reasonable, or is she merely applying a stereotype? Describe the valedictorian(s) of your graduating class.

2. Bailey writes about competition and dating, Nevius about competition and sports, and Lombardi about competition and grades. For each of these three areas, discuss reasons you think competition is dangerous, healthy, or irrelevant.

3. What generalizations is Karen Arnold able to make based on her study about the future achievements of high school valedictorians? If you were an employer trying to choose between two candidates, only one a valedictorian, which would you choose? Is your choice influenced by Arnold's study? Explain.

SECURING THE BENEFITS OF GLOBAL COMPETITION

R. Hewitt Pate

The following is a talk given by R. Hewitt Pate, an Assistant Attorney General for the United States from 2003 to 2005. The talk was sponsored by the US Department of Justice and presented at the Tokyo American Center in Tokyo, Japan, in 2004.

Good afternoon, ladies and gentlemen. I am very pleased to be here today to talk with you about the globalization of competition law. This is my first visit to Japan, on the occasion of the 26th annual US-Japan antitrust consultations. Chairman Takeshima has been a gracious host, and we have had very fruitful discussions over the past two days.

Introduction

Just two weeks ago, the 28th Olympic Games came to a conclusion in Athens, Greece. It was a tremendous event, with more than 10,000 athletes from a record 202 jurisdictions competing. As you know, this year's Olympics were the first to be held in Greece since the modern Olympics Games began in Athens at the end of the nineteenth century. The modern Olympics started in 1896, only six years after the American Sherman Antitrust Act was enacted. Believe it or not, there are some important parallels between the modern Olympics and global competition law.

As for the most basic parallel, the Olympics are a microcosm of globalization and of competition. They are based on the principle that competition creates excellence by providing the incentive to bring out the best capabilities in the athletes. Through the constant challenge of new competitors and new training techniques, world records are made and shattered, and goals once thought impossible are reached and then exceeded. The Olympic Committee and other sports authorities, like antitrust enforcers, attempt to impose certain basic rules to ensure that the competitions are fair, and that cheating—such as fixing the outcome of events or taking banned substances—is not allowed to undermine competitive outcomes. (Like antitrust enforcers, the governing bodies face challenges, and can make no claim to be perfect.)

Participation in the Olympics started slowly. At the first Modern Olympic games in 1896, 241 athletes from 14 nations took part. All of the participants were from Western Europe and North America. One might even say that the early Olympic Games were a regional, rather than a global, market. In 1920, when Ichiya Kumagai won Japan's first Olympic medals—silver medals in singles and doubles men's tennis—the number of participating nations had doubled to 29. Just eight years later, at the 1928 Olympics in Amsterdam, 46 countries competed and Japan won its first gold medals, in the triple jump and in the men's 200 meter breast stroke. At the 1932 Olympics in Los Angeles, a Japanese 14-year-old "new-entrant"—Kusuo Kitamur —won the 1500 meter freestyle swimming competition, to become the youngest male ever to win a gold medal at the Olympics. By 1964, at the Tokyo

"Securing the Benefits of Global Competition" presented at the Tokyo American Center, September 10, 2004 by R. Hewitt Pate, Assistant Attorney General, Antitrust Division, United States Department of Justice.

Olympics, the number of participating nations had doubled again to 93, and Japan—foreshadowing its emergence as a major economic power—was third among all participating nations in the number of gold medals won by its athletes. By the time of the 26th Olympiad in Atlanta in 1996, a truly competitive global athletic market had been established: 10,318 athletes from 197 countries competed in 271 different events, and men and women from 79 different nations won medals.

The Globalization of Competition Law

The history of antitrust laws also started slowly. In the 1890s, only the United States and Canada had comprehensive antitrust laws. It took some time, even in the United States, before enforcement became active or vigorous. By 1950, you still could count on the fingers of both hands the number of countries that were enforcing antitrust laws. Even in the 1970s, by which time many developed countries had adopted comprehensive antitrust laws, efforts by the United States to use our antitrust laws against harmful international cartels were met by strong resistance from our trading partners. US approaches to antitrust law, including the criminalization of cartel behavior and the prosecution of corporate executives, were viewed with puzzlement and suspicion by other governments and their business communities. A number of countries even adopted blocking statutes aimed at thwarting the application of US antitrust laws in the international context. Most countries did not view a law aimed at protecting the competitive process as something that was compatible with their economic or social cultures. And countries that did enact antitrust laws were more concerned with using them to maintain stability in the marketplace than in promoting real competition. In Japan, as we all know, the Antimonopoly Act (AMA) was adopted by the Japanese Diet in 1947. But it was not well accepted by Japanese society, and it was soon subject to amendments that substantially weakened the impact of the AMA on the economy. It was not until the oil shocks of the 1970s that the AMA and the Japan Fair Trade Commission (JFTC) began to be invigorated.

Looking at the global situation today, we see a remarkable change in the global acceptance of antitrust law as a promoter of economic growth and prosperity. More than one hundred countries have adopted antitrust laws, and there is unprecedented cooperation among countries in acting against international cartels. We now have the International Competition Network, an organization composed of antitrust enforcement agencies from, at current count, nearly eighty nations, working to improve our understanding of how best to apply competition laws in an era of globalization.

What happened to cause this remarkable change in the global recognition of the importance of competition law? Probably the most important single event was the triumph of capitalism over the failed command and control model of the Soviet Union. With the dismantling of the Berlin Wall came the realization by many countries that the path to successful economic growth lay in fostering market-based competition, and that one of the building blocks of successful market economies was the protection of the competitive process through strong and well-focused antitrust laws. This was accompanied by a more sophisticated understanding of how markets operate and a greater appreciation of the harm caused to consumers, to the business community, and to our economies as a whole by anticompetitive practices.

In addition, the tensions over US application of its antitrust laws in international matters gradually gave way to increased dialogue and cooperation. This was demonstrated by the antitrust cooperation agreements entered into between the United States and a number of major antitrust enforcing countries in the 1980s and 1990s. Increased cooperation was bolstered by the recommendations of the OECD Council on Cooperation on Restrictive Business Practices affecting International Trade in 1986 and on Hard-Core Cartels in 1998. Around the same time, some highly visible and economically damaging international cartels were uncovered—notably the feed additives, graphite electrodes, and vitamins cartels—that gave concrete evidence of the need for governments to work together and protect their consumers from these harmful global conspiracies.

Antitrust Enforcement Priorities in the United States

For the United States, our reevaluation of the proper role of antitrust law occurred somewhat earlier, in response to advances in economic learning that established the foundation for the landmark Supreme Court decision in the GTE Sylvania case. This reevaluation was based upon the recognition of the importance of promoting business efficiency through market mechanisms. It led to a clarification of the appropriate analytical framework and antitrust enforcement hierarchy for different categories of business conduct, a hierarchy that remains valid today.

At the top of this hierarchy is enforcement against cartels, conduct that is devoid of any efficiency justification and that inflicts tremendous harm on our economy. Our Supreme Court, in its recent *Trinko* decision, described collusive behavior as "the supreme evil of antitrust." Obviously, this is our core priority at the Antitrust Division. Second, we review mergers using the best analytical tools available, and make judgments on whether the effects of the merger may be "substantially to lessen competition or to tend to create a monopoly." If so, we must back up that judgment with a suit in court to block the merger. Third, we analyze unilateral conduct, as well as agreements subject to rule of reason analysis, in a cautious and objective manner. We do this mindful that it is often difficult to tell the difference between good, hard competition and anticompetitive conduct, but knowing that we must be ready to challenge conduct that is harmful to competition.

We need only look at the Olympic gold-medal performances of Mizuki Noguchi (who won the women's marathon) and Kosuke Kitajima (who was victorious in the men's 100 meter and 200 meter breaststroke), to understand how competition produces excellence. To make sure that competition continues to produce excellence in our economies, antitrust enforcers need the most modern investigatory tools and sanctions. The proposals by the JFTC to increase surcharge levels, introduce a corporate amnesty program, and strengthen its investigatory powers are important steps that reflect sound global trends in the antitrust area. They deserve strong support. At the same time, our challenge as antitrust enforcers is to ensure that our antitrust laws are applied in a manner that does not hinder the competitive process. I look forward to working hand-in-hand with the JFTC and our other antitrust colleagues around the world in continuing to promote convergence in the antitrust area and in stoking the flame of competition for the benefit of all our citizens.

Discussion Questions

1. Why does R. Hewitt Pate believe that global competition law is similar to the Olympics?

2. Does the author think these parallels present a positive or negative argument for global competition? Explain the reasons for his evaluation.

3. What connection does Pate draw between capitalism and the global recognition of competition law? Who would be harmed if these laws were not in place? Create a hypothetical example of your own that demonstrates a harmful result you might personally experience without such laws.

4. How do you think Pate would respond to other authors in this section, such as Nevius and Layard, who are less convinced than he is that competition is a positive force in our society?

AN OBJECTIVE LOOK AT THE BENEFITS OF COMPETITION IN THE WORKPLACE

CARMINE COYOTE

Carmine Coyote is the founder and editor of Slow Leadership, *a blog that he discontinued in 2009. Coyote has been an economist and an academic, and he has worked in both the public and private sector. When he retired, he was a partner in one firm and the CEO of another. The following essay appeared in 2008 on a blog.*

Is competition a universal motivator? Is it worth encouraging? Does it work to bring out the best in people?

In business, competition is everywhere: Organizations compete for customers, suppliers compete for orders, and employees compete for attention and promotion. In most organizations, this employee competition is encouraged—even required. But is *more* competition— competition brought about deliberately or enhanced by management efforts—really the best way to motivate people and bring out the best in them? Is it, as conventional management thinking contends, the universal motivator?

Business uses ideas from many sources, but the military and the sports arena are the origin of more business ideas (and downright myths) than anywhere else. Perhaps that's because of the domination of business by men. The military was, until very recently, a male preserve; and sport has long been a staple of male conversation, since the days when it consisted of kicking an enemy's head around a muddy field. Sport has influenced business as much as business has now come to dominate sport.

Competition is essential to sport, whether you play against your own past achievements or another team or individual. Take away the element of competition, and football becomes a group of hooligans in helmets knocking one another over. Golf becomes the stupidest way imaginable for putting a small, white ball into a series of holes in the grass—and why would you want to do that anyway? And tennis . . . why should one person hit a ball to another over a piece of netting, only to have the other person hit the ball right back again?

Business is not a game—though many people treat it as such. It has a purpose, and supposedly that purpose is beneficial. Competition between products or corporations may be essential to prevent monopolistic exploitation in a free market (if only because we accept that organizations will not restrain themselves otherwise—and regulation is often rejected as government interference or frustrated by special interests); but the assumption that putting people into competition against each other inevitably causes them to work harder or better is just that—an assumption.

Outside the sporting arena, most people find that competition increases their anxiety and level of fear. Do people do their best work when they're anxious, frightened, and stressed? Do *you*? If you win, all is well, and you may forget the terror you felt. If you lose . . . well, who cares about losers? I'm not saying competition always has such negative effects, but it's very far from being a universal spur to healthful actions.

For every winner, there must be one or more losers. And before you say losing will spur them to greater efforts next time, think about it. Is that what actually happens? Don't many "losers" resolve never to repeat such humiliation again? Doesn't being branded a loser often cause alienation and wreck people's self-esteem? And doesn't it sometimes drive people to seek to win by any means available, including deceit and even violence?

Of course, competition in sport has another purpose: It's what spectators come to watch. The best game, from the spectators' point of view, is a close-run match where neither player or team seems capable of beating the other. And without spectators and TV audiences, there would be no money. That's why match organizers try so hard to produce games which hang in the balance—even, in the case of some "sports," to the extent of choreographing events and sending players into the game with suitable scripts.

Business isn't—yet—a spectator sport (though Donald Trump and his imitators seem to be trying to make it one), and so rigging the game to win more easily is not much of a problem. If winning is all that counts, as we're often told in the business world, the best game from the player's point of view will always be the one where he or she dominates to such an extent that the opponent never has a chance. Win fast with no effort is the ideal. If you want to be a winner, pick on others who have no chance against you.

That's exactly what happens, only it's usually done by competing against superficially able "opponents" whose ability has been hamstrung in some way—because you're the boss, because you've made it clear you'll destroy their careers if they make you look bad, or because you've rigged the game against them in advance.

Employee competition is rarely "fair" in any objective way. Traditional systems—based as they are on subjective ratings and unstated standards—are heavily rigged in favor of those already in power and their chosen *protégés*. The way to the top depends more on who you know, and how you play the political game, than what you know or how able you are. Businesses are social systems, with all that implies about influence, schmoozing the powerful, and the power of looking good.

Competition for promotion and rewards is often more about how things look than how they are. It's more like a scripted entertainment than a genuine contest. The rules for winning are there, but rarely stated openly, despite all the nonsense about "competencies" and appraisals. Rewards are given out on a largely subjective basis. Those in power make sure the winners are those who they want to win—those who are most useful to them, the ones they like, and probably the ones most like them as well.

Making people compete against one another for rewards, attention, and praise has become traditional, but it's not the only way to set standards or share prizes. There used to be a time when awards were about showing outstanding skill or ability, regardless of other people or winning and losing—when showing your skill and sportsmanship counted for more than coming out on top.

Thanks to the media's obsession with turning everything into a no-holds-barred wrestling match, sport has forgotten sportsmanship, politicians have become die-hard competitors, judges preside over trials that closely resemble gladiatorial contests, and even literary awards are tricked out in the paraphernalia of competition, complete with squabbling judges and post-game slanging matches. And as for the Oscars . . .

It's no surprise that competition has also become the chosen window-dressing of business as well. Let those who don't matter compete as much as possible. They're all "losers" anyway, so who cares who gets hurt? If competition drags out a little extra effort, that's good. If it doesn't, it hardly matters.

The true competition in business has little to do with producing results. It's all about display, playing politics, and destroying those who stand in your way—even if that means hurting the business as well.

In a world of no-holds-barred competition, those who rise to the top are the most ruthless, the most driven, and—all too often—those with the weakest consciences. Who rises to the top? The most able and honorable competitor, or the cheater? Can you tell until it's too late? Does the rash of top executive prosecutions tell you anything about the results of a "winner takes all" outlook?

Competition spurs *some* people to higher effort. It convinces many others it's not worth trying and being humiliated. It causes some to seek to win by honorable means, and others to use every dirty trick they know to cheat their way to the top. When you look at it objectively, competition in business is far from being the best way to encourage individual or team excellence, let alone the only one.

Discussion Questions

1. In what specific ways does competition function in the business world, according to Coyote? Describe specific ways in which you yourself competed or observed someone else compete in a job that you or your acquaintance held.

2. According to Coyote, how do individuals react emotionally to competition? What two rhetorical questions does the author ask about this emotional response? How would you answer each of these questions?

3. What assertions does Coyote make about the value of competition in the business world? Compare his conclusion to the position taken by Pate. Explain your reasons for finding yourself more in agreement with one of these authors than the other.

Assignment #4

"I WISH THEY'D DO IT RIGHT"

This assignment asks you to write an essay in response to Jane Doe's "I Wish They'd Do It Right," an essay that takes up the topic of marriage. Once again, the "Extending the Discussion" section contains several essays that your instructor may assign or that you may read on your own. These essays will help you explore the subject of Doe's argument in greater depth so that you can develop your own ideas on the controversy.

Whether you are assigned to read the supplemental readings or not, we encourage you to continue using all of the prewriting activities provided. They will ensure that you develop your thoughts and organize them within an effective essay format.

I WISH THEY'D DO IT RIGHT

JANE DOE

"Jane Doe" is commonly used as a placeholder name when the identity of a person is unknown. This essay first appeared in the Lakeland Ledger *in 1977, and its author has chosen to remain anonymous.*

My son and his wife are not married. They have lived together for seven years without benefit of license. Though occasionally marriage has been a subject of conjecture, it did not seem important until the day they announced, jubilantly, that they were going to have a child. It was happy news. I was ready and eager to become a grandmother. Now, I thought, they will take the final step and make their relationship legal.

I was apprised of the Lamaze method of natural childbirth. I was prepared by Leboyer for birth without violence. I admired the expectant mother's discipline. She ate only organic foods, abstained from alcohol, avoided insecticides, smog, and trauma. Every precaution was taken to ensure the arrival of a healthy, happy infant. No royal birth had been prepared for more auspiciously. All that was lacking was legitimacy.

Finally, when my grandson was two weeks old, I dared to question their intentions.

"We don't believe in marriage," was all that was volunteered.

"Not even for your son's sake?" I asked. "Maybe he will."

Their eyes were impenetrable, their faces stiffened to masks. "You wouldn't understand," I was told.

And I don't. Surely they cannot believe they are pioneering, making revolutionary changes in society. That frontier has long been tamed. Today, marriage offers all the options. Books and talk shows have surfeited us with the freedom offered in open marriage. Lawyers, psychologists, and marriage counselors are growing rich executing marriage contracts. And divorce, should it come to that, is in most states easy and inexpensive.

On the other hand, living together out of wedlock can be economically impractical as well as socially awkward. How do I present her—as my son's roommate? His spouse? His spice, as one facetious friend suggested? Even my son flounders in these waters. Recently, I heard him refer to her as his girlfriend. I cannot believe that that description will be endearing to their son when he is able to understand.

I have resolved that problem for myself, bypassing their omission, introducing her as she is, as my daughter-in-law. But my son, in militant support of his ideology, refutes any assumption, however casual, that they have taken vows.

There are economic benefits which they are denying themselves. When they applied for housing in the married-students dormitory of the university where he is seeking his doctorate, they were asked for their marriage certificate. Not having one, they were forced to find another, more expensive quarters off campus. Her medical insurance, provided by the company where she was employed, was denied him. He is not her husband. There have been and will be other inconveniences they have elected to endure.

From *New York Times*, September 23, 1997 by Jane Doe, Anonymous.

Their son will not enjoy the luxury of choice about the inconveniences and scurrility to which he will be subject from those of his peers and elders who dislike and fear society's nonconformists.

And if in the future, his parents should decide to separate, will he not suffer greater damage than the child of divorce, who may find comfort in the knowledge that his parents once believed they could live happily ever after, and committed themselves to that idea? The child of unwed parents has no sanctuary. His mother and father have assiduously avoided a pledge of permanency, leaving him drifting and insecure.

more reasons why author objects sons decisions

I know my son is motivated by idealism and honesty in his reluctance to concede what he considers mere ceremony. But is he wise enough to know that no one individual can fight all of society's foibles and frauds? Why does he persist in this, a battle already lost? Because though he rejects marriage, California, his residence, has declared that while couples living together in imitation of marriage are no longer under the jurisdiction of the family court, their relationship is viewed by the state as an implicit contract somewhat like a business agreement. This position was mandated when equal property rights were granted a woman who had been abandoned by the man she had lived with for a number of years.

Finally, the couple's adamance has been depriving to all the rest of the family. There has been no celebration of wedding or anniversaries. There has been concealment from certain family elders who could not cope with the situation. Its irregularity has put constraint on the grandparents, who are stifled by one another's possible embarrassment or hurt.

more reasons why author objects

I hope that one day very soon my son and his wife will acknowledge their cohabitation with a license. The rest of us will not love them any more for it. We love and support them as much as possible now. But it will be easier and happier for us knowing that our grandson will be spared the continued explanation and harassment, the doubts and anxieties of being a child of unmarried parents.

Writing Topic

Why does the author object to her son's decision to cohabitate rather than marry? Do you agree with her position on the issue of marriage versus cohabitation? When responding to these questions, be sure to use examples from your own experiences, observations, or readings.

Vocabulary Check

Good writers choose their words carefully so that their ideas will be clear. In order for you, the reader, to understand an essay and all of the subtleties of its argument, it is important that you be sure about the meanings of words the writer has chosen to represent his or her ideas.

Below are some words that are key to understanding Doe's essay. For each term, find and underline the sentence it appears in in Doe's essay. Look up the word in a dictionary, and then write all of its meanings that are relevant to her ideas.

1. *conjecture*

   definition: _____

   _____

   explanation:

   _____

   _____

   _____

2. *jubilant*

   definition: _____

   _____

   explanation:

   _____

   _____

   _____

3. *Lamaze method*

   definition: _____

   _____

   explanation:

   _____

   _____

   _____

4. *Leboyer*

definition: _____

_____

explanation:

_____

_____

_____

5. *impenetrable*

definition: _____

_____

explanation:

_____

_____

_____

6. *endearing*

definition: _____

_____

explanation:

_____

_____

_____

7. *militant*

definition: _____

_____

explanation:

_____

_____

_____

8. *ideology*

definition: _____

_____

explanation:

_____

_____

_____

9. *assiduous*

definition: _____

_____

explanation:

_____

_____

_____

10. *cohabitation*

definition: _____

_____

explanation:

_____

_____

_____

Questions to Guide Your Reading

Before you begin to answer these questions, review "A Step-by-Step Strategy for Reading Thoughtfully" in Part 1. Use its strategies to analyze "I Wish They'd Do It Right" in preparation for answering the questions here.

Paragraph 1

What event did the author assume would cause her son and his girlfriend to legitimize their relationship? Why do you think she made that assumption?

The event the author assumed would cause her son and his girlfriend to legitamize their relationship? is the birth of a child. I think she made that assumption out of economic benefits

Paragraph 2

What evidence does the author offer to show that the soon-to-be parents are seriously concerned with the welfare of their child?

The evidence that the author offers ~~to show that~~ include

Paragraphs 3–6

What was the gist of the conversation between the author and her son on the topic of marriage?

Paragraph 7

Why does the author say that in today's society "marriage offers all the options"?

Paragraphs 8-10

What economic and social detriments does the author say accompany her son's decision?

Paragraphs 11-12

How will the child be affected by having unmarried parents, according to Doe?

Paragraph 13

How does the state of California view the relationship of cohabiting couples?

Paragraphs 14–15

Why does Jane Doe claim her son's decision hurts the whole family, and how would a legal marriage affect the family's treatment of the couple?

Prewriting for a Directed Summary

Your answers to these questions will provide the specific details necessary for a clear and accurate summary. Remember that you will want to write a *directed* summary, meaning one that responds to the following part of the writing topic.

> first part of the writing topic:
>
> *Why does the author object to her son's decision to cohabitate rather than marry?*

Notice that the question doesn't ask you to summarize the essay or explain the son's attitude toward marriage. Rather, it asks you to explain *why Doe isn't happy with her son's decision* not to marry. Use the questions below to plan your response. They will guide you in identifying Doe's objections.

Don't forget to look back to Part 1's "A Review of the Guidelines for Writing a Directed Summary" as you draft this part of your essay.

Focus Questions

1. According to Doe, in what specific ways can two people who are married live together more cheaply than two unmarried individuals who live together?

2. Whose possible embarrassment and potential emotional damage is Doe strongly concerned about? Explain.

3. Who else might be embarrassed, and even emotionally damaged, by the couple's marital status? Explain.

4. Who else, according to Doe, will be affected by her son's decision not to marry his girlfriend? Why?

Developing an Opinion and Working Thesis Statement

To fully answer the writing topic that follows "I Wish They'd Do It Right," you will have to take a position of your own on the issue Doe addresses. Think about the reasons she presents for supporting her position, and decide whether or not you are convinced that her objections to cohabitation are right. Then, construct a working thesis statement that presents your position on the issue. Use the questions below to help.

> second part of the writing topic:
>
> *Do you agree with her position on the issue of marriage versus cohabitation?*

Although it is likely that you aren't yet sure what position you want to take in your essay, it's a good idea to draft a working thesis now, one based on your initial thinking on the issue and on your own experience and observations. Later in this unit, you will be asked to reexamine the working thesis statement you develop here to see if you want to revise it once you've explored your ideas more systematically.

1. Use the following thesis frame to identify the basic elements of your thesis statement:
   a. What is the issue of "I Wish They'd Do It Right" that the writing topic's first question asks you to consider?

   _____

   b. What is Doe's position on that issue?

   _____

   _____

   c. What is your position on the issue, and will you agree or disagree with Doe?

   _____

   _____

   _____

2. Now use the elements you isolated in 1a, b, and c of the thesis frame to write a thesis statement. You may have to revise it several times until it captures your idea clearly.

   _____

   _____

Prewriting to Find Support for Your Thesis Statement

The last part of the writing topic asks you to support the argument you put forward in your thesis statement.

> writing topic's last question:
>
> *When responding to these questions, be sure to use examples from your own experiences, observations, or readings.*

Use the following questions to develop examples you might use to support your thesis statement.

1. As you begin to develop your own examples, think about how the subject of marriage connects to your own life. In the space below, make a list of personal experiences you have had with married or unmarried couples. How significant are the problems encountered by the unmarried but cohabiting couples you know? Do the couples encounter any of the problems Doe puts forward in her argument? Reflect on your own experiences with dating or with imagining what you want your future to look like if you meet a partner. What might influence your decision to either marry or cohabitate? Any experience you have had that says something about this central idea can provide you with an example to support your thesis. List as many ideas as you can, and freewrite about the significance of each.

   Once you've written your ideas, look them over carefully. Try to group the ideas you've listed or developed in your freewriting into categories. Then, give each category a label. That is, cluster ideas that seem to have something in common and, for each cluster, identify that shared quality by giving it a name.

2. Now make another list, but this time focus on examples from your studies, your reading (especially the supplemental readings in this section), and your knowledge of contemporary society. Do these examples affirm Doe's ideas, or challenge them? For example, do the plots of novels, films, or TV shows you are familiar with depend upon the issue of cohabitation versus marriage; are the parents or children of the couples bothered by the living arrangements? Would these stories have happier endings if the couples got married? Or do most of these examples challenge Doe's ideas and present scenarios in which the couples' parents and children are unconcerned about the couples' cohabitation?

What position on cohabitation do the supplemental essays in this section take? Review their arguments and supporting evidence and compare them to Doe's. Are any of them especially convincing for you? If so, list them here (remember that, if you refer to any of their ideas in your essay, you'll have to cite them carefully). List and/or freewrite about all the relevant ideas you can think of, even those about which you are hesitant.

Once you've written your ideas, look them over carefully. Try to group your ideas into categories. Then, give each category a label. In other words, cluster ideas that seem to have something in common and, for each cluster, identify that shared quality by giving it a title.

3. Once you've created topics by clustering your ideas into categories, go through them and pick two or three specific ones to develop in your essay. Make sure that they are relevant to your thesis and that they have enough substance to be compelling to your reader. Then, in the space below, briefly summarize each item.

Once you've decided which categories and items you will use in your essay, take some time to explain below how each category and its items connect to your thesis statement. You will use these details for the next stage.

Revising Your Thesis Statement

Now that you have spent some time working out your ideas more systematically and developing some supporting evidence for the position you want to take, look again at the working thesis statement you crafted earlier to see if it is still accurate. As your first step, look again at the writing topic and then write your original working thesis on the lines that follow it:

writing topic:

Why does the author object to her son's decision to cohabitate rather than marry? Do you agree with her on the issue of marriage versus cohabitation? When responding to these questions, be sure to use examples from your own experiences, observations, or readings.

working thesis statement:

_____

_____

Remember that your thesis statement must answer the second question in the writing topic while taking into consideration the writing topic as a whole. The first question in the topic identifies the issue that is up for debate, and the last question reminds you that, whatever position you take on the issue, you must be able to support it with specific examples.

Often, after extensive prewriting and focused thought, you will find that the working thesis statement is no longer an accurate reflection of what you plan to say in your essay. Sometimes, only a word or phrase must be added or deleted; other times, the thesis statement must be significantly rewritten. When we draft, we work out our thoughts as we write them down; consequently, draft writing is almost always wordy, unclear, or vague. Look at your working thesis statement through the eyes of your readers and see if it actually says what you want it to say.

After examining your working thesis statement and completing any necessary revisions, check it one more time by asking yourself the following questions:

a. Does the thesis directly identify Doe's argument about cohabitation versus marriage?

b. Do you state your opinion on the issue?

c. Is your thesis well punctuated, grammatically correct, and precisely worded?

Write your polished thesis on the lines below and look at it again. Is it strong and interesting?

_____

_____

Planning and Drafting Your Essay

Now that you have done some prewriting and worked out your thoughts about the issue of cohabitation versus marriage, you are ready to draft your essay. Keep Doe's argument in mind as you respond to the three parts of the writing topic. Don't forget to turn back to earlier pages and use the material you developed there to compose your draft. Once you've completed it, exchange drafts with a classmate and use the peer review activity below to help revise your draft. To use the writing process fully, and produce the most compelling and successful you can, you will have to allow enough time to do at least one thorough revision. It is highly probable that you haven't made your ideas clear enough in your first draft; it's also likely that parts of your essay aren't tied to your thesis, fragmenting your argument overall.

Getting started on the draft is often the hardest part of the writing process. You have to collect all of the sometimes vague or ambiguous ideas that are in your head and written in your prewriting pages, and now you must unify them into a coherent argument. The best way to begin is to construct an outline. This will give you a basic structure for incorporating all the ideas you have developed. Putting together an outline is a handy way to see whether you have a unified, well-developed plan for presenting your argument. Try using the form below.

Creating an Outline for Your Draft

I. Introductory Paragraph

A. An opening sentence that gives the reading selection's title and author, and begins to answer the first question in the writing topic:

_____

B. Main points to include in the directed summary:

1.

2.

3.

4.

C. Write out your thesis statement. It should clearly agree or disagree with the argument in "I Wish They'd Do It Right" and state a clear position using your own words.

_____

II. Body Paragraphs

A. The paragraph's one main point that supports the thesis statement:

_____

1. Controlling idea sentence:

_____

_____

2. Corroborating details:

_____

_____

_____

_____

3. Careful explanation of why the details are significant:

_____

_____

_____

_____

4. Connection to the thesis statement:

_____

_____

_____

_____

B. The paragraph's one main point that supports the thesis statement:

_____

1. Controlling idea sentence:

_____

_____

2. Corroborating details:

_____

_____

_____

_____

3. Careful explanation of why the details are significant:

_____

_____

_____

_____

4. <u>C</u>onnection to the thesis statement:

_____

_____

_____

_____

C. The paragraph's one main point that supports the thesis statement:

_____

1. <u>C</u>ontrolling idea sentence:

_____

_____

2. <u>C</u>orroborating details:

_____

_____

_____

_____

3. <u>C</u>areful explanation of why the details are significant:

_____

_____

_____

_____

4. <u>C</u>onnection to the thesis statement:

_____

_____

_____

_____

D. The paragraph's one main point that supports the thesis statement:

_____

1. <u>C</u>ontrolling idea sentence:

_____

_____

2. Corroborating details:

_____

_____

_____

_____

3. Careful explanation of why the details are significant:

_____

_____

_____

_____

4. Connection to the thesis statement:

_____

_____

_____

_____

Repeat this form for any remaining body paragraphs.

III. Conclusion
   A. Type of conclusion to be used:

_____

   B. Key words or phrases to include:

_____

Use the following guidelines to give a classmate feedback on his or her draft. Read the draft through first, and then answer each of the items below as specifically as you can.

Name of draft's author: _____

Name of draft's reader: _____

Introduction

1. Within the opening sentences,
   a. the author is correctly identified by first and last name   yes   no
   b. the writing selection's title is included and placed within
      quotation marks   yes   no
2. The opening contains a summary that
   a. explains Doe's position on marriage versus cohabitation   yes   no
   b. explains why she thinks marriage is important   yes   no
3. The opening provides a thesis that
   a. makes Doe's conclusions clear   yes   no
   b. gives the draft writer's opinion about those conclusions   yes   no

If the answers to 3 above are yes, state the thesis below as it is written. If the answer is no, explain to the writer what information is needed to make the thesis complete.

_____

_____

_____

Body

1. How many paragraphs are in the body of this essay? _____

2. To support the thesis, this number is   sufficient   not enough

3. Do paragraphs contain the 4Cs?

Paragraph 1	Controlling idea sentence	yes	no
	Corroborating details	yes	no
	Careful explanation of why the details are significant	yes	no
	Connection to the thesis statement	yes	no
Paragraph 2	Controlling idea sentence	yes	no
	Corroborating details	yes	no
	Careful explanation of why the details are significant	yes	no
	Connection to the thesis statement	yes	no

Paragraph 3	Controlling idea sentence	yes	no
	Corroborating details	yes	no
	Careful explanation of why the details are significant	yes	no
	Connection to the thesis statement	yes	no
Paragraph 4	Controlling idea sentence	yes	no
	Corroborating details	yes	no
	Careful explanation of why the details are significant	yes	no
	Connection to the thesis statement	yes	no
Paragraph 5	Controlling idea sentence	yes	no
	Corroborating details	yes	no
	Careful explanation of why the details are significant	yes	no
	Connection to the thesis statement	yes	no

(Continue as needed.)

4. Identify any of the above paragraphs that are underdeveloped (too short). _____

5. Identify any of the above paragraphs that fail to support the thesis. _____

6. Identify any of the above paragraphs that are redundant or repetitive. _____

7. Suggest any ideas for additional paragraphs that might improve this essay.

_____

_____

_____

Conclusion

1. Does the final paragraph avoid introducing new ideas and examples that really belong in the body of the essay?   yes   no

2. Does the conclusion provide closure (let readers know that the end of the essay has been reached)?   yes   no

3. Does the conclusion leave readers with an understanding of the significance of the argument?   yes   no

4. State in your own words what the draft writer considers to be important about his or her argument.

_____

_____

_____

5. Identify the type of conclusion used (see the guidelines for conclusions in Part 1).

_____

Editing

1. During the editing process, the writer should pay attention to the following problems in sentence structure, punctuation, and mechanics:

   fragments
   fused (run-on) sentences
   comma splices
   misplaced, missing, and unnecessary commas
   misplaced, missing, and unnecessary apostrophes
   incorrect quotation mark use
   capitalization errors
   spelling errors

2. While editing, the writer should pay attention to the following areas of grammar:

   verb tense
   subject-verb agreement
   irregular verbs
   pronoun type
   pronoun reference
   pronoun agreement
   irregular verbs
   noun plurals
   dangling and misplaced modifiers
   prepositions

Content

_____ My essay has an appropriate title.

_____ I provide an accurate summary of Doe's position on the issue presented in "I Wish They'd Do It Right."

_____ My thesis states a clear position that can be supported by evidence.

_____ I have enough paragraphs and argument points to support my thesis.

_____ Each body paragraph is relevant to my thesis.

_____ Each body paragraph contains the 4Cs.

_____ I use transitions whenever necessary to connect and ideas to each other.

_____ The final paragraph of my essay (the conclusion) provides readers with a sense of closure.

Grammar, Punctuation, and Mechanics

_____ I use the present tense to discuss Doe's argument and examples.

_____ I use verb tenses correctly to show the chronology of events.

_____ I have verb tense consistency throughout my sentences.

_____ I have checked for subject-verb agreement in all of my sentences.

_____ I have revised all fragments and mixed or garbled sentences.

_____ I have repaired all fused (run-on) sentences and comma splices.

_____ I have placed a comma after introductory elements (transitions and phrases) and all dependent clauses that open a sentence.

_____ If I present items in a series (nouns, verbs, prepositional phrases), they are parallel in form.

_____ If I include material spoken or written by someone other than myself, I have correctly punctuated it with quotation marks, using the MLA style guide's rules for citation.

Reviewing Your Graded Essay

After your instructor has returned your essay, you may have the opportunity to revise your paper and raise your grade. Many students, especially those whose essays receive nonpassing grades, feel that their instructors should be less "picky" about grammar and should pass the work on content alone. However, most students at this level have not yet acquired the ability to recognize quality writing, and they do not realize that content and writing actually cannot be separated in this way. Experienced instructors know that errors in sentence structure, grammar, punctuation, and word choice either interfere with content or distract readers so much that they lose track of content. In short, good ideas badly presented are no longer good ideas; to pass, an essay must have passable writing. So even if you are not submitting a revised version of this essay to your instructor, it is important that you review your work carefully in order to understand its strengths and weaknesses. This sheet will guide you through the evaluation process.

You will want to continue to use the techniques that worked well for you and to find strategies to overcome the problems that you identify in this sample of your writing. To recognize areas that might have been problematic for you, look back at the scoring rubric in this book. Match the numerical/verbal/letter grade received on your essay to the appropriate category. Study the explanation given on the rubric for your grade.

Write a few sentences below in which you identify your problems in each of the following areas. Then, suggest specific changes you could make that would improve your paper. Don't forget to use your handbook as a resource.

1. **Grammar/punctuation/mechanics**

   My problem:

   My strategy for change:

2. **Thesis/response to assignment**

   My problem:

   My strategy for change:

3. **Organization**
   My problem:

   My strategy for change:

4. **Paragraph development/examples/reasoning**
   My problem:

   My strategy for change:

5. **Assessment**

In the space below, assign a grade to your paper using a rubric other than the one used by your instructor. In other words, if your instructor assigned your essay a grade of *High Fail*, you might give it the letter grade you now feel the paper warrants. If your instructor used the traditional letter grade to evaluate the essay, choose a category from the rubric in this book, or any other grading scale that you are familiar with, to show your evaluation of your work. Then, write a short narrative explaining your evaluation of the essay and the reasons it received the grade you gave it.

   Grade: _____

   Narrative: _____

   _____

   _____

   _____

   _____

Extending the Discussion: Considering
Other Viewpoints

Readings

"The Downside of Cohabiting before Marriage" by Meg Jay
"The Negative Effects of Cohabitation" by Linda J. Waite
"The Importance of Being Married" by Ninetta Papadomichelaki and Keith Vance
"Defense and Happiness of Married Life" by Joseph Addison

THE DOWNSIDE OF COHABITING BEFORE MARRIAGE

MEG JAY

Meg Jay earned a PhD from UC Berkeley, where she later taught psychology as a member of the adjunct faculty. She is currently a professor of clinical psychology at the University of Virginia. She also works in private practice, makes public speaking appearances, and has written many articles in newspapers and magazines. She is the author of The Defining Decade: Why Your Twenties Matter—and How to Make the Most of Them Now *(2012). The essay below appeared in the* New York Times *online in 2012.*

At thirty-two, one of my clients (I'll call her Jennifer) had a lavish wine-country wedding. By then, Jennifer and her boyfriend had lived together for more than four years. The event was attended by the couple's friends, families, and two dogs.

When Jennifer started therapy with me less than a year later, she was looking for a divorce lawyer. "I spent more time planning my wedding than I spent happily married," she sobbed. Most disheartening to Jennifer was that she'd tried to do everything right. "My parents got married young so, of course, they got divorced. We lived together! How did this happen?"

Cohabitation in the United States has increased by more than fifteen hundred percent in the past half century. In 1960, about 450,000 unmarried couples lived together. Now the number is more than 7.5 million. The majority of young adults in their twenties will live with a romantic partner at least once, and more than half of all marriages will be preceded by cohabitation. This shift has been attributed to the sexual revolution and the availability of birth control, and in our current economy, sharing the bills makes cohabiting appealing. But when you talk to people in their twenties, you also hear about something else: cohabitation as prophylaxis.

In a nationwide survey conducted in 2001 by the National Marriage Project, then at Rutgers and now at the University of Virginia, nearly half of twenty-somethings agreed with the statement, "You would only marry someone if he or she agreed to live together with you first, so that you could find out whether you really got along." About two-thirds said they believed that moving in together before marriage was a good way to avoid divorce.

But that belief is contradicted by experience. Couples who cohabit before marriage (and especially before an engagement or an otherwise clear commitment) tend to be less satisfied with their marriages—and more likely to divorce—than couples who do not. These negative outcomes are called the cohabitation effect.

Researchers originally attributed the cohabitation effect to selection, or the idea that cohabiters were less conventional about marriage and thus more open to divorce. As cohabitation has become a norm, however, studies have shown that the effect is not entirely explained by individual characteristics like religion, education, or politics. Research suggests that at least some of the risks may lie in cohabitation itself.

As Jennifer and I worked to answer her question "How did this happen?" we talked about how she and her boyfriend went from dating to cohabiting. Her response was consistent with studies reporting that most couples say it "just happened." "We were sleeping over at each other's places all the time," she said. "We liked to be together, so it was cheaper and more convenient. It was a quick decision, but if it didn't work out, there was a quick exit."

She was talking about what researchers call "sliding, not deciding." Moving from dating to sleeping over to sleeping over a lot to cohabitation can be a gradual slope, one not marked by rings or ceremonies or sometimes even a conversation. Couples bypass talking about why they want to live together and what it will mean.

When researchers ask cohabiters these questions, partners often have different, unspoken—even unconscious—agendas. Women are more likely to view cohabitation as a step toward marriage, while men are more likely to see it as a way to test a relationship or postpone commitment, and this gender asymmetry is associated with negative interactions and lower levels of commitment even after the relationship progresses to marriage. One thing men and women do agree on, however, is that their standards for a live-in partner are lower than they are for a spouse.

how cohabitation views differ btwn men and women and what Ideas both men, women share in regards to cohabitation

Sliding into cohabitation wouldn't be a problem if sliding out were as easy. But it isn't. Too often, young adults enter into what they imagine will be low-cost, low-risk living situations only to find themselves unable to get out months, even years, later. It's like signing up for a credit card with zero percent interest. At the end of twelve months when the interest goes up to twenty-three percent, you feel stuck because your balance is too high to pay off. In fact, cohabitation can be exactly like that. In behavioral economics, it's called consumer lock-in.

Potential Problems w/ cohabitation

Lock-in is the decreased likelihood to search for, or change to, another option once an investment in something has been made. The greater the setup costs, the less likely we are to move to another, even better, situation, especially when faced with switching costs, or the time, money, and effort it requires to make a change.

Cohabitation is loaded with setup and switching costs. Living together can be fun and economical, and the setup costs are subtly woven in. After years of living among roommates' junky old stuff, couples happily split the rent on a nice one-bedroom apartment. They share wireless and pets and enjoy shopping for new furniture together. Later, these setup and switching costs have an impact on how likely they are to leave.

talks about how cohabitation is filled w/ complicata and is likely to lead to couples splitting up

Jennifer said she never really felt that her boyfriend was committed to her. "I felt like I was on this multiyear, never-ending audition to be his wife," she said. "We had all this furniture. We had our dogs and all the same friends. It just made it really, really difficult to break up. Then it was like we got married because we were living together once we got into our thirties."

I've had other clients who also wish they hadn't sunk years of their twenties into relationships that would have lasted only months had they not been living together. Others want to feel committed to their partners, yet they are confused about whether they have consciously chosen their mates. Founding relationships on convenience or ambiguity can interfere with the process of claiming the people we love. A life built on top of "maybe you'll do" simply may not feel as dedicated as a life built on top of the "we do" of commitment or marriage.

The unfavorable connection between cohabitation and divorce does seem to be lessening, however, according to a report released last month by the Department of Health and Human Services. More good news is that a 2010 survey by the Pew Research Center found that nearly two-thirds of Americans saw cohabitation as a step toward marriage.[1]

states positive benefits of cohabitation

This shared and serious view of cohabitation may go a long way toward further attenuating the cohabitation effect because the most recent research suggests that serial cohabiters, couples with differing levels of commitment, and those who use cohabitation as a test are most at risk for poor relationship quality and eventual relationship dissolution.

advice for couples who are thinking about cohabitation

Cohabitation is here to stay, and there are things young adults can do to protect their relationships from the cohabitation effect. It's important to discuss each person's motivation and commitment level beforehand and, even better, to view cohabitation as an intentional step toward, rather than a convenient test for, marriage or partnership. It also makes sense to anticipate and regularly evaluate constraints that may keep you from leaving.

Thesis

I am not for or against living together, but I am for young adults knowing that, far from safeguarding against divorce and unhappiness, moving in with someone can increase your chances of making a mistake—or of spending too much time on a mistake. A mentor of mine used to say, "The best time to work on someone's marriage is before he or she has one," and in our era, that may mean before cohabitation.

Notes:
[1] Pew Research Center, January 6, 2011. http://www.pewresearch.org/daily-number/cohabitation-a-step-toward-marriage/

Discussion Questions

1. How have the statistics regarding cohabitation in the United States changed since 1960? What reasons are generally given to account for the change? What other factors do you think cause unmarried couples to avoid cohabitation? Discuss the single most important consideration for you in this situation.

2. According to Meg Jay, how do researchers describe the different agendas for men and women regarding cohabitation? What is the one thing, however, on which the genders agree? Tell about a cohabiting relationship you have observed, personally or on television or in a movie. Did you notice differing agendas for the individuals who are cohabiting? What is the status of the relationship now? What are your long-term expectations for the couple?

3. What steps can cohabiting couples take to protect their relationships? Do you think Jane Doe, author of "I Wish They'd Do It Right," would be satisfied if her son and his partner were responsible in these ways? Explain your answer.

THE NEGATIVE EFFECTS OF COHABITATION

LINDA J. WAITE

Linda J. Waite earned a PhD from the University of Michigan and is a professor of sociology at the University of Chicago. She writes and speaks on social issues such as aging, family, health, and work. She and coauthor Maggie Gallagher published The Case for Marriage *in 2000. Subsequently, Waite delivered, to an audience at Brigham Young University, a speech based on her book; the following reading is taken from that speech.*

[authors def not cohabitation]

Americans often talk as if marriage were a private, personal relationship. But when two people live together for their own strictly private reasons, and carve out their own, strictly private bargain about the relationship, we call that relationship not marriage but "cohabitation." In America, it is now more popular than ever. More men and women are moving in together, sharing an apartment and a bed, without getting married first. The latest Census Bureau figures show four million couples living together outside of marriage (not counting gay couples), eight times as many as in 1970. And many more people have cohabited than are currently doing so; recent figures show that almost two-thirds of young adult men and women chose to cohabit first rather than marry directly.

[Cohabitation is quickly becoming trend]

Most cohabitations are quite short-lived; they typically last for about a year or a little more and then are transformed into marriages or dissolve. Although many observers expected the United States to follow the path blazed by the Nordic countries toward a future of informal but stable relationships, this has not happened. We see no sign that cohabitation is becoming a long-term alternative to marriage in the US. It has remained a stage in the courtship process or a temporary expediency, but not typically a stable social arrangement. Thus, by resembling marriage in some ways and differing from it in others, cohabitation brings some but not all of the costs and benefits of marriage.

[downsides of cohabitation]

Cohabitation is a tentative, nonlegal coresidential union. It does not require or imply a lifetime commitment to stay together. Even if one partner expects the relationship to be permanent, the other partner often does not. Cohabiting unions break up at a much higher rate than marriages. Cohabiters have no responsibility for financial support of their partner, and most do not pool financial resources. Cohabiters are more likely than married couples to both value separate leisure activities and to keep their social lives independent. Although most cohabiters expect their relationship to be sexually exclusive, in fact they are much less likely than husbands and wives to be monogamous.

[more downsides of cohabitation]

A substantial proportion of cohabiting couples have definite plans to marry, and these couples tend to behave like already-married couples. Others have no plans to marry and these tentative and uncommitted relationships are bound together by the "cohabitation deal" rather than the "marriage bargain." In fact, couples may choose cohabitation precisely because it carries no formal constraints or responsibilities.

[States reason why couples would want to cohabitate]

But the deal has costs. The tentative, impermanent, and socially unsupported nature of cohabitation impedes the ability of this type of partnership to deliver many of the benefits of marriage, as do the relatively separate lives typically pursued by cohabiting partners. The uncertainty about the stability and longevity of the relationship makes both investment in the relationship and specialization with this partner much riskier than in marriage. Couples who expect to stay together for the very long run can develop some skills and let others atrophy because they can count on their spouse (or partner) to fill in where they are weak. This specialization means that couples working together in a long-term partnership will produce more than the same people would working alone. But cohabitation reduces the benefits and increases the costs of specializing—it is much safer to just do everything for yourself since you don't know whether the partner you are living with now will be around next year. So cohabiting couples typically produce less than married couples.

[handwritten: States drawbacks of cohabitation]

The temporary and informal nature of cohabitation also makes it more difficult and riskier for extended family to invest in and support the relationship. Parents, siblings, friends of the partners are less likely to get to know a cohabiting partner than a spouse and, more important, less likely to incorporate a person who remains outside "the family" into its activities, ceremonies, and financial dealings. Parents of one member of a cohabiting couple are ill-advised to invest in the partner emotionally or financially until they see if the relationship will be long term. They are also ill-advised to become attached to children of their child's cohabiting partner because their "grandparent" relationship with that child will dissolve if the cohabitation splits up. Marriage and plans to marry make that long-term commitment explicit and reduce the risk to families of incorporating the son- or daughter-in-law and stepchildren.

[handwritten: more draw back of cohabitation]

The separateness of cohabiters' lives also reduces their usefulness as a source of support during difficult times. Julie Brines and Kara Joyner, writing in the *American Sociological Review*, argue that cohabiters tend to expect each person to be responsible for supporting him or herself, and failure to do so threatens the relationship. The lack of sharing typical of cohabiters disadvantages the women and their children in these families relative to the men, because women typically earn less than men—and this is especially true for mothers.

Another drawback of cohabitation is that it seems to distance people from some important social institutions, especially organized religion. Most formal religions disapprove of and discourage cohabitation, making membership in religious communities awkward for unmarried couples. The result is that individuals who enter a cohabitation often reduce their involvement in religious activities. In contrast, people who get married and those who become parents generally become more active. Finally, while young men and women who define themselves as "religious" are less likely to cohabit, those who do cohabit subsequently become less religious.

Cohabitation has become an increasingly important—but poorly delineated—context for child rearing. One quarter of current stepfamilies involve cohabiting couples, and a significant proportion of "single-parent" families are actually two-parent cohabiting families. The parenting role of a cohabiting partner toward the child(ren) of the other person is extremely vaguely defined. The nonparent partner—the man in the substantial majority of cases—has no explicit legal, financial, supervisory, or custodial rights or responsibilities regarding the child of his partner. This ambiguity and lack of enforceable claims by either cohabiting partner or child makes investment in the relationship dangerous for both parties and makes "Mom's boyfriend" a weak and shifting base from which to discipline and guide a child.

[handwritten: Why cohabitation is bad for children]

As the previous section shows, marriage fosters certain behavioral changes—by both the couple and those around them—that cohabitation simply doesn't encourage: Each partner can specialize; in-laws can get involved; children and their parent's spouse can invest in a mutual relationship; and so on. What, though, are the empirical results of these behavioral changes, and of the many other ways in which the two options differ?

Before seeking to answer this question, we must first acknowledge that cohabiting couples, especially those with no plans to marry, tend to differ from married couples even before the cohabitation begins. Living with someone rather than marrying attracts people less committed to marriage, and less likely to be successful at it. Thus, selection of people with less to offer a partner and less to gain from marriage accounts for some of the poorer outcomes of cohabiters. But, as we shall see, at least some of the evidence suggests that cohabiting itself also contributes to those outcomes.

cohabitors are still more likely to commit violence than married couples even if you consider outside factors

A recent Census Bureau report speculates that perhaps so many children were being born to unmarried mothers because women were avoiding marriage out of fear of domestic violence and child abuse. Is this a reasonable fear? My own analysis of data from the 1987/88 National Survey of Families and Households shows that married people are about half as likely as cohabiting couples to say that arguments between them and their partner had become physical in the previous year (eight percent of married women compared to sixteen percent of cohabiting women). When it comes to "hitting, shoving, and throwing things," cohabiting couples are more than three times more likely than the married to say things get that far out of hand. One reason cohabiters are more violent is that they are, on average, younger and less educated. But even after controlling for education, race, age, and gender, people who live together are 1.8 times more likely to report violent arguments than married people.

Choosing whether to cohabitate w/wo intent to marry important

It matters a great deal, however, whether cohabiting couples have definite plans to marry. Engaged cohabiters are no more likely to report violence than married couples, but cohabiters with no plans to marry are twice as likely to report couple violence as either married or engaged couples. Women in uncommitted cohabiting relationships seem to be especially at risk of violence directed toward them. The well-being of married and engaged cohabiting couples is substantially higher on this dimension than uncommitted cohabiting couples. Some researchers suggest that commitment to the relationship and to the partner reduces violence. These differentials seem to support that view.

Sex appears to be a key part of the cohabiting "deal." According to the 1992 National Health and Social Life Survey, cohabiting men and women make love on average between seven and seven and a half times a month, or about one extra sex act a month than married people. But cohabiting men and women are less likely than those who are married to be monogamous, although virtually all say that they expect their relationship to be sexually exclusive. Renata Forste and Koray Tanfer find in the National Survey of Women that four percent of married women had a secondary sex partner compared to twenty percent of cohabiting women and eighteen percent of dating women. Women's behavior changed dramatically when they married, with a huge decline in the chances of having a secondary sex partner. Forste and Tanfer conclude that marriage itself increases sexual exclusivity; cohabitation is no better than "dating" on this dimension.

Women who are living with men tend to do more housework than women living alone or with other women. A recent study by Scott South and Glenna Spitze shows that once they take into account the presence of children and others and characteristics of the partners, married women spend fourteen hours more than married men do. Women who are cohabiting spend about ten hours more on housework than cohabiting men. On this dimension, then, cohabitation would seem to be a better deal for women than marriage. Some economists, however, would argue that husbands compensate their wives for their time in work for the family by sharing their income with them, while cohabiting women generally don't share their partner's earnings, so they may be doing extra housework without extra pay.

Married couples link their fates—including their finances. This is a more attractive proposition if one's intended has a decent income and few debts. But if not, living together is a way to avoid taking on the debts—current or future—of the partner. It also allows couples to avoid the "marriage penalty" in tax code—an issue for two-worker couples with fairly equal incomes (but couples with unequal earnings could see tax benefits if they marry and share income). Since the income of one's spouse (but not one's cohabiting partner) is counted in determining eligibility for benefits under government programs like Food Stamps and the Earned Income Tax Credit, the implicit tax on marriage in these programs can be very high, as C. Eugene Steuerle has pointed out in "A Comprehensive Approach to Removing Marriage Penalties."

Selection of those with few resources into cohabitation—and/or the negative effects of the cohabitation bargain—combine to leave couples who are living together with relatively little money. LingXin Hao, writing in *Social Forces*, shows that among all families with children, cohabiting couples have the lowest average level of wealth, comparable to families headed by a single mother. Intact two-parent families and stepfamilies have the highest level of wealth, followed at a distance by families headed by a single father. Unlike single-parent families, cohabiting couples have two potential earners, so their very low levels of wealth are less expected. But expected or not, they are a cause for concern, especially for the children living in these families.

Marriage is, by design and agreement, for the long run. Married people, thus, see their relationship as much more stable than cohabiting couples do. And for any couple, thinking that the relationship is likely to break up has a dampening effect on the spirits. The result: Cohabiters show lower psychological well-being than similar married people. Specifically, cohabiters report being more depressed and less satisfied with life than do married people. And according to sociologist Susan Brown, worrying that one's relationship will break up is especially distressing for cohabiting mothers, who show quite high levels of depression as a result. *[thesis]*

Perhaps, however, cohabiting people are more depressed because depressed and dissatisfied people have trouble getting married. Not so, says Brown. She found that cohabiters' higher levels of depression are not explained by their scores before the start of the union. Rather it is a person's perception of the chances that the relationship will break up that seems to be the chief culprit in his or her poor emotional well-being.

People often believe that living together in a "trial marriage" will tell potential partners something about what marriage would be like. The information gained could help couples make good choices and avoid bad ones; cohabiting before marriage could lead to better marriages later. Evidence from the National Survey of Families and Households shows how widespread this belief is. Most cohabiters say that making sure that they are compatible before marriage is an important reason that they wanted to live together. *[Evidence says that cohabiting could be test for marriage.]*

But a large body of recent evidence now shows quite consistently that people who cohabit and then marry are much more likely to divorce than people who marry without living together. An initial conclusion might be that cohabitation changes people's attitudes in ways that make them less committed to the institution of marriage. However, research conducted by Lee Lillard, Michael Brien, and me shows that people who cohabit have other characteristics that both lead them to cohabit in the first place and make them poor marriage material. Thus, in the case of divorce, selection would seem to account for the differences between marriage and cohabitation. *[recent evidence contradicts prior belief]*

In the end
cohabitation has
Proven to be
inferior to
marriage despite
Positive benefits
In long run,
Cohabitation
doesn't seem
to work

The cumulative evidence clearly suggests that compared to marriage, uncommitted cohabitation—cohabitation by couples who are not engaged—is an inferior social arrangement. Couples who live together with no definite plans to marry are making a different bargain than married couples or engaged cohabiters. The bargain is very much not marriage, and is "marriage-like" only in that couples share an active sex life and a house or apartment. Cohabiting men tend to be quite uncommitted to the relationship; cohabiting women with children tend to be quite uncertain about its future. Levels of domestic violence are much higher in these couples than in either married or engaged cohabiting couples. Children in families headed by an unmarried couple do much worse than children in families with married parents. Uncommitted cohabitation delivers relatively few benefits to men, women, or children. This social arrangement also probably benefits communities less than marriage does.

Clearly, the men and women who choose uncommitted cohabitation do not have the same characteristics as those who marry without first living together or who live together while planning their wedding. This selection into cohabitation of people less likely to build a successful marriage seems to account for their higher chances of divorce should they ultimately marry. But cohabitation itself seems to cause attitudes to change in ways inimical to long-term commitment, to damage emotional well-being, and to distance people from religious institutions and from their families. There is also some evidence that cohabitation is less beneficial for children than marriage is. And there is some suggestion that marriage—but not uncommitted cohabitation—reduces domestic violence.

If cohabitation is inferior to marriage, then we as a society would benefit from more of the latter and less of the former. Encouraging marriage over cohabitation involves undoing a whole series of legal and social changes that have undercut the privileged status of marriage. This doesn't mean we should encourage a return to the old model of marriage and the family. But in the justified effort to overcome the sexism and inflexibility of the "1950s" marriage, we may have been too willing to throw the baby out with the bathwater. If we wish to retrieve for more people the benefits that marriage delivers that cohabitation does not, it is important to begin the process of re-privileging marriage now.

Discussion Questions

1. In what way does Linda J. Waite claim that cohabitation in the United States differs from cohabitation in Nordic countries? What outside factors in the cultures do you think might account for this difference? Discuss another country whose culture is familiar to you in terms of its attitude toward cohabitation.

2. List the negative costs of the "cohabitation deal," and offer a reasonable counterargument for as many of them as you can.

3. List the products of cohabitation that Waite discusses. Which ones do you think are likely to concern Jane Doe regarding her son's relationship? Explain your reasons for choosing those and your reasons for not selecting the others.

THE IMPORTANCE OF BEING MARRIED

NINETTA PAPADOMICHELAKI AND KEITH VANCE

Keith Vance and Ninetta Papadomichelaki are faculty members in the University Writing Program at the University of California, Riverside. They have published Compass: Paths to Effective Reading *and* Compass: Guidebook to English Grammar.

The debate over gay marriage, many believe, is one of the most divisive factors in American society today, and a plethora of essays has been written either decrying such marriages as abominations or supporting them as the evolution of human relationships and communities. Here follow some of the most pertinent arguments of both sides. On the one side, marriage conservatives feel that 1) marriage is rooted in male/female sexuality and is thus meant to exist between a man and a woman; 2) marriage between a man and a woman is a religious sacrament; 3) marriage serves as a stabilizing institution in society; 4) also for some, most homosexuals cannot handle the responsibilities of marriage. On the other side of the debate, proponents of same sex marriages vehemently refute these claims. They argue that for significant portions of the population, same sex sexuality is equally as strong as the heterosexual one. They believe that equality before the law mandates that the state broaden its legislation to include same sex unions while they promote the expansion of the same idea for religious ceremonies. They scorn the argument that homosexuals lack responsibility by pointing out that same sex partnerships can be equally as durable and strong as heterosexual unions. Besides, if homosexuals are considered competent enough to hold posts of responsibility at all levels of society, why would they be less capable within marriage?

The problem, however, with this debate is that it is asking the wrong question. Instead of "why should homosexuals marry," one should ask, "why should anyone get married?" What is it that makes marriage such an important or even mandatory institution today? To begin to answer these questions, one should look for the essence of marriage in the origins of its modern conceptualization. While people have been "marrying" even before the Romans controlled the world, the formulation of the modern institution of marriage derived from the tradition of Western romantic love in the Middle Ages. In the thirteenth and fourteenth centuries, medieval authors produced an array of what were called "romance" manuscripts that included new notions of romantic love. Indeed, Chrétien de Troyes and other figures created numerous such stories—about knights and their damsels falling in love despite social forces that might be aligned to stop them—whose *dénouement* is a hoped-for marriage. Undoubtedly, the most famous story of Western romantic love is Shakespeare's *Romeo and Juliet,* in which the two title characters, despite the warring family history, secretly marry and thereafter consummate their love. It is mainly through these romances that marriage became figured as the conclusion of romantic love whereby partners choose each other for life. One need only look at modern romantic comedies churned out by Hollywood by the score to find this prevalent notion that love is inextricably connected to marriage. Love is still supposed to bring couples together, and its suitable social culmination is marriage.

Despite, however, the literary efforts of poets from the past, marriage for much of its history was not about love at all. Marriage was primarily about economics and alliances. When two people married, their families were combined, and property changed hands. Even in the Middle Ages, despite the literature of the period, marriage was typically arranged by the parents as more of a combination of the resources of the two families than anything remotely relevant to love. So, while many people focus on Romeo and Juliet's undying love for each other, what is so often missed about *Romeo and Juliet* is the underlying premise of the play: the massive traditional social forces of tradition and economics aligned against love. Contributing to this traditional idea of marriage as an economic transaction was also the institution of dowry, the ceremonial gift of goods and money along with the bride. Even today, in some countries, dowries still constitute an important part of the ritual of marriage, providing the contractual backbone to the rite.

[handwritten margin note: Initially marriage was about money and power]

Of course, today and for most of the US, marriage has changed quite a bit from its roots as a fundamentally economic institution. Today, a dowry has become an outdated custom or a joke rather than a necessary component of marriage; only few parents arrange the marriages of their sons or daughters; and certainly neither women nor their property is any longer relegated as the legal property of the father or of the husband. Since women have the same rights as men, it is entirely possible for single women to exist outside the structure of marriage; they can be financially independent, and they can have fulfilling careers and access to their own funds. Marriage doesn't even provide a tax break because in many cases couples pay the so-called "marriage penalty" by being charged more taxes than if they filed as individuals. So marriage is no longer the bulwark of economic security that it once was reputed to be.

[handwritten margin note: talks about how marriage has changed and evolved]

However, one can argue that the significance of marriage as a predominant social institution remains intact. True, besides its economic significance, one other major reason for marriage has been its role in cementing social relationships and providing the only acceptable path towards creating a family. In tighter communities, everyone knows what they are supposed to do, the road they are supposed to follow, and the social roles they have been assigned; in these societies, marriage is one of the stepping stones into adult life, and the family unit is the primary organizing feature of society. However, any society, including the American one, could be organized on the principle of a commune with groups of ten or fifteen people sharing finances, property, and workload duties, but it is not. Instead, the most prevalent institution in our society is the "nuclear" family whose symbol is marriage. Indeed, statistics from the Census Bureau show that 96.7% of Americans will marry at least one time during their lives.

[handwritten margin note: addresses counterargument of marriage]

Even the social dimension of marriage might be on the wane. Divorce statistics hover around 50%, and there has been a 40% rise since 1990 in the number of couples who live together but are not married in the US. In Europe, this trend is even more pronounced. In a 2006 survey conducted by the German Federal Statistics Office, only 38% of German women and 30% of German men thought marriage was necessary for creating a union. Even having children out of wedlock, which has been one of the primary reasons for marrying, is no longer socially stigmatized but rather legally facilitated and socially more accepted. Across Europe, for instance, one in three children is born to unwed parents, which reflects the sixfold increase in the number of unwed parents since the 1970s; at the same time, most of these births take place in unmarried households by choice.

So why would anyone get married nowadays if it is no longer about fusing two families economically, if women have the economic power to live on their own, if no social stigma attaches to having children outside of marriage? The practical significance of marriage as an

[handwritten margin note: address practical thesis of being married]

institution has definitely waned and will continue to do so once legislation awards unwed-ded unions of both heterosexual and homosexual couples and single parent families with the same legal privileges that it awards families of married heterosexuals. Indeed, it is mostly these privileges and perhaps a remainder of the medieval notion of romantic love, as well as religious convictions that still grant the institution of marriage such importance. However, if there were no legal differentiation, couldn't two people "love" each other without the ritual and the paper? So why should anyone, including same sex partners, desire to participate in a social institution that is slowly becoming obsolete? ⌉

Discussion Questions

1. Why do the authors claim that the debate about same sex marriage is focusing on the wrong question? What, in their opinion, is the right question? Do you think that chang-ing the question may change the way people on both sides of the debate feel about legal-izing gay marriage? Why?

2. Do you think that Doe should be categorized as a marriage conservative or a marriage liberal? Why? Which, if any, of the reasons the authors cite as the fundamental arguments of the marriage conservatives are used by Doe to make her case to her son? Which ones are irrelevant to her son's situation? Why do you think Doe does not discuss the other reasons listed in defense of the institution of marriage?

3. Which of the reasons Doe uses to convince her son to marry might explain the desire of some same sex couples to be legally married? How do these reasons support or change your own position on gay marriage?

DEFENSE AND HAPPINESS OF MARRIED LIFE
FROM THE SPECTATOR, NO 5000

JOSEPH ADDISON

Joseph Addison was born in Wiltshire, England, in 1672. He had a long career in English politics and held many offices, including Secretary of Ireland and Secretary of State. Addison was a member of the Anglican church and worked in his political life for the equality of humans, a constitutional government, and a free, commercial society. He is most remembered for his eloquent prose, and most of his essays were published in the Spectator, *a popular periodical he founded with his friend Richard Steele. Addison used these light, satirical essays to educate the English middle class in manners and morals.*

—Huc natas adjice septem,
Et totidem juvenes, et mox generosque nurusque.
Quaerite nunc, habeat quam nostra superbia causam.[1]
OVID *Metamorphosis.*

Sir,[2] You who are so well acquainted with the story of Socrates, must have read how, upon his making a Discourse concerning Love, he pressed his Point with so much Success that all the Batchelors in his Audience took a Resolution to Marry by the first Opportunity, and that all the married Men immediately took Horse and galloped home to their Wives. I am apt to think your Discourses, in which you have drawn so many agreeable Pictures of Marriage, have had a very good Effect this way in England. We are obliged to you at least, for having taken off that Senseless Ridicule, which for many Years the Witlins of the Town have turned upon their Fathers and Mothers. For my own part, I was born in Wedlock, and I don't care who knows it: For which Reason, among many others, I should look upon my self as a most Insufferable Coxcomb,[3] did I endeavour to maintain that Cuckoldom was inseparable from Marriage, or to make use of Husband and Wife as Terms of Reproach. Nay, Sir, I will go one Step further, and declare to you before the whole World, that I am a married Man, and at the same time I have so much Assurance as not to be ashamed of what I have done.

Among the several Pleasures that accompany this State of Life, and which you have described in your former Papers, there are two you have not taken Notice of, and which are seldom cast into the Account, by those who write on this Subject. You must have observed, in your Speculations on Human Nature, that nothing is more gratifying to the Mind of Man than Power or Dominion, and this I think my self amply possessed of, as I am the Father of a Family. I am perpetually taken up in giving out Orders, in prescribing Duties, in hearing Parties, in administering Justice, and in distributing Rewards and Punishments. To speak in the Language of the Centurion,[4] I say unto one, go and he goeth, and to another come and he cometh, and to my Servant do this and he doeth it. In short, Sir, I look, upon my Family as a Patriarchal Sovereignty, in which I am my self both King and Priest. All great Governments are nothing else but Clusters of these little private Royalties, and therefore I consider the Masters of Families as small Deputy-Governors presiding over the several little Parcels and Divisions of their Fellow Subjects. As I take great Pleasure in the Administration of my

Government in particular, so I look upon my self not only as a more useful, but as a much greater and happier Man than any Batchelor in England of my own Rank and Condition.

There is another accidental Advantage in Marriage, which has likewise fallen to my Share, I mean the having a multitude of Children. These I cannot but regard as very great Blessings. When I see my little Troop before me, I rejoice in the Additions which I have made to my Species, to my Country, and to my Religion, in having produced such a number of reasonable Creatures, Citizens, and Christians. I am pleased to see my self thus perpetuated, and as there is no Production comparable to that of an human Creature, I am more proud of having been the Occasion of ten such glorious Productions, than if I had built an hundred Pyramids at my own Expence, or published as many Volumes of the finest Wit and Learning. In what a beautiful Light has the Holy Scripture represented Abdon, one of the judges of Israel, who had forty Sons and thirty Grandsons, that rode on Threescore and Ten Ass-Colts, according to the Magnificence of the Eastern Countries? How must the Heart of the old Man rejoice, when he saw such a beautiful Procession of his own Descendents, such a numerous Cavalcade of his own raising? For my own part, I can sit in my Parlour with great Content, when I take a Review of half a dozen of my little Boys mounted upon Hobby-Horses, and of as many little Girls tutoring their Babies, each of them endeavouring to excell the rest, and to do something that may gain my Favour and Approbation. I cannot question but he who has blessed me with so many Children, will assist my Endeavours in providing for them. There is one thing I am able to give each of them, which is a virtuous Education. I think, it is Sir Francis Bacon's Observation, that in a numerous Family of Children the eldest is often spoiled by the Prospect of an Estate, and the youngest by being the Darling of the Parent; but that some one or other in the middle, who has not perhaps been regarded, has made his Way in the World, and over-topp'd the rest. It is my Business to implant in every one of my Children the same Seeds of Industry, and the same honest Principles. By this Means I think I have a fair Chance, that one or other of them may grow considerable in some or other way of Life, whether it be in the Army, or in the Fleet, in Trade, or any of the three learned Professions;[5] for you must know, Sir, that from long Experience and Observation, I am perswaded of what seems a Paradox to most of those with whom I converse, namely, that a Man who has many Children, and gives them a good Education, is more likely to raise a Family, than he who has but one, notwithstanding he leaves him his whole Estate. For this Reason I cannot forbear amusing my self with finding out a General, an Admiral, or an Alderman of London, a Divine, a Physician, or a Lawyer, among my little People who are now perhaps in Petticoats; and when I see the Motherly Airs of my little Daughters when they are playing with their Puppets,[6] I cannot but flatter my self that their Husbands and Children will be happy, in the possession of such Wives and Mothers.

If you are a Father, you will not perhaps think, this Letter impertinent; but if you are a single Man, you will not know the Meaning of it, and probably throw it into the Fire; whatever you determine of it, you may assure your self that it comes from one who is Your most humble Servant and Well-wisher, Philogamus.[7]

Endnotes

[1] To this add seven daughters,/And just as many sons, and soon the sons and daughters-in-law,/Ask now whether my pride has its cause.

[2] Addison here impersonates a married man.

[3] Fool.

[4] Commander of one hundred men in the Roman army.

[5] Law, medicine, and religion.

[6] Dolls.

[7] Lover of marriage.

Discussion Questions

1. Do you think the title Addison gives this essay appropriately represents the contents of the essay?

2. What are the additional pleasures of marriage that Addison lists? Do you consider these two things to be convincing arguments for marriage? Why?

3. Now that you have read "Defense and Happiness of Married Life," which of the two—Jane Doe, or her son—would be more likely to use Addison as an authority figure to support his or her position on marriage? Which part would you expect to see quoted?

Assignment #5

"THE AMERICAN PARADOX"

This assignment focuses on the subject of food and its complex and significant impact on our world and on each of us individually. The lead reading selection that you will respond to is written by Michael Pollan, who has written widely on the subject. Read his essay carefully to determine the particular argument he is making in this relatively short essay. After reading Pollan's essay, look carefully at the writing topic that follows it; your assignment in this unit is to respond to this writing topic. As you have done in the previous assignments, be sure to make good use of the pages that follow Pollan's essay. They will help you to understand his ideas and develop your own argument in response to the writing topic.

The reading selections in "Extending the Discussion: Considering Other Viewpoints" may be especially important for this assignment because many of you probably know little about the issues that surround the topic of food. We think you will be interested to learn of some of the back stories on the food you eat. The propagation and distribution of food are determined by a host of priorities, necessities, vested interests, and traditions that most of us haven't given all that much thought to, but which make up a wide net of influence over our environment, our ethics, and our physical and mental health.

The prewriting exercises in this unit will take you through the writing process and help you work through some of these vital issues. Again, be sure to complete all of the pages, carefully following the directions and guidelines. But don't be afraid to move beyond them, too, now that you have become familiar with this book's strategies, so that your writing process is enriched as much as possible.

THE AMERICAN PARADOX

Michael Pollan

Michael Pollan is a professor of journalism at the University of California, Berkeley. He has written often about what he sees as mistakes in the way Americans think about, produce, and eat their food. He has won numerous awards from organizations such as the American Booksellers Association and the Humane Society of the United States. The following selection is adapted from his book In Defense of Food: An Eater's Manifesto *(2008).*

The scientists haven't tested the hypothesis yet, but I'm willing to bet that when they do, they'll find an inverse correlation between the amount of time people spend worrying about nutrition and their overall health and happiness. This is, after all, the implicit lesson of the French paradox, so called not by the French but by American nutritionists, who can't fathom how a people who enjoy their food as much as the French do—who blithely eat beef and cheese and drink red wine—can have substantially lower rates of heart disease than we do on our elaborately engineered low-fat diets. Maybe it's time we confronted the American paradox: a notably unhealthy population preoccupied with nutrition and the idea of eating healthily.

True, as omnivores—creatures that can eat just about anything nature has to offer and that in fact need to eat a wide variety of different things in order to be healthy—the "What to eat" question is somewhat more complicated for us than it is for, say, cows. Yet for most of our history, humans have navigated the question without expert advice. To guide us we had, instead, culture, which, at least when it comes to food, is really just a fancy word for your mother. What to eat, how much of it to eat, what order in which to eat it, with what and when and with whom have for most of human history been a set of questions long settled and passed down from parents to children without a lot of controversy or fuss. But over the last several decades, moms have lost much of their authority over the dinner menu, ceding it to scientists and food marketers—often an unhealthy alliance of the two—and, to a lesser extent, to the government, with its ever-shifting dietary guidelines, food-labeling rules, and perplexing pyramids. Think about it: Most of us no longer eat what our mothers ate as children or, for that matter, what our mothers fed us as children. This is, historically speaking, an unusual state of affairs.

What is driving such relentless change in the American diet? One force is a thirty-two-billion-dollar food-marketing machine that thrives on change for its own sake. Another is the constantly shifting ground of nutrition science that, depending on your point of view, is steadily advancing the frontiers of our knowledge about diet and health or is just changing its mind a lot because it is a flawed science that knows much less than it cares to admit. Part of what drove my grandparents' food culture from the American table was official scientific opinion, which, beginning in the 1960s, decided that animal fat was a deadly substance. And then there were the food manufacturers, who stood to make very little money from my grandmother's cooking, because she was doing so much from scratch—up to and including rendering her own cooking fats. Drawing on then-current science, they managed to sell her daughter on the virtues of hydrogenated vegetable oils, the trans fats that we're now learning may be, well, deadly substances.

Sooner or later, everything solid we've been told about the links between our diet and our health seems to get blown away in the gust of the most recent study. Consider the latest findings. In 2006 came news that a low-fat diet, long believed to protect against cancer, may do no such thing—this from the massive, federally funded Women's Health Initiative, which has also failed to find a link between a low-fat diet and the risk of coronary heart disease. Indeed, the whole nutritional orthodoxy around dietary fat appears to be crumbling. In 2005, we learned that dietary fiber might not, as we'd been confidently told for years, help prevent cancers and heart disease. And then, in the fall of 2006, two prestigious studies on omega-3 fats published at the same time came to strikingly different conclusions. While the Institute of Medicine at the National Academy of Sciences found little conclusive evidence that eating fish would do your heart much good, a Harvard study brought the hopeful piece of news that simply by eating a couple of servings of fish each week you could cut your risk of dying from a heart attack by more than a third.

The story of how the most basic questions about what to eat ever got so complicated reveals a great deal about the institutional imperatives of the food industry, nutrition science, and—ahem—journalism, three parties that stand to gain much from widespread confusion surrounding the most elemental question an omnivore confronts. But humans deciding what to eat without professional guidance—something they have been doing with notable success since coming down out of the trees—is seriously unprofitable if you're a food company, a definite career loser if you're a nutritionist, and just plain boring if you're a newspaper editor or reporter. And so, like a large, gray cloud, a great Conspiracy of Scientific Complexity has gathered around the simplest questions of nutrition, much to the advantage of everyone involved—except, perhaps, the supposed beneficiary of all this advice: us, and our health and happiness as eaters. For the most important thing to know about the campaign to professionalize dietary advice is that it has not made us any healthier. To the contrary: Most of the nutritional advice we've received over the last half century has actually made us less healthy and considerably fatter.

Nutrition science on one side and the food industry on the other have fostered needless complications around eating. Because in their view food is foremost a matter of biology, they preach that we must try to eat "scientifically"—by the nutrient and the number and under the guidance of experts. If such an approach to food doesn't strike you as the least bit strange, that is probably because nutritionists' thinking has become so pervasive as to be invisible. We forget that, historically, people have eaten for a great many reasons other than biological necessity. Food is also about pleasure, about community, about family and spirituality, about our relationship to the natural world, and about expressing our identity. As long as humans have been taking meals together, eating has been as much about culture as it has been about biology.

That eating should be foremost about bodily health is a relatively new and, I think, destructive idea—destructive not just of the pleasure of eating, which would be bad enough, but paradoxically of our health as well. Indeed, no people on earth worry more about the health consequences of their food choices than we Americans do—and no people suffer from as many diet-related health problems. We are becoming a nation of people with an unhealthy obsession with healthy eating.

Writing Topic

According to Pollan, what is wrong with the way Americans think about eating today? Do you agree with him? As you develop your argument, be sure to support your position with specific examples from your own experience, your observation of others, or your reading.

Vocabulary Check

Good writers choose their words carefully so that their ideas will be clear. In order for you to understand any reading selection, it is important to think about its key vocabulary terms and the way they are used by the author. Words can have a variety of meanings, or they can have specialized meanings in certain contexts. Look up the definitions of the following words or phrases from the essay. Find each word in "The American Paradox," and then choose the meaning that you think Pollan intended when he selected that particular word for use in his essay. Then, explain the way that the meaning or concept behind the definition is key to understanding his argument.

1. *inverse*
   definition: _____

   _____

   explanation: _____

   _____

   _____

   _____

2. *correlation*
   definition: _____

   _____

   explanation: _____

   _____

   _____

   _____

3. *implicit*
   definition: _____

   _____

   explanation: _____

   _____

   _____

   _____

4. *blithe*

definition: _____

_____

explanation: _____

_____

_____

_____

5. *elaborate*

definition: _____

_____

explanation: _____

_____

_____

_____

6. *paradox*

definition: _____

_____

explanation: _____

_____

_____

_____

7. *perplexing*

definition: _____

_____

explanation: _____

_____

_____

_____

8. *relentless*
   definition: _____

   _____

   explanation: _____

   _____

   _____

   _____

9. *orthodoxy*
   definition: _____

   _____

   explanation: _____

   _____

   _____

   _____

10. *foster*
    definition: _____

    _____

    explanation: _____

    _____

    _____

    _____

11. *pervasive*
    definition: _____

    _____

    explanation: _____

    _____

    _____

    _____

Questions to Guide Your Reading

Answer the following questions to gain a thorough understanding of "The American Paradox."

Paragraph 1

What relationship does Pollan believe exists between general well-being and a focus on nutrition?

Paragraph 2

According to Pollan, in the past, who and/or what governed what we ate? How does he think the entities that governed what we ate have changed?

Paragraph 3

What are the two main factors responsible for this change, according to Pollan?

Paragraph 4

How does the dietary controversy example highlight the problematic relationship Pollan sees between nutritional science and good nutrition?

Paragraph 5

a. What are some of the historic reasons for what and how we eat, according to Pollan? Explain the correlation Pollan finds between the historic reasons and the biological ones.

b. How can privileging science become harmful, in Pollan's view?

Prewriting for a Directed Summary

Now that you have used the questions above to understand "The American Paradox" as a whole, use the following questions as a guide to focus your attention on a particular perspective in the essay. This perspective will be important when you are working on your own essay in response to the writing topic for this assignment. Be sure to use the answers you give below when it is time to write a clear and coherent directed summary in response to the writing topic's first question.

first question in the writing topic:

According to Pollan, what is wrong with the way Americans think about eating today?

Although this question asks you to explain Pollan's views, it doesn't ask you to summarize the entire reading selection. Be sure to keep the question in mind as you present his ideas.

Hint

Be sure to look back to Part 1 and reread "A Review of the Guidelines for Writing a Directed Summary."

Focus Questions

1. When Pollan talks about the past, how does he think Americans decided the type and amount of food they ate, and the time and place to eat it?

2. What is responsible for the changes in the way Americans think about food, according to Pollan?

3. How can focusing on the nutritional value of foods be harmful to the health of Americans, in Pollan's view?

Developing an Opinion and Working Thesis Statement

The second question in the writing topic for "The American Paradox" asks you to take a position of your own. Your response to this part of the writing topic will become the thesis statement of your essay, so it is important to spend some time ensuring that it is fully developed and that it accurately reflects your position on the issue Pollan addresses. Use the framework below to develop your working thesis, but keep an open mind as you complete the prewriting pages that follow this one, and as you read and discuss the positions other writers take in the "Extending the Discussion" section of this chapter. You may find that, after giving more thought to the issue of food, you want to modify your position.

second part of the writing topic:

Do you agree with him?

Now that you have spent some time with "The American Paradox," you should have some idea about whether or not you are convinced by his argument. Remember that, at this stage of the writing process, you will develop only a working thesis statement. It will capture your position now, early in the thought process, and it may very well change as you do more exploration of the issue. Do you agree with Pollan?

Hint

It is a good idea to go back and review your answers to the "Questions to Guide Your Reading" to remind yourself of Pollan's central claim and his supporting evidence.

1. Use the following thesis frame to identify the basic elements of your working thesis statement:

   a. What is the issue of "The American Paradox" that the writing topic asks you to consider?

   _____

   b. What is Pollan's position on that issue?

   _____

   c. What is your position on the issue, and will you agree or disagree with Pollan's opinion?

   _____

   _____

   _____

2. Now use the elements you isolated in 1a, b, and c to write a thesis statement. You may have to revise it several times until it captures your idea clearly.

   _____

   _____

Prewriting to Find Support for Your Thesis

The last part of the writing topic asks you to support the position you put forward in your thesis statement. Well-developed ideas are crucial when you are making an argument because you will have to be clear, logical, and thorough if you are to be convincing. As you work through the exercises below, you will generate much of the 4Cs material you will need when you draft your essay's body paragraphs.

the writing topic's last part:

As you develop your argument, be sure to support your position with specific examples from your own experience, your observation of others, or your reading.

1. As you begin to develop your own examples, consider the ways in which you, your family, and your friends make choices about the food you eat. In the space below, list or freewrite about personal experiences that involved you, your friends, or your family in making decisions about food and diet. For example:

   List your favorite places to eat, favorite meals, or favorite food-related TV shows, movies, or books. What characteristics do they have that make them a favorite for you?

   Do you and your friends and family discuss food—for example, what to have for dinner, or what to prepare for a holiday or family celebration? Are decisions made solely on the basis of taste, or do other factors weigh into the discussions and ultimate decisions?

   Do you see any health factors in your friends and family that are related to the decisions they make about eating?

Keep in mind Pollan's idea that Americans have an "unhealthy obsession with healthy eating." Feel free to include any experience, however minor or incidental.

Once you've written your ideas, look them over carefully. Try to group your ideas into categories. Then, give each category a label. In other words, cluster ideas that seem to have something in common and, for each cluster, identify that shared quality by giving it a title.

2. Now broaden your focus; list or freewrite about examples from your studies, your readings, and your general knowledge of current events. For example:

> What are some of the food-related presentations commonly found in the media, say, in commercials, TV movies, talk shows, etc.? What is the overall message of these presentations?

> List any of the popular food trends that you've noticed over the past several years, such as the promotion of low-fat, low-carb, or high-protein diets. What is the effect of these trends, and what is the basis for your evaluation?

> Consider the food for sale in a local mall or downtown area where you live. Sit on a bench and observe how many of the people who walk by appear to have food-related health issues. Does the way that food is promoted and sold in these busy centers seem to support or contradict Pollan's view that Americans have an "unhealthy obsession with healthy eating"?

Once you've written your ideas, look them over carefully. Try to group your ideas into categories. Then, give each category a label. In other words, cluster ideas that seem to have something in common and, for each cluster, identify that shared quality by giving it a title.

Once you've created topics by clustering your ideas into categories, go through them and pick two or three specific ones to develop in your essay. Make sure that they are relevant to your thesis and that they have enough substance to be compelling to your reader. Then, in the space below, briefly summarize each item.

Hint

Once you've decided which categories and items you will use in your essay, take some time to explain below how each category and its items connect to your thesis statement. You will use these details for the next stage.

Revising Your Thesis Statement

Now that you have spent some time working out your ideas more systematically and developing some supporting evidence for the position you want to take, look again at the working thesis statement you crafted earlier to see if it is still accurate. As your first step, look again at the writing topic, and then write your original working thesis on the lines that follow it:

writing topic:

According to Pollan, what is wrong with the way Americans think about eating today? Do you agree with him? As you develop your argument, be sure to support your position with specific examples from your own experience, your observation of others, or your reading.

working thesis statement:

_____

_____

Remember that your thesis statement must answer the second question in the writing topic while taking into consideration the writing topic as a whole. The first question in the topic identifies the issue that is up for debate, and the last question reminds you that, whatever position you take on the issue, you must be able to support it with specific examples.

Often, after extensive prewriting and focused thought, you will find that the working thesis statement is no longer an accurate reflection of what you plan to say in your essay. Sometimes, only a word or phrase must be added or deleted; other times, the thesis statement must be significantly rewritten. The subject or the claim portion may be unclear, vague, or even inaccurate. When we draft, we work out our thoughts as we write them down; consequently, draft writing is almost always wordy, unclear, or vague. Look at your working thesis statement through the eyes of your readers and see if it actually says what you want it to say.

After examining it and completing any necessary revisions, check it one more time by asking yourself the following questions:

a. Does the thesis statement directly identify Pollan's argument?

b. Does your thesis state your position on the issue?

c. Is your thesis well punctuated, grammatically correct, and precisely worded?

Write your polished thesis on the lines below and look at it again. Is it strong and interesting?

_____

_____

Planning and Drafting Your Essay

Getting started on the draft is often the hardest part of the writing process because this is where you move from exploring and planning to getting your ideas down in a unified, coherent shape. Creating an outline will give you a basic structure for incorporating all the ideas you have developed in the preceding pages. An outline will also give you a bird's-eye view of your essay and help you spot problems in development or logic.

Hint

This outline doesn't have to contain polished writing. You may want to fill in only the basic ideas in phrases or terms.

Creating an Outline for Your Draft

I. Introductory Paragraph:

    A. An opening sentence that gives the reading selection's title and the author's full name, and that begins to answer the first question in the writing topic:

    _____

    B. Main points to include in the directed summary:

       1.

       2.

       3.

       4.

    C. Write out your thesis statement. (Look back to "Revising Your Thesis Statement," where you reexamined and improved your working thesis statement.) It should clearly agree or disagree with "The American Paradox" and state a clear position using your own words.

    _____

II. Body Paragraphs

    A. The paragraph's one main point that supports the thesis statement:

    _____

       1. Controlling idea sentence:

       _____

       _____

2. <u>C</u>orroborating details:

_____

_____

_____

_____

3. <u>C</u>areful description of why the details are significant:

_____

_____

_____

_____

4. <u>C</u>onnection to the thesis statement:

_____

_____

_____

_____

B. The paragraph's one main point that supports the thesis statement:

_____

1. <u>C</u>ontrolling idea sentence:

_____

_____

2. <u>C</u>orroborating details:

_____

_____

_____

_____

3. <u>C</u>areful description of why the details are significant:

_____

_____

_____

_____

4. Connection to the thesis statement:

_____

_____

_____

_____

C. The paragraph's one main point that supports the thesis statement:

_____

1. Controlling idea sentence:

_____

_____

2. Corroborating details:

_____

_____

_____

_____

3. Careful description of why the details are significant:

_____

_____

_____

_____

4. Connection to the thesis statement:

_____

_____

_____

_____

D. The paragraph's one main point that supports the thesis statement:

_____

1. Controlling idea sentence:

_____

_____

2. Corroborating details:

_____

_____

_____

_____

3. Careful description of why the details are significant:

_____

_____

_____

_____

4. Connection to the thesis statement:

_____

_____

_____

_____

III. Conclusion

A. Type of conclusion to be used:

_____

B. Key words or phrases to include:

_____

Use the following guidelines to give a classmate feedback on his or her draft. Read the draft through first, and then answer each of the items below as specifically as you can.

Name of draft's author: _____

Name of draft's reader: _____

The Introduction

1. Within the opening sentences,
    a. Pollan is correctly identified by first and last name.   yes   no
    b. the writing selection's title is included and
        placed within quotation marks.   yes   no
2. The opening contains a summary that
    a. explains what Pollan means by the term
        "the American paradox"   yes   no
    b. explains why he thinks Americans have an
        "unhealthy obsession with healthy eating"   yes   no
3. The opening provides a thesis that
    a. makes Pollan's conclusions clear.   yes   no
    b. gives the draft writer's opinion about those conclusions.   yes   no

If the answers to #3 above are yes, state the thesis below as it is written. If the answer to one or both of these questions is no, explain to the writer what information is needed to make the thesis complete.

_____

_____

_____

The Body

1. How many paragraphs are in the body of this essay? _____

2. To support the thesis, this number is   sufficient   not enough

3. Do paragraphs contain the 4Cs?

Paragraph 1	Controlling idea sentence	yes	no
	Corroborating details	yes	no
	Careful description of why the details are significant	yes	no
	Connection to the thesis statement	yes	no

Paragraph 2	Controlling idea sentence	yes	no
	Corroborating details	yes	no
	Careful description of why the details are significant	yes	no
	Connection to the thesis statement	yes	no
Paragraph 3	Controlling idea sentence	yes	no
	Corroborating details	yes	no
	Careful description of why the details are significant	yes	no
	Connection to the thesis statement	yes	no
Paragraph 4	Controlling idea sentence	yes	no
	Corroborating details	yes	no
	Careful description of why the details are significant	yes	no
	Connection to the thesis statement	yes	no
Paragraph 5	Controlling idea sentence	yes	no
	Corroborating details	yes	no
	Careful description of why the details are significant	yes	no
	Connection to the thesis statement	yes	no

(Continue as needed.)

4. Identify any of the above paragraphs that are underdeveloped (too short). _____

5. Identify any of the above paragraphs that fail to support the thesis. _____

6. Identify any of the above paragraphs that are redundant or repetitive. _____

7. Suggest any ideas for additional paragraphs that might improve this essay.

_____

_____

_____

The Conclusion

1. Does the final paragraph avoid introducing new ideas and examples that really belong in the body of the essay?	yes	no
2. Does the conclusion provide closure (let readers know that the end of the essay has been reached)?	yes	no
3. Does the conclusion leave readers with an understanding of the significance of the argument?	yes	no

4. State in your own words what the draft writer considers to be important about his or her argument.

_____

_____

_____

5. Identify the type of conclusion used (see the guidelines for conclusions in Part 1).

_____

Editing

1. During the editing process, the writer should pay attention to the following problems in sentence structure, punctuation, and mechanics:
   fragments
   fused (run-on) sentences
   comma splices
   misplaced, missing, and unnecessary commas
   misplaced, missing, and unnecessary apostrophes
   incorrect quotation mark use
   capitalization errors
   spelling errors

2. While editing, the writer should pay attention to the following areas of grammar:
   verb tense
   subject-verb agreement
   irregular verbs
   pronoun type
   pronoun reference
   pronoun agreement
   noun plurals
   misplaced and dangling modifiers
   prepositions

Final Draft Checklist

Content

_____ My essay has an appropriate title.

_____ I provide an accurate summary of Pollan's position on the issue presented in "The American Paradox."

_____ My thesis states a clear position that can be supported by evidence.

_____ I have enough paragraphs and argument points to support my thesis statement.

_____ Each body paragraph is relevant to my thesis.

_____ Each body paragraph contains the 4Cs.

_____ I use transitions whenever necessary to connect ideas to each other.

_____ The final paragraph of my essay (the conclusion) provides readers with a sense of closure.

Grammar, Punctuation, and Mechanics

_____ I use the present tense to discuss Pollan's argument and examples.

_____ I use verb tenses correctly to show the chronology of events.

_____ I have verb tense consistency throughout my sentences.

_____ I have checked for subject-verb agreement in all of my sentences.

_____ I have revised all fragments and mixed or garbled sentences.

_____ I have repaired all fused (run-on) sentences and comma splices.

_____ I have placed a comma after introductory elements (transitions and phrases) and all dependent clauses that open a sentence.

_____ If I present items in a series (nouns, verbs, prepositional phrases), they are parallel in form.

_____ If I include material spoken or written by someone other than myself, I have correctly punctuated it with quotation marks, using the MLA style guide's rules for citation.

Reviewing Your Graded Essay

After your instructor has returned your essay, you may have the opportunity to revise your paper and raise your grade. Many students, especially those whose essays receive nonpassing grades, feel that their instructors should be less "picky" about grammar and should pass the work on content alone. However, most students at this level have not yet acquired the ability to recognize quality writing, and they do not realize that content and writing actually cannot be separated in this way. Experienced instructors know that errors in sentence structure, grammar, punctuation, and word choice either interfere with content or distract readers so much that they lose track of content. In short, good ideas badly presented are no longer good ideas; to pass, an essay must have passable writing. So even if you are not submitting a revised version of this essay to your instructor, it is important that you review your work carefully in order to understand its strengths and weaknesses. This sheet will guide you through the evaluation process.

You will want to continue to use the techniques that worked well for you and to find strategies to overcome the problems that you identify in this sample of your writing. To recognize areas that might have been problematic for you, look back at the scoring rubric in this book. Match the numerical/verbal/letter grade received on your essay to the appropriate category. Study the explanation given on the rubric for your grade.

Write a few sentences below in which you identify your problems in each of the following areas. Then, suggest specific changes you could make that would improve your paper. Don't forget to use your handbook as a resource.

1. **Grammar/punctuation/mechanics**
   My problem:

   My strategy for change:

2. **Thesis/response to assignment**
   My problem:

   My strategy for change:

3. **Organization**
     My problem:

     My strategy for change:

4. **Paragraph development/examples/reasoning**
     My problem:

     My strategy for change:

5. **Assessment**

In the space below, assign a grade to your paper using a rubric other than the one used by your instructor. In other words, if your instructor assigned your essay a grade of *High Fail*, you might give it the letter grade you now feel the paper warrants. If your instructor used the traditional letter grade to evaluate the essay, choose a category from the rubric in this book, or any other grading scale that you are familiar with, to show your evaluation of your work. Then, write a short narrative explaining your evaluation of the essay and the reasons it received the grade you gave it.

     Grade: _____

     Narrative: _____

     _____

     _____

     _____

     _____

Extending the Discussion: Considering Other Viewpoints

Readings

"Why Study Food?" by Warren Belasco

"Loving Animals to Death" by James McWilliams

"Science Says There's No Such Thing as 'Comfort Food.' We All Beg to
  Differ." by Emma Brockes

"Food as Myth" by Marcel Danesi

"Subsistence Hunting" by Gary L. Comstock

WHY STUDY FOOD?

WARREN BELASCO

Warren Belasco is a professor of American studies at the University of Maryland, Baltimore County, and editor of the journal Food, Culture & Society. *His books on American food production and consumption, and the relation of these to history, culture, and the environment, have contributed to the recent emergence of food studies as an academic subject for study at American colleges and universities. The following reading selection is from his book* Food: The Key Concepts *(2008).*

Food is the first of the essentials of life, the world's largest industry, our most frequently indulged pleasure, the core of our most intimate social relationships. It's very hard to imagine a positive social experience that does not involve the sharing of food—whether a simple cup of tea with an acquaintance, a lunchtime "bite" with colleagues, or a sumptuous lobster dinner with a lover. On a broader level, civilization itself is impossible without food: With the invention of agriculture some ten thousand years ago came city states and empires, art, music, and organized warfare. Agriculture remade the world, both physically and culturally, transforming landscapes and geography, subsidizing soldiers and poets, politicians and priests (Diamond 1999: 236).

For French epicure Brillat-Savarin, we are what we eat—and for Lucretius, we are what we won't eat. Our tastes are as telling as our distastes. To be a member of the Parakana people of the Amazon rain forest is to relish roasted tapir and to despise monkey meat, while the neighboring Arara feel quite the reverse (Rensberger 1991: A3). Food identifies who we are, where we come from, and what we want to be. "Food reveals our souls," sociologist Gary Alan Fine writes. "Like Marcel Proust reminiscing about a madeleine or Calvin Trillin astonished at a plate of ribs, we are entangled in our meals" (1996:1). Food is "a highly condensed social fact," anthropologist Arjun Appadurai observes, "and a marvelously plastic kind of collective representation" (1981: 494).

Food is also the object of major anxiety, for what and how we eat may be the single most important cause of disease and death. We can't live without food, but food also kills us. As psychologist Paul Rozin puts it, "Food is fundamental, fun, frightening, and far-reaching" (1999: 9-30). And probably nothing is more frightening or far-reaching than the prospect of running out of food. "A hungry stomach will not allow its owner to forget it, whatever his cares and sorrows," Homer wrote almost three thousand years ago. Even in good times, we are not allowed to forget our deeply rooted heritage of food insecurity. "When thou hast enough," Ecclesiasticus warned, *c.*180 BCE, "remember the time of hunger." As if to take advantage of the brief break from habitual scarcity, our bodies store up fat for the next famine—hence the current obesity crisis—while our prophets warn us against complacency. For much of history, the search for sufficient food drove the conquest and colonization of continents—and the enslavement or eradication of entire populations. Food matters. It has weight, and it weighs us down.

And yet, until recently, scholars were amazingly reluctant to study food, especially the aspect closest to our hearts (and arteries): food consumption. To be sure, food *production* has received considerable attention in established disciplines such as economics, chemistry, agronomy, engineering, marketing, and labor relations. Scientists have long explored the negative pathologies of malnutrition, hunger, and adulteration. But when it comes to analyzing the more positive and intimate features of what, how, and why we eat, academics have been considerably more reticent. Even now, with the rising interest in food studies, a serious analysis of family dinner rituals, cookbooks, or the appeal of fast food may still evoke surprise and even scorn. "Do professors really study *that*!" your friends and family ask. "If you're going to go around telling your colleagues you are a philosopher of food," philosopher Lisa Heldke writes, "you [had] better be prepared to develop a thick skin—and start a wisecrack collection" (2006: 202). Why this reluctance to address the wider meaning of our food behaviors? Why is food taken for granted, at least in academia?

For one thing, intellectuals are heirs to a classical dualism that prizes mind over body. In *Cooking, Eating, Thinking*, Heldke and her colleague Deane Curtin write, "Our tradition has tended to privilege questions about the rational, the unchanging, and the eternal, and the abstract and the mental; and to denigrate questions about embodied, concrete, practical experience" (Curtin and Heldke 1992: xiv). Philosopher Carolyn Korsmeyer agrees that "Taste and eating [are] tied to the necessities of existence and are thus classified as lower functions . . . operating on a primitive, near instinctual level" (1999: 1). There may indeed be some archetypal, dualistic disdain for something as mundane, corporeal, even "animalistic" as eating. "Put a knife to thy throat," urges Proverbs 23:2, "if thou be a man given to appetite." "Reason should direct and appetite obey," Cicero counseled in 44 BCE (Egerton 1994: 17). "Govern thy appetite well," advised Puritan poet John Milton, "lest Sin Surprise thee, and her black attendant Death" (Egerton 1994: 18). To some extent, we may still live with the prejudices of the nineteenth century, which gave birth to so many modern institutions, ranging from research universities to dinner parties. Genteel Victorians constructed such elaborate dining rituals partly because they harbored a deep suspicion of eating, which—like sex—they viewed as basically uncivilized. The novelist Joyce Carol Oates characterizes that attitude nicely: "Civilization is a multiplicity of strategies, dazzling as precious gems inlaid in a golden crown, to obscure from human beings the sound of, the terrible meaning of, their jaws grinding—the meaning of man's place in the food cycle that, by way of our imaginations, we had imagined might not apply to us" (1993: 25). In other words, food is gross.

Food scholarship has also been hindered by another Victorian relic, the "separate spheres"—the idealized bourgeois division between the private female sphere of *consumption* and the more public male sphere of *production*. While the concept did not reflect the daily realities for most women—to this day, women are major food producers across the globe—the ideological polarization certainly influenced the development of middle-class academia, for it effectively segregated women professionals in less valued "domestic" disciplines, particularly dietetics, home economics, social work, and nutrition education (along with elementary school teaching, nursing, and library science). Conversely, the male-dominated realms of industrial agriculture, food technology, mass retailing, and corporate management *have* generally received more public respect and academic prestige.

This institutionalized bias delayed serious attention to food even after the women's movement obliterated the separate spheres. While more women began to enter all fields of academia in the 1960s, it took several decades before scholars could begin to consider the traditional female ghetto of domesticity without Victorian-era blinders and prejudices, and even today, feminists who do treasure their cooking heritage and skills may risk the hostility of colleagues who feel that women should move on to more "serious" pursuits. In recent years, there have been significant and largely sympathetic reappraisals of women's food work (e.g., Strasser

1982, Cowan 1983, Shapiro 1986, 2004, DeVault 1991, Mennell et al. 1992, Avakian 1997), but the identification of food with oppression still slants the scholarship—as evidenced, perhaps, by the fact that there may be more research devoted to women's eating disorders than to women's positive connections to food.

The association of cooking with women's enslavement leads to another major reason for food's relative invisibility: technological utopianism. For millennia, food *has* meant unrelenting drudgery, not just for cooks, but also for all food workers—farmers, field laborers, butchers, grocers, clerks, servers, and so on. Since at least the nineteenth century, many reformers have attempted, in a sense, to "disappear" food, to make it less visible and less central as a burden or concern. Progressives applauded the modern economic shift from messy food production to automated manufacturing and white collar office jobs. Feminist utopians embraced almost any idea that would get food out of the home and thus free up women: the meal in a pill, foods synthesized from coal, centralized kitchens, and "self-service" electric appliances and convenience foods. For example, in 1870, novelist Annie Denton Cridge dreamed of a large, mechanized cooking establishment that, by feeding an eighth of Philadelphia's population at one seating, would give housewives time to read, think, and discuss big ideas—and all at a cost lower "than when every house had its little, selfish, dirty kitchen" (Belasco 2006a: 110). Similarly, farmer-utopians dreamed of push-button, fully automated factory farms as a way to save their children from back-breaking labor and rural isolation. Today we can recognize that those dreams came true; sort of. Whereas once most people were farmers, now a relative handful of highly mechanized farmers grows almost all our food, and in providing over fifty million meals a day, McDonald's comes very close to Cridge's "one big kitchen" vision. But the result has been further distancing from the traditional rituals, sensibilities, and practices of food production—as well as some negative consequences for our health and environment.

Even more important in distancing us from nature and tradition have been the efforts of the food industry to obscure and mystify the links between the farm and the dinner table. While these efforts were stepped up in the mid-nineteenth century (reflected in the above-mentioned, gendered separation of production from consumption), they date at least as far back as the first global food conglomerate, the East India Company, which was dedicated to bringing exotic foodstuffs to European dining rooms and whose annual report in 1701 observed, "We taste the spices of Arabia yet never feel the scorching sun which brings them forth." In other words, this food company was rather proud that thanks to its noble service in distant lands, affluent consumers did not have to experience the strenuous and often violent production processes by which their sausage got peppered or their tea sweetened. Perhaps the most vivid recent example of how we no longer have to feel the "scorching sun" of food production is the meat-packing industry, whose main thrust over 150 years has been to insulate consumers from any contact with the disassembly of warm-blooded mammals into refrigerated, plastic-wrapped chops and patties. "Forget the pig as an animal," a modern livestock management journal advises. "Treat him just like a machine in a factory" (Byrnes 1976: 30). In his environmental history of Chicago, *Nature's Metropolis*, William Cronon writes that the meat-packing industry of the late nineteenth century actively encouraged such "forgetfulness." "In the packers' world it was easy not to remember that eating was a moral act inexorably bound to killing" (Cronon 1991: 256).

By the 1920s, the relationship between supplier and customer, plow and plate, was largely anonymous, as noted by agricultural geneticist Edward East: "Today [1924] one sits down to breakfast, spreads out a napkin of Irish linen, opens the meal with a banana from Central

America, follows with a cereal of Minnesota sweetened with the product of Cuban cane, and ends with a Montana lamb chop and cup of Brazilian coffee. Our daily life is a trip around the world, yet the wonder of it gives us not a single thrill. We are oblivious" (East 1924: 64). If consumers in the 1920s were already complacent about what East called the "globe-girdling" food supply system, they are even more "oblivious" now, when the "forgetfulness" applies not just to spices, sugar, or meat, but to virtually everything we consume: tomatoes, bread, pasta, shrimp, apple juice, grapes, cornflakes, and so on. Food is so vague in our culture in part because, thanks to processing, packaging, and marketing, it *is* an abstraction—an almost infinite set of variations on a theme of corn, which, Michael Pollan demonstrates, is the basis of so many modern foodstuffs, from Big Macs to Twinkies (Pollan 2006: 15–31). According to farmer-poet Wendell Berry, the ideal corporate customer today is the "industrial eater . . . who does not know that eating is an agricultural act, who no longer knows or imagines the connections between eating and the land, and who is therefore necessarily passive and uncritical" (1989: 126). And furthering the critical challenges to those attempting to uncover the complex commodity chains connecting field and fork is the fact that people may not eat as regularly or as socially as they used to. Given that modern meals themselves are so ephemeral, it is not surprising that it takes some effort to see food as a subject worthy of serious social analysis.

Yet, despite these difficulties and delays, there is no question that more people are studying food than ever before. While it may be premature to announce the birth of a new discipline of food studies, signs of increased activity are everywhere. In addition to the food-related papers now presented regularly at mainstream academic conventions, there have been a number of major international conferences devoted entirely to food, and these have, in turn, resulted in published collections (e.g., Lentz 1999, Grew 1999, Mack 1999, Dietler and Hayden 2001, Belasco and Scranton 2002, Jacobs and Scholliers 2003). New academic journals are appearing, culinary history societies are mushrooming, and publishers are announcing food series. There is also a lively market for food-related memoirs, essays, and annotated historical recipes. Serious analyses of the food system by Michael Pollan, Eric Schlosser, Laura Shapiro, and Marion Nestle straddle both "trade" (general) and textbook audiences. There are dozens of excellent websites devoted to the disciplined exploration of foodways, not to mention the thousands of sites dedicated to cooking, gastronomy, nutrition, and restaurant reviews. As hundreds of professors offer undergraduate food-related courses, several universities have established food studies concentrations and degrees, while other students seek to "do food" within conventional disciplines such as history, anthropology, and literary studies.

Trend-watchers might ask, why now? In part, scholarship is following wider urban middle-class culture, which, since the 1970s, has become much more interested in food-related matters of taste, craft, authenticity, status, and health. Food scholars belong to the same affluent social class that has fueled an unprecedented expansion and elaboration of restaurant and supermarket options, and this well-educated, trend-conscious public is literally hungry for analysis and perspective. Enthusiastic journalists and documentary filmmakers popularize the new work of food scholars. Socially conscious food professionals—chefs, managers, cookbook writers, etc.—also mingle and exchange ideas with food professors. Furthermore, as the world seems to spin helplessly from one major political crisis to another, large segments of the public look for ways to assert some control over their lives—and watching what you eat may be one such way to feel in charge of your destiny. Along these lines, the academic left has found food studies to be a fertile base for activist analysis of hunger, inequality, neo-colonialism, corporate accountability, biotechnology, globalization, and ecological sustainability. These concerns underlie much of the food scholarship today and animate many new food studies courses, in which students often attempt to recover and illuminate the invisible links in the global food chain. Finding out where our food comes from is an important step toward taking responsibility for our food's true *cost,* which Henry David Thoreau defined as "the amount of life exchanged for it, immediately or in the long run" (Orr 1994: 172).

So while food studies is now "respectable," it is also inherently subversive. To study food often requires us to cross disciplinary boundaries and to ask inconvenient questions. The food supply belongs to us all, yet in the past one hundred years or so, we have delegated the responsibility for understanding and controlling just about every step of the metabolic process to highly credentialed experts. These specialists have managed to mystify food so thoroughly that many people simply throw up their hands in justifiable confusion when it comes to understanding essential issues of health, agriculture, and business, not to mention cooking and taste. Michael Pollan writes, "Somehow this most elemental of activities—figuring out what to eat—has come to require a remarkable amount of expert help." Decrying "our national eating disorder," Pollan asks, "How did we ever get to a point where we need investigative journalists to tell us where our food comes from and nutritionists to determine the dinner menu?" (Pollan 2006: 1). Yet all too often the experts have led us astray—as for example the period after the Second World War, when specialists with endowed chairs at elite universities assured us that the first modem pesticide, DDT, was perfectly safe, that the Basic Four Food Groups constituted the best diet, and that in the near future, we'd be defeating world hunger with steaks made from algae, yeast, and coal dust. Specialists are useful to have around, of course, since modern life is far too complex for us to understand everything. But the problem with relying entirely on specialists is that sometimes they're wrong. Or worse, they tend to disagree. So to help us sort out the issues and gain some needed perspective, we need generalists—people with a decent grounding in science *and* poetry, agriculture *and* philosophy, who are not afraid to question assumptions, values, and methods. True, we may not understand all the biochemistry involved in nutrition, but we can speculate about why certain foods "taste good" at particular times and to particular people. We may not be able to explain why one pesticide works better on mites than another, but we can still ask why farm workers' children seem especially cancer-prone. We may not fully understand how genetic engineering works, but we still can wonder whether it is necessary in the first place. Such issues require that we think about matters political, historical, economic, sociocultural, and scientific *all at once.* As generalists, we study food as a *system.* Such holistic thinking actually restores our sense of power and humanity, for when it comes to eating, humans *are* generalists, i.e., omnivores.

While interdisciplinary study may entail a freewheeling crossing of disciplinary boundaries, it also requires a careful integration of themes or models on which to hang all these disparate ideas and insights. One needs to avoid the smorgasbord approach to learning—a little of this, a little of that. Or, to use another food metaphor, you can't leave a supermarket without bags to put all the groceries in; otherwise, you have a big mess on the floor. The inquiry needs sturdy containers in which to carry all that stuff away. To organize our inquiry, this book begins with the single question, "So what's for dinner?" Deciding what to eat may not be as simple as it sounds, for "Since Eve ate apples," Byron quipped, "much depends on dinner." Eating entails a host of personal, social, and even global factors that, in their entirety, add up to a complex *food system.* To sort out these variables, imagine a triangle with one point at the top and two on the bottom. Focus first on the baseline: Call the left point "Identity;" the right "Convenience." And call the apex "Responsibility."

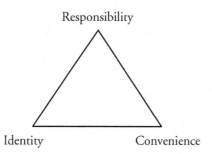

Responsibility

Identity   Convenience

For the most part, people decide what to eat based on a rough negotiation—a pushing and tugging—between the dictates of identity and convenience, with somewhat lesser guidance from the considerations of responsibility. (The triangle is thus not quite equilateral, though the moralist might wish it were so.)

"Identity" involves considerations of personal preference, pleasure, creativity, the sense of who and where you are. Identity includes factors such as taste, family and ethnic background, personal memories (the association between particular foods and past events, both good and bad). The cultural aspects of identity include widely shared values and ideas, extravagant notions about the good life, as well as a community's special food preferences and practices that distinguish it from other communities—for example, those tapir-relishing Parakana versus the tapir-hating Arara. Gender also matters considerably in many cultures, as foods are often grouped as "male" and female"—for example, steaks versus salads. Deeply rooted in childhood, tradition, and group membership, the culinary dictates of identity are hard to change because they raise questions such as "How do I eat it?," "Should I like it?," "Is this *authentic*?," and "Is this what people like me eat?" At the identity point, food choices are expressed through rituals, etiquette, symbols, and arts. In studying food and identity, we look at what, where, and how people eat— and *don't* eat. And we examine how they represent, play with, and think about their food.

"Convenience" encompasses variables such as price, availability, and ease of preparation, which are all related to the requirements of energy, time, labor, and skill. In other words, convenience involves concerns such as "Can I get it?, " "Can I afford it?," and "Can I make it?" Accounting for these all-important factors of convenience will lead us to look at the global food chain—the series of steps and processes by which food gets from farm to fork. Hence, we should examine the role of the people and institutions that make food accessible to us—e.g., farmers, migrant workers, processors, supermarkets, and restaurants. By smoothing food's flow from field to plate, for a price, the food industry sells us convenience. To be sure, there are enormous differences in the degree of convenience afforded different consumers. Some of us in the world have almost instant access to an unprecedented array of meal options, while other people's choices are severely restricted by economics, environment, and social structure. Such differences are starkly presented in *Hungry Planet,* where thirty families from all over the world are lined up separately behind a week's worth of food. Families from North America, Europe, Australia, and Kuwait are almost hidden by immense piles of plastic-wrapped "convenience foods," while people from Mali, Ecuador, and India seem much larger than the baskets of unprocessed grains and produce they consume. Somewhere in between, representing the world's "middle class," families from the Philippines, China, and Egypt stand around tables covered with raw fruits and grains as well as bottled soft drinks and bags of snacks (Menzel and D'Aluisio 2005).

And then, there's the matter of responsibility, which I put at the apex of the triangle not because it is the strongest factor but because maybe it *should* be. Responsibility entails being aware of the consequences of one's actions—both personal and social, physiological and political. It can involve short-term, acute consequences: Will this meal make me sick tomorrow? And it can involve long-term effects: Will it make me sick thirty years from now? Being responsible means being aware of one's place in the food chain—of the enormous impact we have on nature, animals, other people, and the distribution of power and resources all over the globe. It means feeling that "scorching sun" of the East India Company's Arabian enterprises; or appreciating Thoreau's "amount of life exchanged" to get your meal from farm to fork; or calculating, as the Great Law of the Iroquois Confederacy once attempted, "the impact of our decisions on the next seven generations." In eating even the simplest dish, we join a chain of events linking people and places across the world and across time, too—past and future. "We are paying for the foolishness of yesterday while we shape our own tomorrow," environmentalist William Vogt wrote in 1948. "Today's white bread may force a break in the levees and flood New Orleans next spring. This year's wheat from Australia's eroding slopes may flare into a Japanese war three decades hence." Having a sense of responsibility entails both remembering how the food got to you (the past) and anticipating the consequences down the line (the future). "We must develop our sense of time and think of the availability of beefsteaks not only for this Saturday but for the Saturdays of our old age, and of our children" (Vogt 1948: 285, 63). Ultimately, assigning responsibility is a political process, for it entails sorting out the separate duties of individual consumers, food providers, and government. The poet-farmer Wendell Berry writes that "To eat responsibly is to understand and enact, as far as one can, the complex relationship" between the individual and the food system (Berry 1989: 129).

Although I have placed responsibility at the apex of my triangle, it is often the weakest of the three forces pulling at the individual food consumer. Still, many of us do want to be "conscientious consumers." "The unexamined life is not worth living," Socrates argued on behalf of acute self-consciousness. Also, knowing that "there's no free lunch," few of us want to be considered "deadbeats"—irresponsible people who skip out on the check, or worse, let our children pay our debts and then leave them worse off. "We're committing grand larceny against our children," was the charge put by environmental moralist David Brower when describing our reliance on wasteful, unsustainable resources and technologies. "Ours is a chain-letter economy, in which we pick up early handsome dividends and our children find their mailboxes empty" (as cited in McPhee 1971: 82). We must consider some of the consequences—personal and political, immediate and distant—of our food choices and practices.

To illustrate the complexities and rewards of taking this type of comprehensive, multidisciplinary approach to food, let's think about the simple act of toasting a piece of sliced white bread. Start with identity: Where does toast fit in the morning meal rituals of certain peoples? Why have so many cultures traditionally valued processed white grains over more nutritious whole grains, while wholegrain bread is now an elite marker? Why do we like the crunchy texture ("mouth feel") of toasted foods, and is the fondness for toasted *bread* widespread or, as one encyclopedia suggests, "Anglo-bred"? (Tobias 2004: 122). Why is wheat bread the "staff" of life in some cultures, while others put rice or corn tortillas in that central position? "No foodstuff bears greater moral and philosophical burden" than bread, food writer Tom Jaine observes (1999: 97). Who invented the sandwich, and what social function does it serve? Why do some cultures prefer wraps to sandwiches?

Then there are the convenience factors: Who grew, gathered, milled, and packaged the wheat? Who baked the bread? How did bread get so cheap? To turn the wheat into inexpensive sliced bread required the coordinated efforts of numerous companies specializing in food transportation, storage, processing, and marketing, as well as many others involved in manufacturing and selling tractors, trucks, slicers, and so on. Who invented sliced bread, anyway? When did store-bought white bread replace homemade whole wheat? When did they start putting vitamins back in white bread, and why? And who invented the pop-up toaster, and why?

And as for responsibility, think of toast's enormous "ecological footprint" (Wackernagel and Rees 1996). Growing that wheat helped some farmers pay their bills while also polluting their water supply with fertilizers and pesticides, eroding their soil, and, if they used irrigation, lowering their region's water table. The land used to grow the wheat had been acquired—or seized—long ago from other living creatures, human and otherwise, and converted to growing a grass that had originated as a weed in the Middle East and had been gradually domesticated and improved by five hundred generations of gatherers, peasants, farmers, and, only just recently, scientists. By extending the bread's shelf life, the plastic wrapping lowered costs, raised consumer convenience, and increased profits for corporate processors, distributors, and supermarkets. That packaging also helped to put thousands of neighborhood bakers out of business. Making the plastic from petrochemicals may have helped to foul Cancer Alley in Louisiana, and if the oil came from the Middle East, may have helped to pay for the restoration of royalty in Kuwait, which was destroyed several years ago by an Iraqi army *also* financed by petrochemical bread wrappers. (Or perhaps the oil came from Venezuela, where it paid for Hugo Chavez's left-leaning reorganization of the oligarchy.) The copper in the toaster and electrical wiring may have been mined during the dictatorships of Pinochet in Chile, Mobutu in Zaire, or Chiluba in Zambia. The electricity itself probably came from a power plant burning coal, a source of black lung, acid rain, and global warming. And so on. All of this—and much more—involved in making toast. And we have not even mentioned the butter and jam!

While the variables affecting our decision to toast bread are complex, they are relatively uncontroversial compared with the triangle of tense contradictions surrounding the decision to eat another central staple, meat. Identity: The ability to afford meat has long served as a badge of success, health, and power, especially for men. Throughout the world, economic mobility has almost invariably meant an increase in meat consumption—a process called a "nutrition transition" (Sobal 1999: 178). Given the prestige accorded beef, particularly in the West, it is not surprising that the "cowboy"—a Spanish invention *(vaquero)*—has achieved mythical status. While some cultures accord culinary primacy to cattle, others prize pigs, sheep, poultry, fish, and rodents, and some eat no meat at all. Westerners have long denigrated vegetarian cuisines, and such prejudices have even been reflected in medical texts, as in a 1909 text: "White bread, red meat, and blue blood make the tricolor flag of conquest." "The rice-eating Hindoo and Chinese, and the potato-eating Irish are kept in subjection by the well-fed English," influential Victorian physician George Beard agreed. Conversely, vegetarians may frame meat-eaters as less "civilized," as in George Bernard Shaw's famous prediction, "A hundred years hence a cultivated man will no more dream of eating flesh or smoking than he now does of living, as [Samuel] Pepys's [seventeenth century] contemporaries did, in a house with a cesspool under it." Whether staple or taboo, animal foods carry significant cultural meaning throughout the world (Belasco 2006a: 8, 10). Convenience: Biologically, meat may be prized because it offers a compact package of nutrients. It can be relatively easy to cook, especially if it is of the well-fatted, grain-fed variety produced by the modern livestock industry. Meat production has long been the focus of many laborsaving innovations—hence the early rise of the slaughterhouse "disassembly" line, which in turn became the model for so many other mass production industries. A significant proportion—perhaps even most—of modern agricultural science is devoted to devising ever more efficient ways to grow cheap corn and soy for livestock, especially fat-marbled beef. And making this meat convenient—cheap, easy, and accessible—is also a primary goal and achievement of the fast food industry.

But the responsibility considerations are enormous: acute poisoning from "dirty beef"; chronic heart disease from animal fats; the possible mistreatment of animals and workers in animal factories; the immediate and long-term impact on the environment in terms of energy, groundwater pollution, soil loss, and even climate change. The resource-intensive nature of animal production has been known for centuries. William Paley's 1785 *Principles of Moral and Political Philosophy* observes: "A piece of ground capable of supplying animal food sufficient for the subsistence of ten persons would sustain, at least, the double of that number with grain, roots, and milk." In 1811, radical publisher Richard Phillips argued that British farmers could potentially feed 47,000,000 vegetarians "in abundance," "but they sustain only twelve millions *scantily*" on animal products (Belasco 2006a: 5).

In addition, there are the conflicts ensuing from differences in diet, especially meat-eaters vs. vegetarians. In Plato's *Republic*, written over 2,400 years ago, Socrates argued that because domesticated meat production required so much land, it inevitably led to territorial expansion and war with vegetarian neighbors (Adams 1992: 115). *In Guns, Germs, and Steel*, Jared Diamond suggests that Eurasia—Plato's home region—was the origin of many expansionist empires precisely because it harbored such an abundance of domesticated mammals (1999: 157-175). According to medievalist Massimo Montanari, invasion of the declining, and still largely vegetarian, Roman Empire by northern, meat-eating "barbarians" brought widespread deforestation and consolidated landholding to accommodate larger herds of livestock (1999: 77-78). Following the adoption of this Germanic model, environmental historian William Cronon observes, "domesticated grazing animals—and the tool which they made possible, the plow—were arguably the single most distinguishing characteristic of European agricultural practices." And after 1492, European livestock may have done more to destroy Native American ecosystems than all the invading armies combined (1983: 128). "The introduction of livestock proved to be the greatest success story in the culinary conquest of America," Jeffrey Pilcher observes in his history of Mexican foodways. "Herds [of cattle] overran the countryside, driving Indians from their fields" (1998: 30).

Differences in gender attitudes toward meat also have had important consequences. Men have long invoked their power over women as a rationalization for having the best cuts of scarce meat, and such differences in nutrition may indeed have made men more powerful than women deprived of iron, protein, and calcium. In short, with so much at stake in our steaks, there is an almost classic conflict between the rich rewards and stark consequences of an animal-based diet. Such conflicts make for exciting drama—and interesting study. . . .

But perhaps the best place for the individual consumer to begin to reconcile the contradictory tugs of identity, convenience, and responsibility is in the kitchen. As I tell my students at the end of my food course, if you want to create a better future, start by learning to cook. In our quick-and-easy age, it's one of the more subversive things you can do, for when you cook you take control of a piece of the food chain. Moreover, you may start to wonder how the food got to your kitchen—and that's a really good question.

Works Cited

Adams, Carol J. (1992), *The Sexual Politics of Meat: A Feminist-Vegetarian Critical Theory*, New York: Continuum.

Appadurai, Arjun (1981), "GastroPolitics in Hindu South Asia," *American Ethnologist* 8(3): 494–511.

Avakian, Arlene Voski (ed.) (1997), *Through the Kitchen Window: Women Writers Explore the Intimate Meanings of Food and Cooking*, Boston: Beacon Press.

Belasco, Warren, and Scranton, Philip (eds), (2002), *Food Nations: Selling Taste in Consumer Societies*, New York: Routledge.

Belasco, Warren, (2006), *Meals to Come: A History of the Future of Food*, Berkeley: University of California Press.

Berry, Wendell (1989), "The Pleasures of Eating," *Journal of Gastronomy* 5(2): 125–31.

Byrnes, J. (1976), "Raising Pigs by the Calendar at Maplewood Farm," *Hog Farm Management* (September): 30.

Cowan, Ruth Schwartz (1983), *More Work for Mother: The Ironies of Household Technology from the Open Hearth to the Microwave*, New York: Basic Books.

Cronon, William (1983), *Changes in the Land: Indians, Colonists, and the Ecology of New England*, New York: Hill and Wang.

Cronon, William (1991), *Nature's Metropolis: Chicago and the Great West*, New York: Norton.

Curtin, Deane, and Heldke, Lisa M. (eds) (1992), *Cooking, Eating, and Thinking: Transformative Philosophies of Food*, Bloomington, IN: Indiana University Press.

DeVault, Marjorie L. (1991), *Feeding the Family: The Social Organization of Caring as Gendered Work*, Chicago: University of Chicago Press.

Diamond, Jared (1999), *Guns, Germs, and Steel: The Fates of Human Societies*, New York: Norton.

Dietler, Michael, and Hayden, Brian (eds) (2001), *Feasts: Archaeological and Ethnographic Perspectives on Food, Politics, and Power*, Washington, DC: Smithsonian Institution Press.

East, Edward M. (1924), *Mankind at the Crossroads*, New York: Charles Scribner's Sons.

Egerton, March (ed.) (1994), *Since Eve Ate Apples*, Portland, OR: Tsunami Press.

Fine, Gary Alan (1996), *Kitchens: The Culture of Restaurant Work*, Berkeley: University of California Press.

Grew, Raymond (ed.) (1999), *Food and Global History*, Boulder: Westview Press.

Heldke, Lisa (2006), "The Unexamined Meal Is Not Worth Eating, or Why and How Philosophers (Might/Could/Do) Study Food," *Food, Culture, and Society: An International Journal of Multidisciplinary Research* 9(2): 201–19.

Jacobs, Marc, and Scholliers, Peter (eds), (2003), *Eating Out in Europe*, Oxford: Berg.

Jaine, Tom (1999), "Bread," in Alan Davidson (ed.), *Oxford Companion to Food*, New York: Oxford University Press, pp. 95–8.

Korsmeyer, Carolyn (1999), *Making Sense of Taste: Food and Philosophy*, Ithaca, NY: Cornell University Press.

Lentz, Carola (ed.) (1999), *Changing Food Habits: Case Studies from Africa, South America, and Europe*, Amsterdam: Harwood.

Mack, Arien (ed.) (1999), "Food: Nature and Culture," *Social Research* 66(1).

McPhee, John (1971), *Encounters with the Archdruid: Narratives about a Conservationist and Three of His Natural Enemies*, New York: Farrar, Straus & Giroux.

Mennell, Stephen, Murcott, Anne, and van Otterloo, Anneke (1992), *The Sociology of Food: Eating, Diet, and Culture*, London: Sage.

Menzel, Peter, and D'Aluisio, Faith (2005), *Hungry Planet*, Berkeley: Ten Speed Press.

Montanari, Massimo (1999), "Food Systems and Models of Civilization," in Jean-Louis Flandrin and Massimo Montanari (eds), *Food: A Culinary History from Antiquity to the Present*, New York: Columbia University Press, pp. 69–78.

Oates, Joyce Carol (1993), "Food Mysteries," in Daniel Halpern (ed.), *Not for Bread Alone*, Hopewell, NJ: Ecco Press, pp. 25–37.

Orr, David (1994), *Earth in Mind: On Education, Environment, and the Human Prospect*, Washington, DC: Island Press.

Pilcher, Jeffrey M. (1998), *Que Vivan los Tamales! Food and the Making of Mexican Identity*, Albuquerque, NM: University of New Mexico Press.

Pollan, Michael (2006), *The Omnivore's Dilemma: A Natural History of Four Meals*, New York: Penguin.

Rensberger, Boyce (1991), "Anthropology: Diets that Define Amazon Tribes," *Washington Post*, December 30, p. A3.

Rozin, Paul (1999), "Food is Fundamental, Fun, Frightening, and Far-Reaching," in Mack, Arien (ed.), "Food: Nature and Culture," *Social Research* 66(1), pp. 9–30.

Shapiro, Laura (1986), *Perfection Salad: Women and Cooking at the Turn of the Century*, New York: Farrar, Straus & Giroux.

Shapiro, Laura (2004), *Something from the Oven: Reinventing Dinner in 1950s America*, New York: Viking.

Sobal, Jeffrey (1999), "Food System Globalization, Eating Transformations, and Nutrition Transitions," in Raymond Grew (ed.), *Food in Global History*, Boulder, CO: Westview, pp. 171–93.

Strasser, Susan (1982), *Never Done: A History of American Housework*, New York: Pantheon Books.

Tobias, Ruth (2004), "Toast," in Andrew Smith (ed.), *Oxford Encyclopedia of Food and Drink in America*, New York: Oxford University Press, p. 122.

Vogt, William (1948), *The Road to Survival*, New York: William Sloane Associates.

Wackernagel, Mathis, and Rees, William (1996), *Our Ecological Footprint: Reducing Human Impact on the Earth*, Gabriola Island, BC: New Society Publishers.

Discussion Questions

1. Explain Warren Belasco's statement that "civilization is impossible without food." Imagine a world without any industry or cultural traditions related to food. Describe the changes in daily living that would result. After doing this mental exercise, why do you think that Belasco's statement is or is not basically correct?

2. What reasons does Belasco give to explain the previous lack of any serious study of food? Why do you think that currently there is an increase in food studies? What would Pollan say?

3. Reproduce Belasco's food pyramid. Explain each point on the triangle in relation to the *food system*. Now discuss these labels in relation to your own diet. Consider which point most often governs your food choices, and tell why you do or do not feel physically, emotionally, and intellectually satisfied with your diet.

4. Belasco refers, in "Why Study Food," to Pollan, and summarizes some of what Pollan argues in "The American Paradox." Go back and review what Belasco says about Pollan's view. Make two lists, one itemizing Pollan's basic assertions, and the other itemizing Belasco's. Compare the two lists. What ideas do these two writers share? Do you find any areas of disagreement? Explain.

LOVING ANIMALS TO DEATH

JAMES McWILLIAMS

James McWilliams earned a PhD in history from Johns Hopkins University, and is an American history professor at Texas State University, San Marcos. He has written numerous books and articles, and he has published several editorials on food in publications such as the New York Times *and* USA Today. *His books include* A Revolution In Eating: How the Quest for Food Shaped America *(2005) and* Just Food: Where Locavores Get It Wrong and How We Can Truly Eat Responsibly *(2009). The following is an article from the* American Scholar, *and was published in 2014.*

Bob Comis of Stony Brook Farm is a professional pig farmer—the good kind. Comis knows his pigs, loves his pigs, and treats his pigs with uncommon dignity. His animals live in an impossibly bucolic setting and "as close to natural as possible" (Comis). They are, he writes, so piggy that they are Plato's pig, "the ideal form of the pig" (Comis). Comis's pastures, in Schoharie, New York, are playgrounds of porcine fun: "They root, they lounge, they narf, they eat, they forage, they sleep, they wallow, they bask, they run, they play" (Comis). And when the fateful day of deliverance arrives, "they die unconsciously, without pain or suffering" (Comis).

Comis's patrons—educated eaters with an interest in humanely harvested meat—are understandably eager to fill their forks with Comis's pork. To them, Comis represents a new breed of agrarian maverick intent on bucking an agricultural-industrial system so bloated that a single company—Smithfield Foods—produces six billion pounds of pork a year. Comis provides a welcome alternative to this industrial model, and if the reform-minded Food Movement has its way, one day all meat will be humanely raised and locally sourced for the "conscientious carnivore."

Except for one problem: Comis the humane pig farmer believes that what he does for a living is wrong. Morally wrong. "As a pig farmer, I live an unethical life," he wrote recently on the *Huffington Post (Comis)*. He's acutely aware that he "might indeed be a very bad person for killing animals for a living" (qtd. in Southan). Comis's essential objection to his line of work is that he slaughters sentient and emotionally sophisticated beings. His self-assessment on this score is unambiguous. His life is one that's "shrouded in the justificatory trappings of social acceptance" (Comis). To those who want their righteous pork chop, he asserts that "I am a slaveholder and a murderer" and that "what I do is wrong" (Comis). Even if "I cannot yet act on it," he concludes, "I know it in my bones" (Comis).

The Food Movement

Chances are good that you've never heard of Bob Comis. The carnivorously inclined Food Movement would like to keep it that way. With his confession of ethical transgression, he has strayed dangerously from the movement's script. To appreciate the full impact of Comis's defection, it helps to understand something about the Food Movement itself—a loosely organized but powerful coalition of progressive interests, or "a big, lumpy tent," as the phenomenon's leader, author Michael Pollan, calls it ("Food Movement"). Its members aim to localize, downsize, and decentralize the North American food system in order to usher consumers "beyond the barcode" and into a world of wholesome whole food ("Food Movement").

The movement's reformist concerns are more structural than dietary. What ultimately matters to its followers is where their food comes from and how it's prepared rather than what exactly they're eating. You want to eat hog testicles (which a waitress at an upscale Austin, Texas, restaurant recently urged me to order)? Go for it—but just make sure they come from a nonindustrial, local, and humane farm. Craving a plate of "fried pig head"? Sure thing. But it had better come from a venue such as Grange Kitchen and Bar, Ann Arbor's haven of, as one local blogger calls it, "slow foodie mentality." In a noble quest to end the abuses of an overly industrialized agribusiness machine that churns out foodlike substances, the movement—with libertarian-like zeal—fosters a radical freedom of culinary choice. *Dietary restriction* is a phrase generally absent from its lexicon.

But there are standards. Off-grid food freedom should be exercised at the Saturday farmers market or by a slow-food chef rather than in the sterile aisles of a fluorescent-lit Walmart Supercenter. This message is reiterated at every farmers market in the country: Eat all the animals you want—and every part!—so long as they come from Bob Comis and not Oscar Mayer. Do that, and you will not only do right by animals and the small farms that nurture them, but you will also be making important political contributions to the future of real food. You will be creating a food culture in which you can eat the whole hog and, at the same time, put the Chinese-owned Smithfield Foods out to pasture. That aspiration, especially if you enjoy the taste of meat, has become increasingly popular and hard to resist.

Sometimes the movement's rhetoric gets ahead of itself. It can overstate the connection between processed junk food and historically complex social problems ("the advent of fast food," Pollan has written, "has, in effect, subsidized the decline of family incomes in America") ("Food Movement"). And the movement's well-to-do spokespeople can exhibit a tin ear when it comes to the politics of inclusion (restaurateur Alice Waters: "Some people want to buy Nike shoes—two—pairs—and other people want to eat Bronx grapes, and nourish themselves") (qtd. in Birdsall). That said, few conscientious followers of food politics disagree with the movement's core principles, especially when they're articulated by likable ambassadors such as Pollan (a gifted writer), the avuncular Wendell Berry (a contemporary Thoreau), and even Waters herself, who has been known to weep when the integrity of slow food is challenged.

All of which is to say that the Food Movement, despite its missteps and melodrama, is a relatively new but quite formidable force generally pushing the right kind of goals. Consumers with an interest in food justice should root for it to succeed. Who, after all, doesn't think it's a noble idea to eliminate food deserts, serve local broccoli to school kids, make fresh and healthful food more accessible, eliminate pink slime from the food chain, grow kale in the Midwest, and not have a secretary of agriculture from a corn-and-soy state? These are benevolent objectives by any standard.

But still, some skeptics have wondered whether any of the Food Movement's reforms are even remotely achievable if reformers continue to ignore the ethical considerations involved in eating meat. Simply put, when it comes to the Food Movement's long-term viability, could it be that changing what we eat is more important than improving its source? Might the only way to reform our food system—rather than simply providing alternatives—be to stop raising animals for consumption? Pollan has addressed these questions by explaining, "what's wrong with animal agriculture—with eating animals—is the practice, not the principle" (*Omnivore's* 328). But what if he's got that backward? What if, when it comes to eating animals, the Food Movement's principles are out of whack?

The Omnivore's Contradiction

Tacking his rogue thesis—*raising and killing my happy pigs is unethical*—to the doors of the Food Movement's church, Comis creaked those doors open for a philosophical investigation into the principle of killing animals for food we do not need. For an earnest movement aiming to radically alter the way we feed ourselves, this self-exam is long overdue. From Jeremy Bentham's famous moral distinction—"The question is not 'Can [animals] reason,' nor 'Can they talk,' but 'Can they suffer?'"—to Peter Singer's *Animal Liberation* to Tom Regan's *The Case for Animal Rights,* philosophers have, through various perspectives, been building a multifaceted and daunting case that animals have relevant interests and, as a result, deserve a basic level of moral consideration. It may very well follow that because of this moral consideration, we cannot justifiably raise sentient animals and kill them for food when we could replace them with plant-based substitutes. Granted, few philosophers would maintain that it's *always* unethical to eat animals—there may be persuasive cases for doing so under certain circumstances. However, after two centuries of debate on the issue, their arguments do show that the bar has been set higher than most of us acknowledge. In short, it matters to a pig that it leads a pleasurable life. On what grounds can we ignore that interest, kill the animal, and make a pork chop?

This is not a parlor game. Indeed, Comis's call for a more philosophical approach to animal agriculture is neither an arbitrary nor an academic appeal to an abstract notion of animal rights. Instead, it's grounded in the humble workings of daily life, especially the humble, if complex, workings that bring to our plate animal protein—which has been shown to be not only unnecessary but often harmful to human health. A secular and religious consensus exists that living an ethical life means accepting that my own interests are no more important than another's simply because they are mine. Basic decency, not to mention social cohesion, requires us to concede that like interests deserve equal consideration. If we have an interest in anything, it is in avoiding unnecessary pain. Thus, even though a farm animal's experience of suffering might be different from a human's experience of suffering, that suffering requires that we consider the animal's interest in not being raised and eaten much as we would consider our own interest in not being raised and eaten. Once we do that, we would have to demonstrate, in order to justifiably eat a farm animal, that some weighty competing moral consideration was at stake. The succulence of pancetta, unfortunately, won't cut it.

The Food Movement should be game for a serious discussion of this issue. Its own rhetoric urges us to "know where [our] food comes from" and to trace our ingredients "from farm to fork" (McWilliams 2, 26). Leading figures in the movement would thus seem poised to embrace this line of ethical inquiry as a critical step in the larger effort to reform our "broken food system" (McWilliams 2). Animal agriculture is at the heart of almost every major ill that plagues industrial agriculture. Identify an agrarian problem—greenhouse gas emissions, overuse of antibiotics and dangerous pesticides, genetically modified crops, salmonella, *E. coli,* waste disposal, excessive use of water—and trace it to its ultimate origin, and you will likely find an animal. Given that centrality, it's reasonable to expect the Food Movement to leap at the opportunity to grapple with the implications of Comis's conundrum. Research shows that veganism, which obviates the inherent waste involved in growing the grains used to fatten animals for food in conventional systems, is seven times more energy efficient than eating meat and, if embraced globally, could reduce greenhouse gas emissions from conventional agriculture by ninety-four percent. Any pretext to explore meat-eating's moral underpinnings—and possibly land upon an excuse for pursuing a plant-based diet as a viable goal—would be consistent with the movement's anticorporate, ecologically driven mission.

But with rare exception, those in the big, lumpy tent have thrown down a red carpet for "ethical butchers" while generally dismissing animal rights advocates as smug ascetics (which they can be) and crazed activists (ditto) who are driven more by sappy sentiment than rock-ribbed reason. It's an easy move to make. But the problem with this dismissal—and the overall refusal to address the ethics of killing animals for food—is that it potentially anchors the Food Movement's admirable goals in the shifting sands of an unresolved hypocrisy. Let's call it the "omnivore's contradiction."

Conscientious carnivores will argue that we can justify eating animals because humans evolved to do so (the shape of our teeth proves it); that if we did not eat happy farm animals, they'd never have been born to become happy in the first place; that all is fine if an animal lives well and is "killed with respect"; that we need to recycle animals through the agricultural system to keep the soil healthy; that animals eat animals; and that in nature, it's the survival of species and not of individuals that matters most. These arguments create room for a productive conversation. But none of them carry real weight until the Food Movement resolves the contradiction raised by Bob Comis: How do you ethically justify both respecting and killing a sentient animal?

Killing Them with Kindness

Consider why those in the Food Movement want to end the abuses of industrial animal agriculture in the first place: environmental, health, and labor conditions, for starters. As conventional agriculture's damaging effects on natural resources, obesity rates, and workplace justice and safety become increasingly obvious, angry consumers want alternatives. Gargantuan corporate consolidation—which seems only to intensify the worst aspects of industrial agriculture—generates further popular outrage. Even higher on the list for most concerned consumers, though, is the mistreatment of the animals. What makes us cringe is their incessant abuse. How can it ever be okay to chop off an animal's tail without anesthesia, lock it in a cage so tight it cannot turn around, toss live male chicks into a grinder, or jam an electric prod into a cow's anus—all of which are standard procedures on industrial farms? Everyone gets the point intuitively: No self-aware creature should be subjected to this relentless gauntlet of abuse—especially when the purpose of that suffering is merely to satisfy our palates. If only by virtue of our own moral gag reflex, then, we have granted animals a basic level of moral consideration.

The Food Movement's popularity is built upon this idea: that animals raised in factory farms have *qualities* that make them worthy of our moral consideration. Animals are not objects, and their welfare matters to the extent that they should not suffer the abusive confines of factory farms. They deserve the time, space, and freedom to exist as the creatures they were born to be. These concerns assume that farm animals—given their ability to experience suffering in industrialized settings—have authentic emotional lives and intrinsic worth. Our belief that they should not suffer abuse in confinement recognizes their fundamental moral status as sentient beings. They *can* suffer, and as a direct result, we *should*, whenever possible, avoid inflicting suffering upon them. If animals didn't matter to us in a moral sense, then the harm systematically inflicted upon them in industrial operations would pose no ethical concerns whatsoever. We'd be indifferent to their abuse.

If the Food Movement's stance on animals raised in factory farms is clear, it grows murky when applied to nonindustrial, more humane, farms. Indeed, that's where the omnivore's contradiction comes into sharp focus. The Food Movement's premises about farm animals are (we will assume for now) adequately met on most small, sustainable, humane farms. Still, there's no denying that even on the most impressive of these farms—no matter how much their owners talk about a respectful death—animals are raised for the ultimate purpose of being killed and turned into commodities. The Food Movement habitually minimizes this reality, but the fact remains: Just as on factory farms, animals on humane farms are, on slaughter day, transformed through raw violence into objects, after which they are commodified, consumed, and replaced with all the efficiency of car parts.

Ethically speaking, matters at this point become significantly more complicated. This is where, after all, practice and principle suddenly converge, revealing the heart of the hypocrisy: the elevation of *how* animals are raised as a moral consideration (poorly in factory farms; well on humane farms) above *why* we are raising them (to kill and eat them in both cases). It is at this crucial moment in a farm animal's life—the human choice to slaughter the beast against its will—that the moral consideration so effectively deployed to condemn the factory farming of animals loses its punch and its plausibility. Which, again, brings us to the contradiction.

It seems not only reasonable but essential to ask: How can a movement claim to care so deeply about farm animals that it wants to restructure all of animal agriculture to ensure their happiness but, at the same time, turn those same animals into an eleven-dollar appetizer plate of fried pig head? What moral principle could possibly accommodate such a whiplash-inducing shift in practice? And if there were such a principle, would you ever want it to guide your life? Bob Comis, who embodies the omnivore's contradiction with such self-awareness, articulates the problem this way in a recent interview with *Modern Farmer* magazine:

> [L]ivestock farmers lie to their animals. We're kind to them and take good care of them for months, even years. They grow comfortable with our presence, and even begin to like us. But in the end, we take advantage of the animals, using their trust to dupe them into being led to their own deaths.

With kindness, they kill them.

Writing Death out of Life

The Food Movement's failure to recognize this contradiction is most obvious in the culturally pioneering work of its well-known leading tastemakers: Pollan, food journalist Mark Bittman, and novelist Jonathan Safran Foer. Together, these writers embody the omnivore's contradiction by evading the question. They are quick to put down factory farming and insist that farm animals have intrinsic worth. Animals are not objects. They have feelings. They suffer inexcusable pain and frustration. But their eloquent screeds ring hollow the moment they use the horrors of factory farming to justify artisanal production and its ultimate aim: *nicer* killing: More palatable killing. More attractive and marketable killing.

Writing about pigs housed in concentrated animal feeding operations (CAFOs), Pollan, in *The Omnivore's Dilemma*, nails it. He offers genuinely empathetic observations, writing how radical hog confinement causes a "depressed pig," a "demoralized pig," a pig divorced from his "natural predilections" (Pollan 218, 219). He laments the way pigs in CAFOs are "crowded together beneath a metal roof standing on metal slats suspended over a septic tank" (Pollan, *Omnivore's* 218). After visiting a free-range farm where privileged pigs were being happy pigs, Pollan admitted that he "couldn't look at their spiraled tails … without thinking about the fate of pigtails in industrial hog production" (where tails are docked) (Pollan, *Omnivore's* 218). Explaining how pigs in confinement experience a "learned helplessness," he writes, "It's not surprising that an animal as intelligent as a pig would get depressed under these circumstances" (Pollan, *Omnivore's* 218).

Bittman, the influential *New York Times* "Minimalist" food columnist, has regularly reported on the dreadful fate of animals on factory farms. The author of *How to Cook Everything Vegetarian,* he routinely arms his readers with disturbing facts and figures. We learn that the number of cows and broiler chickens housed in factory farms doubled between 1997 and 2007, and that the number of "large livestock operations" almost quadrupled between 1982 and 2002 (Bittman, "Is the U.S."). And Bittman connects these numbers to the emotional turmoil experienced by the animals themselves. "Until a couple of years ago," he confessed in 2012, "I believed that the primary reasons to eat less meat were environment—and health—related" (Bittman, "Human Cost"). While acknowledging that such rationales remain valid, he added, "But animal welfare has since become a large part of my thinking as well" (Bittman, "Human Cost").

As with Pollan, Bittman has experienced an epiphany in realizing that the animals we eat have critical interests in avoiding pain. An undercover Humane Society video of a Smithfield Foods hog facility exposing the chilling abuse of pigs left the columnist, a thoroughly seasoned food writer, "pretty much speechless" (Bittman, "Is Factory Farming"). He lambastes Smithfield Foods for its "infuriating disregard for the welfare of their animals" (Bittman, "Is Factory Farming"). He even suggests that animal abuse in factory farming quietly damages the human psyche, exhorting readers "to look at how we treat animals and begin to change it" (Bittman, "Human Cost").

Foer has also influenced the public's disdain for factory farming—perhaps even more than Pollan and Bittman. Foer's best-selling book *Eating Animals* brought the condemnation of industrial agriculture into more impressively detailed and thoughtful territory. Young people in particular were moved to forgo meat by Foer's nuanced but accessible analysis. He quotes an industrial poultry farmer who explains how turkey hens are killed after a year of life "because they won't lay as many eggs in the second year" (Foer, *Eating Animals* 60). It is, the farmer continues, "cheaper to slaughter them and start over than it is [to] feed and house birds that lay fewer eggs" (Foer, *Eating Animals* 60). Through revealing anecdotes such as this one, Foer illuminates the icy banality of animal objectification, showing how easy it is to overlook the suffering of animals raised on factory farms in the full knowledge of those who perpetuate it. After an overview of the egg industry as a whole, Foer concludes with an appropriate sense of disgust: "I didn't ever want to eat a conventional egg again" (Foer, *Eating Animals* 60).

"Nothing we do," Foer also writes, "has the direct potential to cause nearly as much animal suffering as eating meat" (Foer, *Eating Animals* 73–74). and he makes those words sing when he wonders, "What is suffering? I'm not sure *what* it is, but I know that suffering is the name we give to the origin of all the sighs, screams, and groans—small and large, crude and multifaceted—that concern us" (Foer, *Eating Animals* 77). Suffering is Foer's focus and motivation, the basis of the idea that farm animals are entitled, at the least, to enjoy their lives and not have them arbitrarily cut short for a back-yard barbecue. His message was shrill enough for Pollan to reduce his thoughts on Foer's book to two words in a *New York Review of Books* essay: "vegetarian polemic" ("Food Movement").

Given all this, it's not unreasonable to expect that these writers might advocate an end to raising and killing animals for food. But they are not prepared to take that stand. This decision—this curious dodge—is bound to rot the movement from within. It's a typical sleight of hand of which Pollan is a master. To wit, he explained to Oprah Winfrey in 2011 that after deliberating about the legitimacy of eating meat, "I came out thinking I could eat meat in this very limited way, from farmers who were growing it in a way that I could feel good about how the animals lived" ("Best of Oprah").

How is it possible to ethically raise, love, and then kill an animal "in this very limited way"? If Pollan really does want to "feel good" about an animal's quality of life—much in the way he would, say, his pet dog's—then what's the exact justification for cutting that life short (by something like seventy-five percent) for a menu choice? Wouldn't it be better to spare the pseudo-philosophizing and just admit (as Comis did, until he announced on his blog in February that he had become a vegetarian) that he likes meat too much to stop consuming it? And if *that's* the competing consideration—loving meat—then all humanitarian ballyhooing over animals in factory farms becomes meaningless, as do the arguments over animal suffering in general.

Bittman also dances a version of this dance, writing that "meat-eating may be too strong [a habit] for most of us to give IT up" ("Human Cost"). But this is patronizing. Millions of consumers have given up meat, and many go further by giving up dairy and all animal products. Bittman, himself, kind of joined them by claiming to embrace "semi-veganism": no animal products before dinnertime; carnivorism afterward ("No Meat"). It's a confabulation, a dubious premise that purports to achieve the unachievable—that is, getting to a "place where we continue to eat animals but exchange that privilege . . . for a system in which we eat less and treat [animals] better" (Bittman, "Human Cost"). Bittman's use of "privilege" here is telling, granting as it does special immunity to "responsible" meat-eaters who, unlike Comis or the 7.3 million other vegetarians in the United States, have faced the ethical conundrum.

Foer's own decision to promote the consumption of animals from humane farms in the wake of a book that turned a lot of people into vegetarians is especially confounding. In October 2012, he responded to a question about the morality of killing animals for food by saying, "The answer doesn't really matter. Maybe it's fun, intellectually, to consider the question. But let's talk about what's actually in front of us" (Foer, "Does Jonathan"). Back to that whole principle and practice thing. A few months before making this remark, Foer could be found (briefly) on YouTube promoting a Farm Forward app informing concerned consumers where to buy the right kind of chicken. Foer, who has explicitly exposed the horror of death for industrial chickens, wants us to know where to get humanely killed poultry because, it is assumed, that's the choice that's "actually in front of us."

But is that all that's in front of us?

What Else Is "Actually in Front of Us"?

Look, I get it. These writers are being pragmatic and, for better or worse, pragmatism is persuasive and professional. Their habitual appeal to more humane alternatives, and their tacit rejection of a plant-based diet as an explicit path to food reform, is an example of preventing, as the saying goes, the perfect from being the enemy of the good. Plus, industrial agriculture is so obviously antithetical to animal welfare that any nonindustrial operation by definition will appear to be superior and, in turn, garner public support. Why bother with the heavy lifting of moral consistency when consumers can salve their consciences about continuing to eat animals in a way that's socially acceptable?

This question—and the logic behind it—has not only shaped the message of our leading "agri-intellectuals," but it has even inspired global organizations with a professional stake in animal welfare—the Humane Society of the United States, for one—to support small-scale, humane animal agriculture as an end in itself rather than as a stepping stone to eliminating animals from our diets. "We at HSUS," according to its president and CEO, Wayne Pacelle, "embrace humane farmers and an alternative production strategy to factory farming." The Humane Society is advocating eating animals? Well, yes. They do so because, as a personal choice, eating less meat is perceived to be easier than eating no meat.

Foer asks us to consider the reality we live in when evaluating our position on eating animals. So let's end by doing that. Let's consider the nature of nonindustrial animal agriculture, bringing the same level of scrutiny to those operations that we bring to factory farms. Do this, and two damning realities begin to emerge. Together, they emphasize the consequences of the movement's failure to follow the logic of its own findings and to promote, as it should, the end of animal agriculture as a revolutionary path to agrarian reform, one with the potential to meet the movement's most passionately articulated goals.

The first is that the economics of nonindustrial animal agriculture doesn't work. Consolidation pays. Pasture-based systems are a costly alternative to factory farming and will by necessity appeal primarily to Bittman's "privileged" consumers rather than have broad appeal to the carnivorous masses. In perhaps the most important and overlooked book published on animal agriculture in a generation, Jayson Lusk and F. Bailey Norwood's *Compassion, by the Pound,* the authors—agricultural economists—document the hard economic reality of humane farming. They show beyond a doubt that Plato's pig requires the riches of Croesus and a horde of foodies willing to pay a mint for meat. Of course, many carnivores will happily do that. Niche support for humane meat, however, will do very little to challenge the overall allure of cheap protein churned out by agribusiness. Most consumers will always rally around the lowest price. If there is no stigma against eating animals, the cheapest options will prevail. And so will agribusiness. Simply put: You can't beat the devil at his own game.

The second unrecognized reality is that although nonindustrial animal agriculture might appear to be substantially more humane than industrialized agriculture, small farms are only nominally more accommodating of farm animals' full interests. My research for a book looking into the downside of small-scale animal agriculture has revealed that problems reminiscent of factory farms readily plague many of their smaller counterparts, too. Owning animals for the purposes of slaughter and consumption means that ethical corners will be cut to enhance the bottom line. As competition for privileged consumers increases, this corner cutting can be expected only to intensify.

A short list of routine and sometimes unavoidable problems prevalent on nonindustrial animal farms, all noted by farmers themselves, includes the following: excessive rates of pastured animals being killed by wild and domestic animals, mutilation of pig snouts to prevent detrimental rooting, castration without anesthesia, botched slaughters, preventive (and illicit) antibiotic use, outbreaks of salmonella and trichinosis, acute pasture damage, overuse of pesticides and animal vaccines, and routine separation of mothers and calves. Animals granted a little more space, in other words, still suffer the negative consequences of being owned for exploitation. Given that they are destined to be commodities, not companions, this should not come as a surprise. Hence the ultimate cost of failing to address the omnivore's contradiction: the ongoing suffering of the animals that farmers and foodies say they care so much about.

Nobody is envisioning the immediate liberation of farm animals. We will never realistically face a scenario in which the billions of animals we now kill for food roam the landscape in search of sanctuary. But what we can envision—and what the Food Movement should envision—is a radical shift in agricultural practice initiated by a radical shift in what enlightened consumers agree not to eat. This transition would primarily favor far more diversified systems of production focused on growing plants for people to consume (right now, seventy-five percent of all the world's calories in food production comes from corn, rice, wheat, and soy, and the bulk of all corn and soy goes to livestock). Necessarily complementing this shift would be a gradual but sharp reduction in the practice of raising animals for the purposes of killing them for food, with smaller, more humane farms serving as a necessary but temporary phase in the larger mission of ending animal agriculture altogether.

Once these two related developments are complete, or at least well underway, the Food Movement could then initiate useful debates over the residual uses of animals in food production. If we keep chickens to help fertilize the soil or to be our pets, can we justify eating their eggs? Should we establish municipal programs to process road kill into safe culinary options? Should we eat animals such as jellyfish that proliferate in ecologically dangerous ways? These discussions are all worth having, but not until we make genuine progress toward ending the agricultural tradition of raising animals capable of suffering and then eating them.

"I Have This Thing for Cows"

In addition to insisting that it "doesn't really matter" whether it's morally wrong to raise and kill animals, Foer also explained that this "question is the least relevant to the choices we make on a daily basis" ("Does Jonathan"). In other words, because our culture is so deeply infused with animal products, it makes little practical sense to investigate the morality of eating animals. People don't care. I might have agreed with Foer before last semester, when I helped teach a course called Eating Animals in America. But in that class, something happened that opened my eyes to the Food Movement in a new way. We had read Timothy Pachirat's *Every Twelve Seconds,* a graphic look into the workings of an industrial slaughterhouse. In our discussion, one student—an elaborately tattooed Iraqi war veteran, Purple Heart, competitive weight lifter, and active Texas rancher—told his classmates, all of whom were disgusted by what they'd read, that there was a better way. There was, he insisted, an entirely different way to go about treating cattle. My colleague and I asked this student—let's call him Mike—if he'd be willing to open the next class by describing how he handles slaughtering cattle on his family's ranch, where they kill two cows a year for personal consumption. He generously agreed.

Mike began by explaining how horrified he was by Pachirat's description of the way that the industrial operation's cattle were treated. He was visibly angered. His hands were balled in fists. Having grown up around cattle and admitting that "I have this special thing for cows," even more than his dogs, he said that slaughtering his animals with dignity was of the utmost importance. Mike described how his family cared for the calves, nurtured maternal bonds, made sure that the animals had access to open pasture during nice weather and shelter from storms, monitored feed, never had to administer antibiotics or vaccines, and showered the animals with physical affection. Lots of scratches and rubs. And then he took a deep breath, looked at the class with icy blue eyes, and began to explain how, to kill the cow humanely, you had to create a quiet atmosphere, make sure the knife was sharp, gather the whole family around, and . . and then he paused. He looked shocked for a second as his voice caught in his throat. His eyes darted around the room at his fellow students, who were dead silent. He took another deep breath and began to talk about severing the spinal cord. And then he was overcome. I sensed that a cathartic moment was coming and so looked hard at his eyes as they began to fill up with tears. The only thing I remember thinking was that this rancher is seeking a new path that nobody is providing. And that there's no way he is alone.

Works Cited

"Best of Oprah—Oprah & 378 Staffers Go Vegan: The One-Week Challenge." *The Oprah Winfrey Show*. 1 Feb. 2011. Television.

Birdsall, John. "Cheap Drama at Slow Food." *The Chow Blog*. CBS Interactive Inc., 14 Dec. 2011. Web. N.d. <http://www.chow.com/food-news/101027/slow-food-usa/>.

Bittman, Mark. "The Human Cost of Animal Suffering." *New York Times*. The New York Times Company, 13 Mar. 2012. Web. N.d.

—. "Is Factory Farming Even Worse Than We Know?" *Markbittman.com*. N.p., 15 Dec. 2010. Web. N.d. <http://markbittman.com/horrific-animal-abuses-uncovered-at-smithfiel/>.

—. "Is the U.S. One Big Factory Farm?" *Markbittman.com*. N.p., 3 Dec. 2010. Web. N.d. <http://markbittman.com/america-the-sht-factory/>.

—. "No Meat, No Dairy, No Problem." *New York Times*. The New York Times Company, 29 Dec. 2011. Web. N.d.

Comis, Bob. "The Importance of Our Evolution beyond Killing for Food." *Huffington Post*. TheHuffingtonPost.com, Inc., 3 Jan. 2014. Web. N.d.

Foer, Jonathan Safran. "Does Jonathan Safran Foer Believe It's OK to Kill Animals?" Interview by the Beet-Eating Heeb. *Thebeeteatingheeb.com*. N.p., 24 Oct. 2012. Web. N.d. <http://thebeeteatingheeb.com/2012/10/>.

—. *Eating Animals*. New York: Little, Brown, 2009. Print.

McWilliams, James E. *Just Food: Where Locavores Get It Wrong and How We Can Truly Eat Responsibly*. New York: Little, Brown, 2009. Print.

Pacelle, Wayne. "*The Modern Farmer* Interview: Wayne Pacelle." By Twilight Greenaway. *Modern Farmer*. Modern Farmer Media, 24 May 2013. Web. N.d.

Pollan, Michael. "The Food Movement, Rising." Review. *New York Review* of Books 10 June 2010. Web. N.d. ,http://www.nybooks.com/articles/archives/2010/jun/10/food-movement-rising/>.

—. *The Omnivore's Dilemma: A Natural History of Four Meals*. New York: Penguin, 2006. Print.

Southan, Rhys. "Farm Confessional: I Raise Livestock and I Think It May Be Wrong." *Modern Farmer*. Modern Farmer Media, 5 Feb. 2014. Web. N.d. <http://modernfarmer.com/2014/02/farm-confessional-raise-livestock-think-may-wrong/>.

Discussion Questions

1. What are the goals of the Food Movement? Do you think the achievement of these goals is possible in the near future? Explain.

2. Do you think McWilliams would ever be able to fit under, in Michael Pollan's words, the "big, lumpy tent" that characterizes the various interests that constitute the Food Movement? Explain.

3. Define the "omnivore's contradiction," and list the justifications given by Food Movement adherents for ignoring it. Explain your own reasons for finding their responses either convincing, or, as McWilliams does, hypocritical.

4. Retell the two examples in this article of individuals who had a change of heart about killing animals for food. Why did you find them more or less convincing than the other facts and quotations in the article?

SCIENCE SAYS THERE'S NO SUCH THING AS "COMFORT FOOD." WE ALL BEG TO DIFFER.

EMMA BROCKES

Emma Brockes graduated from Oxford University and is a writer and a journalist. She writes on a number of subjects. Her first book, What Would Barbra Do? *(2007), explores her great affection for, and interest in, stage musicals. Her most recent book,* She Left Me the Gun: My Mother's Life before Me *(2014), is a memoir that traces Brockes's journey to South Africa after her mother's death to find out what drove her mother to emigrate from Johannesburg to London. The following reading is from her blog, which is published by the* Guardian, *an online weekly newspaper.*

Most of us know this intuitively—that comfort and junk foods are subtly distinct. The former is an emotional as well as a nutritional unit, and the latter is merely a sugar rush. Besides which, no cookbook would dare put the word "junk" in its title, but whole shelves are devoted to the art of the comfort food. If, after a hard day, you make yourself mashed potatoes with gravy, or mac and cheese with brown sauce, or scrambled eggs with the consistency of an Ultimate Frisbee, it is probably because someone once made it for you exactly that way. And while no two people's comfort foods are alike, the terrain is broadly the same: sloppy food you can spoon-feed yourself, with at least one element everyone else finds revolting.

For this reason, other people's comfort food has an editorial interest. It has a story, as Mark Bittman reflected recently in the *New York Times* in a charming piece about bagels and lox. Or it adds a certain humanity to high office. Madeleine Albright, in an interview I did with her many years ago, volunteered that after a rough day, "I come home, put on a flannel nightgown, [and] make myself the most disgusting thing, which is cottage cheese with ketchup." If one needs further evidence for how fascinating other people's food choices are, one need only look at all the websites devoted to death row inmates' last meals.

So it is with some surprise, then, that we greet research coming out of the University of Minnesota this month suggesting that our faith in certain foods to lift our spirits and soothe our feelings is entirely without cause. In a study presented at a meeting of the Association for Psychological Science, subjects were asked to come up with two foods—one they thought of as a "comfort" food—which is to say a food which they said had the power to change their moods—and one that they liked but which had no emotional resonance. As in a scene from *A Clockwork Orange*, subjects were then shown a video designed to disturb them in some way and, after it was over, asked how they felt (which was always unhappy). They were then given either their self-identified comfort food, the other food, a granola bar (as a kind of kill-joy control), or nothing at all—and again asked how they were feeling. The results surprised even the researchers. Irrespective of which food they ate, three minutes after the test, all participants in the study had cheered up. "People can develop these very unhealthy habits, where they just immediately reach for these yummy foods when they feel sad," said researcher Hather

Scherschel Wagner. It makes no sense, she said, because "whether it's your comfort food, or it's a granola bar, or if you eat nothing at all, you will eventually feel better. Basically, comfort food can't speed up that healing process."

I have several problems with the methodology of this study, chief among them what happens when you ask people to self-report feelings. As we know from the way we ourselves might lie or exaggerate in a private journal, the very fact of studying one's own reaction to something changes its nature. Secondly, an artificially-induced feeling of crappiness is, one would think, completely different to the multi-layered and highly personal reasons one might turn to comfort food in regular life—a specific response to a specific and complicated psychological state that it is almost impossible to recreate in lab conditions.

Then again, the phenomenon of comfort food is barely complicated enough to merit study. When you are threatened, you retreat in your mind to places of happiness. Comfort food is merely an *aide-mémoire* that uses more than one of your senses.

None of this undermines the fact that most comfort foods are very bad for you and are only supposed to be a once-in-a-while measure. (Michelle Obama, writing in the *New York Times* on Thursday, reminded us of this by castigating the food lobbies for undermining efforts to promote healthy eating among children: "Remember a few years ago when Congress declared that the sauce on a slice of pizza should count as a vegetable in school lunches?")

But since comfort food really is just a route back into memory, it seems odd to reject it as meaningless—even if it is a placebo. As unfashionable cuisines come back into style—artisanal gefilte fish, anyone? —promoted by the grandchildren of their original enthusiasts, the overlap between food, family, and feeling is as strong as it ever was. Bread sauce the consistency of glue, fish finger sandwiches, shepherd's pie with meat and potato that can be mashed into a brown paste and other people at the table shout at you—it might not present well in research, but most of us know that happiness is made of exactly this.

Discussion Questions

1. Discuss the difference between comfort food and junk food. Give examples of things you have seen other people eat while under emotional stress. Describe your reaction to their choices.

2. What were the findings of the University of Minnesota's study on comfort foods? Why does Emma Brockes question the validity of this study? If you were conducting your own study on this topic, describe the changes you would make. Would Pollan agree with Brockes, or would he agree with the findings of the study?

3. What is an *aide-mémoire* is? How can food serve as an *aide-mémoire*? Identify a food and explain the reason that it functions as your *aide-mémoire*. Tell about a recent time when you enjoyed this particular food. How did eating it make you feel at that time?

4. Review Michael Pollan's essay and then list the points from his essay that you think Brocke would agree with. Compare the tone and development of the two readings. Do you think Brocke and Pollan are writing with the same readership in mind? Explain.

5. If Brocke decided to rewrite her essay for submission to a scholarly journal, what might her thesis statement look like? Draft one possible version.

FOOD AS MYTH

MARCEL DANESI

Marcel Danesi is a professor at the University of Toronto and the director of its program in semiotics and communication theory. The following reading selection is an excerpt from his book Of Cigarettes, High Heels, and Other Interesting Things: An Introduction to Semiotics *(1999).*

Mythic thinking is now largely unconscious, but it shows up nevertheless in social rituals, performances, and spectacles that are shaped by its themes. Even if we live in a culture that is based largely on rational thinking—for example, we plan our days around a series of socially fixed events, we mark time precisely, we live by the principles of science and technology—the mythic form of thinking and communicating has not disappeared from our system of everyday life. Its remnants are everywhere: We give cards with poetic, mythic messages on them, we tell nursery rhymes and fairy tales to our children, we read the horoscope daily, and so on. And, as the semiotician Roland Barthes shows, the presence of myth can be detected even in such an apparently idiotic spectacle as commercial wrestling. This spectacle is emotionally involving for many people because it represents a mythic fight between good and evil.

Barthes suggests that virtually anything that we consume or take part in communally continues to have mythic connotations that recall the kinds of beliefs that ancient people had. To grasp what he means, consider the kinds of attitudes people show towards food. In Canada and the United States, we tend not to eat rabbits, keeping them instead as pets. Why? The reason, Barthes would no doubt suggest, is that rabbits have a mythic status in our unconscious mind—think of all the stories we tell our children with rabbits in them as heroic figures (for example, the Easter Bunny). For this reason, we do not think of rabbit meat as edible in the same way as we do other kinds of animal meats that we routinely ingest, such as lamb meat, poultry meat, and especially cow meat. In North American culture, not only rabbits but also foxes and dogs are not eaten because they resonate with mythological meanings by way of our tales, legends, and traditions.

Similarly, the act of eating in a public setting typically reflects a ritualistic structure. We do not gobble food when others are around; we do it according to an *eating code*. The predictable routines leading up to the eating event at a high-class restaurant, for instance, are suggestive of an intrinsic need for ritual. There is no motive for eating at such places, really, other than to engage with our eating partner or partners in an act of symbolic acknowledgment that eating is basic to our existence, both biologically and symbolically.

So, what about fast food? How does it fit in with the theme of myth? In a society where "fast living" and "the fast lane" are appropriate metaphors for the system of everyday life, everything seems indeed to be "moving too fast," leaving little time for mythic rituals. However, this is not the case. Since the middle part of the twentieth century, the fast-food industry has become a multi-billion-dollar business. Why do people go to fast food restaurants, the semiotician would ask. Is it because of the food? Is it to be with friends and family? Is it because the food is affordable and the service fast? Is it because the atmosphere is congenial?

Most people would answer these questions affirmatively. The fast food restaurant seems to provide an opportunity to stay awhile with family or friends, and most people would acknowledge that the food at a McDonald's or a Wendy's is affordable and that the service is fast and polite. Indeed, many people today probably feel more at home at a McDonald's restaurant than in their own households. This is, in fact, the semiotic key to unlocking the mythic meaning of fast food restaurants.

Consider the case of McDonald's. As of 1973, one new McDonald's outlet was being opened every day. Today, billions of McDonald's hamburgers are sold every month. Ronald McDonald is as much a cultural icon and childhood mythological figure as is Santa Claus. The McDonald's "golden arches" logo is now one of the more recognized ones in the world. The mythology of eating has, clearly, not disappeared. It has been revamped by marketers and advertisers to meet new demands, new social realities.

The message underlying the McDonald's symbolism is one basically of Puritan values: law and order, cleanliness, friendliness, hospitality, hard work, self-discipline, and family values. In a society that is on the verge of shedding its traditional puritanical heritage and value systems, McDonald's comes forward as a savior which claims to "do it all for you." Eating at McDonald's is, like any religious ceremony, imbued with ritual and symbolism. The golden arches, like the arches of ancient cities, herald a new age, one based on traditional values. By satisfying a "Big Mac attack," you are, in effect, satisfying a deep metaphorical need to eat symbolically. From the menu to the uniforms, McDonald's imposes standardization, just as do the world's organized religions. As with any ritualistic experience, the eating event at McDonald's is designed to be cathartic and redeeming.

The success of McDonald's is tied, of course, to changes in society. The socioeconomic need to have a two-person, working household led to radical changes in the traditional family structure in the late 1960s. Fewer and fewer North American families had the time to eat meals together within the household, let alone the energy to prepare elaborate dinners. In modern-day households, meals are routinely consumed in front of television sets and, given the increasing number of such sets in the house, family members may not even be in the same place at dinner. The home, ironically, has become a place where very busy people now tend to eat separately. Enter McDonald's (or Wendy's, or Burger King) to the rescue! Eating out at such fast-food places—which are affordable, quick, and cheery—brings the family together, at the same table, under the same roof.

Discussion Questions

1. What mythic forms of communication does Marcel Danesi identify in our present society? Give and explain some other examples of common activities you think, after reading this article, might have mythic significance.

2. Discuss Danesi's thinking about the way myth designates what and how we eat. How do you think some of the other authors in this unit who advocate a vegetarian diet could incorporate an understanding of the mythology of food into their arguments?

3. Analyze the success of McDonald's in terms of the mythology of eating.

4. How does Danesi's idea that "mythic thinking" informs our eating patterns lend support to Pollan's claim that our food choices should be based, not on science or government regulation, but on tradition and culture?

SUBSISTENCE HUNTING

GARY L. COMSTOCK

Gary L. Comstock is a professor of philosophy at North Carolina State University. He is interested in ethical aspects of the biological sciences, and his book Vexing Nature? On the Ethical Case against Agricultural Biotechnology *is a groundbreaking work on genetically modified foods. The following reading is an article he wrote for* Food for Thought: The Debate over Eating Meat *(2004), a collection of readings edited by Steve F. Sapontzis.*

For many centuries, indigenous people along the United States's northwest coastline hunted gray whales for food and fiber. Enveloped in religious mythology and using handheld harpoons, the Makah braved choppy waters in slim boats to bring whale meat to shore. By the 1970s, commercial whaling had decimated whale populations and, with all eight great whale species listed as endangered, the International Whaling Commission (IWC) issued a moratorium. The Makah ceased whaling. Within three decades, however, whale numbers had recovered sufficiently to support a modest kill rate. In 1995, five Makah men petitioned the IWC to allow them to revive their tradition. Asking permission to use rifles to shoot five animals per year, the Makah expressly connected their request to a desire to restore an ancient tribal custom.[1] They argued that it was necessary to reinstitute the hunt for their group to survive as a distinctly Makah people.[2]

Many cultures have engaged, and still engage, in subsistence hunting; suppose someone pondering subsistence whaling were to read the words of the former chair of the US Marine Mammal Commission: "Whales are different. They live in families, they play in the moonlight, they talk to one another, and they care for one another in distress. They are awesome and mysterious. They deserve to be saved."[3] Convinced that whales should not be killed—except, perhaps, in situations where human life depends on it—the animal defender decides to try to intervene to stop the Makah. Could such intervention be justified by arguments analogous to those used to justify interventions to stop slavery, apartheid, or female circumcision? Or would any such intervention inevitably be yet another misguided case of cultural imperialism, the defender failing to respect cultural diversity while trying to force foreign values on autonomous peoples?

Our answer will turn on our views about the relative strength of the duty to defend innocent animal life compared to the duty to respect other cultures. Before we examine those two values, however, let us bring the act itself into sharper focus.

A: Definitions

There are many forms of hunting. *Trophy* hunters hunt for the sheer pleasure of the pursuit and kill, with no intent to use the carcass except perhaps to display the preserved head. Trophy hunting is not necessary for subsistence. Like trophy hunters, *sport* hunters hunt for the pleasure of the act; hunting is not necessary for them to survive. Unlike trophy hunters, however, sport hunters consume the meat. Unlike trophy and sport hunters who hunt habitually, *emergency* hunters kill animals only under the extremely rare condition that the hunters must do so to preserve their life in the short term; they do not hunt as a way of life. *Therapeutic* hunters hunt to preserve the health or integrity of an ecosystem, killing individual animals as a way, as Gary Varner writes, "to see the aggregate welfare of the target species, the integrity of its ecosystem, or both."[4]

Subsistence hunters, unlike any of the previous hunters, must habitually kill animals for one of two reasons: either to survive or to preserve intact their traditional way of life. Subsistence hunting is the traditional practice, often imbued with religious significance, of habitually killing animals at a sustainable rate to feed one's self and one's family when no other adequate sources of protein are available.

B: FOUR CASES

Should we condone such hunting? To begin to unpack the myriad morally relevant considerations, allow me to direct attention away from the facts of the Makah case toward the imagined features of several fictional cases. I will return eventually to the Makah proposal and in conclusion make some remarks about other real-life cases.

Case 1: The Relaxed Cannibals

The Relaxed Cannibals (RCs) command a vast expanse of rich, arable land. Rather than peacefully raising crops, they hunt, kill, and eat humans of a different ethnic origin residing within RC territory. The cannibals call their prey Meat Men (MM). RCs eat only a fraction of the carcasses of the MM they kill. Ruling males oppose all efforts to foreswear cannibalism in favor of farming because they think farming an effeminate way of life unbecoming of them as warriors. There is no critical discussion about the hunting.

There are at least three good reasons to justify intervention in the lives of the RCs, reasons centering on the importance of the interests of the hunted group, the relatively minor consequences to the RCs of ceasing hunting, and environmental benefits.

1. Interests of the hunted: Like the cannibals, the people being hunted have serious interests they wish to pursue, including a basic interest in continuing to live. Like the cannibals, the people being hunted should be free to pursue their interests. If the RCs were acting in self-defense, if the MM were also hunting them, the RCs might be able to justify the RC actions. But the RC reason for hunting—to continue a way of life—is an interest the satisfaction of which is not necessary for the satisfaction of other important RC interests. The interest of the MM in living is necessary for the satisfaction of other important MM interests. The interests of the hunted are more basic than, and therefore trump, the interests of the cannibals.

2. Consequences to the group: A decision about whether to intervene will also depend upon an assessment of the beneficial and harmful consequences of the act. Since the RCs have plenty of land available for productive agriculture, giving up cannibalism would not deprive them of the ability to feed themselves. At worst, ceasing hunting would take away one of the RCs' recreational activities, an activity presumably that could be replaced by other forms of entertainment. And there are benefits. Abandoning the hunting of MM will not only improve the RCs' view of MM and similar groups; it is also likely to improve the RCs' view of one another.

3. Environmental benefits: Humans constantly on the run and fearful of being killed are likely to have little regard for conservation of natural resources. Hunters who have no regard or use for the lives or carcasses of those they kill are unlikely to be concerned with the health of their ecosystems. If RCs give up hunting MM, both groups will have more energy, resources, and time to devote to conserving a diverse environment.

These three considerations establish a presumption in favor of intervention. But one might raise either of two objections: that intervention will restrict RC autonomy, or that the RCs possess no reasons to change their behavior. Let us consider each in turn.

Successful intervention certainly will curtail the RCs' autonomy, especially harming those whose livelihood depends on hunting and who celebrate it in art, dance, and legend. Autonomy, the ability to make one's own choices and pursue one's own interests, is a valuable good. All other things being equal, the burden of proof is on outsiders proposing to curtail the range of a group's freedoms.

We protect freedom because it is a necessary condition for the development of other traits of human excellence, intellect, and character. Humans are not only the sorts of creatures who enjoy pleasure, contentment, and the satisfaction of a comfortable existence. We are also capable of making meaningful plans, deliberating about and settling upon a vision of the good life, and giving our existence significance by ordering our priorities and forgoing trivial satisfactions to pursue more significant ones. Moral reflection profitably begins with a presumption in favor of respecting others' capacity to set their own goals for growth and development simply because of the kind of beings we are: beings capable of forming ground projects, overall plans for how we wish to conduct our lives.[5] The first argument against intervention seeks to protect the RCs' consciously chosen way of life.

The second argument against intervention concerns motives for changing behavior. When there are no reasons internal to one's culture to change, change inevitably appears as an imposition from the outside and, as such, a serious impediment to one's moral development. Given what we have been told about the RCs, we have no reason to believe that there are resources in their traditions to explain or motivate a more peaceful way of life.

How should we weigh these two arguments against intervention? Let us begin by distinguishing several kinds of interests.

Categorical interests are overarching interests or ground projects by which we shape our lives. Categorical interests are long-term projects that give our life meaning when we devote ourselves to them: raising children well, composing string quartets uniquely, playing cello in accordance with appropriate standards of excellence, designing quilts creatively, fulfilling one's institutional duties better than expected. While categorical interests are consciously chosen, one can live to an old age without having pursued them. However, as we are beings capable of pursuing categorical interests, it is not possible to live well without having pursued some such interest or other.

Basic interests are biological interests that must be satisfied if one is to satisfy any other interest whatsoever. These include interests in having access to clean drinking water, an adequate amount of nutritional food, and an intact, efficiently operating physiological system. Unlike categorical interests, basic interests must be satisfied if we are to continue to exist.

Serious interests are goals at which we consciously aim but which are neither basic nor categorical, such as being able on a regular basis to exercise, play a musical instrument, or read recreationally. The satisfaction of serious interests is more important to our welfare than the satisfaction of *trivial* interests, which are mere wishes or whims, such as a desire to have the opportunity to buy light green rather than dark green napkins.

Now, the RCs might claim, their interest in cannibalism is a necessary part of their way of life, a part of the ground project that gives their lives meaning. Granting this claim, we have a conflict between a *categorical* interest of the RCs and a *basic* interest of the MM. When the satisfaction of one human's categorical interest (call this human #1) requires the sacrifice of another human's basic interest (call this human #2), we ought always to act to satisfy the interest of human #2. Here is the argument for this principle.

The two humans in question each have basic and categorical interests, for a total of four interests. All other things being equal, the best world is one in which all four interests are satisfied. If a situation arises in which one interest must be sacrificed, however, it is better to choose a course that will satisfy more rather than fewer interests.[6] To allow human #1 to satisfy a categorical interest that entails depriving human #2 of the ability to satisfy basic interests deprives human #2 both of the ability to satisfy basic interests *and* categorical interests, since, by definition, satisfying basic interests is necessary to the satisfaction of any other interest whatsoever. Should human #1 be allowed to kill human #2, only two interests are satisfiable: human #1's basic and categorical interests. On the other hand, to deny human #1 the ability to satisfy his categorical interest while allowing #2 to satisfy both basic and categorical interests produces an overall rise in utility. In this case, both humans remain alive to satisfy their basic interests, and #2 can also satisfy categorical interests, for a total of three interests being satisfied.

We have agreed to grant (although I have my doubts about the validity of) the RCs' claim that hunting MM is an essential component of their vision of the good life. Even so, we may deny the RCs of the opportunity to hunt MM without preventing them from satisfying their basic interests. One may plausibly add, given the plasticity of categorical interests, that depriving RCs of the ability to pursue a particular categorical interest need not deprive them of the ability to pursue any categorical interest. The RCs, no doubt, can imagine many ground projects not involving cannibalism.

True, intervening with the RCs restricts their liberty. But this cost does not outweigh the virtue of preserving the ability of the MM to satisfy their basic and categorical interests, since freedom is not always good, not good in itself, especially when it is used to compromise the freedoms of others. The argument that we should not intervene with the RCs because they should be free to pursue their traditional way of life is a nonstarter for anyone interested in protecting the lives of the so-called MM.

Case 2: The Hunters of the Misfortunates

Many generations pass, and the RCs continue their cannibalism. Due to years of inbreeding, however, the identity of the prey changes. MM suffer a debilitating narrowing of their gene pool; all children are now born with serious genetic abnormalities. All are able to feed themselves, associate with others, flee the RCs, reproduce, and care for their young. However, none has the mental sophistication to form plans that reach more than thirty or forty minutes into the future. Consequently, none is capable of subordinating simple current interests in favor of more complex longer-term interests. Today's relaxed cannibals hunt and kill these pitiable people, the Misfortunates, for sport, just as their ancestors once hunted MM. In so doing, however, they are not depriving the Misfortunates of the opportunity to pursue categorical desires since the Misfortunates have no categorical desires.

Are there morally relevant differences between cases 1 and 2? An obvious difference is in the mental capacities of the hunted. Whereas the MM were the intellectual equals of the cannibals in every way, the Misfortunates do not have similar sophisticated mental capacities. Like fortunate humans, Misfortunates have basic interests. But they lack the cognitive agility and higher-order thoughts required to form categorical interests. Misfortunates have serious interests, and they include avoiding capture, finding places of safety, experiencing the companionship of others, and feeding their offspring. They can take conscious pleasure in enjoying the warmth of the sun on a pleasant afternoon. They can experience contentment in knowing—and the reverie that potentially accompanies such knowing—that predators are satiated and not on the hunt. Misfortunates have a serious interest in being able to enjoy such experiences. Is the killing of a Misfortunate any less a harm than the killing of an MM? It would seem so, for if death harms some individuals more than others, then death is, all else being equal, worse for an ordinary human than it is for a Misfortunate. Death for a Misfortunate, therefore, constitutes less harm for the Misfortunate than does death for an ordinary human being.

There are reasons to believe death is a variable harm if death is worse for a healthy 23-year-old pregnant woman than for either a 23-day-old fetus or a 103-year-old woman. One reason is that each individual is variably related to her future. The strength of the pregnant woman's psychological internal relatedness to her future self is different, because more intense and complex, than the elderly woman's relatedness to her future self. A pregnant woman has strong ties to the person she will be in a year, or two, or twenty when, for example, her baby will be maturing into a young woman. Envisioning the role that she will play in her child's future life, the mother has powerful reasons to take an urgent interest in her own future. For these and other reasons, death during pregnancy is one of the worst tragedies imaginable. To kill a pregnant woman is to inflict grave harm upon her.

On the other hand, a very old woman has by comparison much weaker internal psychological relatedness to the person she will be in twenty years, or even in two years. Perhaps she has little interest in the person she will be even two months into the future. While the very old may well take an interest in continuing to live, this interest cannot reasonably be as longterm, complex, or intense as the interest taken by the young pregnant woman. Therefore, while death surely harms the very old, it is not as great a harm as it is to those in the prime of their lives. Arguably, a three-week-old fetus has at most a biological tie to the person it will be in the future. It cannot have any conscious psychological ties to its future person because it is not (yet) conscious. Therefore, death is less of a harm to the fetus than to either the pregnant or elderly.

In the same way, death is less of a harm to a Misfortunate than it is to an ordinary human being. Since the Misfortunates lack categorical interests, the strength of the psychological relatedness to their future selves is far weaker than that of the humans in the prime of their lives. But it is important here to remain clear about the question we are addressing. If we had to decide whether to kill an MM or a Misfortunate, we would do less harm, all other things being equal, by killing the Misfortunate because the MM is capable of pursuing ground projects, whereas the Misfortunate is not.

But that is not the question on the table. We are rather concerned to discover whether the killing of a Misfortunate is justified by the categorical interest of the RCs in hunting them. I know of no good reasons to think such killing justified, and many good reasons for thinking it unjustified. The hunters of Misfortunates need not hunt them to survive, and they have alternative ways of life open to them to supply them with food. They, like their ancestors, are cruel, unjust, and unfeeling. Defenders of Misfortunates would be well justified in intervening.

Case 3: The Bonobo Hunters

Bonobo Hunters (BHs) hunt, kill, and eat bonobos, highly intelligent apes, for reasons similar to those that motivate RCs. BHs eat only a fraction of the meat they kill; they are killing their prey at such a rate that they may eventually reduce the target population below a sustainable level; and whereas there is much land available to them for agriculture, the males who rule the BHs are opposed to farming. There is no discussion among the BHs about their hunting traditions; questioning voices are ruthlessly repressed.

There are at least four good reasons to justify intervention.

1. Moral standing of animals: The defender of bonobos has good reasons to think that the harm of death to a bonobo is similar to the harm of death to a Misfortunate. Bonobos possess complex brains and sophisticated neurological systems, and they exhibit pain-avoiding and pleasure-seeking behaviors. Such evidence strongly suggests the capacity of bonobos to take a serious interest in enjoying companionship and sex, forming familial bonds, and rearing offspring. If Misfortunates should not be killed for the kinds of reasons that the hunters of Misfortunates provide, then it is equally true that bonobos should not be killed for the kinds of reasons that the BHs provide.

2. Consequences to the group: To insist that the BHs give up hunting and develop alternative sources of food production would entail, at worst, the BHs' losing this one particular activity from their tradition. The significance of this loss could be minimized by the group's developing other ways of celebrating its past, passing on its legends, and entertaining itself. Arable land is available to develop other sources of protein, and abandoning the killing of bonobos would almost certainly stimulate new traditions, stories, and rituals, and, to be sure, a more peaceful way of life.

3. Consequences to the environment: The BHs are currently taking bonobos at rates that apparently cannot be sustained. Ceasing hunting bonobos will lead to a more stable ecosystem and diverse environment and promote the conservation of resources.

4. Autonomy of humans: The BHs have not arrived at their practice of subsistence hunting through a reflective democratic procedure of considering their options and autonomously selecting a path. Societies should provide all citizens with an opportunity to learn about and influence policy. Minority voices should be respected, not silenced.

Not many animals have the mental sophistication of pygmy chimpanzees. To finish sharpening our concepts, therefore, consider one last fictional case.

Case 4: The Confined Clammers

The Confined Clammers (CCs) are coastal people who gather and eat clams and other animals lacking consciousness. CCs will kill and eat only animals without brains. Indeed, traditional lore expressly forbids killing bears, seals, elk, and octopuses. The CCs regularly engage in public conversations about their practices and have on occasion considered the possibility of growing beans as an alternative source of protein. However, such a plan is not open to them since they are physically hemmed in by groups that have reacted menacingly in the past whenever the CCs have expressed a desire to purchase arable areas. CCs cannot cease clamming; they must habitually hunt the animals they hunt.

There are four good reasons to believe that an animal defender would not be justified in intervening to change the CCs' way of life.

1. Moral standing of animals: We have good reasons to believe the CCs' target species are animals without serious, much less categorical, interests. Clams do not have brains that are, for all we know, necessary to support even as low a mental state as reverie or contentment. Neither do they possess neurological systems sufficiently sophisticated to bring the kind of information out of which a brain, were it present, could form concepts, beliefs, and desires—the stuff of which serious interests are made. While clams have welfare or biological interests—interests in being covered in water rich in nutrients, for example— such interests do not by themselves suffice to establish moral standing. And, like early fetuses, clams have only biological relatedness—no internal psychological relatedness—to the clams they will be in the future. While whales and bonobos apparently have the physiological hardwiring necessary to support internal psychological relatedness between their selves in the present and their selves, say, twenty minutes from now, clams lack the sort of hardwiring necessary for any mental states at all. As such, whales and bonobos, but not clams, are in the same position as Misfortunates. Death is a serious harm for whales and bonobos because they have serious interests. Death is not a serious harm for clams because they do not have serious interests.

2. Consequences for the group: To insist that the CCs quit clamming and develop alternative sources of food production would not only require the CCs to give up their way of life; it would also require that they leave the place that provides them with coherence, self-sufficiency, and the memories and wisdom of ancestors. To be required to pack up and move, to quit clamming, would entail that the CCs lose irrevocably their vision of the good life in this place. Loss of place—and loss of a sense of one's place—is a tragic, because categorical, loss.

3. Consequences for the environment: There are no reasons to think that giving up clamming will lead to a more diverse environment. The CCs take clams at a sustainable rate, so it is plausible to wonder whether they do not in fact stimulate biodiversity in their coastal basins. The CCs may, as far as we know, be engaged in a form of therapeutic hunting, keeping a target population from overshooting its range.

4. Autonomy of humans: CCs have not been coerced in developing their practice of subsistence hunting, and they do not hunt this way unreflectively. They regularly follow transparent, democratic procedures to discuss their behavior, inviting all interested parties to contribute opinions. Clamming is consistent with respect for the autonomy of individuals and minorities.

C: The Makah

Finally, let us return to the Makah, who have petitioned for permission to shoot five animals per year. Those speaking for the group claim the rifle hunt is not only consistent with tribal values but required for the survival of the Makah *as* the Makah. Is this convincing?

Unlike thought experiments, real cases are messy, complex, and not designed for tidy analysis. At the risk of putting on full display my general ignorance about the facts of the Makah case, let me attempt to make some concluding remarks about the kinds of questions we would at least want to have answered before making anything like a final judgment about the Makah. For the sake of argument, I will also hazard my own tentative conclusions.

1. *Moral Standing of Humans*

   How did the Makah arrive at their decision? Did those petitioning for permission to kill whales actively solicit widespread input, carefully weighing contrary opinions? Or did they act as lone rangers, circumventing an open process of inviting all parties to contribute their opinions? When the Makah suggest that they wish to reinstitute the hunt because their identity as a people is at stake, what are the grounds of this claim? If the Makah will literally cease to exist if whaling is not resumed, why have they not ceased to exist in the two decades when they have not been whaling? Is shooting a whale with a rifle from a motorboat consistent with the ancient practice of spearing it with a harpoon from a paddled craft? Perhaps these questions can all be satisfactorily answered in terms favorable to the Makah's petition. In that case, whaling might be a genuine categorical interest of the group.

   If, on the other hand, the answers to these questions suggest that whale-shooting is a serious rather than a categorical interest of the Makah, then these considerations would be less weighty in favor of allowing the hunt. If whaling is a historic, enjoyable practice that will, among other things, teach children important social lessons about the group's history and environment, then we can ask whether there are not nonlethal ways of achieving the same goals.

   Lacking information about whether the petitioners genuinely speak for the entire group or whether the practice proposed is consistent with the past, let us presume positive answers to both questions and, giving the Makah the benefit of the doubt, presume they have a consensus about the desire to reinstitute whaling.

2. *Moral Standing of Animals*

   The Makah hunt whales. Whales are more like bonobos than clams. Like all mammals, whales have the physiological equipment—brains, sensory receptors, neural transmitting and processing systems, etc.—to support arguments from analogy that they are sentient. They also engage in behaviors suggesting they are capable of having a set of serious interests analogous to those of bonobos or Misfortunates. The way seems prepared, therefore, to argue for a presumption against killing them except for reasons that would justify killing Misfortunates. The reasons offered by the Makah for killing whales would not justify the Makah in killing Misfortunates. For reasons presented above, the whales should be considered the moral equivalents of misfortunate humans. The Makah must explain why this claim is not true if they want to overcome this hurdle.

3. *Consequences for the Group*

   To insist that the Makah give up whaling and develop alternative sources of food production would entail, at best, that the group might lose a measure of self-sufficiency and become dependent on trading with other cultures if we assume there is no arable land available to them within their own borders. At worst, abandoning whaling could lead to the group's demise, a catastrophic consequence from the group's perspective. On balance, therefore, and assuming that whale shooting counts as traditional whale hunting and that Makah have a consensus about their interest in reinstituting the practice, the group consequences would argue for allowing the Makah to resume whaling.

4. *Consequences for the Environment*

If the gray whale has recently been delisted from the endangered species list, then killing five whales would not seem to be an environmental cost. On the other hand, it appears that while the gray whale is not endangered, neither has it recovered the robust numbers it once had. Killing additional whales will at best retard the rate at which the stocks recover. Not killing additional whales will speed up that rate. Killing whales is not necessary to keep the species from overshooting its range, nor will killing lead to a more diverse environment or better conservation of resources. Not killing whales may eventually lead to those outcomes. On balance, the environmental arguments seem to lean against whaling resumption.

5. *Motivating Reasons*

During the decades when whaling was not allowed, the Makah must have developed explanations for how their identity could survive decades of nonwhaling. These explanations might not suffice to explain how their identity can survive a permanent cessation of whaling, but they at least provide a resource for dealing with a further extension of the period of nonwhaling. The consensus of Makah opinion to begin whaling, coupled with the successful ability to have withstood together an extended period of nonwhaling, would presumably be useful in assisting the culture to endure a few more years of continued frustration in its desire to resume hunting. While a nonwhaling policy decision would be an unwelcome imposition from the outside, it would not be utterly unintelligible, nor would it seem a decision impossible for the Makah to honor as a single people. Therefore, there appear to be resources within the culture that will allow the Makah to continue as the Makah without whale shooting.

Our tentative answers to the Makah case mirror our answers to the cases in which Misfortunates and bonobos are hunted, except that the consequences to the Makah group might be worse than in either of those cases, assuming the Makah are of a common mind about the importance of whaling. Even granting that assumption, however, the balance of arguments inclines toward deciding the Makah case in the way we decided the Misfortunates and bonobos cases.

Are we justified in intervening in cultures that practice subsistence hunting? It will depend on the particular facts of each case and on the nature of the specific human and animal interests in conflict. Subsistence hunting of animals without serious interests will be the easiest to justify. Subsistence hunting of animals with serious interests is most likely to be justifiable if necessary to serve basic human interests. It may be justified if necessary to serve a categorical interest that cannot be satisfied in any other way. It is unlikely to be justifiable if it serves serious human interests for which the group could substitute alternative, equally serious interests.

Notes:

1. D. J. Orth, "Marine Mammal Protection and Management: A Case Study," *Ag Bioethics Forum* 9.2 (November 1997): 2.

2. Cetacean Society International, "Makah Whaling Stopped, For Now," *Whales Alive!* 12 (January 2003), http://csiwhalesalive.org/csi03 109.html.

3. Orth, "Marine Mammal Protection and Management," p. 2. Orth does not provide the name of the commission chair.

4. Gary Varner, *In Nature's Interests? Interests, Animal Rights, and Environmental Ethics* (New York Oxford University Press, 1998), p. 100.

5. See Bernard Williams, *Moral Luck* (Cambridge: Cambridge University Press, 1981), pp. 12-13; Tom Regan, *The Case for Animal Rights* (Berkeley: University of California Press, 1983); Varner, *In Nature's Interests?* pp. 88–93.

6. See Varner, *In Nature's Interests?* "Perry's Principle of Inclusiveness," pp. 80-88. Varner cites Ralph Barton Perry, *General Theory of Value* (New York: Longman's, Green, and Co., 1926).

Discussion Questions

1. Explain the various kinds of hunters defined by Gary L. Comstock. In terms of these categories, discuss the five Makah men who have petitioned to hunt whales. Consider their past method and tradition of hunting and their current proposal as well. Do the variations make any difference?

2. Summarize the situations of the four different groups of hunters in the case studies. What was your initial reaction as you read about each of them?

3. In the end, what does the author conclude about our right to intervene in cultures that practice subsistence hunting? Choose another author you have read in this unit, and explain the reason you believe this other author would agree or disagree with Comstock's conclusion. How do you feel about his conclusion?

Assignment #6

"COLLEGE IN AMERICA"

This assignment requires you to write a response to the central argument in Caroline Bird's reading selection "College in America." Be sure to read the essay carefully and think about its ideas as you complete the supporting activities. Also, carefully read the background readings in the "Extending the Discussion" section to see what others have to say about college in America. After you have read critically and done the prewriting activities in this section, you will be ready to develop your own essay in response to the writing topic that follows Bird's reading selection.

COLLEGE IN AMERICA

Caroline Bird

Caroline Bird (1915–2011) earned a BA in American history from the University of Toledo in 1938 and an MA in comparative literature from the University of Wisconsin in 1939. Bird's controversial 1975 book The Case Against College *is still an influential work that generates discussion and debate. She is also known for her feminism and writings on women's issues; her book* Born Female: The High Cost of Keeping Women Down *broke new ground in 1968, and she later wrote books and articles about issues concerning women and aging. The following is taken from a* Psychology Today *essay that Bird wrote in 1975.*

The premise that college is the best place for all high school graduates grew out of a noble American ideal. Just as the United States was the first nation to aspire to teach every small child to read and write, so during the 1950s we became the first and only great nation to aspire to higher education for all. During the 1960s, we damned the expense and built great state university systems as fast as we could. And adults—parents, employers, high-school counselors—began to push, shove, and cajole youngsters to "get an education."

We have come to expect that we can bring about social equality by putting all young people through four years of academic rigor. However, at best, this use of college is a roundabout and expensive way to narrow the gap between the highest and lowest in our society. At worst, equalizing opportunity through universal higher education pressures the whole population to do a type of intellectual work natural only to a few. Moreover, it violates the fundamental principle of respect for the differences between people because it leads to the assumption that academic work in college is the only way to establish one's identity in society.

Of course, most parents aren't thinking of the "higher" good at all. They send their children to college because they are convinced young people benefit financially from those four years of higher education. But if money is the only goal, college is the dumbest investment one can make. If a 1972 Princeton-bound high-school graduate had put the $34,181 that his four years of college would have cost him into a savings bank at 7.5% interest compounded daily, he would have had at age sixty-four a total of $1,129,200, or $528,200 more than the earnings of a male college graduate, and more than five times as much as the $199,000 extra the more educated man could expect to earn between twenty-two and sixty-four.

Of course, some people would argue that college is the doorway to the elite professions, especially medicine and law. But only a minority of college graduates can enter law or medical school, and many experts have begun to wonder whether society will support so many lawyers and doctors once they graduate. The American Enterprise Institute estimated in 1971 that there would be more than the target ratio of one hundred doctors for every hundred thousand people in the population by 1980. And the odds are little better for would-be lawyers. Law schools are already graduating twice as many new lawyers every year as the Department of Labor thinks will be needed, and the oversupply is growing every year.

It could be argued that many Americans today are looking less to high status and high pay than to finding a job that is "interesting," that permits them "to make a contribution, express themselves" and "use their special abilities." They think college will help them find it. But

From *Psychology Today,* May 1975 by Caroline Bird.

colleges fail to warn students that jobs of these kinds are hard to come by, even for qualified applicants, and they rarely accept the responsibility of helping students choose a career that will lead to a job. When a young person says he is interested in helping people, his counselor tells him to become a psychologist. But jobs in psychology are scarce. The Department of Labor, for instance, estimated there would be 4,300 new jobs for psychologists in 1975, while colleges were expected to turn out 58,430 BAs in psychology that year.

And it's not at all apparent that what is actually learned in the process of majoring in a field like engineering is necessary for success. Successful engineers and others I talked to said they find that on the job they rarely use what they learned in school. In order to see how well college prepared engineers and scientists for actual paid work in their fields, the Carnegie Commission queried all the employees with degrees in these fields in two large firms. Only one in five said the work they were doing bore a "very close relationship" to their college studies, while almost a third saw "very little relation at all." An overwhelming majority could think of many people who were doing their same work, but had majored in different fields.

Majors in nontechnical fields report even less relationship between their studies and their jobs. Charles Lawrence, a communications major in college and now the producer of *Kennedy & Co.*, the Chicago morning television show, says, "You have to learn all that stuff and you never use it again. I learned my job doing it." Others employed as architects, nurses, teachers, and other members of the so-called learned professions report the same thing.

If college is so expensive and contributes so little to what happens after graduation, how can society justify spending so much money on it? More importantly, how can we defend the immense social pressures—pressures generated by that investment—that manipulate many young people's priorities so that they go to college against their better judgment? We ought to find alternative ways for young people to grow into adulthood, and we ought to give them more realistic preparation for the years ahead.

Writing Topic

Why does Bird think that a college education may not be the best choice for all high school graduates? Does her argument, written in 1975, apply to high school graduates in the twenty-first century? Be sure to support your position with specific examples drawn from your observations, experiences, and readings.

Vocabulary Check

In order for you to understand a reading selection, it is important to think about its key vocabulary terms and the way they are used by the writer. Words can have a variety of meanings, or they can have specialized meanings in certain contexts. Look up the definitions of the following words or phrases from the reading. Choose the meaning that you think Bird intended when she selected that particular word or phrase. Then explain the way the meaning or concept behind the definition is key to understanding her argument.

1. *premise*

   definition: _____

   _____

   explanation: _____

   _____

   _____

   _____

2. *aspire*

   definition: _____

   _____

   explanation: _____

   _____

   _____

   _____

3. *cajole*

   definition: _____

   _____

   explanation: _____

   _____

   _____

   _____

4. *elite*

   definition: _____

   _____

explanation: _____

_____

_____

_____

5. *apparent*

definition: _____

_____

explanation: _____

_____

_____

_____

6. *manipulate*

definition: _____

_____

explanation: _____

_____

_____

_____

Questions to Guide Your Reading

Answer the following questions so you can gain a thorough understanding of "College in America."

Paragraphs 1–2

Explain the reason that Americans believe every high school graduate should attend college. Trace the educational history that resulted in this egalitarian ideal.

Paragraph 2

In what way does Bird think that sending all young people to college fails to respect difference? Consider some of the ways this argument could be used to help or hurt some of the youth.

Paragraph 3

Why, according to the author, do most parents want their children to go to college? If your parents have encouraged you to continue your education at a four-year college, what were their reasons? Do their reasons support Bird's assertion?

Paragraph 4

According to the author, why might an education preparing for the legal and medical professions be a poor investment? How would you respond to her contention?

Paragraph 5

What other kinds of jobs do Americans believe going to college will help them find? Why does the author think this belief is a false one?

Paragraphs 6–7

Why does the author find a college education to be useless in preparing people for careers in engineering, science, and nontechnical fields? How well do you feel she supports her assertion about the relationship between college and these jobs?

Paragraph 8

In her conclusion, what change does the author want us to make?

Prewriting for a Directed Summary

The first part of the writing topic that follows "College in America" asks you about a central idea from Bird's essay. To answer this part of the writing topic, you will want to write a *directed* summary, meaning one that responds specifically to the writing topic's first question.

first question in the writing topic:

Why does Bird think that a college education may not be the best choice for all high school graduates?

Focus Questions

1. What does Bird find inherently disrespectful about the ideal that prompts Americans to believe that all students should go to college after high school?

2. What do most people say is the major benefit of a college education, and why does Bird find that idea unsound?

3. Why are some of the other reasons for attending college equally false, according to Bird?

Developing an Opinion and Working Thesis Statement

The second question in the writing topic for "College in America" asks you to take a position of your own. Your response to this part of the writing topic will become the thesis statement of your essay, so it is important to spend some time ensuring that it reflects the position you want to take on the importance of a college education in today's world.

The framework below will help you develop your working thesis. But keep an open mind as you complete the prewriting pages that follow this one and read the positions other writers take in the essays in the "Extending the Discussion" section of this chapter. You may find that, after giving more thought to the issue, you want to modify your position.

writing topic's second question:

Does her argument, written in 1975, apply to high school graduates in the twenty-first century?

Do you agree with Bird that going on to four years of college may not be the best choice for all high school graduates and that we should encourage some to find alternative ways to prepare for adulthood? As you think about the position you want to take in your working thesis statement, keep in mind Bird's ideas, the ideas of some of the writers in the "Extending the Discussion" section of this unit, and your own experiences.

1. Use the following thesis frame to identify the basic elements of your working thesis statement:

   a. What is the issue of "College in America" that the writing topic's first question asks you to consider?

   _____

   b. What is Bird's position on that issue?

   _____

   c. Will your position be that Bird's claim about high school graduates going to college applies, or doesn't apply, to high school graduates today? _____

   _____

   _____

2. Now use the elements you isolated in 1a, b, and c to write a thesis statement. You may have to revise it several times until it captures your idea clearly.

   _____

   _____

Prewriting to Find Support for Your Thesis Statement

The last part of the writing topic asks you to support the position you put forward in your thesis statement. Well-developed ideas are crucial when you are making an argument because you will have to be clear, logical, and thorough if you are to be convincing. As you work through the exercises below, you will generate much of the 4Cs material you will need when you draft your essay's body paragraphs.

writing topic's last question:

Be sure to support your position with specific examples drawn from your observations, experiences, and readings.

Complete each section of this prewriting activity; your responses will become the material you will use in the next stage—planning and writing the essay.

1. As you begin to develop your own examples, think about how going to college connects to your own life and the lives of those you know. In the space below, make a list of personal experiences you or others have had with making choices after high school. How significant are Bird's observations when it comes to your life and in the lives of those you know? What strategies have you or others used to make choices about your futures? Any experience you have had that says something about this central idea can provide you with an example to support your thesis. List as many ideas as you can, and freewrite about the significance of each.

   Once you've written your ideas, look them over carefully. Try to group your ideas into categories. Then, give each category a label. In other words, cluster ideas that seem to have something in common and, for each cluster, identify that shared quality by giving it a title.

2. Now make another list, but this time focus on examples from your studies, the media, your reading (especially the supplemental readings in this section), and your knowledge of contemporary society. Do any of these examples affirm Bird's ideas? Do any of the examples challenge her views? As you think about society as a whole, consider the many ways people make a living, and the skills they need to do a good job. Think, too, about how you might rank some of those jobs in terms of their importance to society. Do you think a college degree is essential to high achievement in most or all of those jobs you consider to be important? Be sure to note your ideas as fully as possible.

What views do the supplemental essays in this section take? Review their arguments and supporting evidence, and compare them to Bird's. Are any of them especially convincing for you? If so, list them here. (If you refer to any of their ideas in your essay, be sure to cite them.) List and/or freewrite about all the relevant ideas you can think of, even those about which you are hesitant.

Once you've written down your ideas, look them over carefully. Try to group your ideas into categories. Then, give each category a label. In other words, cluster ideas that seem to have something in common and, for each cluster, identify that shared quality by giving the group of ideas a title.

3. Now that you've developed categories, look through them and select two or three to develop in your essay. Make sure they are relevant to your thesis and are important enough to persuade your readers. Then, in the space below, briefly summarize each item in your categories and explain how it supports your thesis statement.

The information and ideas you develop in this exercise will become useful when you turn to planning and drafting your essay.

Revising Your Thesis Statement

Now that you have spent some time working out your ideas more systematically and developing some supporting evidence for the position you want to take, look again at the working thesis statement you crafted earlier to see if it is still accurate. As your first step, look again at the writing topic, and then write your original working thesis on the lines that follow it.

writing topic:

Why does Bird think that a college education may not be the best choice for all high school graduates? Does her argument, written in 1975, apply to high school graduates in the twenty-first century? Be sure to support your position with specific examples drawn from your observations, experiences, and readings.

working thesis statement:

_____

_____

Remember that your thesis statement must answer the second question in the writing topic, but take into consideration the writing topic as a whole. The first question in the topic identifies the issue that is up for debate, and the last question reminds you that, whatever position you take on the issue, you must be able to support it with specific examples.

Take some time now to revise your thesis statement. Consider whether you should change it significantly because it no longer represents your position, or whether only a word or phrase should be added or deleted to make it clearer.

Now, check it one more time by asking yourself the following questions:

a. Does the thesis statement directly identify Bird's argument?

b. Does your thesis state your position on the issue?

c. Is your thesis well punctuated, grammatically correct, and precisely worded?

Add any missing elements, correct the grammar errors, and refine the wording. Then write your polished thesis on the lines below. Try to look at it from your readers' perspective. Is it strong and interesting?

_____

_____

Planning and Drafting Your Essay

You may not be in the habit of outlining or planning your essay before you begin drafting it, and some of you may avoid outlining altogether. If you haven't been using an outline as you move through the writing process, try using it this time. Creating an outline will give you a clear and coherent structure for incorporating all of the ideas you have developed in the preceding pages. It will also show you where you may have gone off track, left logical holes in your reasoning, or failed to develop one or more of your paragraphs.

Your outline doesn't have to use Roman numerals or be highly detailed. Just use an outline form that suits your style and shows you a bird's-eye view of your argument. Below is a form that we think you will find useful. Consult the academic essay diagram in Part 1 of this book, too, to remind yourself of the conventional form of a college essay and its basic parts.

Creating an Outline for Your Draft

I. **Introductory Paragraph**

    A. An opening sentence that gives the reading selection's title and author and begins to answer the first part of the writing topic:

    _____

    B. Main points to include in the directed summary:

       1.

       2.

       3.

       4.

    C. Write out your thesis statement. (Look back to "Revising Your Thesis Statement," where you reexamined and refined your working thesis statement.) It should clearly whether Bird's claim about high school graduates going to college applies, or doesn't apply, to high school graduates today.

    _____

II. **Body Paragraphs**

    A. The paragraph's one main point that supports the thesis statement:

    _____

       1. Controlling idea sentence:

       _____

       _____

2. <u>C</u>orroborating details:

_____

_____

_____

_____

3. Careful explanation of why the details are significant:

_____

_____

_____

_____

4. Connection to the thesis statement:

_____

_____

_____

_____

B. The paragraph's one main point that supports the thesis statement:

_____

1. <u>C</u>ontrolling idea sentence:

_____

_____

2. <u>C</u>orroborating details:

_____

_____

_____

_____

3. <u>C</u>areful explanation of why the details are significant:

_____

_____

_____

_____

4. Connection to the thesis statement:

_____

_____

_____

_____

C. The paragraph's one main point that supports the thesis statement:

_____

1. Controlling idea sentence:

_____

_____

2. Corroborating details:

_____

_____

_____

_____

3. Careful explanation of why the details are significant:

_____

_____

_____

_____

4. Connection to the thesis statement:

_____

_____

_____

_____

D. The paragraph's one main point that supports the thesis statement:

_____

1. Controlling idea sentence:

_____

_____

   2. <u>C</u>orroborating details:

   _____

   _____

   _____

   _____

   3. <u>C</u>areful explanation of why the details are significant:

   _____

   _____

   _____

   _____

   4. <u>C</u>onnection to the thesis statement:

   _____

   _____

   _____

   _____

Repeat this form for any remaining body paragraphs.

III. Conclusion

   A. Type of conclusion to be used:

   _____

   B. Key words or phrases to include:

   _____

Getting Feedback on Your Draft

Use the following guidelines to give a classmate feedback on his or her draft. Read the draft through first, and then answer each of the items below as specifically as you can.

Name of draft's author: _____

Name of draft's reader: _____

The Introduction

1. Within the opening sentences:
   a. Bird's first and last name are given.   yes   no
   b. Bird's title is given and placed within quotation marks.   yes   no
2. The opening contains a summary that:
   a. explains Bird's position on going to college.   yes   no
   b. explains why Bird takes this position.   yes   no
3. The opening provides a thesis that makes clear the writer's opinion regarding Bird's argument.   yes   no

If the answer to #3 above is yes, state the thesis below as it is written. If the answer is no, explain to the writer what information is needed to make the thesis complete.

_____

_____

_____

The Body

1. How many paragraphs are in the body of this essay? _____
2. To support the thesis, this number is   sufficient   not enough
3. Do paragraphs contain the 4Cs?

Paragraph 1	Controlling idea sentence	yes	no
	Corroborating details	yes	no
	Careful explanation of why the details are significant	yes	no
	Connection to the thesis statement	yes	no
Paragraph 2	Controlling idea sentence	yes	no
	Corroborating details	yes	no
	Careful explanation of why the details are significant	yes	no
	Connection to the thesis statement	yes	no
Paragraph 3	Controlling idea sentence	yes	no
	Corroborating details	yes	no

	Careful explanation of why the details are significant	yes	no
	Connection to the thesis statement	yes	no
Paragraph 4	Controlling idea sentence	yes	no
	Corroborating details	yes	no
	Careful explanation of why the details are significant	yes	no
	Connection to the thesis statement	yes	no
Paragraph 5	Controlling idea sentence	yes	no
	Corroborating details	yes	no
	Careful explanation of why the details are significant	yes	no
	Connection to the thesis statement	yes	no

(Continue as needed.)

4. Identify any of the above paragraphs that are underdeveloped (too short). _____

5. Identify any of the above paragraphs that fail to support the thesis. _____

6. Identify any of the above paragraphs that are redundant or repetitive. _____

7. Suggest any ideas for additional paragraphs that might improve this essay.

_____

_____

_____

The Conclusion

1. Does the final paragraph avoid introducing new ideas
and examples that really belong in the body of the essay?   yes   no
2. Does the conclusion provide closure (let readers know
that the end of the essay has been reached)?   yes   no
3. Does the conclusion leave readers with an understanding
of the significance of the argument?   yes   no

4. State in your own words what the draft writer considers to be important about his or her argument.

_____

_____

5. Identify the type of conclusion used (see the guidelines for conclusions in Part 1).

_____

Editing

1. During the editing process, the writer should pay attention to the following problems in sentence structure, punctuation, and mechanics:

   fragments
   fused (run-on) sentences
   comma splices
   misplaced, missing, and unnecessary commas
   misplaced, missing, and unnecessary apostrophes
   incorrect quotation mark use
   capitalization errors
   spelling errors

2. While editing, the writer should pay attention to the following areas of grammar:

   verb tense
   subject-verb agreement
   irregular verbs
   pronoun type
   pronoun reference
   pronoun agreement
   noun plurals
   misplaced and dangling modifiers
   prepositions

Final Draft Checklist

Content

_____ My essay has an appropriate title.

_____ I provide an accurate summary of Bird's position on the issue presented in "College in America."

_____ My thesis states a clear position that can be supported by evidence.

_____ I have enough paragraphs and argument points to support my thesis.

_____ Each body paragraph is relevant to my thesis.

_____ Each body paragraph contains the 4Cs.

_____ I use transitions whenever necessary to connect ideas.

_____ The final paragraph of my essay (the conclusion) provides readers with a sense of closure.

Grammar, Punctuation, and Mechanics

_____ I use the present tense to discuss Bird's argument and examples.

_____ I use verb tenses correctly to show the chronology of events.

_____ I have verb tense consistency throughout my sentences.

_____ I have checked for subject-verb agreement in all of my sentences.

_____ I have revised all fragments and mixed or garbled sentences.

_____ I have repaired all fused (run-on) sentences and comma splices.

_____ I have placed a comma after introductory elements (transitions and phrases) and all dependent clauses that open a sentence.

_____ If I present items in a series (nouns, verbs, prepositional phrases), they are parallel in form.

_____ If I include material spoken or written by someone other than myself, I have correctly punctuated it with quotation marks, using the MLA style guide's rules for citation.

Reviewing Your Graded Essay

After your instructor has returned your essay, you may have the opportunity to revise your paper and raise your grade. Many students, especially those whose essays receive nonpassing grades, feel that their instructors should be less "picky" about grammar and should pass the work on content alone. However, most students at this level have not yet acquired the ability to recognize quality writing, and they do not realize that content and writing actually cannot be separated in this way. Experienced instructors know that errors in sentence structure, grammar, punctuation, and word choice either interfere with content or distract readers so much that they lose track of content. In short, good ideas badly presented are no longer good ideas; to pass, an essay must have passable writing. So even if you are not submitting a revised version of this essay to your instructor, it is important that you review your work carefully in order to understand its strengths and weaknesses. This sheet will guide you through the evaluation process.

You will want to continue to use the techniques that worked well for you and to find strategies to overcome the problems that you identify in this sample of your writing. To recognize areas that might have been problematic for you, look back at the scoring rubric in this book. Match the numerical/verbal/letter grade received on your essay to the appropriate category. Study the explanation given on the rubric for your grade.

Write a few sentences below in which you identify your problems in each of the following areas. Then, suggest specific changes you could make that would improve your paper. Don't forget to use your handbook as a resource.

1. **Grammar/punctuation/mechanics**
   My problem:

   My strategy for change:

2. **Thesis/response to assignment**
   My problem:

   My strategy for change:

3. **Organization**
   My problem:

My strategy for change:

4. **Paragraph development/examples/reasoning**
   My problem:

   My strategy for change:

5. **Assessment**
In the space below, assign a grade to your paper using a rubric other than the one used by your instructor. In other words, if your instructor assigned your essay a grade of *High Fail*, you might give it the letter grade you now feel the paper warrants. If your instructor used the traditional letter grade to evaluate the essay, choose a category from the rubric in this book, or any other grading scale that you are familiar with, to show your evaluation of your work. Then, write a short narrative explaining your evaluation of the essay and the reasons it received the grade you gave it.

   Grade: _____

   Narrative: _____

   _____

   _____

   _____

   _____

Extending the Discussion: Considering Other Viewpoints

Reading Selections

"The American Scholar" by Ralph Waldo Emerson
"White-Collar Blues" by Benedict Jones
"The Men We Carry in Our Minds" by Scott Russell Sanders
"How to Get a Job at Google" by Thomas L. Friedman
"America's Anxious Class" by Robert Reich
"College Graduates Fare Well in Jobs Market, Even through Recession" by
        Catherine Rampell
"Marketing Techniques Go to College" by Penny Singer
Berkeley College Ad
St. Joseph's College Ad
Virginia Intermont College Ad
Hofstra University Ad
Columbia University Ad

THE AMERICAN SCHOLAR

RALPH WALDO EMERSON

Ralph Waldo Emerson (1803-1882) was an influential American man of letters and an indispensable figure in the Transcendentalist movement. His essay "Self-Reliance" is widely considered a classic. The excerpt below is from another essay, originally a speech given to Harvard's Phi Beta Kappa Society and titled "An Oration Delivered before the Phi Beta Kappa Society, at Cambridge, [Massachusetts,] August 31, 1837." He published the speech under its original title as a pamphlet but later changed the title to "The American Scholar" to broaden its appeal.

Mr. President and Gentlemen,

I greet you on the re-commencement of our literary year. Our anniversary is one of hope, and, perhaps, not enough of labor. We do not meet for games of strength or skill, for the recitation of histories, tragedies, and odes, like the ancient Greeks; for parliaments of love and poesy, like the Troubadours; nor for the advancement of science, like our contemporaries in the British and European capitals. Thus far, our holiday has been simply a friendly sign of the survival of the love of letters amongst a people too busy to give to letters any more. As such, it is precious as the sign of an indestructible instinct. Perhaps the time is already come, when it ought to be, and will be, something else; when the sluggard intellect of this continent will look from under its iron lids, and fill the postponed expectation of the world with something better than the exertions of mechanical skill. Our day of dependence, our long apprenticeship to the learning of other lands, draws to a close.

The millions, that around us are rushing into life, cannot always be fed on the sere remains of foreign harvests. Events, actions arise, that must be sung, that will sing themselves. Who can doubt, that poetry will revive and lead in a new age, as the star in the constellation Harp, which now flames in our zenith, astronomers announce, shall one day be the pole-star for a thousand years?

In this hope, I accept the topic which not only usage, but the nature of our association, seem to prescribe to this day, —the AMERICAN SCHOLAR. Year by year, we come up hither to read one more chapter of his biography. Let us inquire what light new days and events have thrown on his character, and his hopes.

It is one of those fables, which, out of an unknown antiquity, convey an unlooked-for wisdom, that the gods, in the beginning, divided Man into men, that he might be more helpful to himself; just as the hand was divided into fingers, the better to answer its end.

The old fable covers a doctrine ever new and sublime; that there is One Man, —present to all particular men only partially, or through one faculty; and that you must take the whole society to find the whole man. Man is not a farmer, or a professor, or an engineer, but he is all. Man is priest, and scholar, and statesman, and producer, and soldier. In the *divided* or social state, these functions are parceled out to individuals, each of whom aims to do his stint of the joint work, whilst each other performs his. The fable implies, that the individual, to possess himself, must sometimes return from his own labor to embrace all the other laborers. But unfortunately, this original unit, this fountain of power, has been so distributed to multitudes, has been so minutely subdivided and peddled out, that it is spilled into drops, and cannot be gathered. The state of society is one in which the members have suffered amputation from the trunk, and strut about so many walking monsters, —a good finger, a neck, a stomach, an elbow, but never a man.

Man is thus metamorphosed into a thing, into many things. The planter, who is Man sent out into the field to gather food, is seldom cheered by any idea of the true dignity of his ministry. He sees his bushel and his cart, and nothing beyond, and sinks into the farmer, instead of Man on the farm. The tradesman scarcely ever gives an ideal worth to his work, but is ridden by the routine of his craft, and the soul is subject to dollars. The priest becomes a form; the attorney, a statute-book; the mechanic, a machine; the sailor, a rope of a ship.

In this distribution of functions, the scholar is the delegated intellect. In the right state, he is, *Man Thinking*. In the degenerate state, when the victim of society, he tends to become a mere thinker, or, still worse, the parrot of other men's thinking.

In this view of him, as Man Thinking, the theory of his office is contained. Him nature solicits with all her placid, all her monitory pictures; him the past instructs; him the future invites.

Is not, indeed, every man a student, and do not all things exist for the student's behoof? And, finally, is not the true scholar the only true master? But the old oracle said, "All things have two handles: beware of the wrong one." In life, too often, the scholar errs with mankind and forfeits his privilege. Let us see him in his school, and consider him in reference to the main influences he receives.

I. The first in time and the first in importance of the influences upon the mind is that of nature. Every day, the sun; and, after sunset, night and her stars. Ever the winds blow; ever the grass grows. Every day, men and women, conversing, beholding and beholden. The scholar is he of all men whom this spectacle most engages. He must settle its value in his mind. What is nature to him? There is never a beginning, there is never an end, to the inexplicable continuity of this web of God, but always circular power returning into itself. Therein it resembles his own spirit, whose beginning, whose ending, he never can find, —so entire, so boundless. Far, too, as her splendors shine, system on system shooting like rays, upward, downward, without center, without circumference, —in the mass and in the particle, nature hastens to render account of herself to the mind. Classification begins. To the young mind, everything is individual, stands by itself. By and by, it finds how to join two things, and see in them one nature; then three, then three thousand; and so, tyrannized over by its own unifying instinct, it goes on tying things together, diminishing anomalies, discovering roots running under ground, whereby contrary and remote things cohere, and flower out from one stem. It presently learns, that, since the dawn of history, there has been a constant accumulation and classifying of facts. But what is classification but the perceiving that these objects are not chaotic, and are not foreign, but have a law which is also a law of the human mind? The astronomer discovers that geometry, a pure abstraction of the human mind, is the measure of planetary motion. The chemist finds proportions and intelligible method throughout matter; and science is nothing but the finding of analogy, identity, in the most remote parts. The ambitious soul sits down before each refractory fact; one after another, reduces all strange constitutions, all new powers, to their class and their law, and goes on for ever to animate the last fiber of organization, the outskirts of nature, by insight.

Thus to him, to this school-boy under the bending dome of day, is suggested, that he and it proceed from one root; one is leaf and one is flower; relation, sympathy, stirring in every vein. And what is that Root? Is not that the soul of his soul? —A thought too bold, —a dream too wild. Yet when this spiritual light shall have revealed the law of more earthly natures, —when he has learned to worship the soul, and to see that the natural philosophy that now is, is only the first gropings of its gigantic hand, he shall look forward to an ever expanding knowledge as to a becoming creator. He shall see, that nature is the opposite of the soul, answering to it part for part. One is seal, and one is print. Its beauty is the beauty of his own mind. Its laws are the laws of his own mind. Nature then becomes to him the measure of his attainments. So much of nature as he is ignorant of, so much of his own mind does he not yet possess. And, in fine, the ancient precept, "Know thyself," and the modern precept, "Study nature," become at last one maxim.

II. The next great influence into the spirit of the scholar, is, the mind of the Past, —in whatever form, whether of literature, of art, of institutions, that mind is inscribed. Books are the best type of the influence of the past, and perhaps we shall get at the truth, —learn the amount of this influence more conveniently, —by considering their value alone.

The theory of books is noble. The scholar of the first age received into him the world around; brooded thereon; gave it the new arrangement of his own mind, and uttered it again. It came into him, life; it went out from him, truth. It came to him, short-lived actions; it went out from him, immortal thoughts. It came to him, business; it went from him, poetry. It was dead fact; now, it is quick thought. It can stand, and it can go. It now endures, it now flies, it now inspires. Precisely in proportion to the depth of mind from which it issued, so high does it soar, so long does it sing.

Or, I might say, it depends on how far the process had gone, of transmuting life into truth. In proportion to the completeness of the distillation, so will the purity and imperishableness of the product be. But none is quite perfect. As no air-pump can by any means make a perfect vacuum, so neither can any artist entirely exclude the conventional, the local, the perishable from his book, or write a book of pure thought, that shall be as efficient, in all respects, to a remote posterity, as to contemporaries, or rather to the second age. Each age, it is found, must write its own books; or rather, each generation for the next succeeding. The books of an older period will not fit this.

Yet hence arises a grave mischief. The sacredness which attaches to the act of creation, —the act of thought, —is transferred to the record. The poet chanting, was felt to be a divine man: henceforth the chant is divine also. The writer was a just and wise spirit: henceforward it is settled, the book is perfect; as love of the hero corrupts into worship of his statue. Instantly, the book becomes noxious: the guide is a tyrant. The sluggish and perverted mind of the multitude, slow to open to the incursions of Reason, having once so opened, having once received this book, stands upon it, and makes an outcry, if it is disparaged. Colleges are built on it. Books are written on it by thinkers, not by Man Thinking; by men of talent, that is, who start wrong, who set out from accepted dogmas, not from their own sight of principles. Meek young men grow up in libraries, believing it their duty to accept the views, which Cicero, which Locke, which Bacon, have given, forgetful that Cicero, Locke, and Bacon were only young men in libraries, when they wrote these books.

Hence, instead of Man Thinking, we have the bookworm. Hence, the book-learned class, who value books, as such; not as related to nature and the human constitution, but as making a sort of Third Estate with the world and the soul. Hence, the restorers of readings, the emendators, the bibliomaniacs of all degrees.

Books are the best of things, well used; abused, among the worst. What is the right use? What is the one end, which all means go to effect? They are for nothing but to inspire. I had better never see a book, than to be warped by its attraction clean out of my own orbit, and made a satellite instead of a system. The one thing in the world, of value, is the active soul. This every man is entitled to; this every man contains within him, although, in almost all men, obstructed, and as yet unborn. The soul active sees absolute truth; and utters truth, or creates. In this action, it is genius; not the privilege of here and there a favorite, but the sound estate of every man. In its essence, it is progressive. The book, the college, the school of art, the institution of any kind, stop with some past utterance of genius. This is good, say they, —let us hold by this. They pin me down. They look backward and not forward. But genius always looks forward. The eyes of man are set in his forehead, not in his hindhead. Man hopes. Genius creates. To create, —to create, —is the proof of a divine presence. Whatever talents may be, if the man create not, the pure efflux of the Deity is not his; —cinders and smoke there may be, but not yet flame. There are creative manners, there are creative actions, and creative words; manners, actions, words, that is, indicative of no custom or authority, but springing spontaneous from the mind's own sense of good and fair.

On the other part, instead of being its own seer, let it receive from another mind its truth, though it were in torrents of light, without periods of solitude, inquest, and self-recovery, and a fatal disservice is done. Genius is always sufficiently the enemy of genius by over influence. The literature of every nation bear me witness. The English dramatic poets have Shakespearized now for two hundred years.

Undoubtedly there is a right way of reading, so it be sternly subordinated. Man Thinking must not be subdued by his instruments. Books are for the scholar's idle times. When he can read God directly, the hour is too precious to be wasted in other men's transcripts of their readings. But when the intervals of darkness come, as come they must, —when the sun is hid, and the stars withdraw their shining, —we repair to the lamps which were kindled by their ray, to guide our steps to the East again, where the dawn is. We hear, that we may speak. The Arabian proverb says, "A fig tree, looking on a fig tree, becometh fruitful."

It is remarkable, the character of the pleasure we derive from the best books. They impress us with the conviction, that one nature wrote and the same reads. We read the verses of one of the great English poets, of Chaucer, of Marvell, of Dryden, with the most modern joy, —with a pleasure, I mean, which is in great part caused by the abstraction of all *time* from their verses. There is some awe mixed with the joy of our surprise, when this poet, who lived in some past world, two or three hundred years ago, says that which lies close to my own soul, that which I also had wellnigh thought and said. But for the evidence thence afforded to the philosophical doctrine of the identity of all minds, we should suppose some preestablished harmony, some foresight of souls that were to be, and some preparation of stores for their future wants, like the fact observed in insects, who lay up food before death for the young grub they shall never see.

I would not be hurried by any love of system, by any exaggeration of instincts, to underrate the Book. We all know, that, as the human body can be nourished on any food, though it were boiled grass and the broth of shoes, so the human mind can be fed by any knowledge. And great and heroic men have existed, who had almost no other information than by the printed page. I only would say, that it needs a strong head to bear that diet. One must be an inventor to read well. As the proverb says, "He that would bring home the wealth of the Indies, must carry out the wealth of the Indies." There is then creative reading as well as creative writing. When the mind is braced by labor and invention, the page of whatever book we read becomes luminous with manifold allusion. Every sentence is doubly significant, and the sense of our author is as broad as the world. We then see, what is always true, that, as the seer's hour of vision is short and rare among heavy days and months, so is its record, perchance, the least part of his volume. The discerning will read, in his Plato or Shakespeare, only that least part, —only the authentic utterances of the oracle; —all the rest he rejects, were it never so many times Plato's and Shakespeare's.

Of course, there is a portion of reading quite indispensable to a wise man. History and exact science he must learn by laborious reading. Colleges, in like manner, have their indispensable office, —to teach elements. But they can only highly serve us, when they aim not to drill, but to create; when they gather from far every ray of various genius to their hospitable halls, and, by the concentrated fires, set the hearts of their youth on flame. Thought and knowledge are natures in which apparatus and pretension avail nothing. Gowns, and pecuniary foundations, though of towns of gold, can never countervail the least sentence or syllable of wit. Forget this, and our American colleges will recede in their public importance, whilst they grow richer every year.

III. There goes in the world a notion, that the scholar should be a recluse, a valetudinarian, —as unfit for any handiwork or public labor, as a penknife for an axe. The so-called "practical men" sneer at speculative men, as if, because they speculate or *see*, they could do nothing. I have heard it said that the clergy, —who are always, more universally than any other class, the scholars of their day, —are addressed as women; that the rough, spontaneous conversation of men they do not hear, but only a mincing and diluted speech. They are often virtually disfranchised; and, indeed, there are advocates for their celibacy. As far as this is true of the studious classes, it is not just and wise. Action is with the scholar subordinate, but it is essential. Without it, he is not yet man. Without it, thought can never ripen into truth. Whilst the world hangs before the eye as a cloud of beauty, we cannot even see its beauty. Inaction is cowardice, but there can be no scholar without the heroic mind. The preamble of thought, the transition through which it passes from the unconscious to the conscious, is action. Only so much do I know, as I have lived. Instantly we know whose words are loaded with life, and whose not.

The world, —this shadow of the soul, or *other me*, lies wide around. Its attractions are the keys which unlock my thoughts and make me acquainted with myself. I run eagerly into this resounding tumult. I grasp the hands of those next me, and take my place in the ring to suffer and to work, taught by an instinct, that so shall the dumb abyss be vocal with speech. I pierce its order; I dissipate its fear; I dispose of it within the circuit of my expanding life. So much only of life as I know by experience, so much of the wilderness have I vanquished and planted, or so far have I extended my being, my dominion. I do not see how any man can afford, for the sake of his nerves and his nap, to spare any action in which he can partake. It is pearls and rubies to his discourse. Drudgery, calamity, exasperation, want, are instructors in eloquence and wisdom. The true scholar grudges every opportunity of action past by, as a loss of power.

It is the raw material out of which the intellect molds her splendid products. A strange process too, this, by which experience is converted into thought, as a mulberry leaf is converted into satin. The manufacture goes forward at all hours.

The actions and events of our childhood and youth, are now matters of calmest observation. They lie like fair pictures in the air. Not so with our recent actions, —with the business which we now have in hand. On this we are quite unable to speculate. Our affections as yet circulate through it. We no more feel or know it, than we feel the feet, or the hand, or the brain of our body. The new deed is yet a part of life, —remains for a time immersed in our unconscious life. In some contemplative hour, it detaches itself from the life like a ripe fruit, to become a thought of the mind. Instantly, it is raised, transfigured; the corruptible has put on incorruption. Henceforth it is an object of beauty, however base its origin and neighborhood. Observe, too, the impossibility of antedating this act. In its grub state, it cannot fly, it cannot shine, it is a dull grub. But suddenly, without observation, the selfsame thing unfurls beautiful wings, and is an angel of wisdom.

So is there no fact, no event, in our private history, which shall not, sooner or later, lose its adhesive, inert form, and astonish us by soaring from our body into the empyrean. Cradle and infancy, school and playground, the fear of boys, and dogs, and ferules, the love of little maids and berries, and many another fact that once filled the whole sky, are gone already; friend and relative profession and party, town and country, nation and world, must also soar and sing.

Of course, he who has put forth his total strength in fit actions, has the richest return of wisdom. I will not shut myself out of this globe of action, and transplant an oak into a flower-pot, there to hunger and pine; nor trust the revenue of some single faculty, and exhaust one vein of thought, much like those Savoyards, who, getting their livelihood by carving shepherds, shepherdesses, and smoking Dutchmen, for all Europe, went out one day to the mountain to find stock, and discovered that they had whittled up the last of their pine-trees. Authors we have, in numbers, who have written out their vein, and who, moved by a commendable prudence, sail for Greece or Palestine, follow the trapper into the prairie, or ramble round Algiers, to replenish their merchantable stock. If it were only for a vocabulary, the scholar would be covetous of action. Life is our dictionary. Years are well spent in country labors; in town, —in the insight into trades and manufactures; in frank intercourse with many men and women; in science; in art; to the one end of mastering in all their facts a language by which to illustrate and embody our perceptions. I learn immediately from any speaker how much he has already lived, through the poverty or the splendor of his speech. Life lies behind us as the quarry from whence we get tiles and copestones for the masonry of to-day. This is the way to learn grammar. Colleges and books only copy the language which the field and the work-yard made.

But the final value of action, like that of books, and better than books, is, that it is a resource. That great principle of Undulation in nature, that shows itself in the inspiring and expiring of the breath; in desire and satiety; in the ebb and flow of the sea; in day and night; in heat and cold; and as yet more deeply ingrained in every atom and every fluid, is known to us under the name of Polarity, —these "fits of easy transmission and reflection," as Newton called them, are the law of nature because they are the law of spirit.

The mind now thinks; now acts; and each fit reproduces the other. When the artist has exhausted his materials, when the fancy no longer paints, when thoughts are no longer apprehended, and books are a weariness, —he has always the resource to *live*. Character is higher than intellect. Thinking is the function. Living is the functionary. The stream retreats to its source. A great soul will be strong to live, as well as strong to think. Does he lack organ or medium to impart his truths? He can still fall back on this elemental force of living them. This is a total act. Thinking is a partial act. Let the grandeur of justice shine in his affairs. Let the beauty of affection cheer his lowly roof. Those "far from fame," who dwell and act with him, will feel the force of his constitution in the doings and passages of the day better than it can be measured by any public and designed display. Time shall teach him, that the scholar loses no hour which the man lives. Herein he unfolds the sacred germ of his instinct, screened from influence. What is lost in seemliness is gained in strength. Not out of those, on whom systems of education have exhausted their culture, comes the helpful giant to destroy the old or to build the new, but out of unhandselled savage nature, out of terrible Druids and Berserkirs, come at last Alfred and Shakespeare.

I hear therefore with joy whatever is beginning to be said of the dignity and necessity of labor to every citizen. There is virtue yet in the hoe and the spade, for learned as well as for unlearned hands. And labor is everywhere welcome; always we are invited to work; only be this limitation observed, that a man shall not for the sake of wider activity sacrifice any opinion to the popular judgments and modes of action.

I have now spoken of the education of the scholar by nature, by books, and by action. It remains to say somewhat of his duties. They are such as become Man Thinking. They may all be comprised in self-trust. The office of the scholar is to cheer, to raise, and to guide men by showing them facts amidst appearances. He plies the slow, unhonored, and unpaid task of observation. Flamsteed and Herschel, in their glazed observatories, may catalogue the stars with the praise of all men, and, the results being splendid and useful, honor is sure. But he, in his private observatory, cataloguing obscure and nebulous stars of the human mind, which as yet no man has thought of as such, —watching days and months, sometimes, for a few facts; correcting still his old records; —must relinquish display and immediate fame. In the long period of his preparation, he must betray often an ignorance and shiftlessness in popular arts, incurring the disdain of the able who shoulder him aside. Long he must stammer in his speech; often forego the living for the dead. Worse yet, he must accept, — how often! poverty and solitude. For the ease and pleasure of treading the old road, accepting the fashions, the education, the religion of society, he takes the cross of making his own, and, of course, the self-accusation, the faint heart, the frequent uncertainty and loss of time, which are the nettles and tangling vines in the way of the self-relying and self-directed; and the state of virtual hostility in which he seems to stand to society, and especially to educated society. For all this loss and scorn, what offset? He is to find consolation in exercising the highest functions of human nature. He is one, who raises himself from private considerations, and breathes and lives on public and illustrious thoughts. He is the world's eye.

He is the world's heart. He is to resist the vulgar prosperity that retrogrades ever to barbarism, by preserving and communicating heroic sentiments, noble biographies, melodious verse, and the conclusions of history. Whatsoever oracles the human heart, in all emergencies, in all solemn hours, has uttered as its commentary on the world of actions, —these he shall receive and impart. And whatsoever new verdict Reason from her inviolable seat pronounces on the passing men and events of to-day, —this he shall hear and promulgate.

These being his functions, it becomes him to feel all confidence in himself, and to defer never to the popular cry. He and he only knows the world. The world of any moment is the merest appearance. Some great decorum, some fetish of a government, some ephemeral trade, or war, or man, is cried up by half mankind and cried down by the other half, as if all depended on this particular up or down. The odds are that the whole question is not worth the poorest thought which the scholar has lost in listening to the controversy. Let him not quit his belief that a popgun is a popgun, though the ancient and honorable of the earth affirm it to be the crack of doom. In silence, in steadiness, in severe abstraction, let him hold by himself; add observation to observation, patient of neglect, patient of reproach; and bide his own time, —happy enough, if he can satisfy himself alone, that this day he has seen something truly. Success treads on every right step. For the instinct is sure, that prompts him to tell his brother what he thinks. He then learns, that in going down into the secrets of his own mind, he has descended into the secrets of all minds. He learns that he who has mastered any law in his private thoughts, is master to that extent of all men whose language he speaks, and of all into whose language his own can be translated. The poet, in utter solitude remembering his spontaneous thoughts and recording them, is found to have recorded that, which men in crowded cities find true for them also. The orator distrusts at first the fitness of his frank confessions, —his want of knowledge of the persons he addresses, —until he finds that he is the complement of his hearers; —that they drink his words because he fulfills for them their own nature; the deeper he dives into his privatest, secretest presentiment, to his wonder he finds, this is the most acceptable, most public, and universally true. The people delight in it; the better part of every man feels, This is my music; this is myself.

In self-trust, all the virtues are comprehended. Free should the scholar be, —free and brave. Free even to the definition of freedom, "without any hindrance that does not arise out of his own constitution." Brave; for fear is a thing, which a scholar by his very function puts behind him. Fear always springs from ignorance. It is a shame to him if his tranquility, amid dangerous times, arise from the presumption, that, like children and women, his is a protected class; or if he seek a temporary peace by the diversion of his thoughts from politics or vexed questions, hiding his head like an ostrich in the flowering bushes, peeping into microscopes, and turning rhymes, as a boy whistles to keep his courage up. So is the danger a danger still; so is the fear worse. Manlike let him turn and face it. Let him look into its eye and search its nature, inspect its origin, —see the whelping of this lion, —which lies no great way back; he will then find in himself a perfect comprehension of its nature and extent; he will have made his hands meet on the other side, and can henceforth defy it, and pass on superior. The world is his, who can see through its pretension. What deafness, what stone-blind custom, what overgrown error you behold, is there only by sufferance, —by your sufferance. See it to be a lie, and you have already dealt it its mortal blow.

Discussion Questions

1. What, according to Emerson, is the difference between "*Man Thinking*" and "a mere thinker"? Which kind of scholar has your college prepared you to be? How has it taught you to be one or the other?

2. Why does Emerson think that in spite of the many books already in existence, it is essential that each generation write books? Do you think new books need to continually be written? Explain your answer.

3. How does Emerson explain his assertion that books are among both the best and worst of things? What reasons would you offer to explain the value of books in our society?

4. What does Emerson see as the true mission of colleges? How does he think they should accomplish their mission? What should be the goal of a college education? Explain ways your college is succeeding or failing in meeting this goal.

5. In section II, how does Emerson differentiate between talent and genius?

6. Near the end of this section, what does he say is the role of colleges with regard to genius? Do you agree? Explain your answer.

7. What does Emerson feel is the relationship between "nature, books, and action"?

WHITE-COLLAR BLUES

BENEDICT JONES

Benedict Jones received a double bachelor's degree from the University of California, San Diego, and earned an English MA at the University of California, Riverside, where he is now a lecturer in the University Writing Program. His scholarly work focuses on Victorian-era prehistoric fiction and evolutionary theories, but he has written articles, reviews, and conference papers on a variety of topics.

A very smart engineer friend of mine (I'll call him Bob) is fond of saying, "College has ruined many a good truck driver." He doesn't mean that truck drivers shouldn't go to college or that a college-educated truck driver is useless. He means that some people who are cut out to be happy, skilled, and productive blue-collar workers aspire to careers that don't suit their talents, all because American society has filled our heads with all sorts of pro-college, anti-blue-collar snobbery.

Some people disagree with Bob. When he makes his pronouncement in public, I hear shocked responses. One person might offer no constructive criticism or argument and just gasp, "You're so elitist! How can you say that?" Someone else will opine that we *all* need equal access to higher education and to highly valued white-collar, service-sector, and professional jobs. Under the misapprehension that college is for everyone, another person might trot out a perennial motto from the United States Army and argue that every one of our esteemed citizens should have the chance to "be all that they can be." College, they think, will do that for everyone, with few exceptions.

I respect their right to their opinion. But I submit that somewhere along the line, this country ran astray. We've demonized blue-collar jobs and democratized higher education to such an extent that many people see physical work as demeaning and view college—particularly four-year colleges and universities—as the only route to success, respectability, and happiness.

You do remember happiness? That elusive quality that we all pursue, especially if we are fans of the Declaration of Independence? I think that happiness is misunderstood in this country. Things have gotten so bad that instead of looking inside ourselves for fulfillment, we look to the latest deodorant or detergent or designer jeans. We follow the latest gossip on our favorite (or least favorite) celebrities. We invest ourselves in a particular football team. We spend thousands of dollars on cosmetics and gym equipment and even plastic surgery—not so much because we want to see a prettier reflection but so that others will see it.

It doesn't work, of course. Buying the latest version of Sure may stave off sweat for a few hours, but it does not improve us as humans. We get caught up in the lives of public figures and think of them as allies when they don't even know us or care about us. We are elated when "our" team wins the championship or our screen idol wins the Oscar, but we're deflated when "our" side loses. We may eliminate the gray in our hair, but we cannot erase the gray disquiet in our souls.

To achieve true happiness, we have to find our place in life. Most of us want romantic relationships. Family is often a factor. Ethics, religion, or spirituality is usually key. Community can be important. And there's always something to be said for having our basic needs met, not to mention a few little luxuries here and there.

So most of us have to work. But I don't see how anyone can be happy in life who is unhappy in work, and so many Americans today are unsatisfied with their jobs. Too many people try to cram themselves into careers for which they are ill-suited—jobs that will not bring happiness or fulfillment. Some people who would make excellent plumbers, electricians, or technicians are doggedly determined to earn a four-year degree so that they can land a mind-numbing and stultifying desk job that doesn't even begin to capitalize on their real gifts and talents.

I haven't even mentioned the huge number of eighteen-year-old pre-med and pre-law hopefuls whose dearest wish (or their families' dearest wish?) is to earn a professional degree that will grant them money and status. In addition to the enormous expense of graduate and professional schools and the unlikelihood that a reputable program will be thrilled with a 2.7 undergraduate GPA, I suspect that many of these young people have no realistic idea what doctors or lawyers actually do all day. For example, I am consistently amazed by the number of students who dislike reading and have poor writing skills but think they want to be lawyers. In addition, a veterinarian I know recently confided in me that veterinary school had not prepared him for the comparatively little time he would spend with animals, doing actual veterinary work—half of his job entails dealing with people and not their pets. I have no doubt that he enjoys his job, but I am pretty sure that the lower-paid animal health technicians spend more time working with the animals than he does and have less stress and less debt to boot. I wonder whether my own veterinary school hopefuls know this.

Many blue-collar workers are highly skilled and make very respectable incomes. One big problem, in many people's eyes, is that such workers are not "professionals." They work with their hands. They wear work clothes, maybe a uniform. They often get dirty. But think about it: If you're not interested in book learning and are miserable taking two years of general education courses, why not find a hands-on career that will make use of your unbookish talents and truly make you happy? Would you rather be a barely adequate and unfulfilled desk jockey (probably with a huge college loan to pay off), or a skilled, appreciated, and contented electrician, inventory specialist, or welder?

More to the point, for students who aren't academically inclined, would you rather turn your nose up at a practical, hands-on education; rack up tens of thousands in debt because of societal expectations; and only then start investigating other options after you discover that your professional career path really doesn't suit your needs? Or perhaps feel stuck in an unfulfilling career forever? Or would you prefer to keep an open mind and an honest heart, and explore the possibilities before you are disillusioned and heavily in debt?

I realize that the situation is not quite that simple for everyone. I seem to be setting up a false dilemma for some individuals. But I don't mean to imply that all young people must choose between a college education and a job that involves working with their hands. There's no reason artisans, craftsmen, and technicians shouldn't acquire a little more book-learning (or a lot) if the spirit moves them. Education can be valuable for anyone. But it is counterproductive to expect all people to aspire to the same college dream when human beings have such widely varying strengths, abilities, and interests. The college-fits-all approach is especially injurious in the United States, where we claim to celebrate diversity. If we revel in America's sexual, ethnic, racial, and religious differences, we should support occupational variety as well. And that means embracing more occupations that do not require a university degree and take place at a desk.

I'm not singing the praises of unskilled labor or assembly-line jobs requiring limited skills. Nor am I trying to keep people down who are trying to get ahead. I'm talking about people who, in a snobbery-free America, would much prefer jobs requiring hands-on skills and talents—and often creativity. I mean jobs that might require an apprenticeship, on-the-job training, or a degree or credential from a trade school, technical college, or community college. I was once startled to hear that one of my university students wanted to be a chef—an occupation requiring true passion, years of dedication, and specialized training. But he was enrolled in a four-year university with no courses to aid him in his ambition. Further discussion revealed that his parents, expecting him to pursue a more prestigious career, had pushed him into the university and refused to help fund him through culinary school. I have since lost track of this young man, so I don't know how it all worked out. But I often wonder about him.

I have also encountered similar stories from young people who wanted to become artists, musicians, computer technicians, dental assistants, electricians, automobile mechanics, and so on. And these are just the students who haven't quite swallowed the college dream and repressed their true longings. After years of hearing "My parents want me to be a doctor/lawyer/other professional" and seeing the anxiety and discontent of students who no longer know their real gifts and passions, I despair that they will ever be happy.

Bob, too, sees the snobbery at his job every day. In a recent e-mail, he writes that his employer exhibits "a blatant and overt dismissal of 'infrastructure' and 'support' roles . . . as neither important nor career paths." He concludes, "It's a disastrous situation with no remedy in sight, but inculcated at the very highest level." This disaster might be avoided if his employer could resist the seductive concept of universal college education and thus offer respect for expert support personnel. Such workers do know what they are doing, but for the boss, college always trumps knowledge.

Lest anyone think that I, a college instructor with an advanced degree, am romanticizing hands-on workers, I should point out that I was a blue-collar employee for fifteen years and worked for eight years as a skilled printer for an international company. I got up early (or stayed up late, when I worked second shift); wore steel-toed shoes; worked with machinery, ink, and tools; and got dirty every day. I went into printing because I was interested in it. I did always expect to finish college, so I never planned to make a career of printing, but I wound up spending twelve years with the same company, and I retained a sense of pride for the product that I delivered day after day. If this had been my true calling, I would have willingly spent twenty or thirty years at the same job. Although I have traded the physically demanding job for one that is more mentally exhausting, I am proud of my years of craftsmanship, even when other people seemed embarrassed by my work. "You're not planning to do this for the rest of your life, are you?" asked a college student who once temped for us. I hastened to assure her that I was not, but a little voice inside said, "I am good at what I do, even if I don't plan to do it forever. Why be ashamed?" What's important is that the individual be satisfied with what he or she does, regardless of what others might think.

Artisans, craftsmen, support personnel, and technicians have something to offer the world. They have real skills and talents, and we need their services. I am deeply grateful to the plumber who repairs a leak that I haven't the skill to fix. I love the CalTrans workers who improve our freeways at night, when fewer drivers are inconvenienced. I treasure the mechanics who keep my car in top form; like most Southern Californians, I would find it difficult to get around efficiently without my horseless carriage. And who can forget our 9/11 adulation of firefighters, police officers, and EMTs? They're not precisely blue-collar employees, but most of them do not have four-year degrees. Lest you forget, these folks are still going strong, serving America, and saving lives.

It's wrong of us to look down on these workers just because we've all bought into the whole college dream. For many young people, four years of college is a nightmare—one whose poisonous effects can derail them for years (or even for their entire lives) and dissuade them from pursuing fulfilling careers. Those who say otherwise have simply succumbed to the snobbery.

So I'm with Bob. College has ruined many a good mechanic, plumber, contractor, facilities manager, IT technician, chef.

Oh, and don't forget the truck drivers.

Discussion Questions

1. Define the attitude toward certain kinds of occupations that Benedict Jones recognizes in the comment of his friend. To what degree do you feel this attitude is responsible for your choice of going to college and your future career goals?

2. What, according to the author, are the essential elements of happiness? What would you like to add or eliminate from this list? Make a prioritized list of the things that you feel are important for your own happiness.

3. Why does the author claim that education snobbery is detrimental to our society as a whole? Imagine a country where everyone had a college education and a professional career, and then describe some specific problems that would result in everyday life.

4. Study and discuss the following quotations, the first from "Blue-Collar Blues" and the second from "College in America." Then, see if you can find points of agreement between the two writers. Read each passage closely and consider all the nuances of the word choices and expressions, as well as the ideas themselves. Look for common ground, and for possible points of difference. Then discuss your conclusions.

Jones:

"There's no reason artisans, craftsmen, and technicians shouldn't acquire a little more book-learning (or a lot) if the spirit moves them. Education can be valuable for anyone. But it is counterproductive to expect all people to aspire to the same college dream when human beings have such widely varying strengths, abilities, and interests."

Bird:

"It could be argued that many Americans today are looking less to high status and high pay than to finding a job that is 'interesting,' that permits them 'to make a contribution, express themselves' and 'use their special abilities.' They think college will help them find it. But colleges fail to warn students that jobs of these kinds are hard to come by, even for qualified applicants, and they rarely accept the responsibility of helping students choose a career that will lead to a job."

THE MEN WE CARRY IN OUR MINDS

SCOTT RUSSELL SANDERS

Scott Russell Sanders earned a BA from Brown University and a PhD from Cambridge University. For over thirty years, he was a professor of English at Indiana University, and he authored many award-winning works ranging from science fiction and historical novels to personal essays and children's books.

The first men, besides my father, I remember seeing were black convicts and white guards, in the cotton field across the road from our farm on the outskirts of Memphis. I must have been three or four. The prisoners wore dingy gray-and-black zebra suits, heavy as canvas, sodden with sweat. Hatless, stooped, they chopped weeds in the fierce heat, row after row, breathing the acrid dust of boll-weevil poison. The overseers wore dazzling white shirts and broad shadowy hats. The oiled barrels of their shotguns flashed in the sunlight. Their faces in memory are utterly blank. Of course those men, white and black, have become for me an emblem of racial hatred. But they have also come to stand for the twin poles of my early vision of manhood—the brute toiling animal and the boss.

When I was a boy, the men I knew labored with their bodies. They were marginal farmers, just scraping by, or welders, steel workers, carpenters; they swept floors, dug ditches, mined coal, or drove trucks, their forearms ropy with muscle; they trained horses, stoked furnaces, built tires, stood on assembly lines wrestling parts onto cars and refrigerators. They got up before light, worked all day long whatever the weather, and when they came home at night, they looked as though somebody had been whipping them. In the evenings and on weekends, they worked on their own places, tilling gardens that were lumpy with clay, fixing broken-down cars, hammering on houses that were always too drafty, too leaky, too small.

The bodies of the men I knew were twisted and maimed in ways visible and invisible. The nails of their hands were black and split, the hands tattooed with scars. Some had lost fingers. Heavy lifting had given many of them finicky backs and guts weak from hernias. Racing against conveyor belts had given them ulcers. Their ankles and knees ached from years of standing on concrete. Anyone who had worked for long around machines was hard of hearing. They squinted, and the skin of their faces was creased like the leather of old work gloves. There were times, studying them, when I dreaded growing up. Most of them coughed, from dust or cigarettes, and most of them drank cheap wine or whiskey, so their eyes looked bloodshot and bruised. The fathers of my friends always seemed older than the mothers. Men wore out sooner. Only women lived into old age.

As a boy, I also knew another sort of men, who did not sweat and break down like mules. They were soldiers, and so far as I could tell, they scarcely worked at all. During my early school years, we lived on a military base, an arsenal in Ohio, and every day I saw GIs in the guard shacks, on the stoops of barracks, at the wheels of olive drab Chevrolets. The chief fact of their lives was boredom. Long after I left the Arsenal, I came to recognize the sour smell the soldiers gave off as that of souls in limbo. They were all waiting—for wars, for transfers, for leaves, for promotions, for the end of their hitch—like so many braves waiting for the hunt to begin. Unlike the warriors of older tribes, however, they would have no say about when the battle would start or how it would be waged. Their waiting was broken only when they practiced for war. They fired guns at targets, drove tanks across the churned-up fields of the military reservation, set off bombs in the wrecks of old fighter planes. I knew this was all play. But I also felt certain that when the hour for killing arrived, they would kill. When the real shooting started, many of them would die. This was what soldiers were *for*, just as a hammer was for driving nails.

Warriors and toilers: Those seemed, in my boyhood vision, to be the chief destinies for men. They weren't the only destinies, as I learned from having a few male teachers, from reading books, and from watching television. But the men on television—the politicians, the astronauts, the generals, the savvy lawyers, the philosophical doctors, the bosses who gave orders to both soldiers and laborers—seemed as remote and unreal to me as the figures in tapestries. I could no more imagine growing up to become one of these cool, potent creatures than I could imagine becoming a prince.

A nearer and more hopeful example was that of my father, who had escaped from a red-dirt farm to a tire factory, and from the assembly line to the front office. Eventually, he dressed in a white shirt and tie. He carried himself as if he had been born to work with his mind. But his body, remembering the earlier years of slogging work, began to give out on him in his fifties, and it quit on him entirely before he turned sixty-five. Even such a partial escape from man's fate as he had accomplished did not seem possible for most of the boys I knew. They joined the Army, stood in line for jobs in the smoky plants, helped build highways. They were bound to work as their fathers had worked, killing themselves or preparing to kill others.

A scholarship enabled me not only to attend college, a rare enough feat in my circle, but even to study in a university meant for the children of the rich. Here I met for the first time young men who had assumed from birth that they would lead lives of comfort and power. And for the first time, I met women who told me that men were guilty of having kept all the joys and privileges of the earth for themselves. I was baffled. What privileges? What joys? I thought about the maimed, dismal lives of most of the men back home. What had they stolen from their wives and daughters? The right to go five days a week, twelve months a year, for thirty or forty years to a steel mill or a coal mine? The right to drop bombs and die in war? The right to feel every leak in the roof, every gap in the fence, every cough in the engine, as a wound they must mend? The right to feel, when the layoff comes or the plant shuts down, not only afraid but ashamed?

I was slow to understand the deep grievances of women. This was because, as a boy, I had envied them. Before college, the only people I had ever known who were interested in art or music or literature, the only ones who read books, the only ones who ever seemed to enjoy a sense of ease and grace, were the mothers and daughters. Like the menfolk, they fretted about money, they scrimped and made-do. But, when the pay stopped coming in, they were not the ones who had failed. Nor did they have to go to war, and that seemed to me a blessed fact. By comparison with the narrow, ironclad days of fathers, there was an expansiveness, I thought, in the days of mothers. They went to see neighbors, to shop in town, to run errands at school, at the library, at church. No doubt, had I looked harder at their lives, I would have envied them less. It was not my fate to become a woman, so it was easier for me to see the graces. Few of them held jobs outside the home, and those who did filled thankless roles as clerks and waitresses. I didn't see, then, what a prison a house could be, since houses seemed to me brighter, handsomer places than any factory. I did not realize—because such things were never spoken of—how often women suffered from men's bullying. I did learn about the wretchedness of abandoned wives, single mothers, widows; but I also learned about the wretchedness of lone men. Even then, I could see how exhausting it was for a mother to cater all day to the needs of young children. But if I had been asked, as a boy, to choose between tending a baby and tending a machine, I think I would have chosen the baby. (Having now tended both, I know I would choose the baby.)

So I was baffled when the women at college accused me and my sex of having cornered the world's pleasures. I think something like my bafflement has been felt by other boys (and by girls as well) who grew up in dirt-poor farm country, in mining country, in black ghettos, in Hispanic barrios, in the shadows of factories, in Third World nations—any place where the fate of men is as grim and bleak as the fate of women. Toilers and warriors. I realize now how ancient these identities are, how deep the tug they exert on men, the undertow of a thousand generations. The miseries I saw, as a boy, in the lives of nearly all men I continue to see in the lives of many—the body-breaking toil, the tedium, the call to be tough, the humiliating powerlessness, the battle for a living and for territory.

When the women I met at college thought about the joys and privileges of men, they did not carry in their minds the sort of men I had known in my childhood. They thought of their fathers, who were bankers, physicians, architects, stockbrokers, the big wheels of the big cities. These fathers rode the train to work or drove cars that cost more than any of my childhood houses. They were attended from morning to night by female helpers, wives and nurses and secretaries. They were never laid off, never short of cash at month's end, never lined up for welfare. These fathers made decisions that mattered. They ran the world.

The daughters of such men wanted to share in this power, this glory. So did I. They yearned for a say over their future, for jobs worthy of their abilities, for the right to live at peace, unmolested, whole. Yes, I thought, yes yes. The difference between me and these daughters was that they saw me, because of my sex, as destined from birth to become like their fathers, and therefore as an enemy to their desires. But I knew better. I wasn't an enemy, in fact or in feeling. I was an ally. If I had known, then, how to tell them so, would they have believed me? Would they now?

Discussion Questions

1. What were the two work options the young Sanders saw open to the men he knew and the man he imagined he would grow up to be? What other kinds of work did he know that men did do? Why couldn't he imagine himself in one of those jobs?

2. What were the jobs relegated to women in the world of Sanders's childhood? In his eyes, how did the lives of women compare to those of men? Why?

3. When Sanders went away to college, what surprised him about the way most of the women he met thought about men and work? How can these differences be explained? What other students on his campus shared his views? Do you think Betty Friedan would or would not have understood Sanders's position? Explain your answer.

4. Why does Sanders consider himself an ally of the young women he sees on his college campus? Do you think that this alliance is something that binds the men and women on your campus? Explain your answer.

5. What do you think Carolyn Bird would say about Sanders's decision to go to college, and the rewards he associates with earning his degree?

HOW TO GET A JOB AT GOOGLE

Thomas L. Friedman

Thomas L. Friedman earned a BA from Brandeis University and an MA from the University of Oxford. He is an American journalist, a bestselling author, and a longtime columnist and reporter for the New York Times. *Friedman has three times received the Pulitzer Prize, twice for International Reporting and once for Commentary.*

Last June, in an interview with Adam Bryant of the *Times*, Laszlo Bock, the senior vice president of people operations for Google—i.e., the guy in charge of hiring for one of the world's most successful companies—noted that Google had determined that "GPAs are worthless as a criterion for hiring, and test scores are worthless. . . . We found that they don't predict anything." He also noted that the "proportion of people without any college education at Google has increased over time"—now as high as fourteen percent on some teams. At a time when many people are asking, "How's my kid gonna get a job?" I thought it would be useful to visit Google and hear how Bock would answer.

Don't get him wrong, Bock begins, "Good grades certainly don't hurt." Many jobs at Google require math, computing, and coding skills, so if your good grades truly reflect skills in those areas that you can apply, it will be an advantage. But Google has its eyes on much more.

"There are five hiring attributes we have across the company," explains Bock. "If it's a technical role, we assess your coding ability, and half the roles in the company are technical roles. For every job, though, the number one thing we look for is general cognitive ability, and it's not IQ. It's learning ability. It's the ability to process on the fly. It's the ability to pull together disparate bits of information. We assess that using structured behavioral interviews that we validate to make sure they're predictive."

The second, he adds, "is leadership—in particular, emergent leadership as opposed to traditional leadership. Traditional leadership is, were you president of the chess club? Were you vice president of sales? How quickly did you get there? We don't care. What we care about is, when faced with a problem and you're a member of a team, do you, at the appropriate time, step in and lead? And just as critical, do you step back and stop leading, do you let someone else? Because what's critical to be an effective leader in this environment is you have to be willing to relinquish power."

What else? Humility and ownership. "It's feeling the sense of responsibility, the sense of ownership, to step in," he says, to try to solve any problem—and the humility to step back and embrace the better ideas of others. "Your end goal," explains Bock, "is what can we do together to problem-solve? I've contributed my piece, and then I step back."

And it is not just humility in creating space for others to contribute, says Bock; it's "intellectual humility. Without humility, you are unable to learn." It is why research shows that many graduates from hotshot business schools plateau. "Successful bright people rarely experience failure, and so they don't learn how to learn from that failure," says Bock. The least important attribute they look for is "expertise." Says Bock: "If you take somebody who has high cognitive ability, is innately curious, willing to learn, and has emergent leadership skills, and you hire them as an HR person or finance person, and they have no content knowledge, and you compare them with someone who's been doing just one thing and is a world expert, the expert will go: 'I've seen this one hundred times before; here's what you do.'" Most of the time the nonexpert will come up with the same answer, adds Bock, "because most of the time it's not that hard." Sure, once in a while they will mess it up, he says, but once in a while they'll also come up with an answer that is totally new. And there is huge value in that.

To sum up Bock's approach to hiring: Talent can come in so many different forms and be built in so many nontraditional ways today that hiring officers have to be alive to every one—besides brand-name colleges. Because "when you look at people who don't go to school and make their way in the world, those are exceptional human beings. And we should do everything we can to find those people." Too many colleges, he adds, "don't deliver on what they promise. You generate a ton of debt, and you don't learn the most useful things for your life. It's [just] an extended adolescence."

Google attracts so much talent that it can afford to look beyond traditional metrics such as GPA. For most young people, though, going to college and doing well is still the best way to master the tools needed for many careers. But Bock is saying something important to them, too: Beware. Your degree is not a proxy for your ability to do any job. The world only cares about—and pays off on—what you can do with what you know (and it doesn't care how you learned it). And in an age when innovation is increasingly a group endeavor, it also cares about a lot of soft skills—leadership, humility, collaboration, adaptability and loving to learn and relearn. This will be true no matter where you go to work.

Discussion Questions

1. How do a college degree and good grades correlate with the job requirements at Google? Explain why this information is or is not a surprise to you? How does this information impact the way you look at your own education?

2. List the five hiring attributes that Google, as a company, looks for in a job candidate. Explain each of these characteristics as defined by Google. How, as a student, do you think you can develop these attributes?

3. Explain your reasons for thinking that the attributes Google requires would or would not be beneficial in the job(s) you want to apply for after finishing your education.

4. How can it be said that Carolyn Bird, writer of the lead essay in this unit, and Laszlo Bock, the senior vice president of people operations for Google, have similar ideas about the value of the differences among people? Does Jones, in "Blue-Collar Blues," agree, or disagree, with Bird and Laszlo? Find at least one quotation from each of the three readings that supports your answer.

AMERICA'S ANXIOUS CLASS

Robert Reich

Robert Reich earned a bachelor's degree from Dartmouth and a JD from Yale; he also studied at Oxford on a Rhodes Scholarship. He has held professorships at Harvard University and Brandeis University, and he currently teaches at UC Berkeley at the prestigious Goldman School of Public Policy. In addition to serving under Presidents Ford and Carter, he was Secretary of Labor during the first Clinton administration. He is an influential lecturer and writer with over a dozen books, several of them bestsellers on politics and the economy.

The American middle class is disintegrating and turning into three new groups: an underclass largely trapped in central cities and isolated from the growing economy; an overclass profitably positioned to ride the waves of change; and an anxious class, most of whom hold jobs but are justifiably uneasy about their own standing and fearful for their children's future.

What divides the over, the under, and the anxious classes is both the quality of their formal educations and their capacity and opportunity to learn throughout their working lives. Skills have always been relevant to earnings, of course. But they have never been as important as they are today. Only fifteen years ago, a male college graduate earned 49% more than a man with only a high school degree. That's a sizable difference, but it's a divide small enough for both men to occupy terrain each would call middle class. In 1992, a male college graduate outearned his high school graduate counterpart by 83%—a difference so great that they no longer inhabit common territory or share common perspectives. Women are divided along similar, though slightly less stark, lines.

Traditionally, membership in the American middle class included not only a job with a steadily increasing income, but a bundle of benefits that came with employment. But a gap has grown here as well. Employer-sponsored health coverage for workers with college degrees has declined only slightly, from 79% in 1979 to 76% in 1993. But for high school graduates, rates have fallen further: 68% to 60% over the same period. And rates for high school dropouts have plunged—from an already low 52% in 1979 to only 36% last year. . . .

But earnings and benefits don't tell the complete story. Merely getting a job and holding onto it depend ever more on strong skills. In the 1970s, the average unemployment rate for people who had not completed high school was 7%; by 1993 it had passed 12%. Job loss for high school graduates has followed a comparable trajectory. By contrast, the unemployment rate for workers with at least a college education has remained around 3%. . . .

As they take hold in the neighborhoods and workplaces of America, these forces are ominous. Consider the physical separation they have already helped forge. The overclass has moved to elite suburbs—occasionally into their own gated communities or residential compounds policed by their own security forces. The underclass finds itself quarantined in surroundings that are unspeakably bleak and often violent. And the anxious class is trapped, too—not only by houses and apartments often too small for growing families, but also by the frenzy of effort it takes to preserve their standing, with many families needing two or three paychecks to deliver the living standard one job used to supply. In other words, even as America's economic tide continues to rise, it no longer lifts all the boats. Only a small portion of the American population benefited from the economic growth of the 1980s. The restructurings and capital investments launched during the 1980s and continuing through the 1990s have improved the productivity and competitiveness of American industry, but not the prospects of most Americans. And the people left behind have unleashed a wave of resentment and distrust—a wave buffeting government, business, and other institutions that the anxious class believes has betrayed them.

This creates fertile soil for the demagogues and conspiracy theorists who often emerge during anxious times. People in distress, people who fear for their future, naturally cling to what they have and often resist anything that threatens it. People who feel abandoned—by a government that has let them slide or a company that has laid them off—respond to opportunists peddling simplistic explanations and sinister solutions. Why are you having trouble making ends meet? We're letting in too many immigrants. Why are you struggling to pay your bills? Affirmative action tilts things in favor of African Americans and Hispanics. Why is your job at risk? Our trade policies have not been sufficiently protectionist.

As a solution, we can't turn back the clock and return to the safe old world of routine mass production that dominated postwar America. Efforts to do so—say, by keeping foreign investment and goods outside of our borders or by stifling technological advancements—would not resurrect the old middle class. They would only inhibit the ability of every American to prosper and change. The real solution is to give all Americans a stake in economic growth, to ensure that everyone benefits from our newfound competitiveness. This economy will not be at full capacity until we tap the potential of all our citizens to be more productive.

Individuals and families shoulder much of the responsibility here, of course. Ultimately, they must face the realities of the new economy and ensure that they and their children have the basic intellectual tools to prosper in it. Government has a role, too. It can clear away some of the obstacles—improving the quality of public education, setting skills standards, and smoothing the transition from school to work and from job to job. But individuals, however resourceful, and governments, however reinvented, can't build a new middle class on their own. Business has an indispensable role to play. Unless business joins in a compact to rebuild America's middle class—training and empowering ordinary workers to be productive and innovative—this task cannot succeed.

Discussion Questions

1. What three classes does Reich say compose American society? Describe the living conditions and the resulting attitudes from these conditions generally experienced by each class. How does Reich's classification compare with your own experiences of American society?

2. According to Reich, what benefits is a middle-class college-educated worker more likely to receive than a middle-class high-school graduate? Consider his statistics in relation to Bird's, and discuss their similarities and differences. How do you account for any discrepancies you might notice?

3. What does Reich predict from America's rising economic tide? What evidence from your own experience confirms or contradicts his prediction? What role do you think education should play in our country's economic future?

4. What do the ideas of Reich and Bird have in common? Do you think they would generally agree if they met and discussed America's youth and the future prospects of America? Do you see any potential areas of disagreement between them? Explain.

COLLEGE GRADUATES FARE WELL IN JOBS MARKET, EVEN THROUGH RECESSION

CATHERINE RAMPELL

Catherine Rampell graduated from Princeton University and now writes about econom-
ics and the arts for the New York Times. *For the* Times, *she also established an award-*
winning blog, Economix. *Earlier in her career, she wrote for the* Washington Post
and the Chronicle of Higher Education. *The article below appeared in the* New York
Times *in 2013.*

Is college worth it? Given the growing price tag and the frequent anecdotes about jobless graduates stuck in their parents' basements, many have started to question the value of a college degree. But the evidence suggests college graduates have suffered through the recession and lackluster recovery with remarkable resilience.

The unemployment rate for college graduates in April of 2013 was a mere 3.9%, compared with 7.5% for the work force as a whole, according to a Labor Department report recently released. Even when the jobless rate for college graduates was at its very worst in this business cycle, in November 2010, it was still just 5.1%. That is close to the jobless rate the rest of the work force experiences when the economy is good.

Among all segments of workers sorted by educational attainment, college graduates are the only group that has more people employed today than when the recession started. The number of college-educated workers with jobs has risen by 9.1% since the beginning of the recession. Those with a high school diploma and no further education are practically a mirror image, with employment down 9% on net. For workers without even a high school diploma, employment levels have fallen 14.1%.

But just because college graduates have jobs does not mean they all have "good" jobs. There is ample evidence that employers are hiring college-educated workers for jobs that do not actually require college-level skills—positions like receptionists, file clerks, waitresses, car rental agents, and so on. "High-skilled people can take the jobs of middle-skilled people, and middle-skilled people can take jobs of low-skilled people," says Justin Wolfers, a professor of public policy and economics at the University of Michigan. "And low-skilled people are out of luck." In some cases, employers are specifically requiring four-year degrees for jobs that previously did not need them, since companies realize that in a relatively poor job market, college graduates will be willing to take whatever they can find.

That has left those who have spent some time in college but have not received a bachelor's degree to scramble for what is left. Employment for them fell during the recession and is now back to exactly where it began. There were 34,992,000 workers with some college employed in December 2007, and there are 34,992,000 today.

In other words, workers with four-year degrees have gobbled up all of the net job gains. In fact, there are more employed college graduates today than employed high school graduates and high school dropouts put together.

It is worth noting, too, that even young college graduates are finding jobs, based on the most recent data on this subgroup. In 2011, the unemployment rate for people in their twenties with at least a bachelor's degree was 5.7%. For those with only a high school diploma or a GED, it was nearly three times as high, at 16.2%.

Americans have gotten the message that college pays off in the job market. College degrees are much more common today than they were in the past. In April, about 32% of the civilian, noninstitutional population over twenty-five—that is, the group of people who are not inmates of penal and mental facilities or residents of homes for the disabled or aged and who are not on active military duty—had a college degree. Twenty years ago, the share was 22%. Given the changing norms for what degree of educational training is expected of working Americans, employers might assume those who do not have a four-year degree are less ambitious or less capable, regardless of their actual ability.

These forces might help explain why there is so much growth in employment among college graduates despite the fact that the bulk of the jobs created in the last few years have been low-wage and low-skilled, according to a report last August from the National Employment Law Project, a liberal research and advocacy group. Today nearly one in thirteen jobs is in food services, for example, a record share.

Clearly, positions in retail and food services are not the best use of the hard-earned skills of college-educated workers, who have gone to great expense to obtain their sheepskins. Student loan borrowers graduate with an average debt of $27,000, a total that is likely to grow in the future. But nearly all of those graduates are at least finding work and income of some kind, unlike a much larger share of their less educated peers. And as the economy improves, college graduates will be better situated to find promotions to jobs that do use their more advanced skills and that pay better wages, economists say.

The median weekly earnings of college-educated, full-time workers—like those for their counterparts with less education—have dipped in recent years. In 2012, the weekly median was $1,141, compared with $1,163 in 2007, after adjusting for inflation. The premium they earn for having that college degree is still high, though.

In 2012, the typical full-time worker with a bachelor's degree earned 79% more than a similar full-time worker with no more than a high school diploma. For comparison, twenty years earlier the premium was 73%, and thirty years earlier it was 48%. And since a higher percentage of college graduates than high school graduates are employed in full-time work, these figures actually understate the increase in the total earnings premium from college completion, says Gary Burtless, a senior fellow at the Brookings Institution, an independent research organization. So, despite the painful upfront cost, the return on investment on a college degree remains high.

An analysis from the Hamilton Project at the Brookings Institution in Washington estimates that the benefits of a four-year college degree are equivalent to an investment that returns 15.2% a year, even after factoring in the earnings students forgo while in school. "This is more than double the average return to stock market investments since 1950," the report says, "and more than five times the returns to corporate bonds, gold, long-term government bonds, or homeownership."

Discussion Questions

1. Discuss the employment statistics for workers with a college degree in comparison to those with a high school diploma or less. Do you think these statistics bear any responsibility for the attitude of snobbery discussed by Jones in "White-Collar Blues"?

2. What kinds of jobs, however, account for the high employment rate of college graduates? What assumptions about college graduates are employers making that accounts for these positions being filled by people with degrees? Explain why you believe the employers' assumptions are valid.

3. In general economic terms, discuss college as an investment and as a pathway to a relatively high standard of living. Imagine that you are preparing for a debate with Carolyn Bird.

MARKETING TECHNIQUES GO TO COLLEGE

PENNY SINGER

Penny Singer was a journalist who wrote for the New York Times. *This article was published in the* New York Times *in 1987.*

Can colleges be sold like cars? At one time, academics shuddered at the idea, but times have changed. Faced with shrinking pools of students and rising operating costs, educators are finding that advertising their wares is not only respectable but essential.

Colleges and universities from coast to coast are retaining advertising agencies, and are using some of the most sophisticated marketing techniques available, to help them sell in a buyer's market. For instance, what was formerly known as the Admissions Office is now the Office of Enrollment Management at the College of New Rochelle. "Enrollment management involves not only recruiting students but retaining them as well," says Nancy Haiduck, director of college recruitment. "We have adapted marketing principles and practices to our own needs to attract students."

To attract the undergraduate student most likely to spend four years at the College of New Rochelle, Dr. Joan Baily, Assistant Vice President of Academic Affairs and in charge of enrollment management, says the college has combined traditional methods of recruiting—such as maintaining alumni contacts and sending admissions counselors to college fairs and high schools—with untraditional sophisticated advertising and marketing campaigns. "In our marketing campaigns, we use a lot of direct mail," Dr. Baily says. "By taking a rifle approach, we make mailings only to a predefined target audience. We buy our list from the College Board in Princeton, New Jersey, which charges us about fifteen cents for a name. The success of the direct-mail program depends on the quality and quantity of the mailing list. Returns from direct mail are put in with other inquiries to generate our list." The College Board, which prepares the Scholastic Aptitude Test, is one of the largest suppliers of lists to colleges. It has the names of more than a million high school juniors and seniors who have agreed to have their names placed on a computer roster. About nine hundred colleges nationwide buy the names of high school students from the Student Search Service, a lucrative arm of the College Board.

The College of New Rochelle's direct-mail series includes several brochures with information on and pictures of the college, plus direct-mail letters—including one from the college president, one from the director of financial aid, and a personal letter from the chairmen of various departments. The cost of the recruiting effort, according to Dr. Baily's estimate, is about $1,100 per entering freshman. "That places us in the middle range; the average cost of recruiting a student is $1,300 at most private colleges, even higher for the Ivies," she says, citing statistics from the National Association of Colleges.

However, the recruitment effort pays off in more than one way. "It helps us hold our own with admissions in a declining market," Dr. Baily says, "and, most important, our retention rate is very high. Most of our entering freshmen graduate four years later."

Print advertising plays only a small role in the recruitment efforts of the School of Arts and Science and the School of Nursing, the two undergraduate schools that enroll the eighteen- to twenty-two-year-old students on the New Rochelle campus. "We do use some institutional ads for that market," Dr. Baily says, "but most of our advertising is aimed at adult students for our School of New Resources, which is one of the first in the country designed exclusively for adults, and the graduate school."

A number of factors—such as job opportunities in a time of high employment, and a lack of financial aid—have caused enrollments of adult students to decline, Dr. Baily says, and have prompted the recent advertising campaigns by the College of New Rochelle and others. "We're running ads in tune with the times, with emphasis on promoting course offerings aimed at the out-of-work executive that will lead to a second career and teaching degrees, for those looking for career changes. Teachers are in short supply right now. We do use an advertising agency—Ruder Finn & Rotman in Manhattan. We also do some radio advertising for the School of New Resources."

The communications-information office at Pace University's Pleasantville campus can compare with a small outside advertising agency, billing about $5 million a year. Headed by Frances A. Keegan, the vice president for university communications, the department, with forty full-time employees, works with a budget of $3.5 million a year for publications and marketing of the three Pace undergraduate schools and its six graduate schools. Ms. Keegan, who is aided by Herbert Falk, director of information, represents a new breed of university vice president: the marketing professional. Formerly vice president in charge of advertising for the Book of the Month Club, Ms. Keegan, a direct-mail marketing specialist, worked for one of the leading advertising agencies in the field, Wunderman, Ricotta & Kline, for a number of years before she was recruited by the Book-of-the-Month Club. "I came to Pace eight years ago" she says, "originally as a trustee who was asked to help reorganize the university's marketing effort. Then I stayed on as a full-time employee."

According to Ms. Keegan, the competition for students is keen among colleges in the area. "Our chief rivals are Fordham, Iona, St. John's, and the State University of New York at Purchase," she says, "and according to a recent newsletter, the years 1989 and 1990 will be extremely difficult for recruiting; the supply of potential students will hit rock bottom owing to the low birth rate of eighteen years before."

The Pace Communications Office is busy year-round. The first in a series of five mailings to high school students for the freshman class of 1988 was made on November 18, Ms. Keegan says. The College Board is the major supplier of names of high school students to Pace, she says. "We also make mailings for our graduate schools; some 50,000 pieces go to 9,500 adults every year," she says. "We consult with advisers, professors, and deans in each of the graduate schools to get us 'psychographic' profiles of the type of student most likely to be recruited. Then we buy the specially targeted names from a list broker we have under contract. For instance, for the law school we get the names of prelaw students from 2,000 colleges."

The psychographic profile is a refinement of the demographic profile, Ms. Keegan explains, and is especially valuable for use in retaining students. "The more you know about a prospective student, the more successful the retention effort." In addition, Mr. Falk says, "It's one thing to get incoming freshmen, another thing to have outgoing seniors." Achieving that result "is what is meant by enrollment management."

Applications for 1988 at the Pace campuses are up, Ms. Keegan says. "Direct-mail efforts have paid off, judging from the number of inquiries we're getting. Nevertheless, it's hard to estimate how many applications will result in matriculating students. But if we can gauge by demand for dormitory space, which is running surprisingly strong, we should more than hold our own next year in the undergraduate college." With the exception of the Pace Law School in White Plains, which Ms. Keegan says is still getting ample numbers of applications, the numbers of adults returning to school has dropped steadily since 1982, a peak year. "We've earmarked a budget of over a million dollars for advertising to the adult market primarily," she says. "AC&R, a division of Saatchi and Saatchi, handles our newspaper and radio advertising campaign. Adults make the decision to enroll in a particular school fairly quickly. They respond to good advertising."

Discussion Questions

1. What is the answer Penny Singer expects to the rhetorical question she uses to open her essay? How useful, effective, or attention-grabbing do you find her analogy to be?

2. Rampell and Bird mention similar connections; Construct a comparison chart using Reeves, Rampell, and Bird and discuss your findings.

3. As a prospective student, choose from the following advertisements the ones that would have appealed to you the most and the least. Explain the reasons for your selections.

4. In what way does Singer's argument support Bird's? How might Bird respond to college ads such as the ones below?

College Advertisements

Below are some college ads. Examine them carefully and see what messages—directly and indirectly—are contained in their images and text. How are they attempting to "sell" a college degree to prospective students and their parents and families?

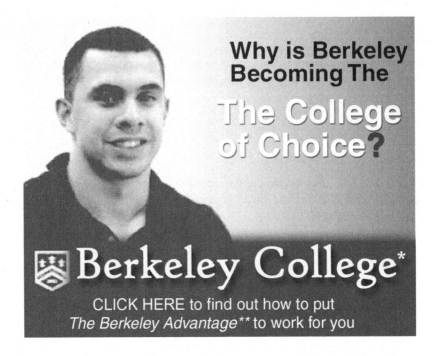

Virginia Intermont College

Assignment # 7

ARGUMENTS IN LITERATURE

This assignment asks you to write an essay that identifies and responds to an argument in Oscar Wilde's "The Nightingale and the Rose." The section begins with an explanation of how arguments are made through literature, some strategies to help you identify them, and an extended example that locates an argument in an excerpt from Charles Dickens's *A Christmas Carol*. After you study this extended example, you will read Oscar Wilde's short story "The Nightingale and the Rose" and write an essay that responds to the writing topic that immediately follows the story. As in previous assignments in *Write It Review*, you will find prewriting and drafting activities following Wilde's story that will help you to respond to the topic in an effective way. We encourage you to take full advantage of these prewriting and drafting activities because they will ensure that you develop your thoughts and organize them within an effective essay format.

Understanding and Responding to Arguments in Literature

One way to talk about a work of literature is to uncover the arguments it makes, arguments that are presented and supported through the elements of the story it tells. An argument is a kind of discussion in which reasons are advanced for (or against) some value or ethical position, often to influence or change people's ideas and actions. The first step to discussing literature as argument is to understand the way literature works *representationally*. In other words, readers are meant to see a fictional story and its characters as dramatizing general human experiences that all of its readers will recognize and understand. Authors hope to use the devices of fiction to capture a representation of life that is insightful and that rings true for readers.

For example, even though Shakespeare's *Romeo and Juliet* is a centuries-old story of two young lovers in a small town in Italy who cannot marry because of an old feud between their families, readers today understand that it is also about the experience of love and the ethical dilemmas we face when our individual desires conflict with the demands of those who have authority over us. We interpret the argument in *Romeo and Juliet* when we decide what the work is saying about this particular ethical dilemma. Those of you who know this play, what do you think it is arguing? That love is more important than duty? That love put over duty to others leads to tragedy? What details about the plot or characters in this play make you answer in the way that you have? As you answer these questions, you begin to see *Romeo and Juliet* as a form of argument. Even though you and your classmates may have different answers, many of your answers may be equally compelling if each person can bring out the elements in the play that support his or her interpretation. One of the reasons that we continue to read works such as *Romeo and Juliet* is that they encourage us to discuss and question our experiences and our beliefs as individuals and as members of human society.

Works of fiction contain one or more themes—in other words, ideas very similar to those in prose essays such as "College in America" and "Competition and Happiness." Instead of stating arguments directly, however, as in prose essays, fiction takes positions on human concerns indirectly, through the tools of fiction. Sometimes, an author's narrator will present a "thesis statement" in a fairly straightforward manner, but more often, the thesis will be implied through the events and characters of the story. Here is a set of strategies that you can use when analyzing the arguments in fiction:

5 Strategies to Identify Arguments in Fiction

1. List the main characters in the story. Briefly summarize their words and actions. What do these things suggest about their personalities and relationships with each other?

2. Identify the main conflict in the story. What is the subject or issue of the conflict? What more general issue is the story *representing* with this conflict?

3. Identify the two or more sides of the conflict. Looking back at the characters you listed in #1, what does each character contribute to the conflict through his or her words or actions? Look carefully at the evidence that each character (including the narrator) presents, and try to determine how the evidence is being linked to support a position.

4. Look over what you wrote for #2 and #3, and then try to state the argument that the story and its characters are representing. This time, try to state the argument in general terms that readers can apply to their own lives.

5. Identify how the story resolves the conflict. This resolution leads directly to the thesis statement, or the story's position in the argument.

Read the following excerpt taken from Dickens's *Christmas Carol*. Pay attention to the conflict between Scrooge's beliefs versus the beliefs of his nephew, two townsmen, and Scrooge's clerk Bob Cratchit. Then use these five steps to see the passage as an argument.

A CHRISTMAS CAROL

CHARLES DICKENS

an excerpt from Chapter 1—"Marley's Ghost"

Once upon a time—of all the good days in the year, on Christmas Eve—old Scrooge sat busy in his counting-house. It was cold, bleak, biting weather: foggy withal: and he could hear the people in the court outside go wheezing up and down, beating their hands upon their breasts, and stamping their feet upon the pavement stones to warm them. The city clocks had only just gone three, but it was quite dark already: It had not been light all day, and candles were flaring in the windows of the neighbouring offices, like ruddy smears upon the palpable brown air. The fog came pouring in at every chink and keyhole, and was so dense without, that although the court was of the narrowest, the houses opposite were mere phantoms. To see the dingy cloud come drooping down, obscuring everything, one might have thought that Nature lived hard by, and was brewing on a large scale.

The door of Scrooge's counting-house was open that he might keep his eye upon his clerk, who in a dismal little cell beyond, a sort of tank, was copying letters. Scrooge had a very small fire, but the clerk's fire was so very much smaller that it looked like one coal. But he couldn't replenish it, for Scrooge kept the coal-box in his own room; and so surely as the clerk came in with the shovel, the master predicted that it would be necessary for them to part. Wherefore the clerk put on his white comforter, and tried to warm himself at the candle; in which effort, not being a man of a strong imagination, he failed.

"A merry Christmas, uncle! God save you!" cried a cheerful voice. It was the voice of Scrooge's nephew, who came upon him so quickly that this was the first intimation he had of his approach.

"Bah!" said Scrooge. "Humbug!"

He had so heated himself with rapid walking in the fog and frost, this nephew of Scrooge's, that he was all in a glow; his face was ruddy and handsome; his eyes sparkled, and his breath smoked again.

"Christmas a humbug, uncle!" said Scrooge's nephew. "You don't mean that, I am sure."

"I do," said Scrooge. "Merry Christmas! What right have you to be merry? What reason have you to be merry? You're poor enough."

"Come, then," returned the nephew gaily. "What right have you to be dismal? What reason have you to be morose? You're rich enough."

Scrooge having no better answer ready on the spur of the moment, said, "Bah!" again; and followed it up with "Humbug."

"Don't be cross, uncle," said the nephew.

"What else can I be," returned the uncle, "when I live in such a world of fools as this Merry Christmas! Out upon Merry Christmas. What's Christmas time to you but a time for paying bills without money; a time for finding yourself a year older, but not an hour richer; a time for balancing your books and having every item in 'em through a round dozen of months presented dead against you? If I could work my will," said Scrooge indignantly, "every idiot who goes about with 'Merry Christmas' on his lips, should be boiled with his own pudding, and buried with a stake of holly through his heart. He should!"

"Uncle!" pleaded the nephew.

"Nephew!" returned the uncle, sternly, "keep Christmas in your own way, and let me keep it in mine."

A Christmas Story by Charles Dickens, 1843.

"Keep it!" repeated Scrooge's nephew. "But you don't keep it."

"Let me leave it alone, then," said Scrooge. "Much good may it do you! Much good it has ever done you!"

"There are many things from which I might have derived good, by which I have not profited, I dare say," returned the nephew: "Christmas among the rest. But I am sure I have always thought of Christmas time, when it has come round—apart from the veneration due to its sacred name and origin, if anything belonging to it can be apart from that—as a good time: a kind, forgiving, charitable, pleasant time: the only time I know of, in the long calendar of the year, when men and women seem by one consent to open their shut-up hearts freely, and to think of people below them as if they really were fellow-passengers to the grave, and not another race of creatures bound on other journeys. And therefore, uncle, though it has never put a scrap of gold or silver in my pocket, I believe that it *has* done me good, and *will* do me good; and I say, God bless it!"

The clerk in the tank involuntarily applauded. Becoming immediately sensible of the impropriety, he poked the fire, and extinguished the last frail spark for ever.

"Let me hear another sound from *you*," said Scrooge, "and you'll keep your Christmas by losing your situation. You're quite a powerful speaker, sir," he added, turning to his nephew. "I wonder you don't go into Parliament."

"Don't be angry, uncle. Come! Dine with us tomorrow."

Scrooge said that he would see him—yes, indeed he did. He went the whole length of the expression, and said that he would see him in that extremity first.

"But why?" cried Scrooge's nephew. "Why?"

"Why did you get married?" said Scrooge.

"Because I fell in love."

"Because you fell in love!" growled Scrooge, as if that were the only one thing in the world more ridiculous than a merry Christmas. "Good afternoon!"

"Nay, uncle, but you never came to see me before that happened. Why give it as a reason for not coming now?"

"Good afternoon," said Scrooge.

"I want nothing from you; I ask nothing of you; why cannot we be friends?"

"Good afternoon," said Scrooge.

"I am sorry, with all my heart, to find you so resolute. We have never had any quarrel, to which I have been a party. But I have made the trial in homage to Christmas, and I'll keep my Christmas humour to the last. So A Merry Christmas, uncle!"

"Good afternoon!" said Scrooge.

"And A Happy New Year!"

"Good afternoon!" said Scrooge.

His nephew left the room without an angry word, notwithstanding. He stopped at the outer door to bestow the greetings of the season on the clerk, who, cold as he was, was warmer than Scrooge; for he returned them cordially.

"There's another fellow," muttered Scrooge, who overheard him: "my clerk, with fifteen shillings a week, and a wife and family, talking about a merry Christmas. I'll retire to Bedlam."

This lunatic, in letting Scrooge's nephew out, had let two other people in. They were portly gentlemen, pleasant to behold, and now stood, with their hats off, in Scrooge's office. They had books and papers in their hands, and bowed to him.

"Scrooge and Marley's, I believe," said one of the gentlemen, referring to his list. "Have I the pleasure of addressing Mr. Scrooge, or Mr. Marley?"

"Mr. Marley has been dead these seven years," Scrooge replied. "He died seven years ago, this very night."

"We have no doubt his liberality is well represented by his surviving partner," said the gentleman, presenting his credentials.

It certainly was; for they had been two kindred spirits. At the ominous word "liberality," Scrooge frowned, and shook his head, and handed the credentials back.

"At this festive season of the year, Mr. Scrooge," said the gentleman, taking up a pen, "it is more than usually desirable that we should make some slight provision for the Poor and destitute, who suffer greatly at the present time. Many thousands are in want of common necessaries; hundreds of thousands are in want of common comforts, sir."

"Are there no prisons?" asked Scrooge.

"Plenty of prisons," said the gentleman, laying down the pen again.

"And the Union workhouses?" demanded Scrooge. "Are they still in operation?"

"They are. Still," returned the gentleman, "I wish I could say they were not."

"The Treadmill and the Poor Law are in full vigour, then?" said Scrooge.

"Both very busy, sir."

"Oh! I was afraid, from what you said at first, that something had occurred to stop them in their useful course," said Scrooge. "I'm very glad to hear it."

"Under the impression that they scarcely furnish Christian cheer of mind or body to the multitude," returned the gentleman, "a few of us are endeavouring to raise a fund to buy the Poor some meat and drink, and means of warmth. We choose this time, because it is a time, of all others, when Want is keenly felt, and Abundance rejoices. What shall I put you down for?"

"Nothing!" Scrooge replied.

"You wish to be anonymous?"

"I wish to be left alone," said Scrooge. "Since you ask me what I wish, gentlemen, that is my answer. I don't make merry myself at Christmas, and I can't afford to make idle people merry. I help to support the establishments I have mentioned: they cost enough: and those who are badly off must go there."

"Many can't go there; and many would rather die."

"If they would rather die," said Scrooge, "they had better do it, and decrease the surplus population. Besides—excuse me—I don't know that."

"But you might know it," observed the gentleman.

"It's not my business," Scrooge returned. "It's enough for a man to understand his own business, and not to interfere with other people's. Mine occupies me constantly. Good afternoon, gentlemen!"

Seeing clearly that it would be useless to pursue their point, the gentlemen withdrew. Scrooge resumed his labours with an improved opinion of himself, and in a more facetious temper than was usual with him.

Meanwhile, the fog and darkness thickened so, that people ran about with flaring links, proffering their services to go before horses in carriages, and conduct them on their way. The ancient tower of a church, whose gruff old bell was always peeping slyly down at Scrooge out of a gothic window in the wall, became invisible, and struck the hours and quarters in the clouds, with tremulous vibrations afterwards as if its teeth were chattering in its frozen head up there. The cold became intense. In the main street, at the corner of the court, some labourers were repairing the gas-pipes, and had lighted a great fire in a brazier, round which a party of ragged men and boys were gathered: warming their hands and winking their eyes before the blaze in rapture. The water-plug being left in solitude, its overflowings sullenly congealed, and turned to misanthropic ice. The brightness of the shops where holly sprigs and berries crackled in the lamp-heat of the windows, made pale faces ruddy as they passed. Poulterers' and grocers' trades became a splendid joke: a glorious pageant, with which it was next to impossible to believe that such dull principles as bargain and sale had anything to do. The Lord Mayor, in the stronghold of the mighty Mansion House, gave orders to his fifty cooks and butlers to keep Christmas as a Lord Mayor's household should; and even the little tailor, whom he had fined five shillings on the previous Monday for being drunk and bloodthirsty in the streets, stirred up tomorrow's pudding in his garret, while his lean wife and the baby sallied out to buy the beef.

Foggier yet, and colder! Piercing, searching, biting cold. If the good Saint Dunstan had but nipped the Evil Spirit's nose with a touch of such weather as that, instead of using his familiar weapons, then indeed he would have roared to lusty purpose. The owner of one scant young nose, gnawed and mumbled by the hungry cold as bones are gnawed by dogs, stooped down at Scrooge's keyhole to regale him with a Christmas carol: but at the first sound of "God bless you, merry gentleman! May nothing you dismay!" Scrooge seized the ruler with such energy of action that the singer fled in terror, leaving the keyhole to the fog and even more congenial frost.

At length, the hour of shutting up the counting-house arrived. With an ill will, Scrooge dismounted from his stool, and tacitly admitted the fact to the expectant clerk in the Tank, who instantly snuffed his candle out, and put on his hat.

"You'll want all day tomorrow, I suppose?" said Scrooge.

"If quite convenient, sir."

"It's not convenient," said Scrooge, "and it's not fair. If I was to stop half-a-crown for it, you'd think yourself ill-used, I'll be bound?"

The clerk smiled faintly.

"And yet," said Scrooge, "you don't think *me* ill-used, when I pay a day's wages for no work."

The clerk observed that it was only once a year.

"A poor excuse for picking a man's pocket every twenty-fifth of December!" said Scrooge, buttoning his great-coat to the chin. "But I suppose you must have the whole day. Be here all the earlier next morning!"

The clerk promised that he would; and Scrooge walked out with a growl. The office was closed in a twinkling, and the clerk, with the long ends of his white comforter dangling below his waist (for he boasted no great-coat), went down a slide on Cornhill, at the end of a lane of boys, twenty times, in honour of its being Christmas Eve, and then ran home to Camden Town as hard as he could pelt, to play at blindman's buff.

Writing Topic

What is Scrooge's attitude toward earning money, and how does it differ from his nephew's? How valid do you find Scrooge's position as he explains it to the various characters in this passage of the story? Be sure to support your position with evidence taken from your experience, your observation of others, the media, and your reading.

Prewriting for a Directed Summary

As in earlier chapters of *Write It Review*, you will use the answers you fill in here when you write a directed summary in response to the first part of the writing topic for this assignment.

first part of the writing topic:

What is Scrooge's attitude toward earning money, and how does it differ from his nephew's?

This question asks you to look at this chapter from two particular points of view: that of the character Scrooge and that of his nephew. It asks you to determine, by these characters' words and actions, their beliefs regarding work and money. To answer this first part of the writing assignment, you will have to look carefully at the conversation between Scrooge and his nephew to understand how each man weighs the importance of these aspects of life. In addition to their discussion, look carefully at the story so as to draw conclusions about the type of life each leads and how their lifestyles underscore their beliefs about work and money.

You will remember from working on the nonfiction essays in the previous chapters that argument works by putting together and linking evidence to support a conclusion. Rather than having a writer's views presented directly, as in "Why We Crave Horror Movies" or "Competition and Happiness," for this assignment you will have to identify the evidence as the writer presents it through the plot and characters in the story. What position does Scrooge represent? What evidence can you gather from his words and actions, and how will this evidence support your interpretation of his beliefs? What position on work and money does Scrooge's nephew represent? What evidence do you find in his words and actions that illustrates his position? Here are the five steps you can use to isolate and identify the two sides of the argument.

1. **List the main characters in the story. Briefly summarize their words and actions. What do these things suggest about their personalities and relationships with each other?**

Scrooge, the owner of the business, does not provide enough coal for his clerk, Bob Cratchit, who is perpetually cold. A little later in the story, Scrooge refuses to help the two portly gentlemen with their charitable efforts, and near the end, he expresses anger and disapproval that Cratchit wants Christmas Day off, particularly since the clerk expects a paid holiday. Scrooge's favorite exclamation is "Bah, humbug!" He says it liberally, especially when people express sentiments of kindness or charity.

His nephew is an irrepressibly jolly young man who wishes his uncle a merry Christmas and looks forward to the holiday because it is a time when people are kind to each other and spend time with loved ones. He married for love. He tries to reason with his uncle but does not have much success.

Uncle and nephew have an unusual relationship. Scrooge cares only for his business and has no regard at all for his nephew, who seems to be a warm and likable person. Scrooge is presented as a hard, intolerant, miserly man whose sole focus is money and who has no interest at all in other people except as they relate to business.

The nephew, on the other hand, seems to have no difficulty in caring about his uncle despite Scrooge's nasty temperament and character. The nephew is a family man, kind, loving, and tolerant of even intolerable people—perhaps his love of family is so strong that he is able to forgive Scrooge for such bad behavior.

Although the clerk (Bob Cratchit) and the two portly gentlemen are not the focus of the writing topic, both parties are presented in opposition to Scrooge. Cratchit is poor and rather pathetic, but he cheers on the nephew. The two gentlemen are presented as humanitarians because they are collecting funds for the poor. They also seem much more reasonable than Scrooge, for they clearly feel that many people are unfortunate through no fault of their own and should not be forced into workhouses and debtors' prisons.

2. Identify the main conflict in the story. What is the subject or issue of the conflict? What more general issue is the story *representing* with this conflict?

Scrooge believes that people should accumulate as much money as they can by working as much as possible. His nephew believes that being with people and giving and receiving kindness are as important as, or more important than, work and money. Their disagreement applies to people in general and how they choose to spend their time. This story makes us think about our own relationship to work and to how important we rate money and earning money versus being with family and friends.

The disagreement between Scrooge and his nephew makes us think about how much of our life and attention should be given to working and earning money. Should the human relationships in our life be placed above work, or should we think first and foremost about working to earn as much money as we can? Does happiness come more from our relationships with people or from our economic accomplishments?

3. Identify the two or more sides of the conflict. Looking back at the characters you listed in #1, what does each character contribute to the conflict through his or her words or actions? Look carefully at the evidence that each character (including the narrator) presents, and try to determine how the evidence is being linked to support a position.

Here is part of their conversation:

> **Scrooge:** "Merry Christmas! What right have you to be merry? What reason have you to be merry? You're poor enough."
>
> **The Nephew**: "Come, then. What right have you to be dismal? What reason have you to be morose? You're rich enough."
>
> **Scrooge**: "What's Christmas time to you but a time for paying bills without money; a time for finding yourself a year older, but not an hour richer; a time for balancing your books and having every item in 'em through a round dozen of months presented dead against you?"
>
> **The Nephew**: "There are many things from which I might have derived good, by which I have not profited, I dare say," returned the nephew: "Christmas among the rest. But I am sure I have always thought of Christmas time, when it has come round—apart from the veneration due to its sacred name and origin, if anything belonging to it can be apart from that—as a good time: a kind, forgiving, charitable, pleasant time: the only time I know of, in the long calendar of the year, when men and women seem by one consent to open their shut-up hearts freely, and to think of people below them as if they really were fellow-passengers to the grave, and not another race of creatures bound on other journeys. And therefore, uncle, though it has never put a scrap of gold or silver in my pocket, I believe that it *has* done me good, and *will* do me good."

Scrooge thinks that, because the nephew is poor, he should be unhappy. The nephew points out that, though Scrooge has plenty of money, he is miserable, so there is no connection between money and happiness. Scrooge answers that money is necessary to pay bills, and that without it, we will not be able to live a comfortable life because we'll always be dodging our creditors. Scrooge feels that Christmas is a waste of time because much money is spent and no work is done. The nephew, however, feels that he gets good from taking time away from thoughts of money and work in order to connect with others and form warm human relationships.

Scrooge appears to be in a bad mood through this part of the story. He is frustrated because, even though he doesn't want to change his lifestyle because of the Christmas holiday, those around him won't allow him to ignore it. The nephew seems cheerful and has a family, and he is able to reach out to his uncle to try and get him to join the holiday celebrations. Yet we learn that the celebration may be costing him money he doesn't have.

We can also look at Scrooge's discussion with the two men collecting money for the poor, and his comments to Bob Cratchit, his clerk. In both cases, Scrooge argues that people should concentrate on earning their living and supporting themselves, rather than taking time away from work to socialize.

4. **Look over what you wrote for #2 and #3, and then try to state the argument that the story and its characters are representing. This time, try to state the argument in general terms that readers can apply to their own lives.**

The interactions of the characters in this section of the story demonstrate that money does not buy happiness. Human relationships make us happy, and people are more important than money. In one way, the story is arguing that helping one another takes precedence over helping ourselves, or maybe that by helping others, we do help ourselves.

5. **Identify how the story resolves the conflict. This resolution leads directly to the thesis statement, or the story's position in the argument.**

In this case, we are working with an excerpt of the story, and there is no clear resolution. Both characters are convinced that their position is the valid one. However, the narrator has a noticeable bias against Scrooge's position. Although the story implies that the nephew might be living beyond his means, the young man is still presented in a positive light. Scrooge could easily be portrayed as a reasonable man with a reasonable preoccupation with his business and income, but he isn't. He is intolerant of his nephew and anyone else who does not see things his way, yet his nephew is tolerant of Scrooge's intolerance and disagreeableness.

Notice that you can use the responses to these five questions to answer the first part of the writing topic: "What is Scrooge's attitude toward earning money, and how does it differ from his nephew's?" If you were writing this essay, you could easily answer this question by rephrasing these answers in a way that answered this question directly.

Hint

Notice that, when writing about fiction, the convention is to use present tense verbs.

Developing an Opinion and Working Thesis Statement

The second question in the writing topic that follows the selection from *A Christmas Carol* asks you to take a position of your own:

> second part of the writing topic:
>
> *How valid do you find Scrooge's position as he explains it to the various characters in this passage of the story?*

Do you agree with the position on work and money that Scrooge represents in the story? To answer this, you would simply use the thesis frame (which you should recognize from previous chapters of this book) to formulate a thesis statement. As you may have done in previous chapters of *Write It Review*, if you're not sure what position you want to take, do some prewriting to develop your ideas, and then come back to writing a working thesis statement.

a. What is the issue of the reading selection that the writing topic asks you to consider? In other words, what is the main topic the essay is about?

It asks whether our lives should focus on earning money and whether money should always be our priority.

b. What is the character Scrooge's opinion about that issue?

He believes that earning money comes first and that nothing should distract us from that concern.

c. What is your opinion about the issue; i.e., will you agree or disagree with him?

In this chapter of Dickens's Christmas Carol, *Scrooge believes that earning money is the most important priority in life, a value system that (add your position on the issue).*

The last part of the writing topic asks you to support the argument you put forward in your thesis statement:

> last part of the writing topic:
>
> *Be sure to support your position with evidence taken from your experience, your observation of others, the media, and your reading.*

If you had to write this essay, the majority of it would be devoted to supporting the position you take in your thesis statement. You would do some prewriting to explore your ideas and develop your supporting topics, and then use an outline to plan and draft your essay. As you can see, even though finding arguments in literature requires you to read with a somewhat different perspective, you can use the same steps of the writing process that you have worked with throughout the writing assignments in *Write It Review*.

The Dickens example is a discussion with several characters that is easily recognizable as a debate, so the argument is fairly clear. But what happens when this is not the case? How do you find the argument when you are asked to look at an extended narrative that uses characters, plot, and setting to present a point of view on an aspect of human life? Go on to the next pages and try out the five steps using a short story, Oscar Wilde's "The Nightingale and the Rose."

THE NIGHTINGALE AND THE ROSE

OSCAR WILDE

"She said that she would dance with me if I brought her red roses," cried the young Student; "but in all my garden there is no red rose."

From her nest in the holm-oak tree the Nightingale heard him, and she looked out through the leaves, and wondered.

"No red rose in all my garden!" he cried, and his beautiful eyes filled with tears. "Ah, on what little things does happiness depend! I have read all that the wise men have written, and all the secrets of philosophy are mine, yet for want of a red rose is my life made wretched."

"Here at last is a true lover," said the Nightingale. "Night after night have I sung of him, though I knew him not: Night after night have I told his story to the stars, and now I see him. His hair is dark as the hyacinth-blossom, and his lips are red as the rose of his desire; but passion has made his face like pale ivory, and sorrow has set her seal upon his brow."

"The Prince gives a ball tomorrow night," murmured the young Student, "and my love will be of the company. If I bring her a red rose, she will dance with me till dawn. If I bring her a red rose, I shall hold her in my arms, and she will lean her head upon my shoulder, and her hand will be clasped in mine. But there is no red rose in my garden, so I shall sit lonely, and she will pass me by. She will have no heed of me, and my heart will break."

"Here indeed is the true lover," said the Nightingale. "What I sing of, he suffers—what is joy to me, to him is pain. Surely Love is a wonderful thing. It is more precious than emeralds, and dearer than fine opals. Pearls and pomegranates cannot buy it, nor is it set forth in the marketplace. It may not be purchased of the merchants, nor can it be weighed out in the balance for gold."

"The musicians will sit in their gallery," said the young Student, "and play upon their stringed instruments, and my love will dance to the sound of the harp and the violin. She will dance so lightly that her feet will not touch the floor, and the courtiers in their gay dresses will throng around her. But with me she will not dance, for I have no red rose to give her"; and he flung himself down on the grass, and buried his face in his hands, and wept.

"Why is he weeping?" asked a little Green Lizard, as he ran past him with his tail in the air.

"Why, indeed?" said a Butterfly, who was fluttering about after a sunbeam.

"Why, indeed?" whispered a Daisy to his neighbor, in a soft, low voice.

"He is weeping for a red rose," said the Nightingale.

"For a red rose?" they cried; "how very ridiculous!" and the little Lizard, who was something of a cynic, laughed outright.

But the Nightingale understood the secret of the Student's sorrow, and she sat silent in the oak tree, and thought about the mystery of Love.

Suddenly, she spread her brown wings for flight, and soared into the air. She passed through the grove like a shadow, and like a shadow she sailed across the garden.

In the center of the grass-plot was standing a beautiful Rose-tree, and when she saw it, she flew over to it, and lit upon a spray.

"Give me a red rose," she cried, "and I will sing you my sweetest song."

But the Tree shook its head.

"My roses are white," it answered; "as white as the foam of the sea, and whiter than the snow upon the mountain. But go to my brother who grows round the old sundial, and perhaps he will give you what you want."

From The Happy Prince and Other Tales by Oscar Wilde, (1888).

So the Nightingale flew over to the Rose-tree that was growing round the old sundial.

"Give me a red rose," she cried, "and I will sing you my sweetest song."

But the Tree shook its head.

"My roses are yellow," it answered; "as yellow as the hair of the mermaiden who sits upon an amber throne, and yellower than the daffodil that blooms in the meadow before the mower comes with his scythe. But go to my brother who grows beneath the Student's window, and perhaps he will give you what you want."

So the Nightingale flew over to the Rose-tree that was growing beneath the Student's window.

"Give me a red rose," she cried, "and I will sing you my sweetest song."

But the Tree shook its head.

"My roses are red," it answered, "as red as the feet of the dove, and redder than the great fans of coral that wave and wave in the ocean cavern. But the winter has chilled my veins, and the frost has nipped my buds, and the storm has broken my branches, and I shall have no roses at all this year."

"One red rose is all I want," cried the Nightingale, "only one red rose! Is there no way by which I can get it?"

"There is a way," answered the Tree; "but it is so terrible that I dare not tell it to you."

"Tell it to me," said the Nightingale, "I am not afraid."

"If you want a red rose," said the Tree, "you must build it out of music by moonlight, and stain it with your own heart's-blood. You must sing to me with your breast against a thorn. All night long you must sing to me, and the thorn must pierce your heart, and your life-blood must flow into my veins, and become mine."

"Death is a great price to pay for a red rose," cried the Nightingale, "and Life is very dear to all. It is pleasant to sit in the green wood, and to watch the Sun in his chariot of gold, and the Moon in her chariot of pearl. Sweet is the scent of the hawthorn, and sweet are the blue-bells that hide in the valley, and the heather that blows on the hill. Yet Love is better than Life, and what is the heart of a bird compared to the heart of a man?"

So she spread her brown wings for flight, and soared into the air. She swept over the garden like a shadow, and like a shadow she sailed through the grove.

The young Student was still lying on the grass, where she had left him, and the tears were not yet dry in his beautiful eyes.

"Be happy," cried the Nightingale, "be happy; you shall have your red rose. I will build it out of music by moonlight, and stain it with my own heart's-blood. All that I ask of you in return is that you will be a true lover, for Love is wiser than Philosophy, though she is wise, and mightier than Power, though he is mighty. Flame-colored are his wings, and colored like flame is his body. His lips are sweet as honey, and his breath is like frankincense."

The Student looked up from the grass, and listened, but he could not understand what the Nightingale was saying to him, for he only knew the things that are written down in books.

But the Oak-tree understood, and felt sad, for he was very fond of the little Nightingale who had built her nest in his branches.

"Sing me one last song," he whispered; "I shall feel very lonely when you are gone."

So the Nightingale sang to the Oak-tree, and her voice was like water bubbling from a silver jar.

When she had finished her song the Student got up and pulled a notebook and a lead pencil out of his pocket.

"She has form," he said to himself, as he walked away through the grove, "That cannot be denied to her; but has she got feeling? I am afraid not. In fact, she is like most artists; she is all style, without any sincerity. She would not sacrifice herself for others. She thinks merely of music, and everybody knows that the arts are selfish. Still, it must be admitted that she has some beautiful notes in her voice. What a pity it is that they do not mean anything, or do any practical good." And he went into his room, and lay down on his little pallet-bed, and began to think of his love; and, after a time, he fell asleep.

And when the Moon shone in the heavens, the Nightingale flew to the Rose-tree, and set her breast against the thorn. All night long she sang with her breast against the thorn, and the cold crystal Moon leaned down and listened. All night long she sang, and the thorn went deeper and deeper into her breast, and her life-blood ebbed away from her.

She sang first of the birth of love in the heart of a boy and a girl. And on the topmost spray of the Rose-tree, there blossomed a marvelous rose, petal following petal, as song followed song. Pale was it, at first, as the mist that hangs over the river—pale as the feet of the morning, and silver as the wings of the dawn. As the shadow of a rose in a mirror of silver, as the shadow of a rose in a water-pool, so was the rose that blossomed on the topmost spray of the Tree.

But the Tree cried to the Nightingale to press closer against the thorn. "Press closer, little Nightingale," cried the Tree, "or the Day will come before the rose is finished."

So the Nightingale pressed closer against the thorn, and louder and louder grew her song, for she sang of the birth of passion in the soul of a man and a maid.

And a delicate flush of pink came into the leaves of the rose, like the flush in the face of the bridegroom when he kisses the lips of the bride. But the thorn had not yet reached her heart, so the rose's heart remained white, for only a Nightingale's heart's-blood can crimson the heart of a rose.

And the Tree cried to the Nightingale to press closer against the thorn. "Press closer, little Nightingale," cried the Tree, "or the Day will come before the rose is finished."

So the Nightingale pressed closer against the thorn, and the thorn touched her heart, and a fierce pang of pain shot through her. Bitter, bitter was the pain, and wilder and wilder grew her song, for she sang of the Love that is perfected by Death, of the Love that dies not in the tomb.

And the marvelous rose became crimson, like the rose of the eastern sky. Crimson was the girdle of petals, and crimson as a ruby was the heart.

But the Nightingale's voice grew fainter, and her little wings began to beat, and a film came over her eyes. Fainter and fainter grew her song, and she felt something choking her in her throat.

Then she gave one last burst of music. The white Moon heard it, and she forgot the dawn, and lingered on in the sky. The red rose heard it, and it trembled all over with ecstasy, and opened its petals to the cold morning air. Echo bore it to her purple cavern in the hills, and woke the sleeping shepherds from their dreams. It floated through the reeds of the river, and they carried its message to the sea.

"Look, look!" cried the Tree, "the rose is finished now"; but the Nightingale made no answer, for she was lying dead in the long grass, with the thorn in her heart.

And at noon the Student opened his window and looked out.

"Why, what a wonderful piece of luck!" he cried; "here is a red rose! I have never seen any rose like it in all my life. It is so beautiful that I am sure it has a long Latin name"; and he leaned down and plucked it.

Then he put on his hat, and ran up to the Professor's house with the rose in his hand.

The daughter of the Professor was sitting in the doorway winding blue silk on a reel, and her little dog was lying at her feet.

"You said that you would dance with me if I brought you a red rose," cried the Student. "Here is the reddest rose in all the world. You will wear it tonight next your heart, and as we dance together, it will tell you how I love you."

But the girl frowned.

"I am afraid it will not go with my dress," she answered; "and, besides, the Chamberlain's nephew has sent me some real jewels, and everybody knows that jewels cost far more than flowers."

"Well, upon my word, you are very ungrateful," said the Student angrily; and he threw the rose into the street, where it fell into the gutter, and a cart-wheel went over it.

"Ungrateful!" said the girl. "I tell you what, you are very rude; and, after all, who are you? Only a Student. Why, I don't believe you have even got silver buckles to your shoes as the Chamberlain's nephew has"; and she got up from her chair and went into the house.

"What a silly thing Love is," said the Student as he walked away. "It is not half as useful as Logic, for it does not prove anything, and it is always telling one of things that are not going to happen, and making one believe things that are not true. In fact, it is quite unpractical, and, as in this age to be practical is everything, I shall go back to Philosophy and study Metaphysics."

So he returned to his room and pulled out a great dusty book, and began to read.

Writing Topic

According to the story, why does the Nightingale, an ideal representation of love, have to die? Do you agree with the story's point of view on love? Be sure to support your position with specific examples drawn from your own experience, your observations of others, and your observations drawn from the media and the larger society and culture to which you belong.

For help in responding to this topic, read the following essay that identifies an argument about love in Shakespeare's *The Taming of the Shrew*. As you read the essay, notice how *The Taming of the Shrew*'s view of love compares to the perspective in "The Nightingale and the Rose." How does your own view of love compare to them?

SHAKESPEARE FLIRTS WITH THE SADISTIC: *THE TAMING OF THE SHREW* AS A REDEFINITION OF LOVE

PAUL A. J. BEEHLER

Dr. Paul Beehler is a faculty member in the University Writing Program at the University of California, Riverside. He has published articles and given conference papers on Shakespeare.

What can one say about love? Love captures our fascination and moves us into a passionate realm, an ecstasy of sorts, that can alter our perception and drastically affect our interaction with the world around us. For many, love binds them in relationships and defines who they are. The force of nature can even penetrate the armor of individual identities as it reshapes all entities in its path like an unrivaled juggernaut. Great crimes in history and fictitious horrors in literature have been perpetrated as a result of, and sometimes on behalf of, love. It is a curious course that Shakespeare charts for love in his renowned drama *The Taming of the Shrew*. Love in the past has always been associated with an intense passion, but it often has accompanied some element of tenderness. Shakespeare offers his audience a new definition and conception of love through the interaction of Katherina and Petruchio, two characters who revel in sadistic love—that is, love which involves pain.

Tension explodes across the stage in even the opening moments with a threat Sly utters against the hostess, "I'll pheeze you, in faith" (*Shr.* 1.1.1), and the two engage in a battle of words. The excitement of the struggle among wills is then advanced when a lord enters the stage comparing the hounds he used during a hunt.

> Lord: Saw'st thou not, boy, how Silver made it good
> At the hedge-corner, in the coldest fault?
> I would not lose the dog for twenty pound.
>
> 1 Hunter: Why, Belman is as good as he, my lord;
> He cried upon it at the merest loss,
> And twice to-day pick'd out the dullest scent.
> Trust me, I take him for the better dog.
> (*Shr.* 1.1.18-25)

The two characters lose themselves in the struggle and pain that defines the hunt; in fact, the hunters take great pleasure in sizing up their dogs' performances. They compare and analyze the beasts, even to the point of placing monetary value on Silver. The thrill of the hunt and the opportunity to have "pick'd out the dullest scent," an act which ultimately leads to the gruesome and painful death of the prey, serves as a more encompassing metaphor in Shakespeare's play: A great love can be born out of pursuit, struggle, and pain. In this opening scene and these opening lines, Shakespeare offers his audience a fragmented and brief glimpse at his new conception of love, sadistic love, which he will investigate at greater length throughout the play.

Sadistic love is a most important component in *The Taming of The Shrew*, and Petruchio offers a wonderful allusion to this end:

> Did ever Dian so become a grove
> As Kate this chamber with her princely gait?
> O, be thou Dian, and let her be Kate,
> And then let Kate be chaste, and Dian sportful!
> (2.1.258-61)

Petruchio desires Kate to transform herself into Diana, a goddess who perhaps is better known as Artemis, so that he might enjoy a "sportful" woman. The word is an interesting one, suggesting a painful and challenging athletic event, like the hunt, but also an amorous interaction. Artemis is in part known for the vengeance she takes upon Actaeon. The goddess notices Actaeon spying on her while she bathes, and her response is to transform the powerful young man into a deer. Actaeon's dogs then mercilessly pursue and eventually savage his flesh in their maws, all to the great delight of Artemis.

This love of savagery and pain, even more than the hunt, is the new love Shakespeare explores in *The Taming of the Shrew*, and the sadistic impulses manifest themselves in a number of characters and actions—far more than can be effectively discussed in this essay. The most potent of these forms, however, is the relationship shared between Petruchio and Katherina. Petruchio initially shows an interest in Kate because of the dowry Baptista offers, but the first scene of act two offers a fiery exchange between the two characters, and Petruchio is very quick to comment on Kate's "virtues," principally her reputation for inflicting harm on those around her. Kate's aptitude for sadistic acts is a quality Petruchio cannot resist as he succumbs to his love for pain and utters those words that will guide his actions throughout the drama: "Myself am mov'd to woo thee for my wife" (*Shr.* 2.1.193).

The young suitor cannot help himself and is "mov'd" beyond his own restraint. Monetary considerations may have enticed him before he meets the shrew, but once in Kate's physical presence, he is trapped like a satellite around a planet. The exchange that immediately ensues between the two characters is spirited, fervent, and unrelenting in the pursuit of pain . . . and both take great pleasure, as contradictory as that statement might be, in the exchange. Petruchio declares directly his goal in that he desires to "bring you from a wild Kate to a Kate/ Conformable as other household Kates" (*Shr.* 2.1.276-77), but he celebrates and indeed privileges the biting exchange with Kate. In the heat of battle, Katherina's animus turns towards a philippic against Petruchio's physical image:

> Petruchio: Why, here's no crab, and therefore look not sour.
> Katherina: There is, there is.
> Petruchio: Then show it me.
> Katherina: Had I a glass, I would.
> Petruchio: What, you mean my face?
> Katherina: Well aim'd of such a young one.
> Petruchio: Now, by Saint George, I am too young for you.
> (*Shr.* 2.1.230-36)

Petruchio enjoys the battle, but more importantly, he relishes the insults that he heaps upon

Kate and that are, in a reciprocal fashion, heaped upon him. This struggle of words places the two in the very throes of love and passion, and the sadism and pain that are inflicted are at the very heart of their attraction—they are, in essence, defining markers of their attraction. The two dance a painful waltz to Shakespeare's newfound music that defines an uncommon love, a love grounded in dysphoria. This scene offers the most intense moments between Kate and Petruchio in the entire play, and, arguably, provides the audience with the closest construction of their unadulterated love, a love for pain.

This deep-seated desire for pain is not limited to the emotional and intellectual banter that Katherina and Petruchio explore. Shakespeare offers hints that his sadistic love ventures into the physical and even sexual. In the midst of their volleys, Petruchio embarks on a provocative attack:

> Petruchio: Who knows not where a wasp does wear his sting?
> In his tail?
> Katherina: In his tongue.
> Petruchio: Whose tongue?
> Katherina: Yours, if you talk of tales, and so farewell.
> Petruchio: What, with my tongue in your tail? Nay,
> come again, Good Kate; I am a gentleman—
> Katherina: That I'll try. *She strikes him.*
> (*Shr.* 2.1.213-19)

This excerpt moves the sadistic play, at the end of the lines, to the realm of the physical when Kate strikes Petruchio. Petruchio is not deterred; in fact, the blow seems to invigorate him as does the debate at hand. Likewise, Kate expresses a passion for inflicting and receiving violence as it is communicated through several media. The other form of violence that Shakespeare considers in this moment is a sexually explicit violence where, in lieu of more common sexual acts (whatever those may be), tongues are placed in tails. The puns are witty, and a clear battle transpires on an intellectual plane, but a heightened sexual (and physical) discomfort also brings great pleasure to the two combatants when considering the seemingly uncomfortable act of inserting a tongue into a tail. I think this revelry in pain and discomfort is extended beyond the characters and into the realm of the audience. Even now, in this moment of critical analysis, a delightful love of pain is expressed through the embarrassing act of discussing tongues in tails. We do not want to hear of such acts, and yet we savor them, and our curiosity urges us to read on if such music be the food of life.

Ultimately, Shakespeare's addition to love, a concept of a "sadistic love," drives the action and intensity in *The Taming of the Shrew*. Both Petruchio and Kate, prime representatives of such newly explored *amour*, are never so much in love as when they seek their most painful exchanges (intellectually, physically, emotionally, and sexually) in the pugnacious dialogue that transpires in the first scene of act two. The thrill of the hunt is no doubt imbued with excitement, but a sadistic love is the underlying force that Shakespeare employs to change the landscape and very definition of love.

Discussion Questions

1. Why does Beehler call the course Shakespeare charts for love in *The Taming of the Shrew* "curious" and "new"? Do you agree that Katherina and Petruchio's relationship is unusual? If you agree, give some examples of similar relationships and in real life. If you disagree, explain your reasons, and offer supporting evidence.

2. In what ways does Petruchio's love for Katherina resemble the Student's love for the daughter of the Professor? In what ways does it differ?

3. Although the Student turns away from love at the end of "The Nightingale and the Rose," Petruchio marries Kate at the end of Shakespeare's play. Which ending do you find more satisfying or more realistic? Explain your answer.

Now go on and complete the prewriting pages for "The Nightingale and the Rose." They will help you further to develop your ideas and draft your essay.

Vocabulary Check

Use a dictionary to define the following words from Oscar Wilde's "The Nightingale and the Rose." Write all meanings that are relevant to the ideas in the passage. Then find each word in his story and underline the sentence that contains it.

1. *wretched*

   _____

   _____

   _____

   _____

2. *seal (not the animal)*

   _____

   _____

   _____

   _____

3. *clasp (verb)*

   _____

   _____

   _____

   _____

4. *gallery*

   _____

   _____

   _____

   _____

5. *courtier*

   _____

   _____

   _____

   _____

6. *throng (verb)*

   _____

_____

_____

_____

7. *cynic*

_____

_____

_____

_____

8. *soar*

_____

_____

_____

_____

9. *sundial*

_____

_____

_____

_____

10. *scythe*

_____

_____

_____

_____

11. *chariot*

_____

_____

_____

_____

12. *frankincense*

_____

_____

_____

_____

13. *pallet*

_____

_____

_____

_____

Questions to Guide Your Reading

Paragraphs 1-2

What is the Student looking for in the garden? Why does he need it? Who overhears the Student in the garden?

Paragraph 3

Does the Student think that his studies have helped him find happiness in life? Why or why not?

Paragraph 4

Why is the Nightingale predisposed to have sympathy for the Student's situation?

Paragraph 5

What is the occasion the Student anticipates, and what are the two alternative experiences he foresees for himself at that time?

Paragraph 6

How does the Nightingale define true love?

Paragraph 7

What are the details of the negative alternative that the Student pictures in his mind, and what is his response to them?

Paragraphs 8-13

How do the other characters in nature feel about the Student's emotional response to the situation? Why does the Nightingale not share their reaction?

Paragraphs 14-26

Why is each of the trees the Nightingale visits unable to give her what she wants?

Paragraphs 27-30

Why does the third tree hesitate to tell the Nightingale about a way to obtain the object the bird seeks?

Paragraph 31

How does the Nightingale reason that it is important to pay the ultimate price for the prize it desires? Is her decision an easy one?

Paragraphs 32-34

What message does the Nightingale sing to the Student? What does the Nightingale ask in return for her sacrifice?

Paragraph 35

How does the Student respond to the Nightingale? Why is that the nature of his response?

Paragraphs 36-40

How does the Oak-tree feel about the Nightingale's plan? What favor does the tree ask of the Nightingale? How does the Student respond to the favor the Nightingale grants the tree?

Paragraphs 41-51

What are the stages that lead to the conclusion of the Nightingale's plan?

Paragraphs 52-54

When does the Student discover the result of the Nightingale's sacrifice? To what does he attribute this result? What action does the Student then take?

Paragraphs 55-60

What does the Student say to the girl? How does she respond? What is his reaction to her response?

Paragraphs 61-62

What conclusion does the Student come to about love? How does this conclusion change his life?

Prewriting for a Directed Summary

Don't forget to look carefully at the writing topic that follows Wilde's story. Notice its three parts. The first part asks you about a central idea in the story—ideal love. Because you are working with literature, you will have to interpret the elements from the story to identify its messages. Remember that you will want to write a *directed* summary, meaning one that responds specifically to the first question in the writing topic. Your answers to the questions below will guide you to discover the story's thesis statement—its position—on the first question regarding ideal love.

> first part of the writing topic:
>
> *According to the story, why does the Nightingale, an ideal representation of love, have to die?*

To answer this question, you must do more than simply retell the plot of the story. Before you can explain the necessity of the Nightingale's death, you must also consider the difference between the Nightingale's definition of love and the love experienced by the Student.

Focus Questions

1. What is the reason that the Student weeps at the beginning of the story? What is it he wants, and what is stopping him from obtaining his heart's desire? Does the Nightingale have the same understanding as the Student of that desire? What general issue is the story representing with this conflict?

2. Why is the Nightingale predisposed to help the Student? Did the Nightingale know the Student before the evening the story takes place?

3. How does the Nightingale provide the Student with the object he seeks? What reasons does the bird give for making the ultimate sacrifice? What characteristics of love does this sacrifice represent?

4. What is the basis of the Student's love for the girl? When he contemplates the character of the object of his love, what qualities does he see in her? In what important way is she different from the Nightingale?

5. Identify the Student's, the Nightingale's, and the girl's view of love in the story. These different views form the terms of the argument. How is each of the main characters aligned in relation to the conflict? That is, examine the words and actions of each character to determine the understanding of love each seems to have, and how these views differ.

6. In the end, what happens to both the token of the Student's love and the love itself?

Before drafting your working thesis statement, spend some time with the "5 Strategies to Identify Arguments in Fiction" that are presented earlier in this unit. They will help you to focus your ideas as you plan your directed summary, and, because they are designed to help you to interpret a work of literature, they will get you thinking about the position you want to take in your thesis statement. Here they are:

5 Strategies to Identify Arguments in Fiction

1. List the main characters in the story. Briefly summarize their words and actions. What do these things suggest about their personalities and relationships with each other?

2. Identify the main conflict in the story. What is the subject or issue of the conflict? What more general issue is the story *representing* with this conflict?

3. Identify the two or more sides of the conflict. Looking back at the characters you listed in #1, what does each character contribute to the conflict through his or her words or actions? Look carefully at the evidence that each character (including the narrator) presents, and try to determine how the evidence is being linked to support a position.

4. Look over what you wrote for #2 and #3, and then try to state the argument that the story and its characters are representing. This time, try to state the argument in general terms that readers can apply to their own lives.

5. Identify how the story resolves the conflict. This resolution leads directly to the thesis statement, or the story's position in the argument.

Developing an Opinion and Working Thesis Statement

The second question in the writing topic asks you to consider the story's position, think about the reasons it presents for taking that position, and decide if you are convinced that the story is right.

second question in the writing topic:

Do you agree with the story's point of view on love?

Make sure you answer this part of the question directly; it is your thesis statement. It is very important that you write a clear thesis statement, one that focuses on the story as a whole.

1. Use the following thesis frame to formulate the basic elements of your thesis statement:
   a. What is the issue of the story that the question asks you to consider?

   _____

   b. What is the story's point of view on that issue?

   _____

   c. What is your position on the issue, and will you agree or disagree with the story's perspective?

   _____

   _____

   _____

2. Now use the elements you isolated in the thesis frame to write a thesis statement. You likely will have to revise it several times until it captures your idea clearly.

   _____

   _____

Prewriting to Find Support for Your Thesis Statement

The last part of the writing topic asks you to develop and support the position you took in your thesis statement by drawing on your own experience and readings.

> third part of the writing topic:
>
> *Be sure to support your position with specific examples drawn from your own experience, your observations of others, and your observations drawn from the media and the larger society and culture to which you belong.*

Use the guiding questions below to develop your ideas and find concrete support for them. The proof or evidence you present is an important element in supporting your argument and a significant aspect of making your ideas persuasive for your readers.

1. As you begin to develop your own examples, think about how important love is in your life and in the lives of those you know. How do you and others imagine ideal love? Does gender affect one's idea of love? Is ideal love found in the relationships you and others have had? Any experience you have had that says something about this central idea can provide you with an example to support your thesis. List as many ideas as you can and freewrite about the significance of each. Is your point of view on love like or unlike that of the story?

   Once you've written your ideas, look them over carefully. Try to group the ideas you've listed or developed in your freewriting into categories. Then, give each category a label. That is, cluster ideas that seem to have something in common and, for each cluster, identify that shared quality by giving it a name.

2. Now make another list, but this time focus on examples from the media and your knowledge of contemporary society. Which of these examples affirm the ideas in Wilde's story, and which ones challenge them? List and/or freewrite about all the relevant ideas you can think of, even those about which you are hesitant.

Once you've written your ideas, look them over carefully. Try to group the ideas you've listed, or developed in your freewriting, into categories. Then, give each category a label. That is, cluster ideas that seem to have something in common and, for each cluster, identify that shared quality by giving it a name.

3. Now that you've developed categories, look through them and select two or three to develop in your essay. Make sure they are relevant to your thesis and are important enough to persuade your readers. Then, in the space below, briefly summarize each item in your categories and explain how it supports your thesis statement.

The information and ideas you develop in this exercise will become useful when you turn to planning and drafting your essay.

Revising Your Thesis Statement

Now that you have spent some time working out your ideas more systematically and developing some supporting evidence for the position you want to take, look again at the working thesis statement you crafted earlier to see if it is still accurate. As your first step, look again at the writing topic, and then write your original working thesis on the lines that follow it.

writing topic:

According to the story, why does the Nightingale, an ideal representation of love, have to die? Do you agree with the story's point of view on love? Be sure to support your position with specific examples drawn from your own experience, your observations of others, and your observations drawn from the media and the larger society and culture to which you belong.

working thesis statement:

_____

_____

Remember that your thesis statement must answer the second question in the writing topic while taking into consideration the writing topic as a whole. The first question in the topic identifies the issue that is up for debate, and the last question reminds you that, whatever position you take on the issue, you must be able to support it with examples.

Now, you should decide whether the working thesis statement that you drafted earlier in this unit should change. Does it still accurately reflect what you plan to say in your essay? Perhaps you will want to change only a word or phrase, but be open to a decision to significantly rewrite it. Draft writing is almost always wordy, unclear, or vague. Look at your working thesis statement through the eyes of your readers and see if it actually says what you want it to say.

After examining it and completing any necessary revisions, check it one more time by asking yourself the following questions:

a. Does the thesis directly identify the story's overall message about love?

b. Does your thesis state your position on love and whether your position agrees or disagrees with the story's?

c. Is your thesis well punctuated, grammatically correct, and precisely worded?

Write your polished thesis on the lines below and look at it again. Is it strong and interesting?

_____

_____

Planning and Drafting Your Essay

Now that you have examined the view of love in "The Nightingale and the Rose" and thought at length about your own view, draft an essay that responds to all parts of the writing topic. Use the material you developed in this section to compose your draft. Don't forget to turn back to Part 1, especially "The Conventional Argument Essay Structure," for further guidance on the essay's conventional structure.

Do take the time to develop an outline because it will give you a basic structure for incorporating all the ideas you have developed in the preceding pages. An outline will also give you a bird's-eye view of your essay and help you spot problems in development or logic. The form below is modeled on "The Conventional Argument Essay Structure" in Part 1, and it can guide you as you plan your essay.

This outline doesn't have to contain polished writing. You may want to fill in only the basic ideas in phrases or terms.

Creating an Outline for Your Draft

I. Introductory Paragraph

A. An opening sentence that gives the reading selection's title and author and begins to answer the writing topic:

_____

B. Main points to include in the directed summary:

1.

2.

3.

4.

C. Write out your thesis statement. (Look back to "Revising Your Thesis Statement," where you reexamined and improved your working thesis statement.) It should clearly agree or disagree with the argument in Wilde's story and state a clear position using your own words.

_____

II. Body Paragraphs

A. The paragraph's one main point that supports the thesis statement:

_____

1. Controlling idea sentence:

   _____

   _____

2. Corroborating details:

   _____

   _____

   _____

   _____

3. Careful explanation of why the details are significant:

   _____

   _____

   _____

   _____

4. Connection to the thesis statement:

   _____

   _____

   _____

   _____

B. The paragraph's one main point that supports the thesis statement:

   _____

   1. Controlling idea sentence:

      _____

      _____

   2. Corroborating details:

      _____

      _____

      _____

      _____

3. Careful explanation of why the details are significant:

_____

_____

_____

_____

4. Connection to the thesis statement:

_____

_____

_____

_____

C. The paragraph's one main point that supports the thesis statement:

_____

1. Controlling idea sentence:

_____

_____

2. Corroborating details:

_____

_____

_____

_____

3. Careful explanation of why the details are significant:

_____

_____

_____

_____

4. Connection to the thesis statement:

_____

_____

_____

_____

  D. The paragraph's one main point that supports the thesis statement:

  _____

  1. Controlling idea sentence:

  _____

  _____

  2. Corroborating details:

  _____

  _____

  _____

  _____

  3. Careful explanation of why the details are significant:

  _____

  _____

  _____

  _____

  4. Connection to the thesis statement:

  _____

  _____

  _____

  _____

Repeat this form for any remaining body paragraphs.

III. Conclusion (Look back to "Conclusions" in Part 1. It will help you make some decisions here about what type of conclusion you will use.)

  A. Type of conclusion to be used:

  _____

  B. Key words or phrases to include:

  _____

Getting Feedback on Your Draft

Use the following guidelines to give a classmate feedback on his or her draft. Read the draft through first, and then answer each of the items below as specifically as you can.

Name of draft's author: _____

Name of draft's reader: _____

The Introduction

1. Within the opening sentences,
   a. the author's first and last name are given.   yes   no
   b. the story's title is given and placed within quotation marks.   yes   no
2. The opening contains a summary that
   a. summarizes the Nightingale's death in the story.   yes   no
   b. interprets the Nightingale's death in terms of what
      it says about ideal love.   yes   no
3. The opening provides a thesis that makes clear the draft
   writer's opinion regarding the view of love in the story.   yes   no

If the answer to #3 above is yes, state the thesis below as it is written. If the answer is no, explain to the writer what information is needed to make the thesis complete.

_____

_____

_____

The Body

1. How many paragraphs are in the body of this essay? _____
2. To support the thesis, this number is   sufficient   not enough
3. Do paragraphs contain the 4Cs?

Paragraph 1	Controlling idea sentence	yes	no
	Corroborating details	yes	no
	Careful explanation of why the details are significant	yes	no
	Connection to the thesis statement	yes	no
Paragraph 2	Controlling idea sentence	yes	no
	Corroborating details	yes	no
	Careful explanation of why the details are significant	yes	no
	Connection to the thesis statement	yes	no

Paragraph 3	Controlling idea sentence	yes	no
	Corroborating details	yes	no
	Careful explanation of why the details are significant	yes	no
	Connection to the thesis statement	yes	no
Paragraph 4	Controlling idea sentence	yes	no
	Corroborating details	yes	no
	Careful explanation of why the details are significant	yes	no
	Connection to the thesis statement	yes	no
Paragraph 5	Controlling idea sentence	yes	no
	Corroborating details	yes	no
	Careful explanation of why the details are significant	yes	no
	Connection to the thesis statement	yes	no

(Continue as needed.)

4. Identify any of the above paragraphs that are underdeveloped (too short). _____

5. Identify any of the above paragraphs that fail to support the thesis. _____

6. Identify any of the above paragraphs that are redundant or repetitive. _____

7. Suggest any ideas for additional paragraphs that might improve this essay.

_____

_____

_____

The Conclusion

1. Does the final paragraph avoid introducing new ideas and examples that really belong in the body of the essay?   yes   no
2. Does the conclusion provide closure (let readers know that the end of the essay has been reached)?   yes   no
3. Does the conclusion leave readers with an understanding of the significance of the argument?   yes   no

4. State in your own words what the draft writer considers to be important about his or her argument.

_____

_____

_____

_____

5. Identify the type of conclusion used (see the guidelines for conclusions in Part 1).

_____

Editing

1. During the editing process, the writer should pay attention to the following problems in sentence structure, punctuation, and mechanics:

   fragments
   fused (run-on) sentences
   comma splices
   misplaced, missing, and unnecessary commas
   misplaced, missing, and unnecessary apostrophes
   incorrect quotation mark use
   capitalization errors
   spelling errors

2. While editing, the writer should pay attention to the following areas of grammar:

   verb tense
   subject-verb agreement
   irregular verbs
   pronoun type
   pronoun reference
   pronoun agreement
   noun plurals
   misplaced and dangling modifiers
   prepositions

Final Draft Checklist

Content

_____ My essay has an appropriate title.

_____ I provide an accurate summary of the position on love that the "The Nightingale and the Rose" takes.

_____ My thesis states a clear position that can be supported by evidence.

_____ I have enough paragraphs and argument points to support my thesis.

_____ Each body paragraph is relevant to my thesis.

_____ Each body paragraph contains the 4Cs.

_____ I use transitions whenever necessary to connect ideas to each other.

_____ The final paragraph of my essay (the conclusion) provides readers with a sense of closure.

Grammar, Punctuation, and Mechanics

_____ I use the present tense to discuss the story's argument and examples.

_____ I use verb tenses correctly to show the chronology of events.

_____ I have verb tense consistency throughout my sentences.

_____ I have checked for subject-verb agreement in all of my sentences.

_____ I have revised all fragments and mixed or garbled sentences.

_____ I have repaired all fused (run-on) sentences and comma splices.

_____ I have placed a comma after introductory elements (transitions and phrases) and all dependent clauses that open a sentence.

_____ If I present items in a series (nouns, verbs, prepositional phrases), they are parallel in form.

_____ If I include material spoken or written by someone other than myself, I have correctly punctuated it with quotation marks, using the MLA style guide's rules for citation.

Reviewing Your Graded Essay

After your instructor has returned your essay, you may have the opportunity to revise your paper and raise your grade. Many students, especially those whose essays receive nonpassing grades, feel that their instructors should be less "picky" about grammar and should pass the work on content alone. However, most students at this level have not yet acquired the ability to recognize quality writing, and they do not realize that content and writing actually cannot be separated in this way. Experienced instructors know that errors in sentence structure, grammar, punctuation, and word choice either interfere with content or distract readers so much that they lose track of content. In short, good ideas badly presented are no longer good ideas; to pass, an essay must have passable writing. So even if you are not submitting a revised version of this essay to your instructor, it is important that you review your work carefully in order to understand its strengths and weaknesses. This sheet will guide you through the evaluation process.

You will want to continue to use the techniques that worked well for you and to find strategies to overcome the problems that you identify in this sample of your writing. To recognize areas that might have been problematic for you, look back at the scoring rubric in this book. Match the numerical/verbal/letter grade received on your essay to the appropriate category. Study the explanation given on the rubric for your grade.

Write a few sentences below in which you identify your problems in each of the following areas. Then, suggest specific changes you could make that would improve your paper. Don't forget to use your handbook as a resource.

1. **Grammar/punctuation/mechanics**
   My problem:

   My strategy for change:

2. **Thesis/response to assignment**
   My problem:

   My strategy for change:

3. Organization
My problem:

My strategy for change:

4. Paragraph development/examples/reasoning
My problem:

My strategy for change:

5. Assessment
In the space below, assign a grade to your paper using a rubric other than the one used by your instructor. In other words, if your instructor assigned your essay a grade of *High Fail*, you might give it the letter grade you now feel the paper warrants. If your instructor used the traditional letter grade to evaluate the essay, choose a category from the rubric in this book, or any other grading scale that you are familiar with, to show your evaluation of your work. Then, write a short narrative explaining your evaluation of the essay and the reasons it received the grade you gave it.

Grade: _____

Narrative: _____

_____

_____

_____

_____

Part 3 contains two case studies made up of reading selections and some sample essays written in response to their writing topics. These essay responses were written by students like you, taking a college-level writing class and using *Write It Review* as their text.

For each case study you are assigned, read the main selection carefully and then annotate each so that you understand its argument and supporting evidence. Then, examine the student essays that follow it. Score each of them, using the scoring rubric in Part 1. Then, discuss each of these student essays with your classmates and identify each essay's strengths and weaknesses. For practice, your instructor may ask you to write a detailed plan identifying the specific steps you would take if you were going to revise one of the essays.

Case Study

Case Study #1: Deborah Tannen's "How Male and Female Students Participate in Class"

The following case study contains an essay written by Tannen, followed by four timed-writing essays written by students like you. You should read the essay and student responses for each, and examine them over for their strengths and weaknesses. A set of study questions follows each student essay to help you evaluate its success.

HOW MALE AND FEMALE STUDENTS PARTICIPATE IN CLASS

Deborah Tannen

Deborah Tannen earned a PhD in Linguistics from the University of California, Berkeley. She is a professor of linguistics at Georgetown University and a best-selling author. She is probably best known for her book You Just Don't Understand: Women and Men in Conversation, *which was on the* New York Times *best seller list for nearly four years. Her most recent book,* You Were Always Mom's Favorite!: Sisters in Conversation throughout Their Lives, *is also a* New York Times *best seller. The following selection appeared in* the Chronicle of Higher Education *in June of 1991.*

The research of sociologists and anthropologists such as Janet Lever, Marjorie Harness Goodwin, and Donna Eder has shown that most girls and boys learn to use language differently in their sex-separate peer groups. Typically, a girl has a best friend with whom she sits and talks, frequently telling secrets. It's the telling of secrets, the fact and the way that they talk to each other, that makes them best friends. For most boys, activities are central: their best friends are the ones they do things with. Boys tend to play in larger groups that are hierarchical; high-status boys give orders and push low-status boys around. So boys are expected to use language to seize center stage by exhibiting their skill, displaying their knowledge, and challenging and resisting challenges.

These patterns have stunning implications for classroom interaction. Most faculty members assume that participating in class discussion is a necessary part of successful performance. Yet speaking in a classroom is more congenial to boys' language experience than to girls', since it entails putting oneself forward in front of a large group of people, many of whom are strangers and at least one of whom is sure to judge speakers' knowledge and intelligence by their verbal display.

Another aspect of many classrooms that makes them more hospitable to most men than to most women is the use of debate-like formats as a learning tool. In his book Fighting for Life, Father Walter Ong shows how our schools pursue knowledge by ritual opposition: public display of information or opinion followed by argument and challenge. Father Ong demonstrates that ritual opposition is fundamental to the way most males approach almost any activity, but ritual opposition is antithetical to the way females learn and like to interact.

When discussing these phenomena with a colleague, I commented that I see these two styles in American conversation: many women bond by talking about troubles, and many men bond by exchanging playful insults and put-downs, and other sorts of verbal sparring. He exclaimed: "I never thought of this, but that's the way I teach: I have students read an article, and then I invite them to tear it apart. After we've torn it to shreds, we talk about how to build a better model." This approach contrasts sharply with the way I teach: I open the discussion of readings by asking, "What did you find useful in this? What can we use in our own theory building and our own methods?" I note what I see as weaknesses in the author's approach, but I also point out that the writer's discipline and purposes might be different from ours. Finally, I offer personal anecdotes illustrating the phenomena under discussion and praise students' anecdotes as well as their critical acumen.

These different teaching styles must make our classrooms wildly different places and therefore hospitable to different students. Male students are more likely to be comfortable attacking the readings and might find the inclusion of personal anecdotes irrelevant and "soft." Women are more likely to resist discussion they perceive as hostile, and, indeed, it is women in my classes who are more likely to offer personal anecdotes. Another colleague who read my book commented that he had always taken for granted that the best way to deal with students' comments is to challenge them; this, he felt it was self-evident, sharpens their minds and helps them develop debating skills. But he had noticed that women were relatively silent in his classes, so he decided to try beginning discussion with relatively open-ended questions and letting comments go unchallenged. He found, to his amazement and satisfaction, that more women began to speak up.

Though some of the women in his class clearly liked this better, perhaps some of the men liked it less. A professor at Hamilton College told me of a young man who was upset because he felt his class presentation had been a failure. The professor was puzzled because he had observed that class members had listened attentively and agreed with the student's observations. It turned out that it was this very agreement that the student interpreted as failure: Since no one had engaged his ideas by arguing with him, he felt they had found them unworthy of attention. Similarly, one young man in my class wrote in praise of a history professor who gave students questions to think about and called on people to answer them: "He would then play devil's advocate . . . i.e., he debated us. . . . That class really sharpened me intellectually. . . . We as students do need to know how to defend ourselves." This young man valued the experience of being attacked and challenged publicly. Many, if not most, women would shrink from such "challenge," experiencing it as public humiliation.

Yet another reason for the different attitudes toward speaking in class that typify women and men is their differing conceptions of how to contribute to the functioning of the class. Students who speak frequently in class, many of whom are men, assume that it is their job to think of contributions and try to get the floor to express them. But many women monitor their participation not only to get the floor but to avoid getting it. Women students in my class tell me that if they have spoken up once or twice, they hold back for the rest of the class because they don't want to dominate. If they have spoken a lot one week, they will remain silent the next. These different ethics of participation are, of course, unstated, so those who speak freely assume that those who remain silent have nothing to say, and those who are reining themselves in assume that the big talkers are self-centered and hoggish.

Writing Topic

According to Tannen, in what ways are men and women likely to think and feel differently about speaking in class? How does her explanation of these differences help you understand student behavior in the classroom? To develop your essay, be sure to discuss specific examples drawn from your personal experience, your observation of others, or any of your reading—including "How Male and Female Students Participate in Class" itself.

First Student Response

In "How Male and Female Students Participate in Class," Deborah Tannen places men and women into two separate, conflicting categories when it comes to learning preferences. She believes that women are more likely to participate in open discussions with a minimum amount of challenges and debates. Men, conversely, appreciate being attacked publicly, and find it more rewarding to debate since it adds to defense skills. I agree with Tannen's representation of behavior in the classroom; men are bolder and willing to stand out while women are more reluctant to participate in class if they believe they will be "attacked."

Tannen attempts to explain the differences between male and female behavior in the classroom by looking at their social demeanor. As small children, girls tend to choose a best friend based on whom she speaks to most frequently and whom she shares "secrets" with. Due to this reason, girls tend to associate with a smaller group. Boys, on the other hand, select a best friend based on who they physically interact with more, making them interact with larger crowds and speak more frequently to capture attention.

As in most cases, there is one individual that desperately tries harder than others to seek any form of attention...the class clown. Sometimes this person's attempts at humor are irritating, but there are also moments when their comedic relief alleviates the blandness of the classroom. I have noticed that usually there is a correlation between class clowns being male. As the school year barely starts, the class clown makes several attempts to receive attention, but they are still controllable. As time progresses, the class clown's peers begin to have higher expectations for him. He is like a controversial rock star, everyone waits for his next scandal, and he is never one to let his audience down. The class clown is not bothered by the fact that he is known as a fool, instead, he prides himself with this reputation. This classroom behavior is typical of men; they are more likely than women to make spectacles of themselves.

As with most cases, one of the requirements is an oral presentation. I have always dreaded the idea of standing in front of my class, speaking to them, and having them judge my work. Regardless, it is something I know I have to do, but again, dread. I normally hope that I am able to present my project and immediately sit down with no questions asked. When I am questioned, I feel an immense amount of anxiety as I try to "defend" my stance.

Men, more often than not, seem pleased with the attention perceived while their ideas are being questioned they perceive this form of attention to be a validation of their ideas. Tannen's representation of behavior in the classroom is not only supported by her evidence and examples, but also from my own experience. Speaking in the classroom was always extremely intimidating for me, and Tannen's explanations of gender differences helped me tie this in to classroom behavior.

Assessment Questions

1. Does this essay have a directed summary that answers the first question in the writing topic?

Yes, the essay has a directed summary that answers the first question

2. Does this essay have a thesis statement that answers the second question in the writing topic?

> Yes the essay has a thesis statement answering the second question

3. Does this essay develop and support its thesis through strong body paragraphs that open with a topic sentence, and present specific examples that support that topic and tie back to the thesis? Evaluate the effectiveness of these examples: is each one detailed, easy to follow, and clearly relevant to the thesis and topic sentence?

> The essay doesnt really develop and support its thesis through body Paragraphs. There are not any clear and specific example and the examples arent really effective

4. Is the essay grammatically correct, well punctuated, and precisely worded, or do significant errors limit the essay's effectiveness?

> The essay is grammatically correct, well Punctuated and Precisely worded and there arent significant errors that limit the essay's effectiveness

5. Using the conventional standards presented in the scoring rubric in Part 1 of this book, what score does this essay deserve? Explain.

> Low Pass, essay indicate satisfactory writing skills but ideas, example arent logically sequenced, lack clarity

Second Student Response

In Deborah Tannen's article "How Male and Female Students Participate in Class," she lists how girls and boys interact differently with their best friends. Girls are more likely to share secrets with their best friends, whereas, boys are more likely to share competitive activities with their best friends. These underlying differences between boys and girls can explain why they think and feel differently about speaking and participating in class. Males respond positively to challenges and females view them as public humiliation in a classroom. Tannen's explanation of these differences clarifies how males and females' behaviors in the classroom are different.

Because of their competitive nature, males use language in the classroom for their advantage. Males view the use of language as a sign of their knowledge and intelligence. The classroom is a setting with many people to judge each other. This is fit for males who want to show their knowledge and intelligence to the other competition. On the other hand, females do not use the classroom to flaunt their knowledge and intelligence, and thus, do not take advantage of a "necessary part of successful [class] performance." In the classroom, many teachers use debates as an effective teaching tool. However, not all students respond uniformly to debates in the classroom. Because of the competitive nature of debates, males uses the opposition to learn. Usually in debates, teachers play the devil's advocate, pressuring the students to defend their personal point of view. However, according to Tannen, females do not like to feel pressured, but would rather speak unopposed. The pressures of debating does not make it an affective learning tool for females.

When females do contribute and speak in class, they often do it differently than the males. Once males start to speak in class, they continue to contribute whenever they can. This is because of their competitive nature and their attempt to make their intelligence known. On the other hand, females do not wan't to be the center of attention. Many women "monitor their participation" and do not allow themselves to be heard more than the other. From speaking with many of my female friends, they have told me that they have no need to participate in class. They can simply be alert, in class, to see if what they would've said out loud is correct or not. It is their secretive nature that allows females to be so silent in class.

The differences between males and females' class participation is attributed to their natural differences. Most males perform better under pressure and when their intelligence is challenged. Females do not react positively to opposition and contribute in class in moderation. Understanding these differences can help teachers teach both their male and female students more effectively.

Assessment Questions

1. Does this essay have a directed summary that answers the first question in the writing topic?

   Yes, essay has directed summary answering first question

2. Does this essay have a thesis statement that answers the second question in the writing topic?

   no essay doesnt have thesis answering second question

3. Does this essay develop and support its thesis through strong body paragraphs that open with a topic sentence, and present specific examples that support that topic and tie back to the thesis? Evaluate the effectiveness of these examples: is each one detailed, easy to follow, and clearly relevant to the thesis and topic sentence?

Essay doesnt develop and support thesis through body paragraphs. Essay doesnt have specific examples and examples arent effective.

4. Is the essay grammatically correct, well punctuated, and precisely worded, or do significant errors limit the essay's effectiveness?

The essay is grammatically correct and there and there arent significant errors that limit essay's effectiveness.

5. Using the conventional standards presented in the scoring rubric in Part 1 of this book, what score does this essay deserve? Explain.

High Fail, essay lacks focus because of no thesis and lacks pattern of organization

Third Student Response

According to Deborah Tannen, in the article, How Male and Female Students Participate in Class, she elaborates on the differences the way men and women think and feel speaking in class. Tannen explains that in general men are very aggressive and women are quiet and soft. Girls have a tendency to easily become friends by telling each other secrets as boys have a tendency to pick on each other. Deborah Tannen's explanation of these differences help me understand student behavior in the classroom not only because of the article but because she states facts that I have even observed in some of my classes. So, is it true what Tannen is elaborating on? Well, I've come to a conclusion that she has a very good perspective on how men and women behave in a classroom.

It is said that girls can sit and chit chat with each other and become the best of friends as boys can do activities together and become friends. I believe if this is true, within a classroom boys would be the dominant one in speaking up first. Why? Well, first because boys generally are comfortable about whats on their mind or how they feel towards something without being "embarrassed." I think that is because boys play a larger role in big groups and some boys are already use to giving orders and pushing people around. So when it comes around to speaking in class, their high status mind speaks freely and no doubt that I've noticed this in my classes as well, especially it is generally the class clown who says anything, even if he is wrong. However, with girls, in my opinion I think because we girls are already soft-speaking we are embarrassed to speak whats on our mind because the thought of being wrong, but of course at times we have those other girls who can speak freely, with confidence in a classroom. But generally speaking in a classroom full of half girls and half boys, the girls are most likely to bond by sharing each others troubles while boys will exchange playful insults and put-downs to each other. Have you noticed girls don't like to be wrong? Well at least in my opinion think girls always think they have to be right. Hence that girls will argue till the person they are arguing with agrees. Well, maybe thats just what I've observed but in this case I also believe because girls like it when they are right, they will only speak up or answer questions in a classroom if they know they are right.

The way a teacher teaches has some effect on the way girls and boys speak about in a classroom as well. If the professor challenges the students, girls and boys have to actually think about what they are being challenged about. This will take effect in two ways either it will be a battle of the sexes, boys versus girls on who is right or no one will say anything. Women usually are relatively silent, but with open-end questions and letting comments go unchallenged more women are likely to speak up, as men like it less. Myself as a girl, admit that I try to avoid the center of attention, I get shy and embarrassed in case I might be wrong. I have a tendency to hold back even if I know the correct answer to a question, I'll just answer the question in my mind. But, of course I am working on this situation. When I came to college, since there was so many students in a classroom, that speaking up makes a differences, even if one is wrong. That's what I've learned, it doesn't matter if your wrong or if it's a dumb question at all. Maybe later in the future, girls will be the dominant one and speak up more. Plus, speaking–up is a challenge, its even a fright or fear to someone but the more one speaks up the more they'll get over their fear. Now, lets not be afraid to speak freely in our classrooms for it doesn't matter if your wrong, we can learn from our mistakes and get use to speaking up at least.

Assessment Questions

1. Does this essay have a directed summary that answers the first question in the writing topic?

   yes, essay has directed summary answering first question

2. Does this essay have a thesis statement that answers the second question in the writing topic?

   The essay has a thesis that answers second question

3. Does this essay develop and support its thesis through strong body paragraphs that open with a topic sentence, and present specific examples that support that topic and tie back to the thesis? Evaluate the effectiveness of these examples: is each one detailed, easy to follow, and clearly relevant to the thesis and topic sentence?

The essay develops and supports thesis through strong body Paragraphs Essay Presents specific examples that support

4. Is the essay grammatically correct, well punctuated, and precisely worded, or do significant errors limit the essay's effectiveness?

Essay is grammatically correct and there went significant errors limiting essay's effectiveness

topic and examples are very effective

5. Using the conventional standards presented in the scoring rubric in Part 1 of this book, what score does this essay deserve? Explain.

Pass, essay has strong writing skills, response thoughtful, appropriate

Fourth Student Response

In the article; "How Male and Female Students Participate in Class," Deborah Tannen describes how boys and girls tend to describe themselves differently, in recognizing their interactions and behaviors. Tannen states how "boys tend to play in larger groups that are hierarchical meaning that they are tendede for the center of attention, and are outgoing in expressing their knowledge and resisting challenges. While girls "bond by talking about troubles," meaning they seem to be more secretive and in classes likely to offer personal anecdotes. Tanner's descriptions of the different reactions between the male and female students helped me realize that male students are more confident while female students are insecure, esp. in class.

While students are not interacting in classrooms, in general, boys tend to play more sports and are more active. There obligations are to choose who is the strongest or best in sports among themselves. On the other hand, girls tend to play with their friends, accessorizing themselves and their dolls. Because women were relatively silent in class, Tanner made an observation to try beginning discussion with relatively open-ended questions, and realized women began to speak up. While men disliked the concept of letting comments go unchallenged.

Throughout my personal experiences, I've seen that their were many different interactions between men & women. As a young girl, I disliked speaking out loud in class. My characteristics were hostile, and I was afraid if I talked too much in class, I would mistakenly shout out the wrong remarks the teacher was leaning towards. Girls tend to get embarrassed more easily.

I agree, with the author that girls tend to be more secure with themselves. Girls are the sexes that usually has a best friend. Someone to talk to and tell secrets with. While boys tend to play sports and enjoy hanging out in larger groups. And being tough. In the article, Tannen describes the differences between how male and female interact in classrooms. "Students who speak frequently in class, many of whom are men, assume that it is their job to think of contributions & try to get the floor to express them. But many women monitor their participation not only to get the floor but to avoid getting it."

Overall, reading this article was interesting I've never observed the differences in how male & female students react. I was able to identify the differences, that female students are usually more quite because they don't want to be dominate, while male students enjoy participation. When female students use examples, usually describe personal experiences, while male students enjoy comparing the effects evolving around the world. That's my thesis for this article.

Assessment Questions

1. Does this essay have a directed summary that answers the first question in the writing topic?

2. Does this essay have a thesis statement that answers the second question in the writing topic?

3. Does this essay develop and support its thesis through strong body paragraphs that open with a topic sentence, and present specific examples that support that topic and tie back to the thesis? Evaluate the effectiveness of these examples: is each one detailed, easy to follow, and clearly relevant to the thesis and topic sentence?

4. Is the essay grammatically correct, well punctuated, and precisely worded, or do significant errors limit the essay's effectiveness?

5. Using the conventional standards presented in the scoring rubric in Part 1 of this book, what score does this essay deserve? Explain.

Case Study #2: "What Management Doesn't Know"

The following case study is based on Devon Hackelton's "What Management Doesn't Know." Read the Hackelton essay and the student responses that follow. Evaluate the strengths and weaknesses of those responses using the scoring rubric that is in Part 1. A set of study questions follows each student essay to help you in evaluating its success.

WHAT MANAGEMENT DOESN'T KNOW

Devon Hackelton

Devon Hackelton graduated from California Polytechnic University, Pomona (1997)
with an MA in rhetoric and composition. He has taught at UCR since 2001, most
recently in the University Writing Program. Before his teaching career, he worked a
variety of blue-collar jobs for eighteen years, from serving chicken to cleaning medical
clinics to repairing industrial air conditioners while attending high school and col-
lege, and later while teaching college level classes part-time. In his spare time, he enjoys
online gaming and writing poetry: His most recent poems, "A Reflection" and "Common
Threads," have appeared in Spring 2012 issue of the Pomona Valley Review.

I worked as an "engineer" for a retail mall for fourteen years, painting and repairing the infrastructure of a one million square foot complex and the surrounding forty-three acres. During
my employment, twelve different mall managers came and went. None of these managers had
ever worked as a security guard, janitor or repair technician: all of them had college degrees,
mostly in business, but even then, only a few had ever worked as a retail salesperson. They
knew about compliance issues, bottom lines, and revenue enhancements, but they didn't know
the first thing about operating a floor buffer, apprehending a shoplifter, replacing an air con-
ditioner motor or selling culottes. They learned about customer service at training seminars
and paraded the employees into the office once a month to remind us we should look neat
and presentable, and we should stop whatever we were doing if a customer needed assistance.

One day, my boss sent me to the food court to fix a leaky hydraulic line in the trash compactor. Now this compactor was about the size of a semi trailer and it was full of discarded
pizza, burgers, ice cream, chow mein, soda, napkins, paper towels from the restroom, and
countless other bits of rotten refuse. And to get to the leaky hose, I had to enter the back of
the machine where all of the grease and sludge had accumulated over the years. Every time I
leaned in to disconnect or connect the hoses, some part of my body or clothing would come
into contact with that feral slime until, by the time the hose was changed, I was a walking,
stinking mess. As soon as I finished, my manager called me over the two-way radio to help a
customer who had dropped his keys in an elevator shaft. I told my boss that I was dirty, but he
said it was an emergency and questioned how dirty could I get by working on the compactor.
After all, he said, the outside of the compactor was hosed down daily. So I went to help the
customer, who was already upset and even more upset when he caught a whiff of me. Within
an hour, the very same manager who ordered me to fix the compactor and then ordered me to
help the customer threatened to fire me for my appearance. The next day I called in sick; in
reality, I had stayed awake all night visualizing different methods of revenge.

Sadly, disconnects like the one between my boss and I occur regularly in the business
world, sometimes with deadly results. In unrelated incidents between July 2nd and 9th, 2003,
three Midwestern employees killed a total of ten coworkers, injured thirteen others, and took
their own lives. All three were targeting bosses or supervisors. The U.S. Bureau of Labor Statistics reports that 709 people were murdered on the job in 1998 and 106 of those people were
killed by employees or former employees. While most employee-employer conflicts are not
this severe, immeasurable working hours are lost annually due to a lack of understanding and
communication between workers and managers.

Communication breakdowns occur, in part, because managers do not understand their employees' jobs and associated stresses. In the last thirty years, most businesses have ended hiring management internally; gone are the hopes of starting in the mailroom and one day being the CEO of a corporation. Fast food restaurants, interestingly, are an exception. Most fast food managers have cooked and cleaned and taken customer orders and unloaded trucks. They know what concerns their employees face in any given task, and the managers are able to offer suggestions and better assign certain employees to certain tasks based on the managers' prior experiences, undoubtedly saving their companies money and allowing for a more smoothly operating workplace.

The only other industry that trains its workforce similarly is education. Teachers know what it means to be a student and know the particular hardships and stresses students face. Students are more likely to complete assignments because they know that their teachers have been assigned and have completed similar tasks in the past. This shared understanding creates a level of respect between student and instructor.

Unfortunately, this respect is seldom found in other professions. Currently, there is a cyclic trend of employees not being promoted to management because they lack some requisite educational degree. Managers and supervisors are hired straight out of college and have little or no understanding of the workings of a company. Strangers make decisions without input from the employees and the employees begin to be suspicious or resentful of management. Then, when there is an opportunity for an employee to advance into management, the employee often refuses to take it in fear of being seen as one of *them*. For instance, one of my relatives has worked for a large railroad for over thirty years. He started as a brakeman, and is now a conductor. His next step should have been engineer and then a possible move into management; however, he chose not to be promoted. Management to him is a dirty word: he says supervisors are book-learned idiots who have no idea about the physical work or dangers involved with operating a two hundred ton locomotive hauling fifty freight cars at seventy miles per hour. He and his co-workers take pleasure in stretching a three-hour job into twelve hours because they are "following the asinine rules of management." He has a plan to increase productivity and cut costs, but when asked why he doesn't present his plan to his bosses, my father-in-law argues that nobody would listen to an uneducated conductor. Instead, he and his cohorts stay bitter, freight moves slowly, business costs increase, and top railroad executives hire new college graduates who have never worked on a train to create cost cutting plans.

It is time for a change. Businesses and corporations should strive to look internally when filling management positions. Bosses should possess some hands-on experience in a variety of jobs that are a part of the business, maybe by working in different departments, even for a short time, before assuming their supervisor role. Workers deserve the reassurance that comes with knowing their bosses understand and have experienced the workers' duties. It just makes ethical and financial sense.

Writing Topic

Why does the author believe managers should have hands-on experience in a variety of jobs that are part of the business before holding supervisor positions? Do you feel that his argument is valid? Support your response using examples from your own experience, observations, and readings.

First Student Response

In the essay "What Management Doesn't Know," the author explains his opinion on the management position. The author explains that managers should get chosen based on experience. Many people may have a great education, but without experience the manager may not understand his/her employees. Another reason for experienced managers is, because they know how to deal with many situations because they themselves have gone through them. The author also states that managers with higher education intimidate those with less education. The authors point of view is valid. If these were managers who could understand their employers communication would be higher. They would also know not to pressure their employers because that can cause a lot of stress in the working environment.

My father works in the Post Office as an electronic technician. He has applied for the supervisors position many times. Every time someone else with less experience get the position because he/she has a higher degree. They may be more educated but they do not know how things work. In order to fix a machine a person needs as much time, depending on how big or small the machine may be, in order to fix it. The person in the higher position may not understand and request something else to be done, yet he/she will want it done quickly. My dad says that he was working on a machine and that his supervisor asked him to work on another machine. My dad went to work on the other machine like an hour later because the machine he was fixing prior to that is much larger. His supervisor got mad and said that he was messing around with the other machine. The supervisor made this big problem that could have been avoide if he/she knew what was going on.

Assessment Questions

1. Does this essay have a directed summary that answers the first question in the writing topic?

2. Does this essay have a thesis statement that answers the second question in the writing topic?

3. Does this essay develop and support its thesis through strong body paragraphs that open with a topic sentence, and present specific examples that support that topic and tie back to the thesis? Evaluate the effectiveness of these examples: is each one detailed, easy to follow, and clearly relevant to the thesis and topic sentence?

4. Is the essay grammatically correct, well punctuated, and precisely worded, or do significant errors limit the essay's effectiveness?

5. Using the conventional standards presented in the scoring rubric in Part 1 of this book, what score does this essay deserve? Explain.

Second Student Response

In "What Management Doesn't Know", Devun Hackleton writes about the communication breakdowns that occur because management doesn't understand their employee's jobs and associated stresses. The author believes that managers should have hands-on experience in a variety of jobs that are part of the business before holding supervisor positions. Managers need hands-on experience so they make correct judgements and decisions, because college degrees can't be substituted for years of experience.

An example of management having experience amounting to a successful business is my father. My father has been in the tire business for 35 years. He started as a mechanic for a large company and through experience, worked his way to the top. After working for many different companies, he gained the experience and opened his own shop. He is an example of effective management because he can do every operation his employees are capable of, and he is always aware of what goes on in his shop. He is capable of overseeing and understanding everything that is done in the shop and is always there to troubleshoot.

Today, companies who are hiring, are making too much emphasis on the education that their future employees hold. For management positions, experience is far more important than the level of education one holds. For management that lacks experience in the field, the basis of the decisions are blind because they are unaware of the circumstances. The management doesn't understand what goes on and shouldn't be able to make decisions that can affect others. For example, in the essay, the mall manager had no idea of the cleanliness of the trash compactor but still sent the author to aid another customer while he was filthy. This shows the lack of knowledge or absent mind of the management because they really don't know what is going on.

The author is correct where he states that companies should fill management jobs internally. Not only does this allow employees to earn higher positions that they have worked hard for, but also allows for effective management. An example of an efficient and lucrative business is the world of fast food. People need to start at the bottom of the chain and work their way up to become apart of management. This situation allows the management to understand and have experienced the worker's duties. If management understands and respects the other employees, there will be a mutual respect which allows for a more efficient workplace.

Managers who have never been in a certain business have no idea what is going on and how to deal with problems. No wonder why employees either hate or plot to kill their bosses due to their ignorance of situations. In order for their to be a safe, lucrative, and efficient business there needs to be management with experience.

Assessment Questions

1. Does this essay have a directed summary that answers the first question in the writing topic?

2. Does this essay have a thesis statement that answers the second question in the writing topic?

3. Does this essay develop and support its thesis through strong body paragraphs that open with a topic sentence, and present specific examples that support that topic and tie back to the thesis? Evaluate the effectiveness of these examples: is each one detailed, easy to follow, and clearly relevant to the thesis and topic sentence?

4. Is the essay grammatically correct, well punctuated, and precisely worded, or do significant errors limit the essay's effectiveness?

5. Using the conventional standards presented in the scoring rubric in Part 1 of this book, what score does this essay deserve? Explain.

Third Student Response

In the essay "What Management Doesn't Know," the author describes the lack of communication between employers and employees and the lack of hands-on experience of many employers. He writes that if employers don't have any experience in the fields they're managing, there is a lack of communication with the employees. Managers do not know the kind of stress and dangers their employees go through every day. This problem occurs because managers and supervisors are hired straight out of college and do not know the workings of a company. Many are also hired straight out of college to create cost-cutting plans. They have no idea how the field works and do not create the most cost effective plans. Employees who have been in the field for a long time are the best for management because of the experience and the knowledge of the tasks involved in the field. Manager should understand and experience the work of their employees before taking the role of a supervisor. I agree with the author's argument because I have been employed in a case where the manager had no hands-on experience and in a case where he did.

Employers should have experience in the jobs of a business before becoming supervisors. I have been employed in a flower distributing company as a filing clerk and the jobs that were given to me were just ridiculous. My manager had no experience in the jobs that I did and was actually hired out of college. There was one task he gave me that really showed he did not understand the difficulties involved in the job. I was told to organize a large file cabinet that was so ridiculously unorganized that not even my manager knew what to do. The files were thrown everywhere with no labels whatsoever. I wasn't familiar with the documents in the cabinet, and my manager didn't realize that the files were impossible to organize. He kept hurrying me and telling me he needed the files organized in a short amount of time. After a few days, my co worker talked to the manager and I was relieved of the job. I saw that the manager wasnt happy but I also knew he had no idea what the difficulties were in the task. I continued to work there and began to realize that the managers did not communicate with their employees and many people were not happy with the way they were treated. This experience definitely shows I agree with the author's position that higher positions should have experience in the field before handling the job as supervisor.

Managers with experience are more communicative and understanding than those without. My second job involved a lot of lifting and moving of heavy boxes. Not only was it strenuous but the warehouse was extremely hot. My manager always told me to take breaks and drink water. He understood the difficulties of the tasks I was doing because he was doing the same tasks before he hired employees. He knew that it was impossible to work in the heat and offered to help me when I needed help. It made the job much easier for me because I had no problems or difficulties with the job. There was a lot of communication between me and my manager. My manager also knew a lot about the business and the most beneficial ways for the company. He knew exactly what to do to keep the employees happy and did his best to keep the company strong. The people with handson experience are better for high positions than those highered straight out of college.

I was much happier at my second job and I agree that managers should have some experience in the field they are supervising. It is essential to the company and for the wellbeing of the employees. The author's argument is definitely valid because I have personally experienced his position on the issue.

Assessment Questions

1. Does this essay have a directed summary that answers the first question in the writing topic?

2. Does this essay have a thesis statement that answers the second question in the writing topic?

3. Does this essay develop and support its thesis through strong body paragraphs that open with a topic sentence, and present specific examples that support that topic and tie back to the thesis? Evaluate the effectiveness of these examples: is each one detailed, easy to follow, and clearly relevant to the thesis and topic sentence?

4. Is the essay grammatically correct, well punctuated, and precisely worded, or do significant errors limit the essay's effectiveness?

5. Using the conventional standards presented in the scoring rubric in Part 1 of this book, what score does this essay deserve? Explain.

Fourth Student Response

In "What Management Doesn't Know", Devin Hackleton explains how managers should have experiences within the particular business before becoming a manager or supervisor. It is not fair for the employees to take orders from a manager that do not even know what to do. A lot of times, managers or supervisors are hire due to the amount of education they have. They may not be experienced and definitely lack skills on the smaller jobs of the company. Even if the managers hold a high position, it does not mean they are well experience or train for the job. What makes these managers different from employees is that managers receive much more education then employees. I believe that Hackelton's argument on managers having more experience within the business before having them promote to higher positions is valid because managers are suppose to know more then the employees.

If managers are hire immediately after they graduate from college, they lack experience and also skills regarding the job. For example, when I was working in a dentist office last summer, my manager was a girl that just graduated from college. She was hired a couple of months after the office hired me. My new manager have no idea on how to manage an office. Therefore, I had to teach her and assisted her on what to do. It did not make any sense to me that I have to listen to someone that knew less then me on what to do in the office. Hackleton states in his essay, "Managers and supervisors are hired straight out of college and have little or no understanding of the workings of a company." It is not reasonable that a complete stranger can become a manager immediately. Where employees do not even get promoted or received a higher raise. Being a manager does not mean they need more education then the employees in the company, but it means that these managers need to have more experiences then the employees. I felt that I had the role of a manager instead, yet I still get pay minimum wage. Also, a lot of times, I had to worked overtime in order to help my so-called manager finish her work.

Managers or supervisors should always start off at the company as employees, and then get promote to a higher position. For example, I used to worked at the doctor's office. My manager was a mid-thirties woman who is extremely intelligent within the company. She knows everything regarding the company. When I was hired, she helped me and assisted me on everything possible. I was amazed on how much information she knew and she was able to train me into a good assistant. Since she used to be an assistant in the office, she knew all the stress I was going through. There was a lot of paperwork and other office-related things to do. Hackleton states, "Communication breakdowns occur because managers do not understand their employee's jobs and associated stresses." Since my manager been through what I was currently going through, she guided me throughout the time I was working there. I am glad that my manager was experienced in the business, because otherwise no one else could had assisted me in the office.

Managers or supervisors should be well-trained and experienced in the company before they get a promotion. The job system in the company should be rank from employees to managers. I do not think it is fair for employees to listen to a complete stranger at work, where the employees will not feel secure. Most of the time, managers will lack skills regarding the business they may be working for. It will make much better sense if an employee is promoted to a manager position because this former employee have experience and been through a long period of training.

Assessment Questions

1. Does this essay have a directed summary that answers the first question in the writing topic?

2. Does this essay have a thesis statement that answers the second question in the writing topic?

3. Does this essay develop and support its thesis through strong body paragraphs that open with a topic sentence, and present specific examples that support that topic and tie back to the thesis? Evaluate the effectiveness of these examples: is each one detailed, easy to follow, and clearly relevant to the thesis and topic sentence?

4. Is the essay grammatically correct, well punctuated, and precisely worded, or do significant errors limit the essay's effectiveness?

5. Using the conventional standards presented in the scoring rubric in Part 1 of this book, what score does this essay deserve? Explain.

Index

CPSIA information can be obtained
at www.ICGtesting.com
Printed in the USA
LVOW01s0803031216
515437LV00003B/11/P